Aprende Ingles

4 Libros En 1

Este Libro Incluye Más De 1000 Palabras En Contexto, Más De 100 Conversaciones, Historias Cortas Para Principiantes Vol. 1-2

Table of Contents

100+ Conversaciones

Aprende Inglés Con Historias Cortas Vol. 2

Aprende inglés para principiantes:

Más de 1000 palabras en inglés fáciles y comunes en contexto para aprender el idioma inglés

By: Paul Car

Introducción

Felicitaciones por descargar su copia de Aprenda inglés para principiantes: más de 1000 palabras en inglés fáciles y comunes en contexto para aprender el idioma inglés. Espero que esté entusiasmado por aprender los conceptos básicos del idioma inglés en la comodidad de su hogar.

En este formato fácil de seguir, aprenderá vocabulario en inglés mientras lee oraciones en contexto. Te divertirás mientras construyes tu vocabulario con palabras que vas a usar todos los días mientras practicas y aprendes inglés.

El libro está dividido en capítulos de categorías de temas comunes que encontrará a lo largo del día. Esto no solo te ayudará a aprender el idioma mientras realizas tus tareas diarias, sino que también te ayudará a solidificar el vocabulario para que puedas usar el idioma mientras viajas o hablas con tus amigos.

Para cada una de las palabras, encontrarás la pronunciación, la traducción al español de la palabra, así como una oración en inglés y español, lo que te ayudará a aprender aún más vocabulario rápidamente. A veces, las oraciones son divertidas y otras, informativas. De cualquier manera, te cautivarán a medida que continúes aprendiendo inglés.

Hay muchos libros sobre cómo aprender inglés, ¡así que gracias de nuevo por elegir este! Se hizo todo lo posible para asegurar que esté lleno de tanta información útil como sea posible.

Adjective — Adjetivo

Afiebrado – feverish

Every time a karate championship ends, it is feverish.

Cada vez que finaliza un campeonato de karate queda afiebrado.

Alerta – alert

At all times, we must remain alert.

En todo momento debemos permanecer alerta.

Algún – some, any, a few

Someday, we will be celebrating the fall of the dictator.

Algún día estaremos celebrando la caída del dictador.

Alucinantes – fantastic, amazing

The experimental sounds that the rock band achieved are amazing.

Los sonidos experimentales que logró la banda de rock son alucinantes.

Amargado – bitter

Nobody wanted to hire him in their company because he had a reputation for being bitter.

Nadie lo quería contratar en su empresa porque tenía fama de amargado.

Amarrado – tight

The guys like it when the girls wear tight pants.

A los chicos les gusta cuando las chicas usan pantalones amarrado.

Amontonado – piled up

They left all the plates and glasses piled up, forming a large pyramid.

Dejaron amontonado todos los platos y vasos formando una gran piramide.

Anciana – elderly, old

That elderly woman escaped from the nursing home last week, and they have not yet noticed her absence.

Esa anciana se escapó del geriátrico la semana pasada y aún no han notado su ausencia.

Anterior – front, previous

The previous boss was much more kind and patient.

El jefe anterior era mucho más amable y paciente.

Antiguos – old, antique

The oldest Egyptian scrolls were found in a sarcophagus in Cairo.

Los más antiguos pergaminos egipcios se encontraron en un sarcófago en el Cairo.

Apasionado – passionate

Nobody was as passionate as when it came to dancing the tango or playing the harmonica.

Nadie era tan apasionado como el a la hora de bailar tango o tocar la armónica.

Arable– especially

That field is especially coveted because its land is totally valuable.

Ese campo es arable codiciado porque su tierra es totalmente valiosa.

Ardiente – passionate

Despite being a 45-year-old woman, she was more passionate than a 20-year-old girl.

A pesar de ser una mujer de 45 años era más ardiente que una chica de 20 años.

Armado – armed

He was strongly armed to rescue his friend who was kidnapped in Morocco.

Se fué fuertemente armado para rescatar a su amigo secuestrado en Marruecos.

Asombroso – amazing

The amazing ship equipped with the highest technology has just arrived.

El asombroso barco equipado con lo más alto de la tecnologíaacaba de llegar.

Asqueroso – disgusting

He looked disgusting, but he had to remain as an undercover agent.

Tenía un aspecto asqueroso, pero debía permanecer así como agente encubierto.

Asustado – scared

I had never been so scared before they told me I would be a Dad.

Nunca antes había estado tan asustado como cuando me dimero que sería Papá.

Atento – attentive, thoughtful

We must be very attentive to the news about the last presidential elections.

Hay que estar muy atento a las noticias sobre las últimas elecciones presidenciales.

Atentos – attentive, thoughtful

Everyone was attentive to the voice of the captain to inform them of the procedures of the trip.

Atentos todos a la voz del capitán que les informara lo procedimientos del viaje.

Atrevido – darling

It was a very bold concept, but they all had a good attitude.

Era un concepto muy atrevido, pero tenían toda la buena actitud.

Bajo – short, low

The degree of alcohol was very low compared to that of the other bottle.

El grado de alcohol era muy bajo en comparación con el de la otra botella.

Biológicamente – biologically

Biologically speaking, these experiments are a bit dangerous.

Biológicamente hablando estos experimentos son un poco peligrosos.

Bonita – pretty

She was the prettiest of the girls in her town and was elected queen of the fair.

Era la más bonita de las chicas de su pueblo y fue elegida reina de la feria.

Borracho – drunk

He was so drunk that he did not know what his name was or how old he was.

Estaba tan borrachoque no sabía ni cómo se llamaba ni que edad tenía.

Bravucón– swaggering

The man was swaggering through the middle of the street like he owned the place.

El hombre se bravucón por el medio de la calle como si fuera el dueño del lugar.

Breve– brief, a short period of time

What seemed like a long and complicated investigation ended up being very brief.

Lo que parecía una investigación larga y complicada terminò siendo muy breve.

Buen humor– good-humored

He woke up in a good-humored mood, and the rest of the day was positive and productive.

Amaneció de buen humor y todoel resto del díafue positivo y productivo.

Bueno– good

He was so good at playing chess that he was paid tribute in Poland.

Era tan bueno jugando a jedrez que le hicieron un homenaje tributo en Polonia.

Cada– every, each

Each of the employees would wear a blue cap with the emblem of the company.

Cada uno de los empleados llevaría una gorraazul con el emblema de la empresa.

Cálido– warm

The warm atmosphere was ideal to rest and clear the mind.

El ambiente cálido era ideal para descansar y despejar la mente.

Cansado– tired

He felt so tired that he had to throw a bucket of cold water on his head.

Se sentía tan cansado que tuvo que arrojarse un balde de agua fría en la cabeza.

Celoso– jealous

He had been warned that if he were still so jealous, she would end the relationship at once.

Le habían advertido que si seguía siendo tan celoso acabaría la relación de una vez.

Cercano– close, nearby

He was the only close relative he had left alive.

Era el único pariente cercano que le quedaba vivo.

Cerrado– closed

It is the third time that I find this mechanical workshop closed.

Es la tercera vez que encuentro cerrado este taller mecánico.

Chiquito– tiny, small

That apartment was so small that only a child or a cat could live there.

Era tan chiquito ese appartamento que sólo podía vivir ahí un niño o un gato.

Chocones– one-legged

The pirate was one-legged and was jumping around until they fashioned a wooden leg.

El pirata solo tenía una sola chocones y estaba saltando hasta que le formaron una pata de palo.

Cláro– clear

Everything had been very clear at the end of the conference.

Todo había quedado muy claro al finalizar la conferencia.

Clasificada– classified

He had access to important classified and confidential information.

Tuvo acceso a una importante información clasificada y confidencial.

Colgante– hanging

The suspension bridge was a brilliant idea of engineers and architects for the city.

El puente colgante fue una brillante idea de los ingenieros y arquitectos para la ciudad.

Completo– complete

If it is not complete, the card deck is useless.

Si no está completo el juego de cartas no sirve para nada.

Corriente– common, ordinary

It was very common to see such conflicts on the block.

Era algo muy corriente ver ese tipo de conflictos en la cuadra.

Cortante– sharp

It was a very sharp response, taking into account what they had spoken before.

Fue una respuesta muy cortante tomando en cuenta lo que habían hablado antes.

Cotidiano– daily

It was designed to be given daily use.

Fue diseñado para que se le diera un uso cotidiano.

Cualquier– any

Any reason or circumstance will be taken very seriously by the board of directors.

Cualquier motivo razón o circunstancia será tomado muy en serio por la junta directiva.

Cubierto– covered

With this last loan, the project is covered completely.

Con este último préstamo el proyecto queda cubierto del todo.

Curioso– curious

It is quite curious that he did not refuse to go to that meeting.

Resulta bastante curioso elhecho de que no se negara a ir a esa reunión.

Debido– due

Due to reasons beyond my control, I must cancel the trip I had planned.

Debido a razones ajenas a mi voluta debo cancelar el viaje que tenía previsto.

Dejado– careless

He did not remember that he had left the keys inside the car.

No recordaba que había dejado las llaves adentro del auto.

Deliciosas– delicious

The cheesecakes of my grandmother are, without a doubt, simply delicious.

Las tortas de queso de mi abuela son sin lugar a dudas simplemente deliciosas.

Delirante– delirious

Of all the artists I have met, this humorist is the most delirious of all.

De todos los artistas que he conocido este humorista es el más delirante de todos.

Demente– crazy, mad

His insane way allowed him to go far and reach his goals.

Su demente forma de ser le permitió llegar muy lejos y alcanzar sus objetivos.

Desaforada– unbridled, boundless

It was a very unbridled discussion, where no agreement was reached.

Fue una discusión muy desaforada en la que no se llegó a ningún acuerdo.

Desagradable– unpleasant

His presence was rather unpleasant as I had to share his space with him.

Bastante desagradable era ya su sola presencia como para tener que compartir con él.

Desastroso– disastrous

His lifestyle is so disastrous that a homeless person is more orderly and balanced than he is.

Su estilo de vida es tan desastroso que un indigente es más ordenado y equilibrado que él.

Desbaratada– corrupted with lewdness

It was the most corrupted idea that had occurred to me so far.

Era la idea más desbaratada que se me había ocurrido hasta el momento.

Descartables– disposable

For me, their opinions were absolutely disposable, and I did not care what happens.

Para mi, sus opiniones eran absolutamente descartables y no me importa lo que pase.

Descomunal– colossal

In a huge and surrealist way, the play finished.

De forma descomunal y surrealista terminó, la obra de teatro.

Deshidratado– dehydrated

He arrived so dehydrated that he looked like a dry and burned leaf.

Llegó tan deshidratado que parecía una hoja seca y quemada.

Desnudo– naked

He thought it was a nudist beach, and when he arrived naked, everyone looked at him scandalized.

Pensó que era una playa nudista y cuando llegó desnudo todos lo miraban escandalizados.

Desordenado– messy, untidy

Having everything messy is a natural state in my life.

Ser y tener todo desordenado es un estado natural en mi vida.

Despreocupado– carefree

His secret to being so happy is that he has always been very carefree.

Su secreto para ser tan feliz es que siempre ha sido muy despreocupado.

Destacado– outstanding, distinguished

The distinguished of the scientific community will meet today secretly.

Lo más destacado de la comunidad científica se reunirá hoy de manera secreta.

Difíciles– difficult

It has been a very difficult year, raising my daughters alone.

Han sido unos años muy difíciles criando yo sólo a mis hijas.

Digno– worthy

There was nothing worthy of him except for his bad reputation.

No había nada digno en él salvo su mala reputación.

Diminuto– tiny, small

It's a problem so tiny that it's not worth to name it here.

Es un problema tan diminuto que no vale la pena ni nombrarloa quí.

Directo– direct, straight

The bullet went straight to the heart and through the lungs.

La bala entró directo al corazón y atravesó los pulmones.

Disfrazado– disguised

He infiltrated the group of Masons in disguise to collect information.

Se infiltrò disfrazado al grupo de los masones para recolectar información.

Distorsionado– twisted, distorted

That band not only played a distorted rhythm, but its appearance was also.

Esa banda no solo tocaba un ritmo distorsionado, sino que su aspectotambién lo era.

Disuelto– dissolved

Unable to make amends, the group had dissolved in the middle of the contract.

Sin poder intentar hacer las paces el grupo se había disuelto a mitad del contrato.

Dulce– sweet

His sweet voice was an advantage when talking and singing, and so he got what he wanted.

Su dulce voz era una ventaja a la hora de hablar y cantar y así conseguía lo que quería.

Egoísta– selfish, egotistical

I had never met someone as selfish as that guy before.

Nunca antes había conocido a alguién tan egoísta como ese sujeto.

Embarazada– pregnant

She was so sexy, sensual, daring, bold, and free that nobody was surprised to see her pregnant.

Era tan sexy sensual, atrevida, osada y libertaria que a nadie le sorprendió verla embarazada.

Enamorado– in love, romantic

He was so in love with her that he had completely forgotten to put on his pants.

Estaba tan enamorado de ella que se había olvidado por completo de ponerse los pantalones.

Encantadores– charming, likeable, delightful, lovely

The lovely children of the chorus sang the Gregorian chants as gods.

Los encantadores niños de la coral cantáron como dioses los cantos gregorianos.

Enfermo– sick person, mental

The atmosphere was so damp that he ended up sick because of the conditions of the place.

El ambiente era tan denso que terminò enfermo por las condiciones del lugar.

Enloquecida– insane, crazy, mad

That crazy way of being so irrational was what made me fall in love with her.

Esa en lo quecida manera de ser tan irracional fue lo que me enamoromás de ella.

Enloquecido– crazed

The crazed day had ended relatively quiet despite the madness.

El en loquecido día había terminado relativamente tranquilo a pesar de la locura.

Enorme– enormous, huge

The effort made by the Red Cross team in the accident was enormous.

Es realmente enorme el esfuerzo que realizó el equipo de la cruzroja en el accidente.

Ensordecedor– deafening

Deafening was the only term that could be used for that kind of music.

Ensordecedor era el único término que se podía utilizar para ese tipo de música.

Enterrado– buried

They had buried him in the Atacama Desert, as was his will.

Lo habían enterrado en el desierto de Atacama como era su voluntad.

Erguido– upright, straight

The soldiers stood straight at attention when the Sergeant walked in the barracks.

Los soldados se mantuvieron erguidos cuando el sargento entró en el cuartel.

Errante– wandering

A wandering Gypsy adventurer was the boyfriend of my daughter.

Un vagabundo aventurero gitano errante fue el novio que se consiguió mi hija.

Escondido– hidden, secret

He had hidden much better than Osama Bin Laden and Chapo Guzman.

Se había escondido mucho mejor que Osama Bin Laden y el Chapo Guzmán.

Espantosa– horrifying, hideous

She was really scary and terribly horrible, but the blind man loved her very much.

Era realmente espantosa y terriblement ehorrible pero el ciego la amaba mucho.

Especial– special

It was a very special moment, and he took full advantage of it.

Era un momento muy especial y lo aprovechó al máximo.

Estrafalaria– eccentric

His clothing was so eccentric that he was mistaken for a hermit.

Su indumentaria era tan estrafalaria que lo confundieron con un ermitaño.

Estrambótico– outlandish

There was no other way to describe his taste that was not outlandish.

No había otra forma de describir su gusto que no fuera estrambótico.

Estruendoso– thunderous

The thunderous storm was heard thousands of kilometers away.

La estruendosa tormenta se escuchó a miles de kilometros de distancia.

Estudiado– studied

The most studied of the participants was a 23-year-old Hindu who was a genius.

El más estudiado de los participantes era un hindú de 23 años que era un genio.

Estudioso– hard working, studious

You had to be very studious to belong to the elite group of the school.

Tenía sque ser muy estudioso para pertenecer al grupo élite de la escuela.

Extraño– strange, odd

It was strange he had arrived as a perfect stranger and now the most popular man in the country.

Era extraño que hubiera llegado como un perfecto desconocido y ahora el hombre más popular del país.

Extraviado– lost

The hiker had gone astray in the middle of the Amazon jungle.

El excursionista se había extraviado en el medio de la selva amazónica.

Fácil– easy, likely

It is really easy to understand the German language; you just have to be drunk.

Es realmente fácil entender el idioma alemán; sólo tienes que estar borracho.

Fallido– failed

It was a failed attempt to enter into negotiations with the Colombian guerrilla.

Fue un intento fallido de entrar en negociación con la guerrilla de Colombia.

Famoso– famous

The most famous of the mobsters died completely old and alone.

El más famoso de los mafiosos murió completamente viejo y sólo.

Fantástica– fantastic

The music was extraordinarily fantastic at that festival that lasted a week.

La música fue extra ordinariamente fantástica en ese festival que duró una semana.

Fija– fixed

A fixed fee was agreed upon in the poker players' club.

Se acordó una cuota fija en el club de jugadores de poker.

Forzoso– obligatory, forced

The forced landing was carried out successfully and without human losses, thanks to the pilot.

El aterrizaje forzoso se realizó con éxito y sin pérdidas humanas gracias al piloto.

Fresca– cool temperature

The night is quite cool today; it's ideal to go camping in the mountains.

La noche está bastante fresca hoy; es ideal para ir a acampar a la montaña.

Frio– cold temperature

Cold black tea is a drink with healing and energetic properties.

El té negro frío es una bebida con propieda descurativas y energéticas.

Galáctico– space-age, galactic

They inaugurated a galactic observatory in the Andean highlands.

Inauguraron un observatorio galáctico en los páramosandinos.

Giratorio– revolving

The stage of the theater had a revolving system for a better acting visual field.

El escenario del teatro tenía un sistema giratorio para un mejor campo visual actoral.

Gorda– fat, thick, big

The fattest of the group was the one who danced better and with more passion.

La más gorda del grupo era la que bailaba mejor y con más pasión.

Gran– grand

The great show of the drums of Japan will take place in the national theater.

El gran espectáculo de los tambores de Japón se llevará a cabo en el teatro nacional.

Griton– loudmouthed

Do not be so loudmouthed that you will deafen your parents and friends.

No seas tan gritón que vas a dejar sordos a tus padres y amigos.

Hecho– made up

The fact is that nobody showed up on time, and everything had to be canceled.

El hecho es que nadie se presentó a tiempo y se tuvo que cancelar todo.

Hediondo– stinky

He was so stinky that even the skunks and the destitute were turning away from him.

Estaba tan hediondo que hasta el mapurite y los indigentes se apartaban de él.

Humilde– humble, modest

The Buddhist teacher told him that he had obtained a lot of intelligence, but he is not humble.

El maestro Budista le dijo que había obtenido mucha inteligencia pero él no es humilde.

Imposible– impossible

If you project it in your mind, and you believe it yourself, nothing is impossible.

Si lo proyectas en tu mente y te lo crees tú mismo, nada es imposible.

Impresionante– impressive

It was really impressive, the virtuosity of the pianist of the new jazz band.

Realmente impresionante, el virtuosismo del pianista de la nueva banda de jazz.

Incomprensible– incomprehensible

It was absolutely incomprehensible the state the car was in.

Absolutamente incomprensibile el estado en que se encontraba el auto.

Indigente– destitute, homeless

The homeless man got a perfect place to spend the night at the train station.

El indigente consiguió un lugar perfecto para pasar la noche en la estación del tren.

Infallible– foolproof, infallible

The plan he had in mind to defraud the swindlers was infallible.

El plan que tenía en mente para estafar a los estafadores era infalible.

Infatigable– tireless

He had not seen a fighter so tireless for years.

Hacía años que no veía en acción a un luchador tan infatigable.

Infernal– hellish

It was quite a hellish experience to attend the meeting of parents and school representatives.

Fue toda una experiencia infernal asistir a la reunión de padres y representantes de la escuela.

Infinita– infinite

With infinite patience, he managed to remain calm in the middle of the earthquake.

Con infinita paciencia, logrópermanecertranquilo en medio del terremoto.

Infinito– infinite

The universe is infinite because it expands and extends, and matter only transforms.

El universo es infinito porque se expande, se extiende y la materia solo se transforma.

Ininterrumpido– uninterrupted

The forty-three uninterrupted cycle classes in a day were completed.

Se completò el ciclo de cuarenta y tres clases ininterrumpidas en un día.

Inmenso– immense, vast

Through the immense sea, there are amazing and dangerous mysteries.

A través del inmenso mar hay misterios asombrosos y peligrosos.

Inocente– innocent

The supreme court of justice declared him innocent and free of all charges.

La corte suprema de justicia lo declaró inocente y libre de todo cargo.

Inquietante– disturbing

The situation that happened today in the assembly was really disturbing.

Verdaderamente inquietante la situación que se vivió hoy en la asamblea.

Insólitos– unusual, extraordinary

He was one of the most unusual writers of his generation.

Fue uno de losescritores más insólitos de su generación.

Inútil– good for nothing, useless

It was so useless that it did not work or serve anything at all.

Era tan inútil que no servía ni para no servir para nada.

Invisible– invisible

He could practically be invisible because he was so unpopular.

Prácticamente podía ser invisible por lo impopular que era.

Izquierdo– left

The left side of the surface of Mars has not yet been explored.

El lad oizquierdo de la superficie de marte aún no se ha explorado.

Joven– young, young person

The casting required young people for the juvenile TV series.

El casting requeria gente joven para la serie de tv juvenil.

Juguetonas– playful

Squirrels are usually very playful, fast, and audacious.

Las ardillas suelen ser muy juguetonas veloces y audaces.

Junto– together

Together with all those people, the dog was hidden.

Junto a toda esa gente, escondido estaba el perro.

Justo– fair, just

Right at that moment, the car got into an accident.

Justo en este momento se me viene a quedar accidentado el carro.

Lanzado– forward, bold

The last shuttle from NASA was launched into space today.

Hoy fue lanzado al espacio el último transbordador de la Nasa.

Largo– length, long

He chose the longest path to meditate and clear his mind.

Escogió el camino más largo para poder meditar y despejar la mente.

Leído– well-informed, well-read

I am well-read in books about philosophy and sex, but none like this.

Soy muy leído en libros sobre filosofía y sexo, pero ninguno como este.

Lejana– distant

It was a very distant land beyond the boundaries of the border.

Era una tierra muy lejana más allá de los límites de la frontera.

Lento– slow

It was a very slow procedure like all bureaucratic systems.

Era un procedimiento muy lento como todos los sistemas burocráticos.

Linda– pretty

They called her pretty, not only because she was cute but because that was her name.

Le decían linda no solo porque fuera linda sino porque ese era su nombre.

Lleno– full

The stadium had a full house with the final of the championship.

El estadio tuvo un lleno total con la final del campeonato.

Mágico– magic, magical

For all the things, however simple, she found the magical side.

A todas las cosas, por muy simples, que fueran ella les encontraba el lado mágico.

Mal– bad, ill

Due to the bad behavior of the group, commercial relationships were broken.

Por el mal comportamiento del grupo se rompieron relaciones comerciales.

Malign– malignant, evil

The whole house had an evil air that made the atmosphere heavier.

Toda la casa tenía un aire maligno que hacía más pesado el ambiente.

Maniáticos– maniac, fanatical

The people whom they call maniacal and crazy are actually the most balanced.

Las personas los llaman maniáticos y locos, son en realidad los más equilibrados.

Maravilloso– wonderful

They found the place so wonderful that they return each year.

Les pareció tan maravilloso el lugar que cada año vuelven.

Mayor– older, larger, bigger

The eldest of the brothers took responsibility for the family and helped his younger brother.

El mayor de los hermanos dió la cara por la familia y ayudó a su hermanito menor.

Mejores– better, best

Since they were 4 years old, Carlos and Juan have been best friends.

Desde que tenían 4 años de edad Carlos y Juan han sido los mejores amigos.

Menor– smaller, younger, lowest

The price is much lower in this store than in the one we visited yesterday.

El precio es mucho menor en esta tienda que en la que visitamos ayer.

Menos– less, fewer

There are fewer bees now in the world than there were five years ago.

Ahora hay menos abejas en el mundo que hace cinco años.

Mismo– same

It is always the same with these condo meetings; nothing is ever solved.

Siempre es lo mismo con estas reuniones de condominio; nunca se soluciona nada.

Místico– mystic

That place had something mystical and was surrounded by a very spiritual atmosphere.

Ese lugar tenía algo místico y estaba rodeado de una atmósfera muy espiritual.

Modern– up to date, modern

The museum of modern art brought the largest collection of surrealist works.

El museo de arte moderno trajo la colección más grande de obras surrealistas.

Mojado– wet

The whole room had been wet from the numerous leaks in the ceiling.

Todo el cuarto había amanecido mojado por las numerosas goteras del techo.

Molestoso– annoying, nuisance

The director of the summer camp was quite annoying.

Era bastante molestoso el director del campamento de verano.

Muchas– many

He had missed many opportunities, and this time, he would be more attentive.

Había dejado pasar muchas oportunidades y esta vez estaría más atento.

Muerto– dead

When the police and the paramedics arrived, he was already dead.

Cuando llegaron los policías y los paramédicos ya estaba muerto.

Mugriento– filthy

That apartment was so filthy that there were six layers of trash on top of the floor.

Ese apartamento estaba tan mugriento que había seis capas de basura antes del piso.

Mundial– worldwide, global

He was saving a whole year to go to the soccer world cup in Russia.

Estuvo ahorrando un año entero para poder ir al mundial de fútbol en Rusia.

Nuevo– new

It was a new cell phone model, and that's why there was a high demand in the store.

Era un modelo nuevo de celular y por eso había alta demanda en el mercado.

Ocultos– hidden

They practiced all kinds of hidden rituals and other strange customs.

Practicaban toda clase de rituals ocultos y otras costumbres extrañas.

Ojeroso– haggard

He spent the whole night partying at a party, drinking everything and waking up haggard.

Pasó toda la noche de fiesta en fiesta bebiendo de todo y amaneció ojeroso.

Onírico– dreamlike

The dream world is something very complex to understand and is an altered state of consciousness.

El mundo onírico es algo muy complejo de entender y es un estadoalterado de conciencia.

Otro– other, another

Another way to cross to that country is crossing the river trail along the border.

Otro modo de cruzar a ese país es atravesando la trocha del río bordeando la frontera.

Pálidos– pale

The house of terror of that fair was so real that they left pale with fright.

La casa del terror de esa feria era tan real que salieron pálidos del susto.

Peleón– aggressive, rough

African bees can be very aggressive.

Las abejas africanas pueden ser muy peleón.

Peor– bad, worse

In some cases, the remedy is worse than the disease because of the pharmaceutical industry.

En algunos casos, el remedio es peor que la enfermedad por culpa de la industria farmacéutica.

Pequeños– young, small in size

The youngest of the group finished all the challenges earlier and more effectively.

Los más pequeños del grupo terminaron antes y con más eficacia todos los retos.

Perplejo– confused, perplexed

After what he saw in that strange country, he was perplexed, dazed, and self-conscious.

Después de lo que vió en ese extraño país, quedó perplejo, aturdido y acomplejado.

Pestilente– foul, pestilent

He was so pestilent, irreverent, cynical, and sarcastic when he spoke.

Era tan pestilente, irreverente, cínico y sarcástico cuando hablaba.

Poco– little, not much, not many

It's very little money because of the amount of forced labor he had to do.

Es muy poco dinero por la cantidad de trabajo forzado que debía realizar.

Poseído– possessed, consumed

It was obvious from the unusual and terrifying behavior that he was possessed.

Por su inusual y aterrador comportamiento era obvio que estaba poseído.

Preciosas– beautiful, precious

They found all kinds of precious jewels in the old, abandoned mine.

Encontraron todo tipo de joyas preciosas en la vieja mina abandonada.

Preocupado– worried, concerned about

I was very worried about the radioactive waste that was thrown into the river.

Estaba muy preocupado por los desperdicios radioactivos arrojados al río.

Preso– imprisoned

He served a ten-year prison sentence for a crime he did not commit.

Cumplió una condena de diez años preso por un crimen que no cometió.

Primer– first, main

First of all, nobody should be in these facilities at this time.

En primer lugar, nadie debería estar en estas instalaciones a estas horas.

Principiantes– inexperienced, beginner

All the critics and specialists were impressed because they earned a few beginner students.

Todosloscríticos y especialistas quedaro nimpresionados porque ganaron pocos estudiantes principiantes.

Propia– own

The happiness and tranquility of having a house of your own is nothing compared to anything.

La felicidad y tranquilidad de tener una casa propia no se compara con nada.

Quemado– burnt, scorched

For being irresponsible and haughty, it resulted in everything being burned.

Por ser irresponsable y altanero, resultó que terminò todo quemado.

Raro– weird, strange, odd

He was so strange that they thought he came from a strange country like Transylvania.

Era tan raro, que pensaban que venía de un paíse xtraño como Transilvania.

Real– real, true

The bomb threat in the courthouse was real.

La amenaza de bomba en el palacio de justicia era real.

Recalcitrante– stubborn

He was quite stubborn in his behavior and attitude.

Era bastante recalcitrante en su comportamiento y en la actitud.

Relajante– relaxing

That kind of music is so relaxing; I only listened to it for ten minutes and slept 12 hours.

Esa clase de música es tan relajante, que solo la escuché diez minutos y dormí 12 horas.

Remote– remote, distant

It was a remote place away from all kinds of civilization.

Era un remoto lugar apartado de todo tipo de civilización.

Retorcido– twisted

He was the most twisted, crazy, and insane patient of the participants.

Era el más retorcido enfermo loco y demente de los participantes.

Revoltoso– rebellious, naughty, troublemaker

The more rebellious the group was, the more they gained fame and publicity.

Mientras más revoltoso fuera el grupo ganaban más fama y publicidad.

Sabio– wise, sensible

The wise person is one who keeps silent walks, and in the midst of silence, helps others.

El sabio es aquel que guarda silenzioso los paseos y en medio del silencio, ayuda a los demás.

Salvaje– savages

The savage way in which the events occurred surprised even the rudest.

La manera salvaje en la que ocurrieron los hechos sorprendió hasta a los másrudos.

Sangrienta– bloody, cruel

It seems to me that the film was unnecessarily bloody without justification.

Me parece que la película fue innecesariamente sangrienta sin justificación.

Seco– dry

The drink was very dry because the barman was an inexperienced rookie.

Estaba muy seco ese trago se ve que el barman era un novato inexperto.

Seguidas– consecutive

The fines earned were consecutive, and that's why the car was confiscated, and the license was taken away.

Fueron mucca multas seguidas y por eso le confiscaro nel carro y le quitaron la licencia.

Seguro– safe, secure

Do not worry; the contract is secure, and everything will start to improve.

No te preocupes; el contrato es seguro y todo empezará a mejorar.

Semejante– similar

Such an idiot could not be the CEO of that prestigious company.

Semejante mamarracho no podía ser el director general de esa prestigiosa compañía.

Sidereal– astral

Astral space is still an infinite and mysterious unknown to the human being.

El espacio sideral es todavía una infinita y misteriosa incógnita para el ser humano.

Sorpresivo– unexpected

The unexpected attack was direct and right on target.

El ataque fue sorpresivo directo y seguro, justo en el blanco.

Subterráneo– underground subway, subterranean

The underground subway was full of graffiti and street musicians from all over the world.

El subterráneo estaba repleto de grafitis y músicos callejeros de todas partes del mundo.

Sufrido– long-suffering, patient

He had suffered so much that he was no longer able to cry or feel anything.

Había sufrido tanto que ya no era capaz de llorar ni de sentir nada.

Sumergido– submerged

He was so immersed in his thoughts that he did not leave his room for a week.

Estaba tan sumergido en sus pensamientos que no salió en una semana de su cuarto.

Supuesto– supposed, alleged

The alleged murder happened on the outskirts of the city at 11 o'clock at night.

El supuesto asesinato sucedió en las afueras de la ciudad a las 11 de la noche.

Temible– fearsome, frightful

The fearsome criminal had finally been captured but escaped after three weeks.

El temible criminal por fín había sido capturado pero se escapó a las tres semanas.

Templadas– lukewarm, mild

Those who chose to camp with the group of the university were in very mild temperatures.

Eran zonas muy templadas las que escogieron para acampar con el grupo de la universidad.

Tenebroso– gloomy, sinister

That gentleman looked so dark that nobody came near him.

Ese señor tenía un aspecto tan tenebroso que nadie se le acercaba.

Terrenal– earthly

Because of his spiritual and mystical faculties, he did not seem an earthly being.

Por sus facultades espirituales y místicas, no parecía un ser terrenal.

Tierna– tender, loving

The sweet and tender way he had to say things opened many doors.

La manera dulce y tierna que tenía de decir las cosas le abría muchas puertas.

Tímido– timid, shy

The shyest of the class became a very controversial comedian years later.

El más tímido de la clase se convirtió años después en un humorista muy polémico.

Todos– total, all

All should attend the anthropology symposium in Mexico.

Absolutamente todos debían asistir al simposio de antropología en México.

Tolerante– tolerant

Despite being the head of the interracial relations department, he was not at all tolerant.

A pesar de ser jefe del departamento de relaciones interraciales no era nada tolerante.

Tonto– foolish, dumb, idiot

The foolish wisdom is the philosophy of the sacred clowns called Heyokas.

La sabiduría del tonto es la filosofía de los payasos sagrados denominados Heyokas.

Torpes– clumsy, dim-witted

Clumsy and careless was how the new members of work were described.

Torpes y descuidados fueron descritos a los nuevos integrantes del trabajo.

Trabajadores– hardworking

The workers argued for hours in the union for their labor rights.

Los trabajadores discutieron por horas en el sindicato por sus derechos laborales.

Tremendous– terrible, enormous

Tremendous seismic movements were recorded yesterday morning.

Tremendos movimientos sísmicos se registraron ayer a primera hora de la mañana.

Triste– sad

There was no human power to take him out of his sad situation.

No había poder humano que lo sacara de su triste situación.

Últimos– last

In the last year, there have been more car accidents and domestic disputes.

En los últimos años han sucedido más accidentes automovilísticos y domésticos.

Única– only, unique

The only way I understand these rituals is by lying when I say I understand them.

La única forma de que yo entienda esos rituales es mintiendo al decir que los entiendo.

Vagabundos– homeless

The homeless people are the most honest and sincere people on the planet.

Los vagabundos son las personas más honestas y sinceras del planeta.

Valiente– courageous, brave

Being brave has nothing to do with being strong and popular.

Ser valiente no tiene nada que ver con ser fuerte y popular.

Veloz- fast

He was a very fast runner even without any kind of training.

Era un corredor muy veloza ún sin tener ningún tipo de entrenamiento.

Venenoso- venomous

They discovered that the contents of that bottle were not poisonous.

Descubrieron que el contenido de ese frasco no era venenoso.

Verdadero– right, real

The feeling she had expressed to her friend was totally real.

El sentimiento que le había manifestado a su amiga era totalmente verdadero.

Viejo– old, old man

That old fisherman knew exactly by looking at the sea if there was to be a storm.

Aquel viejo pescador sabía con exactitud solo con mirar el mar si habría tormenta.

Visto– seen, viewed

What he had seen was not at all a hallucination or the product of alcohol.

Lo que había visto no fue para nada una alucinación ni producto del alcohol.

Vivo– alive

Feeling alive is a fortunate condition in this world of the undead.

Sentirse vivo es una condición afortunada en este mundo de muertos vivientes.

Voluntario– voluntary

It was voluntary work in the oldest hostel in Greece.

Trabaja como voluntario en el hostal más antiguo de Grecia.

Adverbs — Adverbios

Además– besides, in addition

In addition to speaking Japanese and French, he speaks six other languages perfectly.

Además de hablar Japonés y francés habla otros seis idiomas a la perfección.

Abajo– down, below

My cat always likes to hide under my bed.

A mi gato le gusta esconderse siempre abajo de mi cama.

Acá– here, over there

You do not have to move so much, just a little closer over here.

No tienes que moverte tanto, arrímate un poco másacá.

Acertadamente– correctly, appropriately

The group correctly resolved that they would have to renew the contract every three years.

El grupo resolvió acertadamente que tendrían que renovar el contrato cada tresaños.

Adentro– inside, in

All the photographs that they thought were lost were found inside the trunk.

Todas las fotografías que creían que estaban perdidas las encontraron adentro del baúl.

Ahí– there

No one could believe that the famous artist's house was right there in the center of the city.

Nadie podía creer que la casa del famoso artista estaba ahí mismo en el centro de la ciudad.

Ahora– now, in a minute

Now that we are all in agreement with the conditions, we can start the meeting.

Ahora que todos estamos de acuerdo con las condiciones podemos empezar la reunión.

Alrevés– backwards

In this academy, we do things in reverse of how they are supposed to be done.

Es esta academia, hacemos las cosas al revés de como se supone deben hacerse.

Allá- there

Far away in the mountains, you can see the monument of the mountaineer.

Allá a lo lejos en la montaña se puede ver el monumento al alpinista.

Alrededor- around

Everyone held hands and began to dance around the fire.

Todos se tomaron de la mano y comenzaron a bailar alrededor del fuego.

Antes– earlier, soon, before

They had made it very clear that before going to the concert, he had to clean his room.

Le habían dejado muy claro que antes de ir al concierto debía arreglar su habitación.

Aparentemente– apparently

Apparently, they could not cross the border because of diplomatic problems.

Aparentemente no podían cruzar la frontera por problemas diplomáticos.

Apenas– barely, hardly

As soon as you see your sister arrive, please let me know immediately.

Apenas veas que llega tu hermana, me avisas inmediatamente por favor.

Arriba– up, upstairs, above

You should check a little higher where the other suitcases are located.

Debes revisar un poco másarriba donde están las otras maletas.

Atrás– behind, the back of, back, backward

You have to go much further back, so you have more space to run.

Tienes que ponerte mucho más atrás para que tengas más espacio para correr.

Automáticamente– automatically

The money was from the same bank, so it was automatically available.

El dinero se hizo efectivo automáticamente porque era de la misma entidad bancaria.

Bien– well, good

Everything that begins with dedication and enthusiasm ends well.

Todo lo que se comienza con dedicación y entusiasmo termina bien.

Cerca– close, near, nearby

It is necessary to stay close enough to the airport to arrive on time.

Es necesario hospedarnos lo suficientemente cerca del aeropuerto para llegar a tiempo.

Como– how

How can it be possible that at this point, they still have not given us the result of the exam?

¿Cómo puede ser posible que todavía no nos entreguen el resultado del examen?

Debajo– underneath, beneath

Below all these folders, you will find the registration form.

Debajo de todas esas carpetas, encontrarás la planilla de inscripción.

Demasiado– too

It is too early to make such an important and delicate decision.

Es demasiado pronto para tomar una decisión tan importante y delicada.

Dentro– inside, indoors

In ten minutes, we will start the theater event.

Dentro de diez minutos, daremos inicio a la función de teatro.

Después– after, later

We already warned about the procedures they have in the town, so they do not complain later.

Cómo ya le avisamos las conductas que tienen en el pueblo después no se quejen.

Detalladamente– in detail

The detectives investigated the case in detail for two weeks.

Los detectives investigaron el caso detalladamente durante dos semanas.

Detrás– behind

Mt. Everest is behind all of us and can be seen in all its immensity.

Detrás de todos nosotros está el Everest y se puede apreciar en toda su inmensidad.

Diariamente– daily

It was very hard to discover that threats were left daily on the doorstep of the house.

Fue muy fuerte descubrir que nos dejaban amenazas diariamente en la puerta de la casa.

Encima– above, on top

I left the bag on top of the fridge with the food for the trip.

Encima de la nevera te deje la bolsa con la comida del viaje.

Enfrente– in front of

I changed so much in these years that you would not recognize me even when standing right in front of me.

Cambié tanto estos años que no me reconocerías ni estando en frente de mi.

Entonces– then

Only then did I understand that it would be very difficult to forget what happened that afternoon.

Sólo entonces comprendí que sería muy difícil olvidar lo que sucedió aquella tarde.

Fijamente– intently

The hypnotist only had to stare intently at the lady to put her to sleep.

Al hipnotizador solo le bastó mirar fijamente a la señora para ponerla a dormir.

Inmediatamente– immediately

This neighborhood is really very dangerous; let us go immediately from here.

Este barrio es de verdad muy peligroso; vámonos inmediatamente de aquí.

Jamás– never

After what happened, you showed me that I should never trust you again.

Después de lo que pasó me demostraste que jamás debo volver a confiar en ti.

Lejos– far, far away

No place is far away if you intend to arrive with determination.

Ningún lugar está lejos si te propones llegar con determinación.

Lentamente– slowly

We must be very careful and lift the jars slowly because they contain nitrogen.

Debemos tener mucho cuidado y levantar los frascos lentamente porque contienen nitrógeno.

Literalmente– literally

He took everything he heard literally, and that's why everything turned into confusion.

Todo lo que escuchó se lo tomó literalmente y por esotodo se volvió una confusión.

Luego– then, later

After they found the road, they kept driving more calmly.

Luego de que encontraron el camino, siguieron manejando con más tranquilidad.

Más – more

Every day, there are more people who want to legalize marijuana for recreational use.

Cada día, somos más los que queremos que legalicen la marihuana para uso recreacional.

Muy– very

The artistic proposal presented in the national theater was very avant-garde.

La propuesta artística que presentaron en el teatro nacional fue muy vanguardista.

Nuevamente– again

I had to correct my new book six times and ended up rewriting it again.

Mi nuevo libro lo tuve que corregir seis veces y escribirlo nuevamente.

Nunca– never, not ever

I do not think I'll ever find another car like this anymore.

Creo que nunca volveré a encontrar otro automóvil como este ya no los fabrican igual.

Pausadamente– slowly

Approach slowly without making much noise so as not to wake the children.

Vayan acercándose pausadamente sin hacer mucho ruido para no despertar a los niños.

Perfectamente– perfectly

I know that you can perfectly reach all your goals.

Yo sé que tú puedes perfectamente alcanzar todas tus metas.

Precisamente– precisely

Precisely for those same reasons, I do not want to work there again.

Precisamente por esas mismas razones es que no quiero volver a trabajar ahí.

Profundamente– deeply, profoundly

I feel it in my soul deeply, but it is impossible to recover confidence in you.

Lo siento profundamente en el alma, pero es imposible recuperar la confianza en ti.

Quizás– maybe, perhaps

Maybe we can try to fix the old motorcycle that is in the garage.

Quizás podamos intentar arreglar la vieja motocicletta que está en elgaraje.

Rápidamente– quickly, fast

The rescue team acted quickly and saved all the victims of the earthquake.

El equipo de rescate actuó rápidamente y salvaron a todas las víctimas del terremoto.

Realmente– actually, really

I really do not think it's prudent for you to travel in those conditions.

Realmente no creo que sea prudente que viajes en esas condiciones.

Salvajemente– wildly

They made love wildly all night until dawn.

Hicieron el amor salvajemente toda la noche hasta el amanecer.

Seguidamente– next, immediately afterward

Next, we will explain the operation of the power plant.

Seguidamente pasaremos a explicar el funcionamiento de la planta eléctrica.

Seriamente– seriously

It is necessary that you take this job seriously; otherwise, you will not have another opportunity.

Es necesario que te tomes este trabajo seriamente; de lo contrario no tendrás otra oportunidad.

Siempre– always

Whatever happens, whatever it is, we will always be together.

Pase lo que pase, sea lo quesea, estaremos siempre juntos.

Simplemente– simply, just

It just does not seem right to me to leave your work without telling anyone.

Simplemente no me parece correcto que dejes tu trabajo sin avisarle a nadie.

Siquiera– not even

You even thought about it one time before giving that answer so lightly.

Siquiera lo pensaste una véz antes de dar esa respuesta tan a la ligera.

Solamente– only, just

It only takes one more signature, so the contract will be legal.

Solamente hace falta una firma más asíel contrato será legal.

Solo- only

I was thinking for two hours, and I think it's best to travel alone.

Estuve dos horas pensando y creo que lo mejor es viajar solo.

Sucesivamente– in succession, so on

I will go from Colombia to Ecuador, from Ecuador to Mexico, from Mexico to Spain, and so on.

Iré de Colombia a Ecuador de Ecuador a México de México a España y así sucesivamente.

También– also, too

You can be sure that I, too, will be prepared for the fight.

Puedes estar seguro que yo también estaré preparado para la pelea.

Tampoco– neither, nor

It is neither good for you to put on like that, nor exaggerate so much.

Tampoco es para que te pongas así y exageres tanto.

Tanto– so much, very much

I cannot understand how you let go so long without going to the dentist.

No puedo entender cómo dejaste pasar tanto tiempo sin ir al dentista.

Todavía– still, yet

I have not seen the first positive comment about the article you published.

Todavía no he visto el primer comentario positivo sobre el artículo que publicaste.

Totalmente– totally, completely

I totally disagree with what you just said.

Estoy totalmente en desacuerdo con lo que acabas de decir.

Valientemente– bravely

He courageously volunteered to travel and cover the conflict in Palestine.

Valientemente se ofreció como voluntario para viajar y cubrir el conflicto en Palestina.

Verdaderamente– really

What has just happened is truly unusual even for me.

Esto que acaba de ocurrir es verdaderamente insólito hasta para mí.

Action Verbs — Verbos de Acción (Transitive verbs)

Abrir- to open

Opening and closing the door is a safety habit at school.

Abrir y cerrar la puerta es un hábito de seguridad en la escuela.

Acabar- to end, to finish

We have to end this absurd discussion immediately.

Tenemos que acabar con esta absurda discusión inmediatamente.

Acercó– to move closer

He got too close to the fire and had third-degree burns.

Se acercó demasiado al fuego y tuvo quemaduras de tercer grado.

Acompañar- to accompany, to go with

Each child must be accompanied by their parents or representatives.

A cada niño lo deben acompañar sus padres o representantes.

Afinar- to tune

I took a long time to learn how to tune my electric guitar.

Tarde mucho tiempo en aprender a afinar mi guitarra eléctrica.

Agarrar- to grab

The competition is that you must grab as many feathers as possible with one hand.

La competencia es que debes agarrar tantas plumas comoseaposible con una mano.

Alborotar– to disturb

He was imprisoned for disturbing and altering a public order.

Lo metieron preso por alborotar y alterar el orden público.

Amarrar– to tie, to secure

We have to secure the edges of the tree house very well.

Tenemos que amarrar muy bien los bordes de la casa del árbol.

Anulado– to cancel

For obvious reasons already presented, the contract is canceled.

Por razones obvias ya presentadas, el contrato queda anulado.

Armando– to assemble

My son spent all day assembling his lego towers.

Mi hijo se pasó todo el día armando sustorres de lego.

Arreglar- to fix, to repair

It is not at all simple to have to fix the electrical system of the office.

No es nada simple tener que arreglar el sistema eléctrico de la oficina.

Arrugada– to wrinkle

The shirt I wore this morning was more wrinkled than my grandmother's belly.

La camisa que me puse esta mañana estaba más arrugada que la panza de mi abuela.

Atrapar– to catch

No one could catch the thief they called Crazy Legs.

Nadie podía atrapar a ese ladrón al que llamaban el Piernas Locas.

Atravesar– to cross

After traversing the mountains for six days in a row, he reached the top and celebrated.

Después de atravesar las montañas por seis días seguidos, llegó a la cima y celebró.

Bañar– to bathe

The same thing always happens every time I go to bathe the water goes away.

Siempre pasa lo mismo cada vezque me voy a bañar se va elagua.

Beber– to drink

I had no schedules or limitations or any restrictions to drink.

No tenía horarios ni limitaciones ni ningún tipo de restricciones para beber.

Buscar– to search for

Let's all go together to find a good place to camp.

Vamos todos juntos a buscar un buen lugar para acampar.

Cambiar– to change

We have to change some habits in our lives so that different things happen.

Hay que cambiar algunas costumbres en nuestras vidas para que sucedan cosas diferentes.

Cantar– to sing

Since I have use of reason, there is nothing that I like as much as singing.

Desde que tengo uso de razón, no hay nada que me guste tanto como cantar.

Casados- to marry

They have been married so long that they no longer remember if they are spouses, brothers, cousins, or what.

Tienen tanto tiempo casados que ya no se acuerdan si son esposos, hermanos, primos o que.

Cerrar– to close

They were told very clearly that they should make sure to close all the doors.

Se les dijo muy claramente que debían asegurarse de cerrar todas las puertas.

Chiflados- to whistle, to hiss at

The girls hate it when the guys whistle at them while walking down the street.

Las chicas lo odian cuando los chicos chiflados mientras caminan por la calle.

Cocinar– to cook

He was such a spiritual chef that he spent an hour meditating in the kitchen before cooking.

Era un chef tan espiritual que antes de cocinar pasaba una hora meditando en la cocina.

Coleccionar– to collect

I inherited my passion for collecting stamps from my grandfather.

Heredé de mi abuelo la pasión por coleccionar estampillas.

Colocar– to place

We will have to put all the pieces in their place again.

Tendremos que colocar todas las piezas en su lugar de nuevo.

Columpiarse– to swing

There is nothing more amazing when you are a child than to swing.

No hay nada más alucinante cuando se es niño que columpiarse.

Comer– to eat

One of the great pleasures of life is to eat if it does not become gluttony.

Uno de los grandes placeres de la vida es comer, si no se convierte en gula.

Confundir– to confound

Confuse and reign is one of the tactics and strategies of all governments.

Confunde y reinarás es una de las tácticas y estrategias de todos los gobiernos.

Conocer– to meet, to know

There is no worse ignorance than the one who says that he does not need to know anything.

No hay peor ignorante que aquel que dice que no le hace falta conocer nada.

Construer– to build

To build that tourist complex, more than 400 workers were needed.

Para construir ese complejo turístico se necesitaron más de cuatrocientos obreros.

Contar– to count, to tell

The game consisted of counting how many bricks were in the medieval Hohenzollern Castle.

El juego consistía en contar cuántos ladrillos había en el castillo medieval de Hohenzollern.

Contener– to contain

As much as he tried not to ruin the surprise, he could not contain the urge to laugh.

Por más que lo intentò para no arruinar la sorpresa, no pudo contener las ganas de reír.

Contester– to answer

The phone rang more than twenty times, but he was unable to answer.

El teléfono sonaba más de veinte veces, pero él era incapaz de contestar.

Convertir– to turn into

Converting coal into gold or anything into gold was the obsession of the alchemists.

Convertir el carbón en oro o cualquier cosa en oro era la obsesión de los alquimistas.

Cortar– to cut

After seeing myself in the mirror this morning, I knew that I had to cut my hair.

Después de verme en el espejo esta mañana, supe que me debía cortarel pelo.

Cumplir– to achieve

I must meet all the requirements to be admitted to the music academy.

Debo cumplir con todos los requisitos para poder ser admitido en la academia de música.

Deber– to owe, must

We must try to do something to improve the situation in the country.

Es nuestro deber intentar hacer algo para mejorar la situación del país.

Decider– to decide

One of the most difficult things is deciding how to explain political crises to our children.

Una de las cosas más difíciles es decider cómo explicarles la crisis política a nuestros hijos.

Descifrar– to decipher, to figure out

Scientists and Egyptologists came together to decipher the latest archaeological findings.

Los científicos y los egiptólogos se unieron para descifrar los últimos hallazgos arqueológicos.

Decir- to say, to tell

It is very easy to say that you can do anything; the hard part is to fulfill and demonstrate them.

Es muy fácil decir que puedes hacer cualquier cosa; lo difícil es cumplirlas y demostrarlas.

Dejar– to allow oneself, to leave

To allow oneself to stop the habit of smoking when it becomes a vice is something that requires willpower.

Dejar el hábito de fumar cuando se convierte en vicio es algo que requiere fuerza de voluntad.

Demostrar– to prove, to demonstrate

He was such a good politician that nobody could prove anything against him.

Era tan buen político que nadie le pudo demostrar nada en su contra.

Derrochar– to squander, to throw money away

Most people are not used to having money, and they start squandering.

La mayoría de las personas no están acostumbradas a tener dinero y empiezan a derrochar.

Desbaratando– to disrupt

The headlines of the press and social networks announce that Madonna continues to disrupt platforms.

Los titulares de la prensa y redes sociales anuncian que Madonna sigue desbaratando tarimas.

Descomponer– to tear down

After a while, just like the fish, the visit begins to decompose.

Después de un tiempo, al igual que los pescados, la visita se empieza a descomponer.

Descubrir– to discover, to uncover

Astronomers always dream that they are going to discover a new galaxy.

Los astrónomos sueñan siempre que están a punto de descubrir una nueva galaxia.

Despegar- to take off

The passenger plane bound for Nepal could not take off for security reasons.

El avión de pasajeros con destino a Nepal no pudo despegar por razones de seguridad.

Detener- to stop

We have to stop this misfortune once and for all.

Tenemosque detener esta desgracia de una vez por todas.

Devolver- to give back, to return

The shirt was two sizes too small, so it had to be returned.

La camisa era dostallas demasiado pequeñas, por lo que tuvo que devolverla.

Dibujar– to draw

I remember that I started drawing when I was two years old.

Recuerdo que comencé a dibujar cuando tenía dos años de edad.

Dirigir- to run, to manage

Maestro Martelli started managing the national symphony orchestra from 10 years of age.

El maestro Martelli empezó a dirigir la orquesta sinfónica nacional desde los 10 años de edad.

Disponer- to have, to arrange

When you have finished legalizing the contract, you can arrange to dispose of your money.

Cuando se haya terminado de legalizar el contrato podrá usted disponer de su dinero.

Elegida– to choose

She was chosen as the queen of the carnival for two years in a row.

Ella fue elegida como la reina del carnaval por dos años seguidos.

Empujar– to push

There were twelve people in total, pushing the crashed truck on the road.

Fueron doce personas en total empujando al camión accidentado en la carretera.

Encender– to light, to turn on

To light a fire, the wood must be very dry.

Para encender una fogata se necesita que la madera esté muy seca.

Encontrar- to find

They used two private investigators to find lost family members.

Utilizaron dos investigadores privados para encontrar a los familiares perdidos.

Enfrentar– to contront, to face

Today, they will face the two legends of Latin American football, Argentina and Brazil.

Hoy se van a enfrentar las dos leyendas del fútbol latinoamericano Argentina y Brasil.

Enloquecer– to go crazy

It is easy to go mad in the hectic pace of life.

Es fácil enloquecer en el agitado ritmo de vida.

Ensayando– to try out

The theater group was rehearsing all week for the premiere of the play.

El grupo de teatro estuvo ensayando toda la semana para el estreno de la obra.

Entender– to understand

Understanding how all religions work is like understanding what women want.

Entender cómo funcionan todas las religiones es cómo saber qué quieren las mujeres.

Enterar- to inform

Thanks to the bad habit of gossip about what Ricardo has, everyone knew what was happening.

Gracias al mal hábito del chismequé tiene Ricardo todos se enteraban de lo quepasaba.

Escalar- to climb

Climbing Everest was more than a project; it is the dream of his entire life.

Escalar el everest era más que un proyecto; es el sueño de toda su vida.

Escribir- to write

One of the best therapies to perform catharsis is to write.

Una de las majores terapias para hacer catarsis es escribir.

Escuchar- to listen to, to hear

It is easy to maintain healthy and stable relationships; you just need to know how to listen.

Es fácil mantener relaciones sanas y estables; solo hace falta saber escuchar.

Estrellar– to smash, to crash

The stolen motorcycle that the criminal handled came to crash right in the police station.

La moto robada que manejaba el criminal se vino a estrellar justo en la estación de policía.

Estudiar- to study

Of all the weapons and defense systems, studying is the most effective.

De todas las armas y sistemas de defense estudiar es la más efectiva.

Extrañar- to miss

Before I got the news that she would leave, I had already begun to miss her.

Antes de que me dieran la noticia de que ella se iría ya la había empezado a extrañar.

Fabricar– to fabricate

To fabricate these sports facilities, it took four weeks.

Para fabricar esas instalaciones deportivas se necesitaron cuatro semanas.

Fastidiar- to annoy

He was an expert at teasing his younger brother and swearing it was not him.

Era un experto a la hora de fastidiar a su hermano menor y jurar que no había sido él.

Festejar- to celebrate

He was capable of celebrating anything just to drink beer and rum.

Era capaz de festeja rcualquier cosa con tal de beber cerveza y Ron.

Filmar- to film

The production team found the perfect location to shoot.

El equipo de producción encontró las locaciones perfectas para filmar.

Ganar- to win

We are going to win because we deserve it for hard training and dedication.

Vamos a ganar ya que nos los merecemos por el duro entrenamiento y la dedicación.

Girar- to spin, to turn

You had to turn counterclockwise to win this level of the game.

Había que girar en sentido contrario a las agujas del reloj para ganar este nivel del juego.

Grabar- to record

They decided to record the nine scenes that were short despite the bad weather.

Decidieron grabar las nueve escenas que faltaban a pesar del mal clima.

Hacer- to make, to do

Doing everything they ask for in less than forty-eight hours is almost impossible.

Hacer todo lo que piden en menos de cuarenta y ocho horas es casi imposible.

Imaginar- to imagine

Imagining things is the trade of poets, comedians, actors, magicians, children, and madmen.

Imaginar cosas es el comercio de poetas, los humoristas, los actores, los magos, los niños y los locos.

Imitar- to imitate

He was the best at imitating famous people's voices and machine sounds.

Era el major en imitar voces de personas famosas y sonidos de máquinas.

Instalando- to install

They took on more than the bill by installing the cable television antennas.

Se tardaron más de la cuenta instalando las antenas de televisión por cable.

Insultando– to insult, to offend

The humorist Groucho Marx was a teacher, insulting the audience with irony and sarcasm.

El humorista Groucho Marx era un maestro, insultando con ironía y sarcasmo al público.

Intercambiar- to exchange

When I was a kid, I liked to exchange my collectible toys for other models.

Cuando era niño, me gustaba intercambiar mis juguetes de colección por otros modelos.

Inventar- to invent

Inventing has been a curse and a blessing of geniuses such as Da Vinci and Einstein.

Inventar ha sido una maldición y una bendición de genios como Da Vinci y Einstein.

Investigar- to investigate

Since the way things happened was very suspicious, they decided to investigate.

Dado a que la forma en que sucedieron las cosas era muy sospechosa, decidieron investigar.

Lanzar– to throw

Everything was ready to launch the new product to the world market.

Todo estaba listo para lanzar el nuevo producto al mercado mundial.

Leer- to read

Of all the possible ways of transporting, reading is the best way to travel.

De todas las formas posibles de transportarse leer es la mejor forma de viajar.

Levanter - to raise, to lift

To lift that wall, fourteen-thousand seven-hundred bricks and twelve-thousand stones were needed.

Para levantarese muro se necesitaron catorcemilsetecientos ladrillos y docemil piedras.

Limpiar- to clean

My grandmother was obsessed with cleaning everything three times with meticulous revision.

Mi abuela estaba obsesionada con limpiar todo tres veces con meticulosa revisión.

Llenar- to fill

There is nothing that bothers me more than having to fill out forms and surveys.

No hay nada que me moleste más que tener que llenar formularios y encuestas.

Lograr- to reach, to be able to

Sixteen musicians from different genres collaborated to achieve the final result.

Para lograr e lresultado final del disco colaboraron 16 músicos de distintos géneros.

Manteniendo- to maintain

Keeping calm and serene was the only way they managed to escape.

Manteniendo la calma y la serenidad fue la única forma con la que consiguieron escapar.

Memorizer - to memorize

It was a phenomenon; I could memorize all the names and numbers in the phone book.

Era un fenómeno; podía memorizar todos los nombres y números de la guía telefónica.

Mezcladas- to mix

The folders were so mixed up that it took two weeks to verify the information.

Las carpetas estaban tan mezcladas que tardaron dos semanas en verificar la información.

Mirar- to look at

It's awesome how I could not stop looking at the moon.

Es impresionante como no podía dejar de mirar la luna.

Mostrarle- to show

His work was to show all tourist destinations to visitors.

Sus labores estaba la de mostrarle todos los destinos turísticos a los visitantes.

Mover- to move

To move these rocks without the help of any type of machine, 150 workers were needed.

Para mover esas rocas sin ayuda de ningún tipo de máquinas fueron necesarios 150 obreros.

Necesitar- to need

You never know when you're going to need that person you criticize so much.

Nunca sabes cuándo vas a necesitar de esa persona que tanto criticas.

Pensarlo– to think

If you sit to think too much, you never will.

Si te sientas a pensarlo demasiado, nunca lo harás.

Perder- to lose

The more you assimilate how to lose, you will be better prepared for success.

Mientras más asimiles como perder estarás mejor preparado para eléxito.

Perseguido– to pursue

He was a politically persecuted for many years until he was granted amnesty.

Fue durante muchos años un perseguido político hasta que le otorgaron la amnistía.

Fotografíar- to photograph

They sent him to Africa to photograph the behavior of the gorillas.

Lo mandaron al África para fotografiar el comportamiento de los gorilas.

Poder- to be able to

We need to be able to bring together twenty actors of different nationalities with the same physical characteristics.

Necesitamos reunir a veinte actores de diferentes nacionalidades con las mismas características físicas.

Poner- to put

You have to get used to putting things in place in all aspects of life.

Hay que acostumbrarse a poner las cosas en su sitio en todos los aspectos de la vida.

Preparar- to prepare

To start preparing lunch, you need to have all the ingredients.

Para empezar a preparar el almuerzo, es necesario tener todos los ingredientes.

Presenter - to present

There had to be diplomatic apologies for the inconvenience caused.

Había que presentar disculpas diplomáticas por las molestias causadas.

Proteger- to protect

To protect the witnesses, double surveillance had to be reinforced.

Para proteger a los testigos, se tuvo que reforzar la vigilancia al doble.

Provocando– to provoke, to cause

He was sentenced to two years in prison for provoking the church and the government.

Le dieron una sentencia de dos años de prisión por estar provocando a la iglesia y el gobierno.

Querer- to want

Wanting to pretend to be what you do not know should only be done by actors.

Querer pretender ser lo que no se es deberían hacerlo solo los actores.

Recibir – to receive

Receiving the Nobel Prize for Literature helped him to be able to help many more people.

Recibirel premio Nobel de literatura lo ayudó a poder ayudar a muchas más personas.

Repetir- to repeat, to do again

Repeating the same lie more than a hundred times will make it come true.

Repetir la misma mentira más de cien veces hará que se convierta en realidad.

Resolver- to solve

This conflict has to be resolved in the most peaceful way possible.

Todo este conflicto se tiene que resolver de la manera más pacífica posible.

Respetado- to respect

For his bravery, integrity, and honor, he came to be respected even by his friends.

Por su valentía, integridad y honor, llegó a ser respetado hasta por sus amigos.

Robar- to steal

Stealing that old cadillac was his first job in organized crime.

Robarse ese viejo cadillac fué su primer trabajo en el crimen organizado.

Saber- to know, to taste

Knowing how to differentiate lettuce from a beet is a mystery to me.

Saber diferenciar una lechuga de una remolacha es un misterio para mi.

Sacar– to take out, to remove

To take the best advantage of the situation—however bad it may be—is an attitude of winners.

Sacar el mejor provecho de la situación—por mala quesea—es una actitud de vencedores.

Seguir– to follow

To keep insisting on the same subject following the complaints is silly.

Seguir insistiendo en el mismo tema después de las quejas es cosa de necios.

Separar - to separate

The news that the president and his wife are going to separate went viral.

La noticia de que el presidente y su esposa se van a separar se volvió viral.

Soltar– to let go of, to loosen

Releasing all spiritual and material ties brings you closer to transcendence.

Soltar todas las ataduras espirituales y materiales te acerca a la transcendencia.

Soñando– to dream

A dreaming man invented the car, phone, movies, and the plane and went to the moon.

Soñando el hombre inventò el automóvil, el teléfono, el cine, el avión y llegó a la luna.

Sostener– to hold

To hold your principles with total certainty and responsibility is the virtue of a person of integrity.

Sostener con total certeza y responsabilidad tus principios es virtud de gente íntegra.

Subir– to go up

My foot got caught in the escalator as I was going up.

Mi pie quedó atrapado en la escalera mecánica mientras subía.

Subrayar– to underline

When analyzing and diagnosing the factors of separation, we must emphasize the essential.

Al analizar y diagnosticar los factores de la separación, hay que subrayar lo esencial.

Tapar– to cover

They used a hundred meters of plastic to temporarily cover the hole in the roof.

Para tapar el hueco del techo previsionalmente utilizaron cien metros de plástico.

Tardar- to take

It is better that they carry enough supplies because this will take a while.

Es mejor que lleven suficientes suministros porque esto tomará un tiempo.

Temido- to fear

For two decades, he was the most feared bandit in the entire Old West.

Fué por dos décadas, el bandido mást emido de todo el viejo oeste.

Tocarse– to touch

It is advisable to touch your breasts and chest to detect cancer in time.

Es recomendable tocarse los senos y el pecho para detectar a tiempo el cáncer.

Traer- to take

The logistics to bring the whole team of anthropologists is a gigantic task.

La logística para traer a todo el equipo de antropólogos es una labor titánica.

Ubicar- to locate

We are the San Bernabé Coffee Hostel, and we are located in Bogotá.

Somos el Hostal Café san Bernabé y estamos ubicadosen Bogotá.

Usar- to use

In order not to waste anything, we must use all the whole corn dough.

Para no desperdiciar nada, debemos usar toda la masa de maíz.

Vaciar- to empty

You have to empty the entire pantry in order to take a complete inventory.

Hay que vaciar toda la despensa para poder hacer un inventario completo.

Vender- to sell

The winner will be the one who manages to sell more than two hundred shares of the club.

Se premiará al que logre vender más de doscientas acciones del club.

Venerado– to worship, to venerate

He became accustomed to being a kind of god revered by all, and that was his downfall.

Se acostumbró a ser una especie de dios venerado por todos y esa fue su perdición.

Action Verbs — Verbos de Acción (Intransitive verbs)

Acostumbrar- to be used to

I think I will never get used to this climate change.

Pienso que no me voy acostumbrar nunca a este cambio de clima.

Agradar - to please

It is not possible to pretend that one can please everyone.

No es posible pretender que uno le pueda agradar a todo el mundo.

Andar- to take

You have to be careful in these violent times.

Hay que andar con cuidado en estos tiempos violentos.

Aparecer- to turn up, to appear

When the guilty party appeared, all the other suspects felt great relief.

Al aparecer el culpable todos los otros sospechos os sintieron un gran alivio.

Aterrizar- to land

Due to bad weather and lightning storm, the pilot had to land in the jungle.

Debido al mal tiempo y a la ligera tormenta, el piloto tuvo que aterrizar en la selva.

Avanzaba – to advance, to move forward

He moved slowly and safely to the lair of the raccoons.

Avanzaba lento y seguro hasta la guarida de los mapaches.

Bajar- to go down

The further he went down the hill, the more he realized how far he was from the city.

Mientras más bajar la cuesta, más se daba cuenta de lo lejos que estaba de la ciudad.

Brillar- to shine

All his ideas and his passion for art would make him shine like a supernova.

Todas sus ideas y su pasión por el arte lo harían brillar como una supernova.

Caminar- to walk

Besides being a good exercise, walking is a free way to get around.

Además de ser un buen ejercicio caminar es una manera gratis de trasladarse.

Conversando- to talk

They spent almost eight hours talking about the same subject without reaching any agreement.

Pasaron casi ocho horas conversando sobre el mismo tema sin llegar a ningún acuerdo.

Corer - to run

We all started running when we found out about the offer of chocolates.

Todos empezamos a correr cuando nos enteramos de la oferta en chocolates.

Crecer- to grow

I am totally and absolutely sure that growing up is a trap.

Estoy total y absolutamente seguro de que crecer es una trampa.

Creer- to believe

When everything is lost, it is necessary to believe in whatever it is that gives you strength of spirit.

Cuando todo está perdido es necesario creer en lo que sea que te de fortaleza de espíritu.

Desaparecer- to disappear

One or several people disappearing was a daily custom in the 60s and 70s.

Desaparecer a una o varias personas era costumbre diaria en los años 60 y 70.

Dormir- to sleep

I have always liked to sleep in the forest outside, under the trees.

Siempre me ha gustado dormir en el bosque a la intemperie debajo de los árboles.

Durar- to last

Nowadays, cars do not last as long as old cars.

Hoy en día los autos no duran tanto como duraban los autos antiguos.

Empezar- to start, to begin

They all started checking their bills when they heard about the fake scandal.

Todos empezaron a revisar sus billete scuando se enteraron del escándalo de la falsificación.

Fallar- to fail

Never before had anyone seen the Yankees batter in New York fail in that way.

Nunca antes nadie había visto fallar al bateador de los yankees de New York de esamanera.

Flotar- to float

He had the ability to float in the sea like a boat or a duck with total naturalness.

Tenía la capacidad de flotar en el mar como un barco o un pato con total naturalidad.

Gateando– to crawl

The baby crawled out of his room to the kitchen of the house.

El bebé se escapó gateando de su cuarto hasta la cocina de la casa.

Habitar- to live, to inhabit

When they found that the water was drinkable and abundant, they began to inhabit the area.

Cuando comprobaron que el agua era potable y abundante comenzaron a habitar la zona.

Hablar- to speak

I have not been able to talk as much as I would like with my French teacher.

No he podido hablar tanto como quisiera con mi profesora de francés.

Ingresar- to enter

To enter that University, seven admission exams had to be passed with excellence.

Para ingresar a esa Universidad se debían pasar con excelencia siete exámenes de admisión.

Insister - to insist

After insisting, the German said yes to the Mexican and celebrated with beer and guacamole.

De tanto insistir, la Alemana le dijo sí al Mexicano y celebraron con Cerveza y guacamole.

Interesar- to interest

They began to be interested in the proposal that was raised when they learned that he was a millionaire.

Se comenzaron a interesar en la propuesta que planteaba cuando supieron que era millonario.

Ir- to go

We would have to go to the Sonoran Desert in Mexico to see if what they tell me is true.

Habría que ir hasta el desierto de Sonora en México para ver si lo que me cuentan es cierto.

Llegar- to arrive, to come

Arriving at the finish line is not always as important as what you learned on the way.

Llegar a la meta no siempre es tan importante como lo que aprendiste en el trayecto.

Luchar- to fight

He never gave up or ever stopped fighting for his lifelong dreams.

Nunca se rindió ni dejó jamás de luchar por sus sueños de toda la vida.

Marchar- to walk

All groups organized to leave at the same time.

Todos los grupos se organizaron para salir a marchar a la misma hora.

Meditar- to meditate

They say that this Buddhist teacher could meditate twenty hours in a row.

Dicen que ese maestro Budista podía meditar veinte horas seguidas.

Nacer- to be born

Probably one of the greatest mysteries of humanity is to be born.

Probablemente uno de los misterios más grandes de la humanidad es nacer.

Nadar- to swim

It was proposed to swim eight hours without stopping using different swimming techniques.

Se propusonadar ocho horas sin parar utilizando distintas técnicas de nado.

Ocurrir- to occur

Everyone was waiting to see what would occur.

Todos estaban a la expectativa para ver qué es lo que podría ocurrir.

Paseando– to go for a walk

They spent the whole week walking around the city and its surroundings.

Pasaron toda la semana paseando por la ciudad y sus alrededores.

Pasear- to go for a walk

The most anticipated moment for my pet is just when I take it out for a walk.

El momento más esperado por mi mascota es justo cuando la saco a pasear.

Permanecer- to stay

It is recommended to remain calm when being locked in an elevator.

Se recomienda permanecer calmados al quedarse encerrados en un ascensor.

Pertenecer- to belong to

Belonging to that gang and being accepted was their only purpose in life.

Pertenecer a esapandilla y ser aceptado era su único propósito en la vida.

Pesar- to weigh

I was very sorry for the situation that this whole family went through.

Me dió mucho pesar la situación por la que atravesó toda esa familia.

Pestañear– to blink

He had a temper of steel so strong that he decapitated three deer without blinking.

Tenía un temple de acero tan fuerte que decapitò tresvenados sin pestañear.

Quedar- to be left, to stay

They had a suspicion that they could run out of fuel in the middle of nowhere.

Tenían la sospecha de que se podían quedar sin combustible en medio de la nada.

Reaccionar- to react

Nobody knew how the public would react to such a controversial work.

Nadie sabía cómo iría a reaccionar el público ante una obra tan polémica.

Respirar- to breathe

He was in India and learned fifteen different breathing techniques.

Estuvo en la India y aprendió quince técnicas diferentes para respirar.

Responder- to respond

By correctly answering the entire questionnaire, they accepted it without further conditions.

Al responder correctamente todo el cuestionario, lo aceptaron sin más condiciones.

Responder- to answer

Everyone wanted to be present to see what the misfits of the class were responding to.

Todos querían estar presentes para ver a qué respondían los inadaptados de la clase..

Rodar- to roll

They started filming the movie six months ago, and they are almost finished.

Comenzaron a rodar la película hace seis meses y ya casi la terminan.

Salir- to leave

To leave at this time in this city is to sign your death sentence.

Salir a esta hora en esta ciudad es firmar tu sentencia de muerte.

Saltar- to jump

I should practice jumping higher to go to the Olympics next year.

Debo practicar saltar más alto para ir a las olimpiadas el próximo año.

Silbar- to whistle

I will never forget how much time it took for me to learn to whistle.

Nunca voy a olvidar cuánto tiempo me costó aprender a silbar.

Suceder- to happen

What will happen will simply happen one way or another.

Lo que va a suceder simplemente sucederá de una u otra manera.

Terminar- to end, to finish

To finish the concert, they prepared a great surprise for the audience.

Para terminar el concierto, prepararon una gran sorpresa para el público.

Transcurrir- to pass

It would take another twenty years for everything to return to normal.

Habría que transcurrir otros veinte años para que todo vuelva a la normalidad.

Treparse- to climb

Cats are experts at climbing trees and roofs.

Los gatos son expertos para treparse en los árboles y los tejados.

Trepo– to climb

If I climb that roof in less than 15 minutes, you pay for a round of beers.

Si yo me trepo a ese techo en menos de 15 minutos me pagas una ronda de cervezas.

Viajar- to travel

Traveling is the best school; it is a catharsis of the senses.

Viajar es la mejor escuela; es una catarsis de los sentidos.

Volar- to fly

Everything was blown to pieces when the dynamite that was in the basement detonated.

Todo voló en pedazos cuando detonaron la dinamita que estaba en el sótano.

Volver - to return

To return is a symptom of hope and courage.

Volver a empezar es un síntoma de esperanza y coraje.

Question Words — Palabras de Pregunta

¿Cuánto?– how much, how long

How long did it take to build that artificial island so that it seemed so real?

¿Cuánto tiempo tomó construir esa isla artificial para que pareciera tan real?

¿Quién? - who

Who was checking my computer this morning?

¿Quien estuvo revisando mi computadora esta mañana?

¿Qué?- what

What the hell is that weird thing that is coming out of your ear?

¿Que demonios es esa cosa rara que te está saliendo por la oreja?

¿Cuándo? - when

When did they plan to tell me that my pet was dead?

¿Cuándo tenían pensado decirme que mi mascota estaba muerta?

¿Donde?– where, wherever

Wouldn't it be great to know where exactly the soul is located?

¿Sería fantástico saber donde se encuentra exactamente el alma?

¿Por qué? - why

Why don't they come to live here for a while until they get a job?

¿Por qué no se vienen a vivir aquí por un tiempo hasta que consigan trabajo?

¿Cómo? - how

How are we going to explain to the whole world that we lost our party money?

¿Cómo le vamos a explicar a todo el mundo que se nos perdi óel dinero de la fiesta?

Numbers — Numeros

Uno–one

They could eat one of the sandwiches offered on the menu.

Podían comer uno solo de los bocadillos que ofrecía el menú.

Dos- two

Two policemen were found dead on the main avenue.

Dos policías fueron encontrados muertos en la avenida principal.

Tres–three

Three delegates of the anti-bribery commission received their commission in dollars.

Tres delegados de la comisión anti soborno recibieron su comisión en dólares.

Cuatro–four

Four vans with tinted glass arrived in a suspicious manner.

Cuatro camionetas con los vidrios ahumados llegaron de manera sospechosa.

Cinco–five

They were five weeks late because they had traveled by land.

Cinco semanas tardaron en llegar porque habían viajado por tierra.

Seis– six

Six women won the trial, and the rapist received a life sentence.

Seis mujere sganaron el juicio y el violador recibió una sentencia de cadena perpetua.

Siete– seven

It was seven o'clock at night when I realized that I had lost my wallet.

Eran las siete de la noche cuando me dí cuenta que había perdido mi billetera.

Ocho– eight

The number eight player of the Uruguayan soccer team received the golden ball.

El jugador número ocho de la selección de fútbol de Uruguay recibió el balón de oro.

Nueve- nine

Nine times he had to knock on the door until, finally, they opened it.

Nueve veces tuvo que tocar la puerta hasta que por fín le abrieron.

Diez– ten

Ten ancient coins were found by archaeologists responsible for this dig in Egypt.

Diez monedas antiguas encontraron los arqueólogos encargados de esa labor en Egipto.

Veinte– twenty

They charged him twenty dollars for moving the office.

Le cabrarono veinte dólares por hacerle la mudanza de la oficina.

Treinta- thirty

It had been thirty years since there was activity in the Hawaiian volcano.

Hacía treinta años que no se veí a actividad en el volcán de hawai.

Cuarenta– forty

When he was forty years old, he went on a trip to India.

Al cumplir los cuarenta años de edad se fue de viaje a la India.

Cincuenta- fifty

Fifty years had to pass before their ideas were understood.

Cincuenta años tuvieron que pasar antes de que se comprendieran sus ideas.

Sesenta– sixty

Sixty sea turtles were rescued from contaminated beaches.

Sesenta tortugas marinas fueron rescatadas de las playas contaminadas.

Setenta- seventy

Only seventy people attended the poetry recital, much less than last year.

Al recital de poesía sólo asistieron setenta personas, mucho menos que el año pasado.

Ochenta– eighty

Despite being eighty years old, he was healthier and stronger than a teenager.

A pesar de tener ochenta años de edad estabamás lúcido sano y fuerte que un adolescente.

Noventa- ninety

The Criminalistics team found ninety rounds of different bullets.

El equipo de Criminalística encontró noventa cartuchos de balas diferentes.

Cien- one-hundred

The theater group celebrated the 100th performance of their new work.

El grupo de teatro celebró la presentación número cien de su nueva obra.

Mil- one-thousand

More than a thousand new bacteria were discovered by the laboratory's research team.

Más de mil bacterias fueron descubiertos por el equipo de investigación del laboratorio.

Colors — Colores

Amarillo - yellow

The yellow train left early and arrived at its destination without problems.

El tren amarillo salió temprano y llegó a su destino sin problemas.

Roja- red

The nose of the clown is a red ball, like the flag of Japan.

La nariz del payaso es una bola roja como la bandera de Japón.

Negro- black

Black humor is a genre of irreverent comedy.

El humor negro es un género de la comedia irreverente.

Azul- blue

Cinderella's godmother gave her a blue dress.

La madrina de Cenicienta le regaló un vestido azul.

Blanco- white

The White Owl is a mystical and sacred bird of the forest.

El Búho blanco es un ave mística y sagrada del bosque.

Verde- green

The Buffon's costume is green, just like the leaves of the trees.

El traje del Buffon es verde al igual que las hojas de los árboles.

Anaranjado- orange

The twilight is sometimes orange like the tangerine peel.

El crepúsculo es a veces anaranjado como la concha de las mandarinas.

Marron - brown

El bate de béisbol es marróncomo la corteza de losárboles.

The baseball bat is brown like the bark of trees.

Plateado- silver

My cousin's new car is silver like the coins.

El carro nuevo de mi primo es plateado como las monedas.

Morado- purple

That bird has purple feathers on the left wing.

Ese pájaro tiene las plumas de color morado en el ala izquierda.

Rosado- pink

The girlfriend's dress was very long and pink.

El vestido que estrenó la novia era muy largo y de color rosado.

Animals — Los Animales

Mapache- raccoon

The raccoon is a very astute animal, mysterious, and fast.

El mapache es un animal muy astuto misterioso y rápido.

Mono- monkey

The monkey is very naughty and likes to have fun like a rascal.

El mono es muy travieso y le gusta divertirse como un pícaro.

Elefante- elephant

One of the greatest and noblest creatures is the elephant.

Una de las criaturas más grandes y nobles es el elefante.

Araña- spider

The spider is agile, and its attack is fast like the ninjas.

La araña es ágil y su ataque es veloz como los ninjas.

Ardilla- squirrel

A squirrel can collect hundreds of nuts in a day.

Una ardilla pued erecolectar cientos de nueces en un día.

Caballo- horse

The cowboys and the Indians had a great connection with their horses.

Los vaqueros y los indios tenían una gran conexión con sus caballos.

Abeja- bee

If bees disappear from the planet, human beings would have four years to live.

Si las abejas desaparecen del planeta, los seres humanos tendrían cuatro años de vida.

Delfín- dolphin

Dolphins are the most intelligent animals in the world.

Los delfines son los animales más inteligentes de todo el mundo.

Perro- dog

Throughout history, the dog has proven to be the most faithful pet.

A través de la historia el perro ha demostrado ser la mascota más fiel.

Tortuga - turtle

When the turtles breed, they bite and hit their shells.

Cuando las tortugas se reproducen son muerden y golpean sus caparazones.

Gato- cat

The cat climbed into the pantry and ate all the food.

El gato se subió a la despensa y se comió toda la reserva de comida.

Loro- parrot

Without stopping, the parrot repeated absolutely everything that the people said in the house.

El loro repetía sin parar absolutamente todo lo que decían las personas de la casa.

Pescado- fish

On the shore of the beach, the fishermen sell fresh fish.

A la orilla de la playa los pescadores venden el pescado fresco.

Serpiente- snake

Snakes are very elusive, and some are capable of swallowing a complete deer.

Las serpientes son muy escurridizas y algunas son capaces de tragarse un venado completo.

Cocodrilo- crocodile

The crocodiles are very silent and cautious when it comes to stalking their prey.

Los cocodrilos son muy silenciosos y cautelosos a la hora de acechar a su presa.

Salamandra- salamander

The giant salamander of China is on the verge of extinction.

La salamandra gigante de china está al borde de la extinción.

León- lion

The lion is considered, without any doubt, the King of the Jungle.

El león es considerado sin duda alguna comoel Rey de la selva.

Alacrán- scorpion

The scorpion is a great patient and violent stalker that must be respected.

El alacrán es un gran acechador paciente y violento que se debe respetar.

Águila- eagle

The sight and precision of the eagle are its best weapons.

La vista y la precisión del águila son sus mejores armas.

Anguila- eel

I've lost count of how many eels I've run into.

Ya perdí la cuenta de con cuántas anguilas me he topado.

Armadillo- armadillo

There were so many armadillos crossing the street that I thought it was a Pixar movie.

Había tantos armadillos cruzando la calle que pensé que era una película de Pixar.

Burro- donkey

The donkey is a noble and submissive animal with a lot of brute strength.

El burro es un animal noble y sumiso con mucha fuerza bruta.

Cabra- goat

People tend to think that the goats are all crazy, and they are right.

La gente suele pensar que las cabras están todas locas y tienen razón.

Colibri- hummingbird

For the shamans, the hummingbird is the guardian of time by the speed of its flutter.

Para los shamanes el colibrí es el guardián del tiempo por la velocidad de su aleteo.

Conejo- rabbit

The rabbit is cunning and quick and plays tirelessly like humans.

El conejo es astuto y rápido y se reproduce incansablemente como los humanos.

Cucaracha- cockroach

There is a belief that if the world ends, only the cockroaches will survive.

Existe la creencia de que si el mundo se acaba solo sobrevivirán las cucarachas.

Cuervo - crow

The crow is master and lord in the skies, intelligent and bold.

El cuervo es amo y señoren los cielos, inteligente y audaz.

Escarabajo- beetle

There are more than three-hundred and seventy-five thousand different species of beetles.

Existen más de trescientossetenta y cinco mil especies distintas de escarabajos.

Grillo- cricket

The sound that the cricket produces with its legs drives you crazy and does not let you sleep.

El sonido que produce el grillo con suspatas te enloquece y no te deja dormir.

Oruga- caterpillar

The caterpillars are fantastic creatures, tender, and disgusting.

La oruga son unas criaturas fantásticas tiernas y asquerosas.

Halcón- hawk

The falcon is a majestic bird that imposes admiration.

El halcón es un ave majestuosa que impone admiración.

Hipopótamo- hippopotamus

The hippopotamus is considered by many to be Africa's most dangerous animal.

El hipopótamo es considerado por muchos el animal más peligroso de África.

Hormiga- ant

The ants have a huge force and can lift up to ten times their weight.

Las hormigas tienen una fuerza descomunal y levantan hasta diez veces su propio peso.

Iguana- iguana

Iguanas are the only animals that preserve the appearance of dinosaurs.

Las iguanas son los únicos animales que conservan el aspecto de los dinosaurios.

Jirafa- giraffe

Giraffes do not have long necks, just stressed.

Las jirafas no tienen el cuello largo, solo están estresadas.

Lagartija- lizard

The lizard is fast and agile and knows how to hide very well.

La lagartija es veloz, ágil y se sabe esconder muy bien.

Libélula- dragonfly

The dragonfly is considered a sacred and wise insect.

La libélula es considerada un insecto sagrado y sabio.

Mantis- praying mantis

The mantis or mantis are teachers of kung fu.

La mantis religiosa son maestras de kung fú.

Mariposa- butterfly

The butterfly lived a slow and strange process of metamorphosis.

La mariposa vivió un proceso de metamorfosis lento y raro.

Mosca- fly

The fly is the most unfriendly and disrespectful insect that exists.

La mosca es elinsecto más antipático y falta de respeto que existe.

Mosquito- mosquito

The mosquito prefers the small holes in your nose and your ear to annoy you.

El mosquito prefiere los huecos pequeños de tu nariz y tu oído para fastidiarte.

Pájarocarpintero- woodpecker

The woodpecker inspired one of the most beloved characters on TV.

El pájaro carpintero inspiró a uno de los personajes más queridos de la tv.

Paloma- dove

The dove has been used as a messenger throughout the history of humanity.

La paloma ha sido utilizada como mensajera a través de la historia de la humanidad.

Petirrojo- robin

The robin is strange and beautiful and can sometimes be interesting.

El petirrojo es extraño, hermoso y a veces puede ser interesante.

Pezespada- swordfish

The swordfish is the fencing champion of the seven seas.

El pez espada es el campeón de esgrima de los siete mares.

Oso- bear

The bear, under its sweet, chubby, and pretty appearance, is a serial killer.

El oso bajo su apariencia dulce, gordita y bonita es un asesino en serie.

Oveja- sheep

Sheep, like cows, are the animals most abducted by extraterrestrials.

Las ovejas al igual que las vacas son los animales más secuestrados por extraterrestres.

Rana- frog

Some hallucinogenic drugs are made from some frogs and their liquids.

De algunas ranas y sus líquidos se hacen unas drogas alucinógenas.

Rata- rat

The rat has been the animal with which most have experimented in laboratories.

La rata ha sido el animal con el que más han experimentado en laboratorios.

Ratón- mouse

The most famous mouse in the world is called Mickey Mouse.

El ratón más famoso del mundo se llama Mickey Mouse.

Raya- stingray

Be careful around the stingray; it should not be underestimated.

La raya es de cuidado; no se le debe subestimar.

Renacuajo- tadpole

The tadpole is very slippery and will grow into a frog.

El renacuajo es muy resbaladizo y crece en una rana.

Salmón- salmon

Salmon is undoubtedly an exquisite delicacy at every table.

El salmón es sin lugar a dudas un exquisito manjar en toda mesa.

Saltamontes- grasshopper

Grasshoppers are always hyperactive, jumping around.

Los saltamontes siempre andan hiperactivos, saltando por ahí.

Tiburón- shark

The shark is used as a symbol of power and control and causes fear.

El tiburón es utilizado como símbolo de poder, control y causar temor.

Tigre- tiger

Of all the animals of the jungle, the tiger has a reputation for everything.

De todos los animales de la selva, el tigre tiene fama de todo.

Trucha- trout

Trout is a food that only bears can catch easily and have fun with.

La trucha es un alimento que sólo los osos pueden atrapar de manera fácil y divertida.

Vaca- cow

The syndrome and epidemic of the mad cow disease was an invention of the farming industry.

El síndrome y epidemia de la vaca loca fue un invento de la industria farmáceutica.

Venado- deer

The deer is a little animal that everyone wants because of the movie Bambi.

Los venados son animalitos que todo el mundo quiere por culpa de la película Bambi.

Zancudo- mosquito

A simple mosquito can take your nerves apart from stinging and playing with your psyche.

Un simple zancudo te puede sacar los nervios además de picarte y jugar con tu psiquis.

Food — Comida

Arroz- rice

The rice with chicken is accompanied by a great salad.

El arroz con pollo se acompaña con una buena ensalada.

Espinaca- spinach

Spinach cream soup is very healthy food.

La sopa de crema de espinaca es un alimento muy saludable.

Manzana- apple

You can prepare an excellent and delicious cake with apples.

Con las manzanas se puede preparar un excelente y delicioso pastel.

Espagueti- spaghetti

Spaghetti au gratin with bechamel sauce is a good choice for lunch.

El espagueti gratinado con salsa bechamel es una buena opción para el almuerzo.

Huevos- eggs

The eggs can be scrambled or cooked whole with bread for breakfast.

Los huevos pueden ser revueltos o cocidos enteros con pan para el desayuno.

Tamales- tamales

Tamales are a hot dish that is wrapped in leaves.

Los tamales son un plato caliente que viene envuelto en hojas.

Café- coffee

Coffee is a hot drink that is customary to drink first thing in the morning.

El cafées una bebida caliente que se acostumbra tomar a primera hora de la mañana.

Empanada- empanada (pastry)

The empanadas can be stuffed with chicken, cheese, and ham or ground beef.

Las empanadas pueden ser rellenas de pollo, queso con jamón o carne molida.

Arepa- arepa

The arepas are a typical food of Venezuela and Colombia, and it is a tradition at the table.

Las arepas son un alimento típico de Venezuela y Colombia y es tradición en la mesa.

Pollo- chicken

The chicken can be prepared fried or baked and is served with potatoes.

El pollo se puede preparar frito o al horno y es especial servido con papas.

Cerdo- Pork

Roast and stuffed pork is a specialty of our restaurant.

El cerdo asado y relleno es una especialidad de nuestro restaurante.

Hamburguesa- Hamburger

The hamburgers that we prepared for the festival won the first prize.

Las hamburguesas que preparamos para el festival se llevaronel primer premio.

Queso- cheese

The melted goat cheese is a delight that we offer on our menu.

El queso de cabra fundido es una delicia que ofrecemos en nuestro menú.

Frijoles- beans

Eating many beans can send you to the bathroom for three hours.

Comer muchos frijoles te puede mandar al baño por tres horas.

Palomitasde maíz- popcorn

Popcorn should be eaten only in the movies.

Las palomitas de maíz deberían comerse solo en el cine.

Harina- flour

With flour, you can prepare so many things that you do not want to cook.

Con la harina, se pueden preparar tantas cosas que se te quitan las ganas de cocinar.

Pavo- turkey

It is advisable not to think about the life that the turkey had lived before eating it.

Es recomendable no pensar la la vida que llevaba el pavo antes de comerlo.

Accessories — Accesorios

Lentes- glasses

There are lenses for reading and correcting the eyes and some can be bifocals.

Hay lentes para leer, corregir la vista y algunos pueden ser bifocales.

Gafasde sol- sunglasses

Sunglasses were invented to protect us from the sun, but now, they are just a fad.

Las gafas de sol se inventaron para protegernos del sol, pero ahora son solo una moda.

Reloj de pulsera- wristwatch

Just like sunglasses, the wristwatch is no longer to know the time; it's just fashion.

Al igual que las gafas, de sol el reloj de pulse raya no es para saber la hora; solo es moda.

Aretes- earrings

Pirates began wearing earrings much earlier than women.

Los piratas empezaron a usar aretes mucho antes que las mujeres.

Collar- necklace

There are collars valued at an excessive fortune, and others come in a cereal box.

Hayc ollares valorados en una fortuna desmedida y otros vienen en la caja de cereal.

Pulsera- bracelet

Bracelets are a very popular accessory for women and girls.

Las pulseras son prendas muy populares para las mujeres y las niñas.

Bolso- handbag

Handbags are something like a third arm for women.

Los bolsos son algo así como un tercer brazo para las mujeres.

Billetera- wallet

The wallet is an extension of masculinity coveted by women.

La billetera es una extensión de la masculinidad codiciada por las mujeres.

Guantes- gloves

Gloves should only be worn by doctors and boxers.

Los guantes solo los deberían usar los médicos y los boxeadores.

Anillo- ring

The graduation ring and the engagement ring are symbols of old age.

El anillo de graduación y el anillo de compromiso son símbolos de la vejez.

Clothing — Ropa

Zapatos- shoes

The shoes that clowns wear are called chalupas, and they are huge.

Los zapatos que usan los payasos se llaman chalupas y son enormes.

Sombrero- hat

The hat is a very elegant garment worn by gangsters and tango dancers.

El sombrero es una prenda muy elegante usada por los gangster y los bailarines de tango.

Chaqueta- jacket

The jackets have become fashionable, but their main function is to protect us from the cold.

Las chaquetas se han puesto de moda, pero su función principal es protegernos del frío.

Pantalón- pants

Before, women did not wear pants, and nowadays, they wear them more than men.

Antiguamente las mujeres no usaban pantalones y hoy en día los usan más que los hombres.

Corbata- tie

The tie originated in Krakow and expanded to become a masculine symbol.

La corbata se originó en cracovia y se expandió convirtiéndose en símbolo masculino.

Camisa- shirt

There are long-sleeved and short-sleeved shirts and can be combined with everything.

Hay camisas de manga larga y de manga corta y se pueden combinar con todo.

Medias- socks

There are thick, long, and short socks of all colors and some with small toes.

Hay medias largas, cortas gruesas y de todos los colores y algunas con deditos.

Bufanda- scarf

The scarf not only serves to wrap our necks, but it is also a very elegant garment.

La bufandano solo sirve para abrigarnos el cuello, también es una prenda muy elegante.

Botas- boots

The cowboys, the workers, and the military wear boots every day.

Los vaqueros, los obreros y los militares usan botas a diario.

Correa- belt

The belt was formerly used to hold the pants; today, it is used for fashion.

La correa era antiguamente utilizada para sostener el pantalón hoy se usa por estética.

Ropainterior- underwear

Women's underwear comes in more varieties than men's.

La ropa interior femenina viene en más variedades que la masculina.

Vestido- dress

That dress I bought you for our anniversary matches your mother's shoes.

Ese vestido que te compré para nuestro aniversario combina con los zapatos de tu madre.

Falda- skirt

Her skirt was so short that she could see absolutely all her humanity.

Tenía la falda tan corta que se le podía ver absolutamente toda su humanidad.

Pantalonescortos- shorts

The shorts are quite practical and comfortable to go for a walk in the country.

Los pantalones cortos son bastante prácticos y cómodos para ir de paseo al campo.

Traje de baño- swimming suit

When I arrived at the beach, I realized that I forgot the swimsuit.

Cuando llegué a la playa después me di cuenta que olvidé el traje de baño.

Abrigo - coat

There are coats so elegant that you know they used to have a wild life.

Hay abrigos tan elegantes que uno sabe queantes tenían una vida salvaje.

Suéter- sweater

The sweater is a sinister invention of the grandmothers to torment their grandchildren.

El suéter es un siniestro invento de las abuelas para atormentar a sus nietos.

Traje- suit

Wearing a suit is a symbol of elegance and glamor.

Usar traje es símbolo de elegancia y glamour.

Pijamas- pajamas

Pajamas, no matter what they say, do not help us sleep better.

Las pijamas, por más que digan lo que digan, no nos ayudan a dormir mejor.

Pantaleta- pantyhose

The panties are possibly the garment that awakens more of the imagination.

La pantaleta es posiblemente la prenda de vestir que despierta más la imaginación.

Sandalias- sandals

The sandals are so comfortable that one understands that it is better to walk around in.

Las sandalias son tan cómodas que uno comprende que es mejorandar de.

Blusa- blouse

The blouse has an important place, not only in the closet but in the mind of a woman.

La blusa tiene un lugar importante; no sólo en el closet sino en la mente de una mujer.

Cierre- zipper

I have tried to lower this zipper for more time than it took to produce it.

He intentado bajar este cierre durante más tiempo del que se tardó en fabricarlo.

Velcro- velcro

Velcro is a popular choice for some sports shoes.

El cierre mágico es un sistema muy usado para algunos zapatos deportivos.

Weather — Clima

Clima- weather

In general, there are three types of climate—warm, temperate and polar.

En general, existen tres tipos de clima - cálidos, templados y polares.

Tormenta- storm

The storm unleashed with fury and lasted approximately three hours.

La tormenta se desató con furia y duró tres horas aproximadamente.

Tropical- tropical

The tropical climates are the ones in the areas of the planet located in the tropics.

Los climas tropicales es el que tienen las zonas del planeta situadas en los trópicos.

Lluvia - rain

Rainwater is of great benefit to nature.

El agua de la lluvia es de gran beneficio para la naturaleza.

Soleado- sunny

The day started sunny and was ideal for a walk to the beach.

El día comenzó soleado y fue ideal para dar un paseo a la playa.

Nublado- cloudy

It is so cloudy that they suspended all flights until further notice.

Está tan nublado que sus pendieron todos los vuelos hasta nuevo aviso.

Nube- cloud

The clouds scatter all the visible light, and that's why they look white.

Las nubes dispersan toda la luz visible y por eso se ven blancas.

Eclipse- eclipse

The eclipse is a phenomenon in which the light of one celestial body is blocked by another.

El eclipse es un fenómeno en el que la luz de un cuerpo celeste es bloqueada por otro.

Luna- moon

The moon does not have its own light; it only reflects what comes from the sun.

La luna no tiene luz propia; solo refleja la que le llega del sol.

Huracan- hurricane

A hurricane is a severe form of a storm that produces strong winds of 155 miles.

Un huracán es una forma severa de tormenta que produce vientos fuertes de 155 millas.

Sol- sun

The sun was so strong that even with an umbrella and sunscreen, I could not avoid having burns.

El sol era tan fuerte que incluso con un paraguas y un protector solar, no podía evitar las quemaduras.

Estrella - star

Beyond the stars are the infinite dimensions and galaxies yet to be discovered.

Más allá de las estrellas están las infinitas dimensiones y galaxias aún por descubrir.

Viento- wind

Strong winds are capable of causing terrible catastrophes.

Los vientos fuertes son capaces de ocasionar catástrofes terribles.

Aire- air

The air has been around for many years, so it is not air; it is a mixture of several wastes.

El aire hace muchos años ya que no es aire; es una mezcla de varias porquerías.

Inundación- flood

A flood is one of the most common disasters that exist.

Una inundación de agua es uno de los desastres más comunes que existen.

Nieve- snow

Children love to play in the snow; they like it so much that they do not feel the cold.

A los niños les fascina jugar en la nieve; les gusta tanto que no sienten el frío.

Temperatura- temperature

The temperature change affected my grandfather's health terribly.

El cambio de temperatura afectó terriblemente la salud de mi abuelo.

Termómetro- thermometer

Of everything that I should not forget is the precise reading of the thermometer.

De todo lo que no se me debía olvidar precisamente el termómetro se me quedo.

Nebuloso- foggy

The day started foggy, so traffic will be a problem today.

El día amaneció nebuloso por lo que el tráfico será un problema hoy.

Neblina- mist

There was so much mist that it looked like a place for ghosts from a horror movie.

Había tanta neblina que parecía una zona fantasma de una película de terror.

Humedad- humidity

Humidity can cause irreparable damage to the house.

La humedad puede causar daños irreparables en la casa.

Family — Familia

Familia- family

My family is so numerous that for Christmas, we must rent a farm.

Mi familia es tan numerosa que para navidad, debemos alquilar una granja.

Abuelo- grandfather

My grandfather has the biggest stamp collection, and it's a world record.

Mi abuelo tiene la colección de estampillas más grande y es un récord mundial.

Abuela- grandmother

My grandmother is an extraordinary confectioner and also plays the piano perfectly.

Mi abuela es una extraordinaria repostera y también toca el piano a la perfección.

Mamá- mother

My mom spent all night sewing my costume for the school party.

Mi mamá estuvo toda la noche cosiendo mi disfraz para la fiesta del colegio.

Primo- cousin

My cousin won a free week at the amusement park.

Mi primo se ganó una semana gratis en el parque de diversiones.

Papá- father

My dad is a stunt double actor and has been in more than 20 movies.

Mi papa es un actor de doble de acción y ha estado en más de 20 películas.

Hermano- brother

My little brother won the national gold medal for the swimming competition.

Mi hermano pequeño ganó la competencia nacional de natación medalla de oro.

Tia- aunt

My aunt left early this morning for her guitar class.

Mi tía se fue esta mañana temprano a su clase de guitarra.

Padrino- godfather

I have not visited my godfather for a year because he moved to another country.

Hace un año que no voy a visitar a mi padrino porque se mudo a otro país.

Hijo- son

I am very proud of the successes achieved by my son in college.

Estoy muy orgulloso de los éxito sobtenidos por mi hijo en la universidad.

Hija- daughter

My daughter was very happy with the bike I bought her.

Mi hija se puso muy contenta con la bicicleta que le compré.

Hermana- sister

My sister had told me that those doctors were not reliable.

Mi hermana me había dicho que esos doctores no eran confiables.

Madrastra- stepmother

My stepmother did not know anything about my swimming tournaments.

Mi madrastra no sabía nada de mis torneos de natación.

Padrastro- stepfather

My stepfather was approved for the credit to open his spare parts computer store.

A mi padrastro le aprobaron el crédito para abrir su tienda de repuestos de computadoras.

Tío- uncle

My uncle is the world champion of the Olympics in the 100-meter dash category.

Mi tío es campeón mundial de las olimpiadas en la categoría cien metros planos.

Sobrino- nephew

My seven-year-old nephew is more dangerous than a gang of Koreans.

Mi sobrino de siete años es más peligroso que una pandilla de coreanos.

Cuñado- brother-in-law

My brother-in-law is so unbearable that I prefer to visit my mother-in-law.

Mi cuñado es tan insoportable que prefiero visitar a mi suegra.

Cuñada- sister-in-law

My sister-in-law can really make you lose patience in a minute.

Mi cuñada de verdad puede hacerte perder la paciencia en un minuto.

Suegra- mother-in-law

I have seriously decided that my mother-in-law is harmful to my health.

He decidido seriamente que mi suegra es nociva para mi salud.

Suegro- father-in-law

You never know if my father-in-law is about to kill you or fall asleep.

Nunca sabes si mi suegro está a punto de matarte o de dormirse.

Novio- boyfriend

My daughter's boyfriend does not like me so much; I have to have karate classes and weapons management.

El novio de mi hija me cae tan mal que me metí en clases de karate y manejo de armas.

Nuera- daughter-in-law

Frankly, my daughter-in-law is an example that the human being is never perfect.

Francamente, mi nuera es un ejemplo de que el ser humano no es perfecto.

Yerno- son-in-law

My son-in-law should understand that not everything revolves around him.

El yerno debería entender que no todo gira alrededor de él.

Relaciones- relationships

Relationships are more complicated than religions and politics.

Las relaciones son más complicadas que las religiones y la política.

Amigo- friend

My friend told me he would travel to London in two weeks.

Mi amigo me avisó que viajaría a Londres en dos semanas.

Marido- husband

My husband is a test that God has given me to see if I decide to make myself a nun.

Mi marido es una prueba que me ha puesto Dios para ver si me decido a meterme a monja.

Esposa- wife

My wife taught me the importance of silence because she has not spoken to me for two years.

Mi esposa me enseñó la importancia del silencio porque llevados años sin hablarme.

Sobrina- niece

Only for my niece, I am able to support a lot of idiotic teenagers.

Sólo por mi sobrina soy capaz de soportar a un montón de adolescentes idiotas.

Novia- girlfriend

I do not know why my girlfriend only speaks to me in English.

Mi novia no sé por qué extraña manía sólo me habla en inglés.

Fruits — Frutas

Pera- pear

The pear is sweet and juicy; you can eat it with salads or in desserts like ice cream.

La pera es dulce y jugosa; se puede comer con ensaladas o en postres como los helados.

Fresa- strawberry

Strawberries are an excellent complement to accompany meals such as pancakes.

Las fresas son un excelente complemento para acompañar comidas como las panquecas.

Uva- grape

The grapes are nutritious and fundamental for the preparation of the wine.

Las uvas son nutritivas y fundamentales para la preparación del vino.

Banano- banana

Bananas are an excellent compliment with cereal and milk.

Los bananos son un excelente complemento con el cereal y la leche.

Melocotón- peach

Peaches are used in the preparation of different sweets.

Los melocotones se usanen la preparación de diferentes dulces.

Coco- coconut

I had to climb like a monkey up that palm tree to grab three coconuts.

Tuve que trepar como un mono por esa palmera para agarrar tres cocos.

Cereza- cherry

Cherries are usually added to some drinks for flavor.

Las cerezas son colocadas como un bocado en algunas bebidas.

Mango- mango

Despite being very sweet, mango is eaten by some people with salt.

A pesar de ser muy dulce, algunas personas se comenel mango con sal.

Naranja- orange

Oranges have vitamin C and are perfect for preparing juices and smoothies.

Las naranjas tienen vitamina C y son perfectas para preparer jugos y batidos.

Arándano- blueberries

The blueberry cake was the surprise I had for my little sister for her birthday.

La torta de arándanos fue la sorpresa que le tenía a mi hermanita para su cumpleaños.

Vegetables — Vegetales

Tomate- tomato

With a good amount of tomatoes, Napolitana sauce can be prepared.

Con una buena cantidad de tomates se prepara la salsa Napolitana.

Cebolla- onion

Some people generally prefer to order their hot dog without onions.

Algunas personas generalmente prefieren pedir su pancho sin cebolla.

Brócoli- broccoli

Broccoli is an ideal companion for pasta and salads.

Los brócolis son un acompañante ideal para pastas y ensaladas.

Aguacate- avocado

With the avocado, the delicious guacamole is made for several meals.

Con el aguacate, se hace el delicioso guacamole para varias comidas.

Lechuga- lettuce

The lettuce should be washed very well before being consumed.

La lechuga debe estar muy bien lavadas antes de ser consumidas.

Papa- potato

The baked potato chips are very tasty, filled with chicken and cheese.

Las papas al horno son muy sabrosas rellenas de pollo y queso.

Lechosa- papaya

It is known as papaya in Colombia and Frutabomba in Cuba.

A la lechosa se le conoce como papaya en Colombia y Frutabomba en Cuba.

Acelga- chard

Many sauces and creams from very elaborate recipes and gourmet dishes are with chard.

Muchas salsas y cremas para recetas muy elaboradas y platos gourmet son con acelga.

Zanahoria- carrot

Horses and rabbits like carrots as much as people.

A los caballos y a los conejos les gusta tanto la zanahoria como a las personas.

Rábano- radish

The radish has healing properties; many remedies are based on radish.

El rábano tiene propiedades de sanación; muchos remedios son a base de rábano.

Espárrago- asparagus

Asparagus has only 24 calories, is rich in fiber, and contains vitamin A.

Los espárragos proporcionan sólo 24 calorías, es rico en fibra y contiene vitamina A.

Remolacha- beet

Beet is an excellent natural medicine for a cough problem.

La remolacha es una excelente medicina natural para el problema de la tos.

Coliflor- cauliflower

The cauliflower is very healthy and can be seasoned with many spices.

La coliflor es muy saludable y se puede aderezar con muchas especias.

Limón- lemon

With this lemon, it is worth preparing a good lemonade.

Con esté limón vale la pena preparar una buena limonada.

Lima – lime

Lime juice is one of the most refreshing drinks I know.

El jugo de lima es una de las bebidas más refrescantes que conozco.

Condiments — Condimentos

Salsade tomate- ketchup

Tomato sauce is used a lot for hot dogs and hamburgers.

La salsa de tomate se usa mucho para los perros calientes y las hamburguesas.

Mayonesa- mayonnaise

Toasted bread with mayonnaise and garlic is a good choice for pinwheels.

El pan tostado con mayonesa y ajo es una buena opción para pasapalos.

Mostaza- mustard

The mustard gives a touch of special flavor to meals with beef or chicken.

La mostaza le da un toque de sabor especial a las comidas con carne o pollo.

Sal- salt

Tequila is usually taken with a squeeze of lemon and a pinch of salt.

El tequila se suele tomar con un chorro de limón y una pizca de sal.

Pimienta- pepper

The pepper is the perfect complement for the grill.

La pimienta es el complemento perfecto para la parrilla.

Salsa- salsa

There are great varieties of sauces of different flavors to combine in your meals.

Hay grandes variedades de salsas de diversos sabores para combinar en tus comidas.

Miel- honey

Honey is excellent for health and for raising your energy.

La miel es excelente para la salud y para levantar tu energía.

Salsa tártara- tartar sauce

The tartar sauce is the most requested to accompany the empanadas.

La salsa tártara es la más pedida para acompañar las empanadas.

Chimichurri- chimichurri sauce

The chimichurri is the favorite sauce when cooking a barbecue.

El chimichurri es la salsa preferida a la hora de cocinar un asado.

Guacamole- guacamole

Guacamole is used in numerous recipes, especially in Latin America.

El guacamole se utiliza en numerosas recetas, especialmente en Latinoamérica.

Pico de gallo- salad toppings

In Mexico, a variety of regional salads are called pico de gallo.

En México reciben el nombre de pico de gallo una variedad de ensaladas regionales.

Restaurant — Restaurante

Cubiertos- silverware

In restaurants, the hygiene of cutlery is important.

En los restaurantes, es importante la higiene de los cubiertos.

Mesero- waiter

The waiters are a fundamental part of the restaurants.

Los meseros son una parte fundamental en los restaurantes.

Mesa- table

The tables should be impeccable and properly decorated with tablecloths.

Las mesas deben estar impecables y correctamente adornadas con manteles.

Chef- chef

The chef is the master of the kitchen andis responsible for preparing the special dishes.

El chef es el maestro de cocinaque se encarga de elaborar los platos especiales.

Menú- menu

The menu in a restaurant must be understood easily and presented well.

El menú en un restaurante debe ser diverso claro comprensible y bien presentado.

Cocina- kitchen

The kitchen of a restaurant must be in good condition and always clean.

La cocina de un restaurante debe estar en buen estado y limpia permanentemente.

Nevera- refrigerator

It is necessary that restaurants have a sufficiently large and well-stocked fridge.

Es necesario que los restaurantes tengan una nevera suficientemente amplia y bien abastecida.

Plato- plate

The dishes must not only be clean, they must also be of all sizes.

Los platos no solo deben estar limpios también los debe haber de todos los tamaños.

Despensa- pantry

The restaurant's pantry contains the necessary supplies and provisions.

La despensa de los restaurantes contiene los insumos y víveres necesarios.

Ayudantede cocina- kitchen assistant

The kitchen assistants are the ones who support the chef at all times.

Los ayudantes de cocina son los que apoyan al chef en todo momento.

Cuchara- spoon

The spoon was so dirty; it looked like a monkey's finger.

La cuchara estaba tan sucia que parecía el dedo de un mono.

Cuchillo- knife

The knife was sharpened so much that you could cut the hooves of a rhinoceros.

El cuchillo lo afilaron tanto que podías cortar las pezuñas de un rinoceronte.

Tenedor- fork

The kitchen was equipped with everything but did not have a single fork.

La cocina estab aequipada con todo pero no tenía ni un solo tenedor.

Vaso- cup, glass

He cut his hand with the glass tumbler that fell from the pantry.

Se cortó la mano con el vaso de vidrio que se cayó de la despensa.

Cuenco- bowl

The bowl overflowed with water, and the entire floor became wet.

El cuenco se desbordó de agua y todo el piso quedó mojado.

Servilleta- napkin

He liked to draw, paint, and doodle on napkins.

Le gustaba dibujar, pintar y hacer garabatos en las servilletas.

Aperitivo- appetizer

The appetizers have the function of creating the appetite.

Los aperitivos tienen la función de abrir el apetito.

Desayuno- breakfast

Breakfast is the most important meal of the day.

El desayuno es la comida más importante del día.

Postre- dessert

There are people who really should not be allowed to eat dessert.

Hay gente que de verdad no se le debería permitir comer el postre.

Cena- dinner

Dinner should be light simple and humble so as not to have a heavy sleep.

La cena debe ser ligera sencilla y humilde para no tener el sueño pesado.

Almuerzo- lunch

Many people prefer to have lunch on the street rather than in their homes.

Muchas personas prefieren almorzar en la calle que en sus casas.

Platoprincipal- main dish

Most of the time, the main course is not as good as the appetizer.

La mayoría de las vecese el plato principal no es tan bueno como el aperitivo.

Professions — Profesiones

Bombero- firefighter

Firefighters do not always put out fires; they also rescue cats.

Los bomberos no siempre apagan el fuego también rescatan gatos.

Mecánico- mechanic

The mechanic spent six hours checking the engine of that car.

El mecánico estuvo seis horas revisando el motor de ese auto.

Médico- doctor

The doctor told his patient that he should rest for two weeks.

El médico le dijo a su paciente que debía reposar por dos semanas.

Boxeador- boxer

The boxers train very hard and take care of their health to be fit.

Los boxeadores entrenan muy duro y cuidan su salud para estar en forma.

Abogado- lawyer

The lawyer had to investigate the case thoroughly for eight months.

El abogado tuvo que investigar el caso a fondo durante ocho meses.

Veterinario- veterinarian

That veterinarian saved six animals in one day.

Ese veterinario les salvó la vida a seis animales en un día.

Arquitecto- architect

It took four architects to review the plans for that mall.

Se necesitaron cuatro arquitectos para revisar los planos de ese centro comercial.

Dentista- dentist

The dentist attended the conference of dentistry that was held in Italy.

El dentista asistió al congreso de odontología que se realizó en italia.

Astronauta- astronaut

The astronauts spent five months repairing the space station on Mars.

Los astronautas pasaron cinco meses reparando la estación espacial de marte.

Músico- musician

The musicians of the band went on tour in Latin America.

Los músicos de la banda se fueron de gira por Latinoamérica.

Periodista- journalist

The journalist received the Pulitzer Prize for his report on emigrants.

El periodista recibió el premio pulitzer por su reportaje sobre los emigrantes.

Carpintero- carpenter

The carpenter was commissioned to make three beds, two chairs, and a large table.

Al carpintero le encargaron fabricar tres camas ,dos sillas y una mesa grande.

Escritor- writer

The writer finished writing his latest novel and delivered it on time to his publisher.

El escritor terminó de escribir su última novela y la entregó a tiempo a su editorial.

Actor- actor

The acceptance speech of the actor in the Oscar awards ceremony was very emotional.

El discurso de aceptación del actor en la ceremonia de entrega de los premios Oscar fue muy emotivo.

Científico- scientist

The scientific society gave the highest award to the scientist for his contributions to humanity.

La sociedad científica le otorgó el máximo galardón al científico por susaportes a la humanidad.

Cocinero- cook

For the end-of-the-year party, they hired the best chefs in the country.

Para la fiesta de fin de año contrataron a los mejores cocineros del país.

Chofer- chauffeur

The driver drove for 14 straight hours, demonstrating resistance and control.

El chofer manejó durante 14 horas seguidas demostrando resistencia y control.

Piloto- pilot

Commercial aviation pilots have a great deal of responsibility for their passengers.

Los pilotos de aviación comercial tienen una gran responsabilidad para suspasajeros.

Agricultor- farmer

The work of the farmer is very important because, without a field, there is no city.

El trabajo del agricultor es muy importante porque sin campo no hay ciudad.

Docente- teacher

Teachers and professors are responsible for the education of future generations.

Los maestros y maestros son responsables de la educación de las generaciones futuras.

Camionero- truck driver

Truck drivers are the people who eat the most junk food in the whole world.

Los camioneros son las personas que comen más comida chatarra en todo el mundo.

Consejero- counselor

A counselor is someone who teaches better than what they need to learn.

Un consejero es alguien que enseña mejor lo que el mismo necesita aprender.

Enfermero- nurse

The nurse is sometimes much more important than the doctor and works harder.

El enfermero es a veces mucho más importante que el doctor y trabaja más.

Farmacéutico- pharmacist

A pharmacist is an unscrupulous person who negotiates the health of people.

Un farmacéutico es una persona sin escrúpulos que negocia la salud de la gente.

Juez- judge

It is almost science fiction to say that there is a judge who is not corrupt.

Es casi ciencia ficción decir que existe un juezque no sea corrupto.

Padre- priest

Being a father by trade means explaining with faith what he does not understand or practice.

Ser padre de oficio significa explicar con fé lo que el mismo no entiende ni practica.

Transportation — Transporte

Transporte- transportation

Transportation is how objects and people are transferred.

El transporte es cómo se transfieren los objetos y las personas.

Transporteterrestre- land transport

Land transport is carried out on wheels like cars and motorcycles.

El transporte terrestre es el que se realiza sobre ruedas como automóviles y motocicletas.

Señales de tránsito - road signs

Traffic signs are the signs used on public roads to give the correct information.

Las señales de tránsito son los signos usados en la vía pública para dar la información correcta.

Carreteras- highway

A highway is a route of domain and public use built for the movement of vehicles.

Una carretera es una ruta de dominio y uso público construida para el movimiento
de vehículos.

Autopistas- highway

The highways are those that are fast and safe and contain a large volume of traffic.

Las autopistas son aquellas que son rápidas, seguras y con un gran volumen de tráfico.

Autobus- bus

The bus is a vehicle designed to transport many people through urban roads.

El autobús es un vehículo diseñado para transportar numerosas personas por las vías urbanas.

Taxi- taxi

That taxi had a very high fare, and I preferred to take a bus trip.

Ese taxi tenía una tarifa muy alta y preferí hacer el viaje en autobús.

Tren- train

This train is one of the fastest in the world, and the rates are cheap.

Este tren es uno de los más rápidos del mundo y las tarifas son económicas.

Metro- metro

Large cities prefer the underground metro as a transportation option.

Las grandes ciudades prefieren el metro subterráneo como opción de transporte.

Motocicleta - motorcycle

Motorcycles are the ideal means of transport to avoid traffic.

Las motocicletas son el medio de transporte ideal para evitar el tráfico.

Carro- car

The neighbor's car had a broken engine and bumper.

El carro del vecino tenía fallas en el motor y el parachoques roto.

Bicicleta - bicycle

The bicycle is an ecological and sporty transport at the same time.

La bicicleta es un transporte ecológico y a la vez deportivo.

Bote- boat

Every weekend, he took my children for a boat ride.

Todos los fines de semana llevó a mis hijos a pasear en bote.

Ciclomotor- moped

I prefer the moped because it is much faster and safer.

Prefiero el ciclomotor porque es mucho más rápido y seguro.

Park — Parque

Parque - park

The parks are public spaces where you can enjoy nature without leaving the city.

Los parques son espacios públicos en los que se disfruta de la naturaleza sin salir de la ciudad.

Flores- flower

In the parks, a great variety of flowers are usually found.

En los parques suelen encontrarse una gran variedad de flores.

Caminito- pathway

The best part of the park is its multiple paths to walk, play, and exercise.

Lo mejor del parque son sus multiples caminos para pasear, jugar y hacer ejercicios.

Árbol- tree

The trees are the fundamental element of the parks, as they convert the air with their green lungs.

Los árboles son el elemento fundamental de los parques los convierte en un pulmón verde.

Laguna- lagoon

Some parks have beautiful and wide natural or artificial lagoons.

Algunos parques disponen de hermosas y amplias lagunas naturales o artificiales.

Banco- bench

In every park, there is a considerable number of benches ideal for resting or reading.

En todo parque hay un número considerable de bancos ideales para descansar o leer.

Sendero- path

Certain parks have a system of aerial trails as a tourist experience.

Ciertos parques cuentan con un sistema de senderos aéreos como experiencia turística.

Zona deportiva- sports area

The parks have spaces for sports.

Los parques cuentan con espacios habilitados para realizar actividades deportivas.

Aréainfantil- children's area

These are the spaces preferred by children as there are swings, slides, and tires.

Son los espacios preferidos por los niños ya que hay columpios toboganes y ruedas.

Mirador- viewpoint

The viewpoints are special places of the parks since they offer a view of the landscape.

Los miradores son lugares especiales de los parques ya que ofrecen una vista del paisaje.

Bank — Banco

Cuentas de crédito - loan

To start my project of a network of museums, I had to ask for a loan.

Para poder iniciar mi proyecto de una red de museos tuve que pedir un crédito bancario.

Préstamos y créditos - Loans and Credits

Only through a loan and credit system that could I save my business.

Solo mediante un sistema de préstamos y créditos pude salvar mi negocio.

Operacionespasiva - passive operation

The bank obtained a huge amount of money only in passive operations.

El banco obtuvo una enorme cantidad de dinero solo en operaciones pasivas.

Encajebancario - bank reserve

The institution was investigated for alleged misappropriation and deviation of the banking reserve.

La institución fue investigada por presuntas mal versaciones y desviación del encaje bancario.

Tarjeta de débito - debit card

After an hour of standing in line at the cashier, I realized that I was not carrying my debit card.

Después de una hora de hacer fila en el cajero me di cuenta que no llevaba mi tarjeta de débito.

Tarjeta de crédito - credit card

I have exceeded my limit on my credit card, and the bank froze them.

He excedido el límite de mi tarjeta de crédito y el banco los congeló.

Ahorro- savings

In the celebration of my son's birthday, I emptied my savings account.

En la celebración del cumpleaños de mi hijo vacié mi cuenta de ahorro.

Gerente- manager

All responsibility for the seizure fell on the bank manager.

Toda la responsabilidad del embargo recayó sobreel gerente del banco.

Depósitos- deposit

In the afternoon today, they deposited the six months of salary that they owed me.

Hoy en la tarde me depositaron los seis meses de salario que me debían.

Director- CEO

The bank's CEO presented his resignation letter for personal matters.

El director general del banco presentó su carta de renuncia por asuntos personales.

Cuentabancaria- bank account

My bank account had been blocked indefinitely.

Mi cuenta bancaria había sido bloqueada por tiempo indefinido.

Cajero- teller

My debit card got stuck at the ATM yesterday afternoon.

Mi tarjeta de débito se quedó atorada en el cajero ayer por la tarde.

Extracto de cuenta - bank statement

I had serious doubts about the final balance of the account statement.

Tenía serias dudas sobre el balance final del extracto de cuenta.

Tipo de cambio - exchange rate

I realized right away that the exchange rate did not favor me at all.

Me di cuenta en seguida que el tipo de cambio no me favorecía para nada.

Dinero- money

I must be very careful when managing or investing my money.

Debo tener mucha precaución a la hora de administrar o invertir mi dinero.

Sobregiro- overdraft

What had me so worried all week was that overdraft.

Lo que me tenía tan preocupado toda la semana era ese sobregiro.

Bedroom — Cuarto

Cuarto- bedroom

In my room, there are all kinds of coffee cups that I have been collecting on my travels.

En mi cuarto hay toda clase de tazas de café que he ido coleccionando en mis viajes.

Cama- bed

Of the four legs that my bed has, only two are good, as the other two are unstable.

De las cuatro patas que tiene mi cama solo le sirven dos, las otras dos están inestables.

Ventana - window

The window in my room is full of cactus and sunflowers that attract different birds.

La ventana de mi habitación está llena de cactus y girasoles que atraen a diferentes aves.

Cortina- curtain

The curtains that I chose for my room resemble my grandmother's dresses.

Las cortinas que elegí para mi cuarto se parecen a los vestidos de mi abuela.

Piso- floor

On the floor of my room under the bed, you find very interesting and strange things.

En el piso de mi cuarto de bajo de la cama, se encuentran cosas muy interesantes y extrañas.

Vestidor - dressing room

My wife's dressing room was so glamorous that it appeared on the cover of Hola Magazine.

El vestidor de mi esposa era tan glamoroso que salió en la portada de la revista Hola.

Armario- closet, wardrobe

My closet is a mess; there should be only clothes, and there are TV and two microwaves in there.

Mi armario es un desastre; debería haber sólo ropa y hay hasta un televisor y dos microondas.

Perchas- hangers

These very thin hangers will not resist the weight of my jackets and raincoats.

Estas perchas son muy delgadas no resistirán el peso de mis chaquetas y gabardinas.

Espejo - mirror

The mirror we chose for the living room of the apartment is really a good idea.

El espejo que elegimos para la sala del apartamento es de verdad una buena idea.

Despertador- alarm clock

It is the second time in the week that I have to repair the alarm clock.

Es la segunda vez en la semana que debo reparar el despertador.

Escritorio- desk

There are so many books and notebooks on my desk that it looks like a library.

En mi escritorio hay tantos libros y cuadernos que ya parece una biblioteca.

Carteles- posters

The posters with the latest films fit very well as a decoration in the room.

Los carteles decorados con las últimas películas que dan muy bien en el cuarto.

Sábana- bedsheet

This sheet is so big; I think you could wrap eight people.

Esta sábana es demasiado grande, creo que se podrían arropar 8 personas.

Almohada- pillow

I prefer the pillow that is filled with feathers and not cotton balls.

Prefiero la almohada que está rellena de plumas y no la de bolas de algodón.

Manta- blanket

This blanket covers much more than the blanket I bought in Moscow.

Esta manta abriga mucho más que la cobija que compré en Moscú.

Bathroom — Baño

Baño- bathroom

My room has a bathroom that every time I enter, it gives me the feeling that I will die soon.

Mi cuarto tiene un baño que cada vezque entro, me da la sensación de que moriré pronto.

Lavabo- sink

The sink was so dirty; it looked like the underwear of a homeless man.

El lavabo estaba tan sucio que parecía la ropa interior de un indigente.

Ducha- shower

After spending six days in the desert, this shower is the glory.

Después de pasar seis días en el desierto ésta ducha es la gloria.

Bañera- bathtub

The bathtub had so much foam that it could be shaken and shampooed.

La bañera tenía tanta espuma que se podía batir y hacer champú.

Cepillo de dientes- toothbrush

I must change my toothbrush before I go on a trip.

Debo cambiar mi cepillo de dientes antes de irme de viaje.

Pasta dental- toothpaste

I spilled all the toothpaste in the suitcase and stained almost everything.

Se me derramó toda la pasta dental en la maleta y manchó casi todo.

Maquinillade afeitar- razor

I could not find a razor anywhere in that town.

En ninguna parte de ese pueblo pude encontrar una maquinilla de afeitar.

Champú- shampoo

The shampoo had rendered with the foam of the bathtub.

El champú lo habíamos rendido con la espuma de la bañera.

Acondicionador- conditioner

The conditioner that I always use is no longer being manufactured.

El acondicionador que siempre uso ya no lo fabrican más.

Toalla- towel

The towel was still very wet, and I had to dry myself with my shirt.

La toalla estaba todavía muy húmeda y tuve que secarme con mi camisa.

Cepillo- brush

His hair is so tangled that no brush was useful.

Tiene el pelo tan enredado que ningún cepillo le servía.

Secador de pelo- hair dryer

I was almost electrocuted with the hair dryer in the bathroom.

Casi se electrocuta con el secador de pelo en el baño.

Jabón- soap

The natural soap they were using turned out to be not as natural.

El jabón natural que estaban usando resultó no ser tan natural.

Botiquín- medicine cabinet, first aid kit

The first-aid kit only had a pack of condoms.

El botiquín de primeros auxilios solo tenía un paquete de condones.

Barrade cortinas- curtain rod

The curtain rod was totally ruined by cigarette burns.

El cortinero quedó totalmente arruinado con las quemaduras de los cigarrillos.

Desagüe- drain

The drain was covered for four days, and nobody had noticed.

El desagüe estaba tapado desde hace cuatro días y nadie lo había notado.

Gorrode ducha- shower cap

The shower cap had been lost since the last time we went to the pool.

El gorro de ducha se había perdido desde la última vez que fuimos a la piscina.

Kitchen — Cocina

Cocina- kitchen

The kitchen is a laboratory of alchemy for food.

La cocina es un laboratorio de la alquimia de los alimentos.

Sarten- frying pan

Good frying pans are designed to withstand high heat temperatures.

Los buenos sartenes están diseñados para aguantar altas temperaturas de calor.

Hoyas- cooking pot

That cooking pot got so hot that it evaporated all the broth.

Esa hoya se calentó tanto que evaporò todo el caldo.

Hornillas- burner

Modern kitchens have up to eleven burners that light electronically.

Las cocinas modernas tienen hasta once hornillas que encienden electrónicamente.

Horno- oven

By not timing the baking time, the cake exploded in the oven.

Al no calcular el tiempo de cocción, la torta explotó en el horno.

Microonda- microwave

A container with aluminum foil was included in the microwave and melted in seconds.

En el microondas metieron un envase con papel aluminio y se fundió en segundos.

Espátula- spatula

The spatula that I got in the market on Saturdays has lasted me a while.

La espátula que conseguí en el mercado de los sábados me ha durado bastante.

Table de cortar - cutting board

The cutting board was not of good material because, after five days, it was no longer useful.

La tabla de cortar no era de buen material porque a los cinco días, ya no servía.

Jabón para platos - dish soap

Of all the ones I bought at that store, this soap has the best quality.

De todos los que he comprador en esa tienda, este jabón es el de mejor calidad.

Esponja- sponge

It's amazing how long this sponge has lasted despite the excessive use.

Es increíble todo lo que me ha durado esta esponja a pesar del exceso de uso.

Licuadora- blender

The seven-speed blender is the best investment I've made this month.

La licuadora de siete velocidades es la mejor inversión que he hecho este mes.

Abrelatas- can opener

The can opener is the only kitchen utensil that I take on my travels.

El abrelatas es el único utensilio de cocina que siempre viaja conmigo.

Colador- colander

The colander has already been used several times in a week.

El colador ya se ha utilizado varias veces en una semana.

Congelador- freezer

The freezer cooled much more than I had thought.

El congelador enfrió mucho más de lo que tenía pensado.

Destapador- bottle opener

Even using a bottle opener could not open that bottle.

Incluso usar un abrebotellas no podría abrir esa botella.

Escurridor- dish rack

The dish rack melted because it was very close to the stove.

El escurridor se derritió porque estaba muy cerca de la ornilla.

Olla – saucepan, pot

The pot was all greasy and sticky after cooking in the chicken.

La olla quedó toda grasosa y pegostosa después de cocinarel pollo.

Tostador- toaster

The toaster melted from using it so much every day.

El tostador se fundió de tanto usarlo todos los días.

Laundry/Utility Room — Cuarto de Lavado/Limpia

Fregona- mop

I already lost count of how many mops I had to buy for the house.

Ya perdí la cuenta de cuantas fregonas he tenido que comprar para la casa.

Balde- bucket, pail

Five buckets of hot water were needed to bathe the puppies.

Fueron necesarios cinco baldes de aguacaliente para poder bañar a los cachorros.

Escoba- broom

The broom that was used to clean the bathroom was ruined.

La escoba que se utilizó para limpiar el baño quedó arruinada.

Recogedor- dustpan

I think I'm going to need a dustpan to finish cleaning my room.

Creo que voy a necesitar un recogedor para terminar de asear mi habitación.

Bolsas de basura - trash bags

Garbage bags are no longer as strong as they were twenty years ago.

Las bolsas de basura ya no son tan resistente scomo las de hace veinte años.

Lavadora- washing machine

I do not know what's wrong with this washing machine.

No sé qué le pasa a esta lavadora.

Secadora- dryer

It is very strange, but behind the fridge, the clothes dry faster than in the dryer.

Es muy raro, pero detrás de la nevera la ropa seca más rápido que en la secadora.

Tabla de planchar - ironing board

The ironing board has broken legs and has fallen to the ground.

La tabla de planchar tiene las patas rotas y se ha caído al suelo.

Planchar- iron

I did not have time to iron my clothes, and I had to come out with wrinkled clothes.

No tuve tiempo de planchar mi ropa y tuve que salir con ropa arrugada.

Plumero- duster

It took me ten days to realize that my daughter was allergic to the duster.

Tardé diez días en darme cuenta que mi hija era alérgica al plumero.

Calentador de agua - water heater

The water heater broke down and had not been working for a week.

El calentador de agua se averió y no funciona desde hace una semana.

Trapo- rag

Kitchen rags are never clean.

Los trapos de la cocina nunca están limpios.

School — Escuela

Escuela- school

This year, I have missed school six times for health reasons.

Este año he faltado 6 veces a la escuela por razones de salud.

Pupitres- desk

In some schools, the desks are very small and unstable; they are hardly used.

En algunas escuelas, los pupitres son muy pequeños e inestables; ya casi no se usan.

Tiza- chalk

I like the sound of white chalk on the green blackboard, although it gives some chills to some.

Me gusta el sonido de la tiza blanca en el pizarrón verde, aunque a algunos les da escalofríos.

Marcador- marker

Markers and highlighters are useful for school work.

Marcadores y resaltadores de colores son útiles para los trabajos de la escuela.

Lápiz- pencil

Almost no one uses pencils; they have been replaced by pens and computers.

Ya casi nadie usa lápices han sido reemplazados por bolígrafos y computadoras.

Pizarra- chalkboard

The blackboard was full of exercises and mathematical formulas of different levels of difficulty.

La pizarra estaba llena de ejercicios y fórmulas matemáticas de distintos niveles de dificultad.

Libro- book

Books are the treasure of every school; a large library is a temple of wisdom.

Los libros son el tesoro de toda escuela; una gran biblioteca es un templo de sabiduría.

Cuadernos- notebook

Like pencils, notebooks are almost never used to write—only laptops and tablets.

Al igual que los lápicesya casi nadie usa los cuadernos para escribir—solo laptops y tablets.

Maestros- teacher

Teachers are like second parents and personal motivation guides.

Los maestros son como los segundos padres y unos guías de motivación personal.

Busescolar- school bus

Some schools have school bus service for the transfer of students.

Algunas escuelas disponen del servicio de bus escolar para el traslado de los estudiantes.

examenes- exams

Exams are tests that can assess your ability to study but not your intelligence.

Los exámenes son pruebas que pueden evaluar la capacidad de estudio, pero no tu inteligencia.

Matemática- mathematics

I did not like and never will like mathematics.

No me gustaron y nunca me gustarán las matemáticas.

Ciencia- science

Science, art, and religion should make peace and put themselves at the service of creation.

La ciencia el arte y la religión deberían hacer las paces y ponerse al servicio de la creación.

Literatura- literature

Literature is a jealous lover; if you stop writing for a month, it leaves you for a year.

La literatura es una amante celosa; si dejas de escribir un mes te abandona por un año.

Historia- history, story

The story they are about to hear was told to me by my grandfather 35 years ago.

La historia que están a punto de escuchar me la contó mi abuelo hace 35 años.

Idiomaextranjero- foreign language

The man who came to my store earlier spoke in a foreign language.

El señor que se acercó temprano a mi tienda hablaba en un idioma extranjero.

Educaciónfísica- physical education

Of all the subjects, the one I like the least is physical education.

De todas las asignaturas la que menos me gusta es la de educación física.

Música- music

Music is a celebration of the senses and emotions.

La música es una fiesta de los sentidos y de las emociones.

Computadora- computer

My computer is broken after being full of viruses for three days.

Mi computa dora está averiada y llena de virus desde hace tres días.

Principle- principle

The principal said this was the last time he would call me to his office.

El principio decía que esta era la última vez que me llamaría a su oficina.

Recreo- recess

I used my recess time to finish the essay on the Spanish Civil War.

Usé mi tiempo de recreo para terminar el ensayo sobre la guerra civil Española.

Sports & Hobbies — Deportes y Pasatiempos

Fútbol- soccer

Soccer started as a friendly game and became a bloody business.

El fútbol comenzó como un juego amigable y se convirtió en un negocio sangriento.

Baloncesto- basketball

Basketball has been established very well in public schools and universities.

El baloncesto se ha establecido muy bien en las escuelas públicas y universidades.

Tenis- tennis

Tennis has always been like golf—an elite bourgeois and exclusive sport.

El tenis siempre ha sido como el golf—un deporte elite scoburgués y excluyente.

Nadando- swimming

He came to the island of Barbados swimming and received the island with honor.

Nadando llegó hasta la isla de barbados y lo recibieron con honor.

Pista- track

The children ran around the track ten times.

Los niños corrieron alrededor de la pista diez veces.

Béisbol- baseball

Baseball has great fanatics throughout Latin America.

El béisbol cuenta con una gran fanaticada en toda Latino américa.

Fotografía- photography

With savings of two years, I went to study photography in London.

Con los ahorros de dos años, me fuí a estudiar fotografía en Londres.

Danza- dance

To perform this type of dance, more than one hundred genres and styles were studied.

Para realizar este tipo de danza se estudiaron más de cien géneros y estilos.

Dibujo- drawing

No one could believe that this drawing had been made by a three-year-old child.

Nadie podía creer que ese dibujo lo había hecho un niño de tres años.

Ajedrez- chess

The Russian champion and the French champion met in the chess final.

El campeón de Rusia y el campeón de Francia se enfrentaron en la final de ajedrez.

Videojuegos- video games

Video games create addiction and move you away from reading.

Los videojuegos crean adicción y te alejan de la lectura.

Rompecabezas- jigsaw puzzles

It was a challenge to put together the puzzle of 12850246 small pieces.

Fue todo un reto armar el rompecabezas de 12850246 piezas de las pequeñas.

Tarjetas- playing cards

It had the largest collection of cards of all time.

Tenía la más grande colección de tarjetas de todos los tiempos.

Golf- golf

The annual golf tournament was held in the exclusive fields of the city of Dubai.

El torne oanual de golf se celebró en los exclusives campos de la ciudad de Dubai.

Equitación- horseback riding

They chose a thoroughbred specimen for riding lessons.

Escogieron a un ejemplar pura sangre para las clases de equitación.

Natación- swimming

After practicing mountaineering for five years, I practice swimming now.

Después de dedicarme al alpinismo por cinco años, ahora practico natación.

Equipo- team

My volleyball team won the world championship that was held in Brazil.

Mi equipo de voleibol ganó el campeonato mundial que se celebró en brasil.

Musical Instruments — Instrumentos Musicales

Guitarra- guitar

The guitars have six or twelve strings and are acoustic or electric.

Las guitarras tienen seis o doce cuerdas y son acústicas o eléctricas.

Bajo- bass guitar

The bass gives a peculiar and very important rhythmic sound to the accompaniment of music.

El bajo le da un sonido rítmico peculiar y muy importante al acompañamiento de la música.

Violín- violin

Formerly, the violin was associated only with classical music and is now used in rock.

Antiguamente el violín era asociado solo a la música clásica y ya se usa en el rock.

Bateria- drum

The drummers are musicians who exercise and perfect their ability to synchronize.

Los bateristas son músicos que ejercitan y perfeccionan su capacidad de sincronización.

Armónica- harmonica

The harmonica is the most used musical instrument in blues and folk.

La armónica es el instrumento musical más usado en el blues y el folk.

Clarinete- clarinet

The clarinet is an instrument in the family of wind and wood instruments.

El clarinete es un instrumento de la familia de los instrumentos de viento y madera.

Saxofón- saxophone

The saxophone is a key instrument in jazz and Caribbean rhythms like salsa.

El saxofón es un instrumento clave en el jazz y los ritmos caribeños como la salsa.

Violonchelo- cello

In the symphony orchestra, the cellist stood out above all the other musicians.

En la orquesta sinfónica el violonchelista se destacó sobre todos los demás intérpretes.

Contrabajo- double bass

The bassist of the band managed to impress with an avant-garde style in the new song.

El contrabajista de la banda logró imprimirle un estilo vanguardista a la nueva canción.

Cuatro- four string guitar

The cuatro is a typical four-string musical instrument from Venezuela.

El cuatro es un instrumento musical de cuatro curda típico de Venezuela.

Maracas- maracas

The maracas imprint the tropical and folk rhythm in the music of the plains.

Las maracas le imprimen el ritmo tropical y folclórico a la música llanera.

Piano- piano

Beethoven was a genius of music and an almost supernatural pianist since he was two years old.

Beethoven era un genio de la música y un pianista casi sobrenatural desde los dos años.

Teclado- keyboard

Many pop groups use the keyboard or synthesizer as their main instrument.

Muchos grupos de pop utilizan el teclado o sintetizador como instrumento principal.

Timbales- kettledrums

In the rhythms, known as salsa and merengue, timbales are frequent.

En los ritmos conocidos como salsa y merengue son frecuentes los timbales.

Oboe- oboe

The concert pianist of the Philharmonic left the audience speechless with his virtuosity with the oboe.

El concertista de la filarmónica dejó al público sin palabras con su virtuosismo en el oboe.

Flauta- flute

The Pied Piper of Hamelin saved the city from the rats just by playing his flute.

El flautista de Hamelin salvo a la ciudad de las ratas solo tocando su flauta.

Fagot- bassoon

The sound of the bassoon gives the philharmonic orchestra a mystical air.

El sonido del fagot le dá a la orquesta filarmónica un aire místico.

Trompeta- trumpet

The trumpet in a jazz ensemble is the soul of the party.

La trompeta en un conjunto de jazz es el alma de la fiesta.

Movies — El Cine

Cine- movie theater

The art of cinema is a feast of the senses.

El arte del cine es una fiesta de los sentidos.

Director- director

The director had to resort to several techniques to direct the actors.

El director tuvo que recurrir a varias técnicas para dirigir a los actores.

Película- film

The film about autistics had five Oscar nominations.

La película sobre los autistas tuvo cinco nominaciones a los premios Oscar.

Producción- production

The most complicated part of this documentary was the production.

Lo más complicado de este documental fue la producción.

Locación- location

The team visited eight cities before finding the locations of the film.

El equipo visitò ocho ciudades antes de encontrar la locación del filme.

Claqueta- clapperboard

Just before starting to record, the clapper was lost.

Justo antes de comenzar a grabar, se perdió la claqueta.

Actrices- actress

The actresses decided to make a joke to the dresser.

Las actrices decidieron hacerle una broma a la encargada de vestuario.

Actuación- performance

Critics agreed that the performance was extraordinary.

Los críticos estuvieron de acuerdo en que la actuación fue extraordinaria.

Editor- editor

The editor was left with insomnia after several nights editing the movie.

El editor quedó con insomnio después de varias noches editando la película.

Montaje- montage, assembly

The final assembly was quite satisfactory for the cast and the production team.

El montaje final fue bastante satisfactorio para el elenco y el equipo de producción.

Guión- script

It was necessary to write nine different versions before having the final script.

Fue necesario escribir nueve versiones distintas antes de tener el guión definitivo.

Synopsis - synopsis

What seemed a simple synopsis at first was transformed into the movie of the year.

Lo que parecía al principio una simple sinopsis se transformó en la película del año.

Personajes- character

The creation of characters for the development of the plot kept the playwright busy.

La creación de personajes para el desarrollo del argumento mantuvo ocupado al dramaturgo.

Doblaje- dubbing

The dubbing must be in accordance with the interpretation of the actors.

El doblaje debe ser acorde con la interpretación de los actores.

Director de fotografía - director of photography

The director of photography surprised everyone with the final result.

El director de fotografíasorprendió a todo el mundo con el resulta dofinal.

Argumento- plot, story line

The plot of history went through several processes of analysis.

El argumento de la historia pasó por varios procesos de análisis.

Gag- bag, joke

The jokes of Charles Chaplin and Buster Keaton are the most famous gags in history.

El gag de humor más famosos de la historia son los de Charles Chaplin y Buster Keaton.

Reparto- cast

The cast of actors was considered a good choice of the director.

El reparto de actores fue considerado una buena elección del director.

Casting- casting

For the four protagonists of the series, 280 actors were presented for the casting.

Para los cuatro protagonistas de la serie se presentaron 280 actores al casting.

Cámara- camera

The use of four simultaneous cameras gave the cinema new horizons of realization.

El uso de cuatro cámaras simultáneas le dío al cine nuevos horizontes de realización.

Tripode- tripod

The tripod of the camera broke in the middle of filming, and the filming stopped.

El trípode de la cámara se rompió a mitad del rodaje y se paró la filmación.

Subtitulo- subtitle

The film's subtitles in Spanish went backward.

Los subtítulos en español de esta película salieron al revés.

Supermarket — Supermercado

Electrónica- electronics

The electronics department has new merchandise.

El departamento de electrónica tiene mercancía nueva.

Artículos de usodoméstico - household goods

The household goods can be found on the third floor.

Los artículos de uso doméstico los pueden encontrar en el tercer piso.

Artículosdeportivos- sporting goods

The only thing that interested my son in the supermarket was the sporting goods section.

Lo único que le interesaba a mi hijo del supermercado eran los artículos deportivos.

Bebida- beverage

They usually sell many good milk-based fruit drinks.

Suelen vender muchas buenas bebidas de frutas a base de leche.

Comestibles- groceries

The groceries are on sale this month when you present the store card.

Los comestibles están en oferta este mes presentando el carnet.

Garantía de reembolso - money-back guarantee

He demanded very seriously that they give him his money-back guarantee.

Exigió muy seriamente que le dieran su garantía de reembolso.

Reintegrable- refundable

The manager said the item was not refundable.

El gerente dijo que el artículo no era reintegrable.

Panadería- bakery

That bakery was very popular because it was open from five in the morning.

Esa panadería era muy popular porque estaba abierta desde las cinco de la mañana.

Alimentoscongelados - frozen food

Frozen foods are the products mostly bought by singles.

Los alimentos congelados son los productos más comprados por los solteros.

Productoslácteos- dairy products

Long-life dairy products are the most popular.

Los productos lácteos de larga duración son los más llevados.

Productosenlatados - canned goods

I really must consider not buying so many canned products.

De verdad debo considerar no comprar tantos productos en latados.

Suministrosde mascotas - pet supplies

Pet supplies are exhausted by the week of pet adoption.

Los suministros de mascotas están agotados por la semana de adopción de mascotas.

Productoscosméticos - cosmetics

She never spent less than two hours in the area of cosmetic products.

Ella nunca pasaba menos de dos horas en el área de productos cosméticos.

Recibo- receipt

They demanded that he show the receipt in order to make the claim.

Le exigieron que enseñara el recibo para poder hacer el reclamo.

Precio- price

The agreed price is the right thing to pay and is not negotiable.

El precio acordado es lo correcto a pagar y no es negociable.

Ascensor- elevator, lift

Thankfully, there was an elevator to take them to the eighteenth floor.

Afortunadamente había un ascensor para llevarlos al piso dieciocho.

Escaleramecánica - escalator

The escalator is out of service since the accident.

La escalera mecánica está fuera de servicio desde el accidente.

Almacén- warehouse

The warehouse is well-stocked but will remain closed for two weeks.

El almacén está bien abastecido pero permanecerá cerrado dos semanas.

Cliente- customer

The client is always right. When it comes to you, I'll make an exception.

El cliente siempre tiene la razón; tratándose de usted, haré una excepción.

Asistentede ventas - sales assistant

The sales assistant received an award for being the employee of the month.

El asistente de ventas recibió un premio por ser el empleado del mes.

Horariode la tienda- store hours

Everyone was upset because the store schedule had changed nine times.

Todos estában molestos porque el horario de la tienda había cambiado nueve veces.

Carrito de compra - shopping cart

The shopping cart had more children than food.

El carrito de compras tenía más niños adentro qué artículos de comida.

Cestade la compra- shopping basket

The shopping basket was broken by putting more weight than it could handle.

La cesta de la compra se rompió por ponerle más peso del que podía aguantar.

Pasillo- aisle

The aisle was chaotic with children and pets running and jumping everywhere.

El pasillo era un caos niños y mascotas corriendo y saltando por todos lados.

Estante- shelf

By pushing the shopping cart without looking, he knocked down the whole shelf of the tuna.

Por estar empujando el carrito de compras sin mirar, tumbó todo el estante del atún.

Embalaje- packaging

The packaging of the merchandise was damaged by the box knife.

El embalaje de la mercancía fue dañado por la navaja.

Código de barras- barcode

The bar code system was broken for three days, and everything collapsed.

El sistema de código de barras estuvo averiado tres días y todo colapsó.

Informaciónnutricional- nutritional information

People almost never read the nutritional information on the labels of the products.

La gente casi nunca lee la informació nnutricional de las etiquetas de los productos.

Airport — Aeropuerto

Boleto- ticket

It's the most expensive ticket I've bought since the planes were invented.

Es el boleto más caro que he comprado desde que se inventaron los aviones.

Bolso de mano- carry-on

Sir, we inform you that you will only be able to carry the handbag with you.

Señor, le informamos que solo podrá llevar consigo el bolso de mano.

Detectorde metales - metal detector

I went through the metal detector seven times until I remembered my metal implants.

Pasé siete veces por el detector de metales hasta que me acordé de mis implantes de metal.

Guardia- security guard

The guard questioned me for twenty minutes just because he thought my dress was strange.

El guardia me interrogó durante veinte minutos solo porque le pareció rara mi vestimenta.

Maleta- suitcase

I found the suitcase open and established a claim for damages to my property.

La maleta la encontré abierta y establecí una demanda por daños a mi propiedad.

Mostrador de facturación - check-in desk

The girl at the check-in desk seemed familiar to me from somewhere else.

La chica del mostrador de facturación me parecía conocida de alguna otra parte.

Llegadas- arrivals

They announced that arrivals scheduled for nine o'clock at night are delayed.

Anunciaron que las llegadas programadas para las nueve de la noche están retrasadas.

Salidas- departures

I ran to the departure gate so that I would not miss my flight.

Corrí hacia la puerta de salida para no perder mi vuelo.

Colocarse- stand by

As I arrived late at the airport, they put me in place for the next flight.

Como llegué tarde al aeropuerto, me pusieron en colocarse para el próximo vuelo.

Retrasar- delay

They will delay the flight due to weather conditions.

Van a retrasar el vuelo debido a las pésimas condiciones climáticas.

Asiento- seat

Gentlemen, please do not get out of your seats, and use your seatbelt.

Señores, pasajeros por favor no se levanten de sus asientos y usen el cinturón de seguridad.

Aduana- customs

Going through all the procedures of the customs department is the most annoying part of travel.

Pasar por todos los trámites de la aduana es lo más fastidioso de viajar.

Inmigración- immigration

We expect more than twelve hours in immigration due to the negligence of their agents.

Esperamos más de doce horas en inmigración por la negligencia de sus agentes.

The Beach — La Playa

Aletas- flippers

These flippers are already small; I will have to rent or buy another.

Esta saletas ya me quedan pequeñas; tendré que alquilar o comprar otras.

Arena- sand

I have sand everywhere; I always have to rub myself down several times.

Tengo arena por todas partes; siempre tengo que sacudirme varias veces.

Alga- seaweed

The seaweed seems to me the most beautiful and curious.

El alga marina me parece de lo másbonita y curiosa.

Castillo de arena- sand castle

My brother and I are experts at building sand castles.

Mi hermano y yo somos expertos construyendo castillos de arena.

Protectorsolar- sunscreen

The sunscreen was expired, so I got burned.

El protector solar estaba vencido así que me quemé .

Duna- dune

I remember taking more than fourteen photos on that dune.

Recuerdo haberme tomado más de catorce fotos en esa duna.

Marea- tide

The tide was very strong, and the very high waves were ideal for surfing.

La marea estaba muy fuerte y las olas muy altas era ideal para surfear.

Onda- wave

The waves of the sea were very soothing.

Las olas del mar eran muy calmantes.

Orilla- shore

On the shore of the beach, we play ping pong.

En la orilla de la playa, jugamos con nuestro pingpong.

Sombrilla- beach umbrella

Many people use an umbrella on the beach, but I prefer to sunbathe.

Muchas personas usan la sombrilla en la playa, pero yo prefiero tomar el sol.

Nature — Naturaleza

Arbusto- bush

That bush is huge, and my son likes it a lot.

Ese arbusto es enorme y a mi hijo le gusta mucho.

Bulbo- bulb

They found a good number of bulbs in that area of the garden.

Encontraron un buen número de bombillas en esa zona del jardín.

Cactus- cactus

I was able to survive, thanks to the fact that I kept drinking the water from the cactus.

Pude sobrevivir gracias a que me mantuve bebiendo el agua de los cactus.

Enredadera- vine

That was my favorite vine because, for some reason, it reminds me of my grandmother.

Esa era mi enredadera favorita porque por alguna razón me recuerda a mi abuela.

Hoja- leaf

The leaf began to fall slowly from the tree, and the wind took it away.

La hoja empezó a caer lentamente desde el árbol y se la llevó el viento.

Margarita- daisy

There were many daisies in that field.

Había muchas margaritas en ese campo.

Rosa- rose

The rose is the flower that most people give on Valentine's Day and Mothers' Day.

La rosa es la flor que más regalan el día de los enamorados y el día de las madres.

Orquídea- orchid

The orchid I gave her meant a lot to her, and she took care of it with dedication.

La orquídea que le regalé significò mucho para ella y la cuidó con dedicación.

Tallo- stem

The stem was a little mistreated, but with patience, it recovered.

El tallo estaba un poco maltratado, pero con paciencia se recuperó.

Tulipán- tulip

Tulips are beautiful flowers that embellish any landscape.

Los tulipanes son flores hermosas que embellecen cualquier paisaje.

Violeta- violet

Violet is my daughter's favorite flower; she goes crazy every time she sees one.

La violetaes la flor preferida de mi hija; se vuelve loca cada vez que ve una.

Bosque- woods

In the middle of the forest, the ecologists met to talk about their project.

En el medio del bosque, se reunieron los ecologistas para conversar sobre su proyecto.

Pantano- swamp

The swamp is a strange place to go on vacation, but I like it.

El pantano es un lugar extraño para ir a vacacionar, pero a mi me gusta.

Selva- jungle

The expedition that took place in the Amazon jungle concluded successfully.

La expedición que se realizó en la selva amazónica concluyó con éxito.

Montaña- mountain

The seventh meeting of climbers was held on the highest mountain.

En la montaña más alta se llevó a cabo el séptimo encuentro de alpinistas.

Colina- hill

At the top of the hill, they had left several provisions well-hidden for the others.

En la cima de la colina habían dejado varias provisiones bien escondidas para los otros.

Llanuras- plains

I traveled the vast plains on horseback, walking, and cycling.

Recorrí las extensas llanuras a caballo, caminando y en bicicleta.

Río- river

That river was the meeting point of all the years when we were children.

Ese río era el punto de encuentro de todos los años cuando éramos niños.

Roca- rock

On the largest rock, I sat to meditate.

Sobre la roca más grande, me senté a meditar.

Lago- lake

We went to that lake to remember the best moments of our childhood.

Fuimos a ese lago para recordar los mejores momentos de nuestra infancia.

Mar- ocean

It was the first time I saw the sea so close standing on the shore.

Era la primera vez que veía el mar así de cerca parado en la orilla.

Conclusión

Espero que haya disfrutado de su copia de Aprenda inglés para principiantes: más de 1000 palabras en inglés fáciles y comunes en contexto para aprender inglés. Esperemos que te diviertas aprendiendo inglés mientras lees estas divertidas e informativas frases. También espero que tenga más confianza para comprender y leer el idioma inglés.

Recuerde no ser demasiado duro consigo mismo cuando esté aprendiendo cosas nuevas, especialmente un idioma extranjero. Es un proceso que requiere tiempo y práctica. Asegúrate de aprovechar cualquier oportunidad para practicar el idioma durante el día, y esto te ayudará a recordar las palabras mucho más rápidamente.

También es útil involucrar a un miembro de la familia o un amigo para que puedan probarse y practicar juntos. No solo ambos se divertirán mucho aprendiendo, sino que también fortalecerán sus mentes y ampliarán sus horizontes.

Por último, si este libro le resultó útil de alguna manera, ¡siempre se agradece una reseña en Amazon! ¡Gracias!

Aprende Inglés Para Principiantes

Más de 100 conversaciones en inglés fáciles y comunes para aprender inglés

Introducción

Felicitaciones por descargar Aprenda inglés para principiantes: más de 100 conversaciones en inglés fáciles y comunes para aprender inglés, y gracias por hacerlo.

Los siguientes capítulos proporcionarán todo tipo de conversaciones habituales, comunes y básicas en inglés con su respectiva traducción al idioma español para poder leer, hablar, escuchar y lo más importante, comprender el idioma inglés. A través de los capítulos de este libro, puede encontrar diferentes tipos de conversaciones, desde conversaciones personales, conversaciones cotidianas hasta trabajos y conversaciones profesionales. Este es un libro para principiantes, por lo que las conversaciones escritas aquí son básicas. Se recomienda leer varias veces cada una de las conversaciones disponibles en este libro para tener una comprensión clara del significado y contexto de cada una de las palabras en las oraciones y de las oraciones en las conversaciones.

Espero que disfrute de este libro y que sea de gran beneficio para usted. También espero que te sirva de herramienta para alcanzar tu objetivo de aprender el idioma inglés para que puedas hablarlo y entenderlo perfectamente en el futuro.

Hay muchos libros sobre este tema en el mercado, ¡gracias nuevamente por elegir este! Se hizo todo lo posible para garantizar que esté lleno de tanta información útil como sea posible. ¡Por favor, disfruta!

Chapter 1: Conversaciones sobre información personal - Personal information conversations

Introducing to someone - Presentarse a alguien

English

-Alberto: Hello, how are you?
-Juan: Hey. I am good, and you?
-Alberto: Pretty good. What is your name?
-Juan: My name is Juan, and yours?
-Alberto: My name is Alberto. Nice to meet you.
-Juan: Nice to meet you too. How old are you?
-Alberto: I am 34 years old, and you?
-Juan: I am younger. I am 29 years old.
-Alberto: I see.
-Juan: And, where are you from?
-Alberto: I am from Bogota, Colombia, and you?
-Juan: I am from DF, Mexico.
-Alberto: What a coincidence. I have a cousin who is from over there. His name is Luis.
-Juan: Really? Where does he live?
-Alberto: He lives in Tacubaya.
-Juan: Is his last name Rodriguez?
-Alberto: Yes.
-Juan: I know him. He is a friend of mine.

Spanish

-Alberto: Hola, ¿como estas?
-Juan: Hey, muy bien, ¿y tú?
-Alberto: Bastante bien. ¿Cómo te llamas?
-Juan: Mi nombre es Juan, ¿y el tuyo?
-Alberto: Mi nombre es Alberto. Encantado de conocerte.
-Juan: Igualmente. ¿Cuántos años tienes?
-Alberto: Yo tengo 34 años, ¿Tu?
-Juan: Yo soy más joven, yo tengo 29 años.
-Alberto: Ya veo.
.Juan: Y, ¿De dónde eres?
-Alberto: Yo soy de Bogotá, Colombia ¿y tú?
-Juan: Yo soy de DF, México.
-Alberto: Que casualidad, yo tengo un primo que es de allá. Se llama Luis
-Juan: ¿En serio? ¿Dónde vive?

-Alberto: En Tacubaya
-Juan: ¿Su apellido es Rodríguez?
-Alberto: Si.
-Juan: Yo lo conozco, el es amigo mío.

Birthdate - Fecha de nacimiento

English

-Julia: Good morning Alexandra. How are you?
-Alexandra: Good morning. Very good, and you?
-Julia: Excellent.
-Alexandra: Glad to hear.
-Julia: Thank you very much.
-Alexandra: Tell me, what can I do for you?
-Julia: You do have a son, right?
-Alexandra: That is right. Why do you ask?
-Julia: Because there will be an activity at the park for children under 10 years old.
-Alexandra: When will it be? He is going to be 10 years old soon.
-Julia: The event will be on July 15th. What is his birthdate?
-Alexandra: His birthdate is July 13th, 2009.
-Julia: So, he will already be 10 years old the day of the event. I am afraid that he couldn't go.
-Alexandra: You are right.

Spanish

-Julia: Buenos días Alexandra, ¿Cómo estás?
-Alexandra: Buenos días, muy bien, ¿Y usted?
-Julia: Excelente.
-Alexandra: Encantada de oírlo.
-Julia: Muchas gracias.
-Alexandra: Dígame, ¿Qué puedo hacer por usted?
-Julia: Tú tienes un hijo, ¿cierto?
-Alexandra: Eso es correcto, ¿Por qué pregunta?
-Julia: Porque habrá una actividad en el parque para menores de 10 años
-Alexandra: ¿Cuándo va a ser? El va a cumplir los 10 años pronto
-Julia: El evento será el 15 de Julio, ¿Cuál es su fecha de nacimiento?
-Alexandra: Su fecha de nacimiento es el 13 de Julio de 2009.
-Julia: Entonces ya tendrá 10 años el día del evento, me temo que no podrá asistir.
-Alexandra: Tienes razón

Introducing the family - Presentando a la Familia

English

-Tatiana: Hi Isa, welcome to my house. How are you?
-Isa: Hello, Tatiana. Thank you very much for the invitation. Pretty good, and you?
-Tatiana: A bit stressed about the meeting, but I am fine.
-Isa: I imagine. Coordinating a family meeting is a difficult task.
-Tatiana: Exactly.
-Isa: Has someone arrived?
-Tatiana: Yes, follow me. They are in the courtyard.
*At the courtyard...
-Tatiana: Look, Isa. These are my parents. My mother's name is Ana and my father is Carlos.
-Isa: Pleased to meet you. My name is Isa.
-Ana & Carlos: Pleased to meet you too.
-Tatiana: Those two over there are my brothers, Sebastian and Santiago and the girl who is with them is my sister, Mercedes.
-Isa: So, you are four.
-Tatiana: That's right. The ones at that corner are my uncles. Eduardo, Domingo, and Mila are my father's brothers, and Mader is my mother's sister.
-Isa: Got it.
-Tatiana: The kids playing around the table are my cousins. Alejandro is 6 years old, and Samantha is 8. They are Eduardo's kids. Michael is 5 years old, and Pedro is 10. They are Domingo's kids. Diana is 14 years old, and she is Mila's daughter.
-Isa: And Mader has no kids?
-Tatiana: No, she doesn't.
-Isa: And are your grandparents over here?
-Tatiana: Yeah, they are inside resting. I have only 2 grandparents, Carmen and Ruben. They are my father's parents.
-Isa: You are a big family.

Spanish

-Tatiana: Hola Isa, bienvenida a mi casa, ¿Cómo estás?
-Isa: Hola Tatiana, muchas gracias por la invitación. Muy bien, ¿Y tú?
-Tatiana: Un poco estresada por la reunión, pero estoy bien.
-Isa: Me imagino, coordinar una reunión familiar es una tarea difícil.
-Tatiana: Exactamente
-Isa: Y, ¿Ya ha llegado alguien?
-Tatiana: Si, sígueme, están en al patio...
En el patio

-Tatiana: Mira Isa, estos son mis padres, mi mamá se llama Ana y mi papá Carlos.

-Isa: Encantada de conocerlos, mi nombre es Isa.

-Ana y Carlos: Igualmente.

-Tatiana: Esos dos de allá son mis hermanos, Sebastián y Santiago, y la que está con ellos es mi hermana, Mercedes

-Isa: Entonces son cuatro

-Tatiana: Correcto. Los de aquella esquina son mis tíos. Eduardo, Domigo y Mila son los hermanos de mi papá y Mader es la hermana de mi mamá.

-Isa: Entiendo.

-Tatiana: Los niños que están jugando por la mesa son mis primos. Alejandro tiene 6 años y Samantha 8 y son los hijos de Eduardo; Michael tiene 5 años y Pedro 10 y son hijos de Domingo y Diana tiene 14 años y es la hija de Mila.

-Isa: ¿Y Mader no tiene hijos?

-Tatiana: No.

-Isa: ¿Y tus abuelos están por aquí?

-Tatiana: Si, están adentro descansando. Solo tengo 2 abuelos, Carmen y Rubén, son los padres de mi papa.

-Isa: Son una familia grande.

Talking About Relationships - Hablando Sobre Relaciones

English

-John: Hi, Karina, long time no see.
-Karina: Hi, John, certainly.
-John: How have you been?
-Karina: Things have been a little complicated lately.
-John: Why do you say it, Karina?
-Karina: I separated from my husband a year ago. I asked for a divorce, but he hasn't signed yet.
-John: That's bad news. I'm really sorry.
-Karina: Don't worry, that's not the worst.
-John: And what is it?
-Karina: That I've been seeing someone and he asked me to be his girlfriend.
-John: What's wrong with that?
Karina: Until my ex-husband signs the divorce papers, I don't feel comfortable being someone else's girlfriend.
-John: I see, and how long have you been dating?
-Karina: About two months but he had been flirting with me since before.
-John: It's a complicated situation. I think it's best if you talk to him and make things clear.
-Karina: That's what I'll do. Tell me, how is your wife?
-John: She's quite well. She must be picking up the children at school.
-Karina: I'm so glad she's all right. How are the children?
-John: Well, Victor had the flu last week, but he's already recovered, and Jose is excited because he made his debut on the school football team.
-Karina: I'm so happy to have seen you. It's always good to hear from you.
-John: Same here. Good luck to you.

Spanish

-John: Hola Karina, tiempo sin verte.
-Karina: Hola John, ciertamente.
-John: ¿Cómo has estado?
-Karina: Últimamente las cosas han estado un poco complicadas.
-John: ¿Por qué lo dices Karina?
-Karina: Es que me separe de mi esposo hace un año, y pedí el divorcio pero aun no ha firmado.
-John: Que mala noticia, lo lamento mucho.
-Karina: No te preocupes, eso no es lo peor.
-John: ¿Y qué es?
-Karina: Que he estado saliendo con alguien y me pidió que fuésemos novios.
-John: ¿Y qué tiene eso de malo?
-Karina: Que hasta que mi ex esposo no firme los papeles del divorcio no me siento cómoda siendo novia de alguien más.

-John: Ya veo, ¿Y cuanto tiempo tienen saliendo?
-Karina: Como dos meses pero me había estado coqueteando desde antes.
-John: Es una situación complicada, yo creo que lo mejor es que hables con él y aclaren las cosas.
-Karina: Eso hare. Cuéntame, ¿Cómo está tu esposa?
-John: Ella está bastante bien, debe estar buscando a los niños en la escuela.
-Karina: Me alegro mucho de que estén bien. ¿Cómo están los niños?
-John: Bueno, Víctor tuvo gripe la semana pasada pero ya se recupero y José está emocionado porque debutó en el equipo de futbol de la escuela.
-Karina: Me contenta mucho haberte visto, siempre es bueno saber de ti.
-John: Lo mismo digo. Que te vaya bien.
-Karina: A ti igual. Cuídate.

Talking About Hobbies - Hablando Sobre Pasatiempos

English

-Fred: Hey, you're Alex, right?
-Alex: Yes, sir.
-Fred: Nice to meet you. I'm the interviewer.
-Alex: Nice to meet you.
-Fred: Thank you very much.
-Alex: I'm here to ask for a scholarship.
-Fred: I know. I need information about your hobbies and your skills.
-Alex: Perfect. What do you want me to talk to you about first?
-Fred: About your hobbies.
-Alex: Well, I like baseball a lot. I'm on the city team, and I practice every Tuesday and Thursday for two hours. I also like to go jogging in the morning before breakfast for about five kilometers. I was in swimming, but I had to quit because I didn't have enough time.
-Fred: I see you're an athletic person. Don't you like music?
-Alex: Not so much. I took piano lessons for two months and didn't learn much. It's hard for me to learn.
-Fred: I understand. Now tell me a little bit about your skills.
-Alex: I'm very good at drawing, not so good at painting. I know English at an advanced level, and Spanish is my mother tongue.
-Fred: Are you good at math?
-Alex: More or less.
-Fred: That's all. Thank you very much. We'll call you back.
-Alex: Great, thanks to you.

Spanish

-Fred: Hey, tú eres Alex, ¿Cierto?
-Alex: Si señor.
-Fred: Mucho gusto, soy el entrevistador.
-Alex: Un placer conocerlo.
-Fred: Muchas gracias.
-Alex: Estoy aquí para pedir una beca.
-Fred: Lo sé, necesito información sobre tus pasatiempos, y tus habilidades.
-Alex: Perfecto, ¿Sobre qué quiere que le hable primero?
-Fred: Sobre tus pasatiempos.
-Alex: Bueno, me gusta bastante el beisbol, estoy en el equipo de la ciudad y práctico todos los martes y jueves durante dos horas. También me gusta salir a trotar en las mañanas antes de desayunar unos cinco kilómetros. Estaba en natación pero tuve que salirme porque no tenía suficiente tiempo.
-Fred: Veo que eres una persona atlética, ¿qué tal se te da la música?
-Alex: No muy bien, asistí a clases de piano por dos meses y no aprendí mucho. Me cuesta bastante aprender.

-Fred: Entiendo. Ahora háblame un poco sobre tus habilidades.

-Alex: Soy muy bueno para dibujar, no tanto para pintar. Se ingles a nivel avanzado y el español es mi lengua materna.

-Fred: ¿Eres bueno en matemática?

-Alex: Mas o menos.

-Fred: Eso es todo, muchas gracias. Te llamaremos.

-Alex: Genial, gracias a usted

Talking About Pets - Hablando Sobre Mascotas

English

-Doctor: Good afternoon. Sit down.
-Mary: Good afternoon. Thank you very much.
-Doctor: Why are you here?
-Mary: I came here because I've had an allergy on my skin for some time now.
-Doctor: Let's see.
-Mary: This is it.
-Doctor: I see. Do you have pets?
-Mary: Yes doctor, why?
-Doctor: What pets do you have?
-Mary: I have a dog, two cats, two parrots, four fishes, a turtle, a rabbit, a hedgehog, and a few days ago, I rescued a monkey.
-Doctor: How many days do you have an allergy?
-Mary: Five days.
-Doctor: When did you rescue the monkey?
-Mary: Five days ago... Oh, now it makes sense.
-Doctor: Exactly.
-Mary: Thank you very much, doctor.
-Doctor: Don't worry.

Spanish

-Doctor: Buenas tardes, siéntese
-María: Buenas tardes, muchas gracias.
-Doctor: ¿Por qué esta acá?
-María: Vine porque tengo una alergia en la piel desde hace un tiempo.
-Doctor: A ver.
-María: Es esta.
-Doctor: Ya veo. ¿Tiene usted mascotas?
-María: Si doctor, ¿Por qué?
-Doctor: ¿Qué mascotas tiene?
-María: Tengo un perro, dos gatos, dos loros, cuatro peces, una tortuga, un conejo, un erizo y hace unos días rescate a un mono.
-Doctor: ¿Cuántos días tiene con la alergia?
-María: Cinco días.
-Doctor: ¿Cuándo rescato al mono?
-María: Hace cinco días... Ah, ahora tiene sentido.
-Doctor: Exacto.
-Maria: Muchas gracias doctor.
-Doctor: No se preocupe.

Talking About Music - Hablando Sobre Música

English

-Kenya: Sofia, do you know any DJs who could be at today's party?
-Sofia: Yes, I know some.
-Kenya: Which is the best?
-Sofia: Depends. What's your favorite type of music?
-Kenya: Mmm, I don't know. I like pop a lot, but I also love to dance hip-hop.
-Sofia: Perfect. So, DJ Loco is the best.
-Kenya: Although, lately I'm fascinated by the songs they're releasing with Latin singers.
-Sofia: Reggaeton?
-Kenya: I think so. What kind of music do you like?
-Sofia: My favorite is blues and then jazz, but I love rock and techno.
-Kenya: Very varied tastes, isn't it?
-Sofia: Hahaha, that's what I've been told.

Spanish

-Kenia: Sofia, ¿conoces algún DJ que pueda estar en la fiesta de hoy?
-Sofia: Si, conozco varios.
-Kenia: ¿Cuál es el mejor?
-Sofia: Depende, ¿Cuál es tu tipo de música favorito?
-Kenia: Mmm, no lo sé. Me gusta bastante el pop, pero también me encanta bailar hip hop.
-Sofia: Perfecto, entonces DJ Loco es el mejor.
-Kenia: Aunque, últimamente me fascinan las canciones que están sacando con cantantes latinos.
-Sofia: ¿El reggaetón?
-Kenia: Creo que sí. ¿A ti que tipo de música te gusta?
-Sofia: Mi favorito es el blues y luego el jazz, pero amo el rock y la música techno.
-Kenia: ¿Unos gustos muy variados no?
-Sofia: Jajaja, eso me han dicho.

Talking About Cuisine - Hablando Sobre Gastronomía

English

-Hector: Daniela, I'm going to have lunch at the mall. Do you want to come?
-Daniela: Of course. I was about to have lunch too.
-Hector: Great.
-Daniela: What are you going to eat?
-Hector: I was thinking about a hamburger.
-Daniela: Didn't you eat that yesterday?
-Hector: Yes, they're delicious.
-Daniela: I know.
-Hector: And you, what are you going to eat?
-Daniela: I was thinking about eating Venezuelan food. I heard it's very tasty.
-Hector: Really?
-Daniela: Yes, they told me about the pabellon.
-Hector: What's that?
-Daniela: Rice, fried plantains, black beans, and meat.
-Hector: Sounds good. Maybe I'll try it.
-Daniela: Great.
-Hector: What's your favorite type of food?
-Daniela: I love Italian food.
-Hector: I have a weakness for French cuisine.
-Daniela: I don't like it very much. Too sweet.
-Hector: That's why I like it. And I also like German cuisine.
-Daniela: I haven't tried it.
-Hector: You should.
-Daniela: There's a restaurant where they have typical dishes from different countries. I'm going to eat the pabellon there. You can order German food, and I'll order Venezuelan food, so we can try a little of each one.
-Hector: Perfect. Let's go then.

Spanish

-Hector: Daniela, voy a ir a almorzar al centro comercial, ¿Quieres venir?
-Daniela: Si claro, ya estaba por almorzar yo también
-Hector: Genial.
-Daniela: ¿Qué vas a comer?
-Hector: Estaba pensando en una hamburguesa.
-Daniela: ¿No comiste eso ayer?
-Hector: Si, es que son deliciosas.
-Daniela: Lo sé.
-Hector: Y tú, ¿Qué vas a comer?
-Daniela: Estaba pensando en comer comida Venezolana. Escuche que es muy rica.
-Hector: ¿En serio?

-Daniela: Si, me hablaron del pabellón.
-Hector: ¿Y eso que es?
-Daniela: Arroz, plátano frito, caraotas y carne.
-Hector: Suena bien. Quizás lo pruebe
-Daniela: Genial.
-Hector: ¿Cuál es tu tipo de comida favorita?
-Daniela: Amo la comida italiana.
-Hector: Yo tengo debilidad por la cocina francesa.
-Daniela: No me gusta mucho. Muy dulce.
-Hector: Por eso es que me gusta. Y también me gusta la Alemana.
-Daniela: No la he probado.
-Hector: Deberías.
-Daniela: Hay un restaurante donde tienen los platos típicos de distintos países, ahí voy a comer el pabellón. Tú puedes pedir comida alemana y yo la venezolana y así probamos un poco de cada una.
-Hector: Perfecto. Vamos entonces.

Talking about Social Networks - Hablando de redes Sociales

English

- Jessica: Last night at Sebastian's meeting, I met a very handsome boy.
-Veronica: Really? What's his name?
- Jessica: I don't know. We talked a lot, but I didn't ask his name.
-Veronica: And he asked you yours?
- Jessica: Yes, but I didn't give him my number.
-Veronica: How are you going to talk now?
- Jessica: I'll wait for another meeting to see him.
-Veronica: Maybe he'll search for you on social networks.
- Jessica: I don't use that.
-Veronica: None? No Instagram, no Facebook, no Snapchat, no Twitter?
- Jessica: No, I don't know what they are used for.
-Veronica: In Facebook, you add friends, upload photos and videos, texts, photo albums, there are games and other integrated applications. In Instagram, you upload photos and comment on others. In Snapchat, you take photos, and there are many filters to play, and on Twitter, you write your opinion about things or how you feel.
- Jessica: Do you use them?
-Veronica: Sure. And when I want to be added in Instagram, Snapchat, or Twitter, I give my user, and so they look for me.
- Jessica: I see.
-Veronica: Use them and follow me in @Veronica and add me on Facebook as Veronica Marrero.
- Jessica: Perfect.

Spanish

-Jessica: Anoche en la reunión de Sebastián conocí a un chico muy guapo.
-Verónica: ¿En serio? ¿Cómo se llama?
- Jessica: No se, hablamos mucho pero no le pregunte su nombre.
-Verónica: ¿Y el te pregunto el tuyo?
- Jessica: Si, pero no le di mi numero.
-Verónica: ¿Y ahora como van a hablar?
- Jessica: Esperare a otra reunión para verlo.
-Verónica: Quizás te busque por las redes sociales.
- Jessica: Yo no uso eso.
-Verónica: ¿Ninguna? ¿Ni Instagram, ni Facebook, ni Snapchat ni Twitter?
- Jessica: No, no se para que funcionan.
-Verónica: En Facebook agregas amigos, suben fotos y videos, textos, álbumes de fotos, hay juegos y otras aplicaciones integradas; en Instagram se suben fotos y los demás comentan; en Snapchat te tomas fotos y hay muchos filtros para jugar; y en twitter escribes tu opinión sobre cosas o como te sientes.

- Jessica: ¿Tú las usas?

-Veronica: Claro. Y cuando quiero que me agreguen en Instagram, Snapchat o Twitter doy mi usuario y así me consiguen.

- Jessica: Ya veo.

-Veronica: Úsalas y sígueme en @Veronica y agregame en Facebook como Sofia Marrero.

- Jessica: Perfecto.

Talking about feelings - Hablando de sentimientos

English

-Monica: Mom, can we talk?
-Mother: Of course, daughter. What's wrong?
-Monica: I've been feeling sad lately.
-Mother: Why is that?
-Monica: I didn't do well in class.
-Mother: Which ones?
-Monica: In physics, the teacher is a bad teacher and that bothers me.
-Mother: Study on your own.
-Monica: That's what I do, but I despair because I don't understand.
-Mother: What about other subjects?
-Monica: In art, I am happy. Sport always tires me a lot, and mathematics frustrates me.
-Mother: You have to be patient and focused.
-Monica: That's what I'm trying to do, but I feel stuck.
-Mother: Relax daughter, you can do it. Let's go for a walk and have some ice cream to calm you down a bit.
-Monica: Thanks mom, you're the best.

Spanish

-Mónica: Mamá, ¿podemos hablar?
-Madre: Claro hija, ¿Qué pasa?
-Mónica: Es que últimamente me he sentido triste.
-Madre: ¿Y eso porque?
-Mónica: Es que no me ha ido bien en clases.
-Madre: ¿En cuáles?
-Mónica: En física, la profesora es mala enseñando y eso me molesta.
-Madre: Estudia por tu cuenta.
-Mónica: Eso hago, pero me desespero por no entender.
-Madre: ¿Y las demás materias?
-Mónica: En arte soy feliz, deporte siempre me cansa mucho y matemática me frustra.
-Madre: Tienes que ser paciente y enfocarte.
-Mónica: Eso estoy intentando pero me siento atascada.
-Madre: Relájate hija, tu puedes hacerlo. Vamos a pasear y nos comemos un helado para que te calmes un poco.
-Mónica: Gracias mamá, eres la mejor.

Talking about Books - Hablando Sobre Libros

English

-Mother: Daughter, I'm going to a book fair in the square, are you coming?
-Daughter: Of course, mom. You know I love to read.
-Mother: That's my daughter.
-Daughter: Besides, I just finished the last book I bought. I need some new ones.
-Mother: What was it about?
-Daughter: It was a suspense book, but it had a lot of comedy.
-Mother: I see, are those your favorites?
-Daughter: I like them a lot, they entertain me. However, my favorites are those of mysteries and ghosts.
-Mother: I don't like those. I prefer romance and self-help.
-Daughter: They're good, but they bore me.
-Mother: Everyone has their own preferences.
-Daughter: That's right. My father likes fantasies and magic better.
-Mother: And your brother gets bored with biographies and politics.
-Daughter: I don't blame him.

Spanish

-Madre: Hija, voy saliendo a una feria de libros que hay en la plaza, ¿Vienes?
-Hija: Claro má, sabes que me encanta leer.
-Madre: Esa es mi hija.
-Hija: Además, acabo de terminar el último libro que compre. Necesito unos nuevos.
-Madre: ¿De qué se trataba?
-Hija: Era un libro de suspenso pero tenía un montón de comedia.
-Madre: Ya veo, ¿Esos son tus favoritos?
-Hija: Esos me gustan bastante, me entretienen. Sin embargo, mis favoritos son los de misterios y fantasmas.
-Madre: A mí no me gustan esos. Yo prefiero los de romance y los de autoayuda.
-Hija: Son buenos, pero me aburren.
-Madre: Cada quien tiene sus preferencias.
-Hija: Eso es correcto. A mi padre le gustan más los de fantasías y magia.
-Madre: Y a tu hermano se aburre con las biografías y los de política.
-Hija: No lo culpo.

Talking about Politics - Hablando sobre Política

English

-Teacher: Good morning, students. Did you see the films I recommended?
-Student 1: Yes, professor. They give a good idea about the different political systems.
-Professor: Can you tell me what they were?
-Student 2: Monarchy, democracy, republic, dictatorship, fascism, theocracy, and others.
-Professor: Very well. Which is the best?
-Student 3: It's hard to choose one. They all have their pros and cons.
-Teacher: Excellent answer. No political system is perfect.

Spanish

-Profesor: Buenos días estudiantes. ¿Vieron las películas que les recomendé?
-Estudiante 1: Si profesor, es buena la idea que dan sobre los distintos sistemas políticos
-Profesor: ¿Pueden decirme cuales eran?
-Estudiante 2: Monarquía, democracia, republica, dictadura, fascismo, teocracia y otros.
-Profesor: Muy bien. ¿Cuál es el mejor?
-Estudiante 3: Es difícil elegir uno. Todos tienen sus pros y contras.
-Profesor: Excelente respuesta. Ningún sistema político es perfecto.

Talking about Religion - Hablando sobre Religion

English

-Jean: Welcome to my home, my friend.
-Howard: Thank you very much. It looks very nice.
-Jean: Thank you very much. Follow me, here is the library.
-Howard: Perfect.
-Jean: Well, here it is.
-Howard: Wow, you have lots of books.
-Jean: Yeah, my dad reads a lot. He's curious about religions.
-Howard: I'm a Buddhist.
-Jean: Well, my dad would love to meet you. He read a book about Buddhism recently.
-Howard: What are you?
-Jean: We're Christians.
-Howard: I understand.
-Jean: But my dad knows a lot about many religions like Catholicism, atheism, Buddhism, Judaism, Islam, Hinduism, and many others that I don't remember.
-Howard: He must have read a lot.
-Jean: I don't doubt it.

Spanish

-Jean: Bienvenido a mi casa amigo mío.
-Howard: Muchas gracias, está muy bonita.
-Jean: Muchas gracias. Sígueme, por acá esta la biblioteca.
-Howard: Perfecto.
-Jean: Bueno, aquí es.
-Howard: Vaya, tienen montones de libros.
-Jean: Si, mi papá lee bastante. Es curioso con las religiones.
-Howard: Yo soy budista.
-Jean: Que bien, a mi papá le encantara conocerte. Leyó un libro sobre el budismo hace poco.
-Howard: ¿Ustedes que son?
-Jean: Somos cristianos.
-Howard: Entiendo.
-Jean: Sin embargo mi papá sabe bastante sobre muchas religiones como el catolicismo, el ateísmo, el budismo, el judaísmo, el islamismo, hinduismo y muchas otras que no recuerdo.
-Howard: Debe haber leído mucho.
-Jean: No lo dudo.

Documentation - Documentación

English

-Adriana: Good morning. How are you?
-Carlos: Good morning. Very well. How can I help you?
-Adriana: Yesterday, I lost my bag with all my documentation, and I need new documents.
-Carlos: Are you undocumented?
-Adriana: That's right. I need to get my ID, my driver's license, and my credit card.
-Carlos: I can only help you with identification and driver's license.
-Adriana: It's okay.
-Carlos: What was your identification number or identity number?
-Adriana: It was 112398734.
-Carlos: Perfect. Are you Adriana Miller?
-Adriana: Correct.
-Carlos: Done with the identification, now the license.
-Adriana: Thank you very much. Does the credit card have to be in the bank?
-Carlos: That's right.
-Adriana: I also lost my passport. Where can I order a new one?
-Carlos: I have a friend who can help you, let's call him.
-Adriana: Great. You don't know how much I appreciate it.

Spanish

-Adriana: Buenos días. ¿Cómo esta?
-Carlos: Buenos días, muy bien ¿en que la puedo ayudar?
-Adriana: Ayer perdí mi bolsa con toda mi documentación y necesito unas nuevas.
-Carlos: ¿Esta indocumentada?
-Adriana: Así es, necesito sacar mi identificación, mi licencia de conducir y mi tarjeta de crédito
-Carlos: Acá solo puedo ayudarla con la identificación y la licencia de conducir.
-Adriana: Esta bien.
-Carlos: ¿Cuál era su número de identificación o número de identidad?
-Adriana: Era 112398734
-Carlos: Perfecto. ¿Es usted Adriana Miller?
-Adriana: Correcto.
-Carlos: Listo la identificación, ahora la licencia.
-Adriana: Muchísimas gracias. ¿La tarjeta de crédito debe ser en el banco?
-Carlos: Así es.
-Adriana: También perdí mi pasaporte, ¿Dónde puedo pedir uno nuevo?
-Carlos: Tengo un amigo que puede ayudarte, vamos a llamarlo.
-Adriana: Genial. No sabes cuánto lo agradezco.

Phone number - Número telefónico

English

-Valentina: Hi Steve, how are you?
-Steve: Hi Valentina, all right, you?
-Valentina: Today, I'm better. Yesterday, I was nauseous, and I couldn't come to class.
-Steve: That's what I was going to ask you.
-Valentina: What did you do in class yesterday?
-Steve: The professor did a lot of exercises and sent homework.
-Valentina: Can I borrow your notebook to see?
-Steve: It's in my house.
-Valentina: Give me your cell phone number and send me the photos.
-Steve: That's fine. It's 99933441.
-Valentina: Thank you very much.
-Steve: Give me yours in case you forget.
-Valentina: My cell phone number is 99933445, and my home phone number is 88822111.
-Steve: Okay, I'll call you in the afternoon.

Spanish

-Valentina: Hola Steve, ¿Cómo estás?
-Steve: Hola Valentina, todo bien, ¿Tu?
-Valentina: Hoy estoy mejor, ayer tuve nauseas y no pude venir a clases.
-Steve: Eso te iba a preguntar.
-Valentina: ¿Qué hicieron ayer en clases?
-Steve: El profesor hizo un montón de ejercicios y envió tarea para la casa.
-Valentina: ¿Me prestas tu cuaderno para ver?
-Steve: Esta en mi casa.
-Valentina: Dame tu numero celular y me envías las fotos.
-Steve: Me parece bien, es 99933441.
-Valentina: Muchas gracias.
-Steve: Dame el tuyo en caso de que lo olvides
-Valentina: Mi número celular es 99933445 y mi número de teléfono de la casa es 88822111.
-Steve: Vale, te llamo en la tarde.

Email - Correo electrónico

English

-Oswaldo: Good evening. I come to ask for information about the event.
-Manager: Good evening. Which event?
-Oswaldo: From the marketing course.
-Manager: There are three events, one on Saturday, another on Monday, and the last one on Wednesday.
-Oswaldo: What time? Do they cost the same? Who will be the teachers?
-Manager: At this moment, I don't remember. Give me your email, and I can send you the flyers there.
-Oswaldo: Perfect. My email is Oswaldo123@OSW.com
-Manager: Ready.
-Oswaldo: To book can be by mail too, right?
-Manager: Exactly. If you have doubts, you can come again.
-Oswaldo: Perfect. Thank you. Have a nice day.
-Manager: Same as you.

Spanish

-Oswaldo: Buenas noches. Vengo a pedir información sobre un evento.
-Manager: Buenas noches. ¿De cuál evento?
-Oswaldo: Del curso de marketing.
-Manager: Hay tres eventos, uno el sábado, otro el lunes y el ultimo el miércoles.
-Oswaldo: ¿A qué hora? ¿Cuestan lo mismo? ¿Quiénes serán los profesores?
-Manager: En este momento no recuerdo, dame tu correo electrónico y te puedo pasar los flyers por allí.
-Oswaldo: Perfecto, mi correo electrónico es Oswaldo123@OSW.com
-Manager: Listo.
-Oswaldo: Para reservar puede ser por correo también, ¿Cierto?
-Manager: Exacto. Si tienes dudas puedes venir de nuevo.
-Oswaldo: Perfecto; Gracias. Que tenga buen día
-Manager: Igual tu.

Education - Educación

English

Mark: Are you Betty Thompson?
-Betty: Yes, who are you?
-Mark: I'm Mark Jordan. I studied with you in preschool at Chatter School.
-Betty: Ah, I remember you.
-Mark: I'm glad.
-Betty: Why did you leave that school?
-Mark: My parents had to move because of work, and I went with them.
-Betty: I see.
-Mark: Yeah, I loved that school.
-Betty: And where did you go?
-Mark: Well, I finished preschool in New York. Then, I finished elementary school in California, high school in Miami, and I'm studying mechanical engineering at a university here in Michigan.
-Betty: You traveled a lot, didn't you?
-Mark: A lot. It was frustrating. What did you do?
-Betty: I stayed at the Chatter until I finished high school. I took some Web design courses, got certified in German, and I'm studying economics in Orlando. But I came on vacation.
-Mark: Good news. You've made the most of your time.
-Betty: That's right.
-Mark: It was good to see you again.
-Betty: Same here.
-Mark: Success with your studies.
-Betty: Same for you.

Spanish

-Mark: ¿Tú eres Betty Thompson?
-Betty: Si, ¿Quién eres tú?
-Mark: Soy Mark Jordan, estudie contigo en preescolar en la escuela Chatter.
-Betty: Ah ya me acuerdo de ti.
-Mark: Me alegro.
-Betty: ¿Porque te fuiste de esa escuela?
-Mark: Mis padres tuvieron que mudarse por el trabajo y me fui con ellos.
-Betty: Ya veo.
-Mark: Si, me encantaba esa escuela.
-Betty: ¿Y a donde te fuiste?
-Mark: Bueno, termine preescolar en Nueva York; luego termine primaria en California, secundaria en Miami y estoy estudiando ingeniería mecánica en una universidad aquí en Michigan.
-Betty: Viajaste bastante, ¿no?
-Mark: Un montón, era frustrante. ¿Tú qué hiciste?

-Betty: Me mantuve en la Chatter hasta que termine secundaria; hice varios cursos de diseño web, me certifique en alemán y estoy estudiando economía en Orlando. Pero vine de vacaciones.
-Mark: Que buena noticia, has aprovechado tu tiempo.
-Betty: Así es.
-Mark: Fue bueno haberte visto de nuevo.
-Betty: Lo mismo digo.
-Mark: Que tengas éxito con tus estudios.
-Betty: Igual para ti.

Giving my Address - Dando mi dirección

English

-Harry: Good afternoon. I'd like to buy ten family tents.
-Bruce: Good afternoon. Perfect. Do you know about our delivery service?
-Harry: No, is it new?
-Bruce: That's right. We're testing it.
-Harry: Great. My purchase wasn't going to fit in my car.
-Bruce: In order to use the delivery service, you must give me your address.
-Harry: Amazing. I live at 15th Avenue, 4th Street, 8th Condo 6-C in Santiago de Chile, Chile.
-Bruce: Annotated. We will ship tomorrow morning, and it should arrive tomorrow afternoon.
-Harry: Thank you very much. We are in contact.

Spanish

-Harry: Buenas tardes; me gustaría comprar diez carpas familiares.
-Bruce: Buenas tardes; perfecto. ¿Sabe usted de nuestro servicio de entregas?
-Harry: No, ¿Es nuevo?
-Bruce: Así es. Estamos probándolo.
-Harry: Genial, mi compra no iba a caber en mi carro.
-Bruce: Para poder usar el servicio de entregas debe darme su dirección.
-Harry: Asombroso. Yo vivo en la avenida 15, calle 4, edificio 8, piso 6, apartamento C, en Santiago de Chile, Chile.
-Bruce: Anotado. Haremos el envío mañana por la mañana y debe llegar mañana por la tarde.
-Harry: Muchas gracias. Estamos en contacto.

Clothing size - Talla de ropa

English
-Hanna: Sister, are you going to Peter's wedding?
-Allison: Of course. Why?
-Hanna: I don't know what to wear.
-Allison: I'll help you.
-Hanna: Thank you.
-Allison: What do you plan to use?
-Hanna: My white dress.
-Allison: What about the black one?
-Hanna: It's too small for me. Its size S and I'm M.
-Allison: I have a black one, size M.
-Hanna: Can I borrow it?
-Allison: Sure, and can I borrow your white one?
-Hanna: Sure. But I don't have shoes for the black one.
-Allison: What size are you?
-Hanna: Size 8.
-Allison: I use 7. They won't fit you.
-Hanna: Don't worry. My aunt has one size 8.
-Allison: I thought you were size S. What size pants do you wear?
-Hanna: 10.
-Allison: We're the same.

Spanish

-Hanna: Hermana, ¿Tu vas a la boda de Peter?
-Allison: Claro. ¿Por qué?
-Hanna: Es que no se que ponerme.
-Allison: Yo te ayudo.
-Hanna: Gracias.
-Allison: ¿Qué tienes pensado usar?
-Hanna: Mi vestido blanco.
-Allison: ¿Y el negro?
-Hanna: Ya me queda pequeño. Es talla S y yo soy M.
-Allison: Yo tengo uno negro talla M.
-Hanna: ¿Me lo prestas?
-Allison: Claro, y me prestas el tuyo blanco
-Hanna: Seguro. Pero para el negro no tengo zapatos.
-Allison: ¿Qué talla eres?
-Hanna: Talla 8
-Allison: Yo uso 7, no te sirven.
-Hanna: No te preocupes. Mi tía tiene unos talla 8.
-Allison: Pensé que eras talla S. ¿Qué talla de pantalones usas?
-Hanna: 10.
-Allison: Somos iguales.

Medical conditions - Condiciones medicas

English

-Nurse: Good afternoon.
-Chase: Good afternoon.
-Nurse: Can you tell me what you feel?
-Chase: I feel weak and warm.
-Nurse: Have you taken any medication?
-Chase: Not yet.
-Nurse: Do you take any medicine?
-Chase: What do you mean?
-Nurse: If you have a medical condition.
-Chase: What do you mean, like diabetes or something?
-Nurse: Correct.
-Chase: Well, I take pills for cardiac arrhythmia. I'm allergic to broccoli and cats.
-Nurse: Anything else?
-Chase: Sometimes, I have anxiety attacks.
-Nurse: Do you take pills for that?
-Chase: I try not to.
-Nurse: I understand. I'll write your prescription.
-Chase: Thank you very much.

Spanish

-Enfermera: Buenas tardes.
-Chase: Buenas tardes.
-Enfermera: ¿Puede decirme que siente?
-Chase: Me siento débil y acalorado.
-Enfermera: ¿Has tomado algún medicamento?
-Chase: Aun no.
-Enfermera: ¿Tomas algún medicamento?
-Chase: ¿A qué se refiere?
-Enfermera: A si tienes alguna condición médica.
-Chase ¿Cómo diabetes o eso?
-Enfermera: Correcto.
-Chase: Bueno, tomo pastillas para la arritmia cardiaca. Soy alérgico al brócoli y a los gatos.
-Enfermera: ¿Algo más?
-Chase: A veces tengo ataques de ansiedad.
-Enfermera: ¿Tomas pastillas para eso?
-Chase: Intento no hacerlo.
-Enfermera: Entiendo. Ya escribiré su récipe.
-Chase: Muchas gracias.

Characteristics of people - Características de las personas

English

-Nick: Good evening, how are you?
-Carl: Good evening, who is it?
-Nick: I'm in front of you. My name is Nick.
-Carl: I'm sorry, Nick, but I can't see you, I'm blind.
-Nick: Excuse me, sir, I didn't know. I didn't mean to offend you.
-Carl: Don't worry, you didn't.
-Nick: Okay.
-Carl: Tell me, what do you need?
-Nick: It was to ask for an address. But I've located myself.
-Carl: Perfect. Hey Nick, what are you like?
-Nick: What do you mean?
-Carl: Your appearance, your physical characteristics.
-Nick: I'm tall, thin, with brown skin, smooth brown hair, black eyes, no beard, thick lips, small nose, and pointed ears.
-Carl: I see, and how would you describe me?
-Nick: Well, you're short, a bit fat, white-skinned, bald, with a long white beard, small lips, medium nose, and big ears.
-Carl: So I've been told. Thank you very much, boy. Have a good night.
-Nick: Thank you, sir, you too.

Spanish

-Nick: Buenas noches, ¿Cómo esta?
-Carl: Buenas noches, ¿Quién es?
-Nick: Estoy al frente suyo, mi nombre es Nick.
-Carl: Lo lamento Nick, pero no puedo verte, soy ciego.
-Nick: Disculpe señor, no sabía. No era mi intención ofenderlo.
-Carl: No te preocupes, no lo hiciste.
-Nick: Ok.
-Carl: Cuéntame, ¿Qué necesitas?
-Nick: Era para preguntarle una dirección. Pero ya me ubique.
-Carl: Perfecto. Oye Nick, ¿Cómo eres?
-Nick: ¿A qué se refiere?
-Carl: A tu apariencia, tus características físicas.
-Nick: Soy alto, delgado, de piel morena, pelo marrón liso, ojos negros, sin barba, labios gruesos, nariz pequeña y orejas puntiagudas.
-Carl: Ya veo, ¿Y cómo me describirías?
-Nick: Bueno, usted es bajo, un poco gordo, de piel blanca, calvo, con larga barba blanca, labios pequeños, nariz mediana y orejas grandes.
-Carl: Así me han dicho. Muchas gracias muchacho. Que te vaya bien.
-Nick: Gracias señor, a usted también.

Chapter 2: Yendo de Vacaciones - Going on vacations

Packing up - Empacando/Haciendo las maletas

English

-Carla: Good morning, children. Get up. Today we are going on a trip, and we must pack up.
-Noah: Okay, Mom, I'll get up.
-Agatha: It's very early, Mommy, I'll get up later.
-Carla: No daughter, get up now and do that early so we can check if anything is missing.
-Noah: What am I taking, Mommy?
-Carla: Take underwear, some shirts, pants, and sweaters. You can take your laptop and a video game.
-Noah: Okay, what about shoes?
-Carla: Sure, son, I almost forgot, take also some shoes.
-Noah: Should I bring the big suitcase or the small suitcase and a bag?
-Carla: Bring a small suitcase and a bag.
-Noah: Okay.
-Carla: Agatha, get up and pack your bags.
-Agatha: Okay.
-Carla: You take what I told your brother. Take the big suitcase and put everything there. Also, look for towels, sheets, and blankets to sleep on.
-Agatha: Can I take my pillow?
-Carla: I think so, so you can sleep on the plane.
-Agatha: What about medicines and hygiene items?
-Carla: I carry that in my handbag.
-Agatha: It's okay, Mom.
-Carla: Let me know if you need help.
-Agatha: Don't worry, go pack up too.
-Carla: It's okay. Don't forget your bathing suits.
-Agatha and Noah: It's okay.

Spanish

-Carla: Buenos días niños, levántense, hoy nos vamos de viaje y debemos empacar.
-Noah: Esta bien mamá, ya me levanto.
-Agatha: Es muy temprano mami, me levanto luego.
-Carla: No hija, levántate ahorita y haz eso temprano, así podemos revisar si falta algo.

-Noah: ¿Qué me llevo mami?
-Carla: Lleva ropa interior, unas camisas, pantalones y suéteres, puedes guardar tu laptop y un videojuego.
-Noah: Esta bien, ¿Y zapatos?
-Carla: Claro hijo, casi se me olvida, lleva también unos zapatos.
-Noah: ¿Llevo la maleta grande o la maleta pequeña y un bolso?
-Carla: Lleva mejor la maleta pequeña y un bolso.
-Noah: Ok.
-Carla: Agatha levántate y haz tus maletas.
-Agatha: Esta bien.
-Carla: Lleva tu también lo que le dije a tu hermano, agarra la maleta grande y guarda todo allí, también busca toallas, sabanas y cobijas para poder dormir.
-Agatha: ¿Me puedo llevar mi almohada?
-Carla: Creo que sí, para que duermas en el avión.
-Agatha: ¿Y medicinas y artículos de higiene?
-Carla: Eso lo llevo yo en mi bolso de mano.
-Agatha: Esta bien mamá.
-Carla: Avísame si necesitas ayuda.
-Agatha: Tranquila, ve a empacar tu también.
-Carla: Esta bien. No olviden sus trajes de baño.
-Agatha y Noah: Esta bien.

Going to the airport - Yendo al Aeropuerto

English

-Carla: Well, kids, the driver's here. Take the bags out, and we'll put them in the car.
-Noah: I'll look for my suitcase.
-Agatha: I have mine here.
-Carla: All right, daughter, give it to the driver.
-Agatha: Here you go.
-Driver: Thank you. Well, this suitcase is very heavy.
-Agatha: Yes, I bring my favorite blanket and many towels.
-Driver: Did you check if it exceeds the weight limit?
-Agatha: No, I didn't check.
-Carla: How much is the allowed weight?
-Driver: I think it is 25 kilograms.
-Carla: Do you have to weigh?
-Driver: Luckily, I have a portable weighing scale here.
-Carla: Thank you very much.
-Driver: Let's see... It weighs 23 kilograms, almost there.
-Carla: Thank goodness.
-Noah: Here's my suitcase.
-Driver: It's the last one, right?
-Carla: That's right.
-Driver: We can go then.
-Carla: Okay.
...
-Driver: We're almost to the airport. Did you check if you brought everything?
-Carla: Yes, tickets, passports, letters, reservations, and most importantly, my book of 100 conversations in Spanish for beginners.
-Driver: Excellent, I'll leave you at this door. Here, the boys from the airport will help you with your luggage.
-Carla: Thank you very much.
-Driver: At your order. Have a nice trip.
-Carla, Agatha, and Noah: Thank you very much. See you later.

Spanish

-Carla: Bueno hijos, llego el chofer. Saquen las maletas y vamos a montarlas en el carro.
-Noah: Ya busco mi maleta.
-Agatha: Yo tengo la mía aquí.
-Carla: Muy bien hija, entrégasela al chofer.
-Agatha: Aquí tiene.
-Chofer: Gracias. Vaya, está muy pesada esta maleta.

-Agatha: Si, llevo mi cobija favorita y muchas toallas.
-Chofer: ¿Revisaste si excede el límite de peso permitido?
-Agatha: No, no me fije.
-Carla: ¿Cuánto es el peso permitido?
-Chofer: Creo que son 25 kilogramos.
-Carla: ¿Tiene usted para pesar?
-Chofer: Por suerte si, aquí tengo una balanza portátil.
-Carla: Muchas gracias.
-Chofer: Veamos.... Pesa 23 kilogramos, por poco.
-Carla: Menos mal.
-Noah: Aquí tengo mi maleta.
-Chofer: Es la última, ¿Cierto?
-Carla: Así es.
-Chofer: Podemos irnos entonces.
-Carla: De acuerdo.
...
-Chofer: Ya casi llegamos al aeropuerto, ¿Revisaron si trajeron todo?
-Carla: Si, boletos, pasaportes, cartas, reservaciones y lo más importante, mi libro de 100 conversaciones en español para principiantes.
-Chofer: Excelente, los dejaré en esta puerta. Aquí los muchachos del aeropuerto los ayudaran con sus maletas.
-Carla: Muchas gracias.
-Chofer: A su orden. Que tengan un buen viaje.
-Carla, Agatha y Noah: Muchas gracias, hasta luego.

Getting off the plane - Bajandose del avión

English

-Carla: Get ready, children, the plane is going to land.
-Noah: Good. It was time.
-Carla: Agatha?
-Noah: She's asleep.
-Carla: Well, better, so she doesn't feel the landing.
-Noah: I like it.
-Carla: I know.
-Noah: What do we do after landing?
-Carla: We wait to get to the door to disembark. We go and pick up our luggage, and that's it.
-Noah: That's good. What will we do when we leave the airport?
-Carla: I have to call a taxi.
-Noah: I see.
-Carla: Noah, wake up your sister, we're almost at the door to disembark.
-Noah: Agatha, wake up, we're here.
-Agatha: So fast?
-Noah: Did you think it was fast? It took 8 hours.
-Agatha: I think I slept a lot. Hahaha.
-Noah: You slept almost the whole trip. Hahaha.
-Carla: Let's go down, we have to go get the luggage, and we can leave here.
-Agatha: Wait, I need to go to the bathroom.
-Carla: Ask that officer where the bathroom is.
-Agatha: It's okay.
...
-Agatha: Excuse me, where's the bathroom?
-Officer: Pass the food fair, on the left.
-Agatha: Thank you very much.

Spanish

-Carla: Prepárense hijos, el avión va a aterrizar.
-Noah: Que bueno, ya era hora.
-Carla: ¿Agatha?
-Noah: Esta dormida .
-Carla: Bueno, mejor, así no siente el aterrizaje.
-Noah: A mí me gusta.
-Carla: Lo sé.
-Noah: ¿Qué hacemos después de aterrizar?
-Carla: Esperamos que nos dejen el puerta para desembarcar, vamos y buscamos nuestras maletas y listo.
-Noah: Que bien. ¿Qué haremos al salir del aeropuerto?
-Carla: Debo llamar a un taxi.

-Noah: Ya veo.
-Carla: Noah, despierta a tu hermana, ya casi llegamos a la puerta para desembarcar.
-Noah: Agatha despierta, ya llegamos.
-Agatha: ¿Tan rápido?
-Noah: ¿Te pareció rápido? Fueron 8 horas.
-Agatha: Creo que dormí mucho jajaja.
-Noah: Dormiste casi todo el viaje jajaja.
-Carla: Bajémonos, hay que ir a buscar las maletas y ya podremos irnos de aquí.
-Agatha: Espera, necesito ir al baño.
-Carla: Pregúntale a aquel oficial que donde está el baño.
-Agatha: Esta bien
...
-Agatha: Disculpe, ¿Dónde está el baño?
-Oficial: Pasando la feria de comida, a la izquierda.
-Agatha: Muchas gracias.

Calling a taxi - Llamando a un taxi

English

-Carla: Alo, is Frank the taxi driver?
-Frank: Yes, who is this?
-Carla: Hi, it's Carla. My driver gave me your number, said you were his cousin.
-Frank: Ahh yeah. Are you at the airport already?
-Carla: That's right.
-Frank: Perfect, I'm on my way to pick you up.
-Carla: Thank you very much.
-Frank: Where do you want me to take you?
Carla: To the four-star hotel near the city center.
-Frank: The one with the pool or the one without the pool?
-Carla: The one with the pool.
-Frank: Excellent. I know which one. Wait for me outside the airport, I'll be there in 20 minutes.
-Carla: Okay, here we wait.
-Frank: See you.
-Noah: What did the taxi driver just say?
-Carla: To wait for him out here, he was already on his way.
-Noah: How long will it take?
-Carla: He said about 20 minutes.
-Noah: Can I go play with those kids?
-Carla: Yes, but be careful.

Spanish

-Carla: Alo, ¿es Frank el taxista?
-Frank: Si, ¿Quién habla?
-Carla: Hola, soy Carla, mi chofer me dio su número, dijo que usted era su primo.
-Frank: Ahh si, ¿Ya está en el aeropuerto?
-Carla: Así es.
-Frank: Perfecto, voy en camino a recogerla.
-Carla: Muchas gracias.
-Frank: ¿A dónde va a querer que la lleve?
-Carla: Al hotel cuatro estrellas que está cerca del centro de la ciudad.
-Frank: ¿El que tiene piscina o el que no tiene piscina?
-Carla: El que tiene la piscina.
-Frank: Excelente. Ya sé cuál es. Espéreme ahí afuera del aeropuerto, llego en 20 minutos.

-Carla: Ok, aquí lo esperamos.
-Frank: Nos vemos.
-Noah: ¿Qué dijo el taxista?
-Carla: Que lo esperáramos aquí afuera, que ya venía en camino.
-Noah: ¿Cuánto va a tardar?
-Carla: Dijo que como 20 minutos.
-Noah: ¿Puedo ir a jugar con esos niños?
-Carla: Si, pero con cuidado.

I'm a tourist - Soy turista

English

-Noah: Hey, what are you playing?
-Mathias: We are playing La ere.
-Noah: La ere? What's that?
-Mathias: Don't you know what la ere is?
-Noah: No, I've never played it.
-Mathias: Well, whoever is La ere has to run and touch another person so that that person becomes La ere.
-Noah: Ahh, just like the tag game.
-Mathias: The tag game?
-Noah: Yeah, it's just like your game.
-Mathias: I've never heard it before.
-Noah: Where I come from it's called like that.
-Mathias: And where do you come from?
-Noah: Ahh, I didn't tell you. I'm a tourist. I'm not from here.
-Mathias: Oh, got it.

Spanish

-Noah: Hola, ¿Qué juegan?
-Mathias: Jugamos a la ere.
-Noah: ¿La ere? ¿Qué es eso?
-Mathias: ¿No sabes que es la ere?
-Noah: No, nunca lo he jugado.
-Mathias: Bueno, el que sea la ere tiene que correr y tocar a otra persona para que esa persona se convierta en la ere.
-Noah: Ahh, así como las traes.
-Mathias: ¿Las traes?
-Noah: Si, es igualito a ese juego.
-Mathias: Nunca había escuchado.
-Noah: De donde vengo se llama así.
-Mathias ¿Y de dónde vienes?
-Noah: Ahh, no te había dicho, soy turista, no soy de aquí.
-Mathias: Ahh ya.

Getting to the hotel - Llegando al hotel

English

-Frank: We're close to the hotel now.
-Clara: Did you hear, Noah? We're going to get to the hotel.
-Noah: How exciting!
-Agatha: Finally, I don't want to move my luggage anymore.
-Clara: We're almost there, daughter. When we arrive at the hotel, we leave them in the room, and we'll forget about them for a while.
-Agatha: Thank goodness.
-Frank: Well, here we are.
-Clara: Thank you very much, Frank.
-Frank: Don't worry. Let me help you get your luggage down.
-Clara: I'm tired already.
-Frank: I can imagine.
-Clara: See you later, Frank. Be well.
-Frank: See you later, Clara. If you need a taxi, don't hesitate to call me.
-Clara: I'm sure I will.
-Noah: Bye Frank. Thanks for everything.
-Clara: Okay, guys. Let's go in.
-Receptionist: Good afternoon. How can I help you?
-Clara: Good afternoon. My name is Clara Friedman. I made an online reservation for a family room for a period of one month.
-Receptionist: All right, do you have the reservation number?
-Clare: 122333.
-Receptionist: Perfect. Everything is in order, here is the key, and your room is 104.
-Clara: Thank you very much.
-Receptionist: Leave the luggage here. The baggage handler will take it to your room.
-Clara: Really? That's good news. Thank you very much.
-Receptionist: On your order. Enjoy your stay in our hotel.

Spanish

-Frank: Ya estamos cerca del hotel.
-Clara: ¿Escuchaste Noah? Ya vamos a llegar al hotel.
-Noah: ¡Qué emoción!
-Agatha: Por fin, ya no quiero seguir moviendo las maletas.
-Clara: Ya falta poco hija, llegamos al hotel, las dejamos en la habitación y nos olvidaremos de ellas por un tiempo.
-Agatha: Menos mal.
-Frank: Bueno, aquí estamos.
-Clara: Muchas gracias Frank.
-Frank: No se preocupe. Déjeme ayudarla a bajar las maletas.

-Clara: Ya estoy cansada.
-Frank: Me imagino.
-Clara: Hasta luego Frank. Que estés bien.
-Frank: Hasta luego Clara, si necesitas un taxi, no dudes en llamarme.
-Clara: Seguro que lo hare.
-Noah: Chao Frank, gracias por todo.
-Clara: Bueno chicos, entremos.
-Recepcionista: Buenas tardes, ¿en qué puedo ayudarlos?
-Clara: Buenas tardes. Mi nombre es Clara Friedman, hice una reservación por internet de una habitación familiar para un periodo de un mes.
-Recepcionista: Muy bien, ¿tiene el número de reservación?
-Clara: 122333.
-Recepcionista: Perfecto. Todo en orden, aquí tiene la llave, su habitación es la 104.
-Clara: Muchas gracias.
-Recepcionista: Deje las maletas aquí, el encargado de equipaje las llevara a su habitación.
-Clara: ¿En serio? Qué buena noticia, muchísimas gracias.
-Recepcionista: A su orden. Disfrute su estadía en nuestro hotel.

Currencies - Divisas

English

-Carla: Good morning, how are you?
-Receptionist: Good morning. Very well, you? How did you spend the night?
-Carla: Excellent, the beds are super comfortable, the room is very nice, the swimming pool is beautiful, the children are enjoying it very much, and the dinner in the room was the best.
-Receptionist: I'm glad you're enjoying it.
-Carla: Thank you very much. I was told that here in the hotel, there were one or two exchange houses. Is it true?
-Receptionist: That's right. They're on the third floor.
-Clara: Ok, have a nice day.
-Receptionist: You too.
...
-Clara: Good morning. Is this one of the exchange houses?
-Seller: That's right.
-Clara: I would like to know how your service works.
-Seller: You give us the currency you have, you tell us which one you want to change it to, and we make the change.
-Clear: Perfect. What if I need the money on a card?
-Seller: We can lend you one, but you have to pay for the card loan.
-Clara: Very good. Here, I would like to change all this for euros. You give me half in cash and the other half in a card and you charge the loan.
-Seller: Perfect.

Spanish

-Carla: Buenos días, ¿Cómo esta?
-Recepcionista: Buenos días. Muy bien, ¿Usted? ¿Cómo pasaron la noche?
-Carla: Excelente, las camas son súper cómodas, la habitación muy bonita, la piscina hermosa, los niños lo están disfrutando muchísimo y la cena en la habitación fue lo mejor.
-Recepcionista: Me alegra que este disfrutando.
-Carla: Muchas gracias. Me dijeron que acá en el hotel había una o dos casas de cambio, ¿Es cierto?
-Recepcionista: Así es. Están en el tercer piso.
-Clara: Ok, que tenga buen día.
-Recepcionista: Igual usted.
...
-Clara: Buenos días, ¿Esta es una de las casas de cambio?
-Vendedor: Así es.
-Clara: Me gustaría saber cómo funciona su servicio.
-Vendedor: Usted nos da la divisa que tiene, nos dice a cual desea cambiarla y hacemos el cambio.

-Clara: Perfecto. ¿Y si necesito el dinero en una tarjeta?

-Vendedor: Nosotros le podemos prestar una pero tiene que pagar por el préstamo de la tarjeta.

-Clara: Muy bien. Toma, me gustaría cambiar todo esto a Euros, me das la mitad en efectivo y la otra mitad en una tarjeta y te cobras el préstamo.

-Vendedor: Perfecto.

Renting a car - Alquilando un carro

English

-Clara: Guys, I'm going out to rent a car. Stay here in the room until I get back.
-Noah: Can I ask for room service?
-Clara: Yes, but don't ask for too much candy.
-Agatha: Can I order a hot chocolate?
-Clara: Yes.
-Agatha: Great, thanks, mom.
-Clara: Alo, Frank?
-Frank: Hi Clara, tell me.
-Clara: I'm ready for you to take me to rent a car.
-Frank: Well, I'm already outside waiting for you.
-Clara: Yeah, I just saw your taxi.
-Frank: Okay, get in.
-Clara: Where are you taking me?
-Frank: To a friend's car rental, he has a lot of cars and the best rates and plans in the area.
-Clara: Excellent. What car do you think I should rent?
-Frank: I'd say a small one. You're only three, and you won't be traveling as far to ask for an SUV or a van, right?
-Clara: You're right.
-Frank: Ask for my friend Richard.
-Clara: Okay.
-Frank: That's it. I'll leave you here, and you cross the street.
-Clara: Thank you very much.
-Frank: Bye.
...
-Clara: Good afternoon. Is Richard here?
-Richard: Yes, hello, it's me. Tell me.
-Clara: I come from Frank. I'd like to rent a small car for a month.
-Richard: From Frank? We'll give you a discount then.
-Clara: Excellent.
-Richard: Those are all the small cars we have. Which one do you want?
-Clara: I think I'll keep the red, my kids like the red.
-Richard: Good choice, that's the cheapest and it's just been maintained.
-Clara: Lucky you.

Spanish

-Clara: Chicos, voy a salir a alquilar un carro. Quedense aquí en la habitación hasta que regrese.
-Noah: ¿Puedo pedir servicio a la habitación?
-Clara: Si, pero no pidas muchos dulces.

225

-Agatha: ¿Yo puedo pedir un chocolate caliente?
-Clara: Si.
-Agatha: Genial, gracias mamá.
-Clara: Alo, ¿Frank?
-Frank: Hola Clara, dime.
-Clara: Ya estoy lista para que me lleves a alquilar un carro.
-Frank: Que bueno, yo ya estoy afuera esperándote.
-Clara: Si, acabo de ver tu taxi.
-Frank: Vale, súbete.
-Clara: ¿A dónde me llevas?
-Frank: Al alquiler de carros de un amigo, tiene un montón de carros y las mejores tarifas y planes de la zona.
-Clara: Excelente. ¿Qué carro crees que debería pedir?
-Frank: Yo diría que uno pequeño, ustedes son solo tres, y no viajaran tan lejos como pedir una SUV o una van, ¿Cierto?
-Clara: Tienes razón.
-Frank: Pregunta por mi amigo Richard.
-Clara: De acuerdo.
-Frank: Es ahí, te dejo aquí y tu cruzas la calle.
-Clara: Muchas Gracias.
-Frank: Chao.
...
-Clara: Buenas tardes, ¿Esta Richard?
-Richard: Si, hola, soy yo, dígame.
-Clara: Vengo de parte de Frank, me gustaría alquilar un carro pequeño por un mes.
-Richard: ¿De Frank? Le haremos un descuento entonces.
-Clara: Excelente.
-Richard: Esos que ve allá son todos los carros pequeños que tenemos. ¿Cuál quiere?
-Clara: Creo que me quedare con el rojo, a mis hijos les gusta el rojo.
-Richard: Buena elección, ese es el más económico y le acaban de hacer mantenimiento.
-Clara: Que suerte.

Asking for directions - Pidiendo direcciones

English

-Clara: Excuse me, do you know how to get to the nearest bakery?
-Strange: Of course, go straight on this avenue. Three blocks ahead, turn left, go to a fork and take the right, turn around the block, and that's where it is.
-Clara: Great, thank you very much.
-Strange: There's also another one that's near the roundabout. Go straight for about five blocks, and in the roundabout, you'll see the bakery.
-Clear: Ok, I understand.

Spanish

-Clara: Disculpe, ¿Sabe usted como hago para llegar a la panadería más cercana?
-Extraño: Claro, sigue derecho por esta avenida, tres cuadras más adelante gira a la izquierda, avanza hasta una bifurcación y agarras a la derecha, das vuelta a la manzana y allí es.
-Clara: Genial, muchísimas gracias.
-Extraño: También hay otra que está cerca de la redoma, siga derecho como por cinco cuadras y en la redoma de media vuelta y ahí vera la panadería.
-Clara: Ok, entiendo.

Meeting people - Conociendo gente

English

-Clara: Good afternoon.
-Wanda: Good afternoon.
-Clara: Do you often come to this bakery?
-Wanda: Yes, why?
-Clara: I'm here on vacation with my children, and I wanted to bring them something delicious for breakfast, and I don't know what's good.
-Wanda: Aren't you from around here?
-Clara: No.
-Wanda: My name is Wanda. I live nearby. Nice to meet you. What's your name?
-Clara: My name is Clara.
-Wanda: Well, the tastiest thing here are the sandwiches. They are exquisite.
-Clara: Great. Thank you very much.
-Wanda: Clara, take my number, if you need any advice about places or food or whatever, you can write to me, and I will gladly advise you.
-Clear: Wow, it means a lot, thank you seriously.
-Wanda: Don't worry. I hope to hear from you soon.
-Clara: For sure, I will.

Spanish

-Clara: Buenas tardes.
-Wanda: Buenas tardes.
-Clara: ¿Tú vienes frecuentemente a esta panadería?
-Wanda: Si, ¿Por qué?
-Clara: Es que estoy aquí de vacaciones con mis niños y quería llevarles algo delicioso para desayunar.
-Wanda: ¿No eres de por aquí?
-Clara: No.
-Wanda: Mi nombre es Wanda, yo vivo aquí cerca. Encantada de conocerte. ¿Cómo te llamas?
-Clara: Mi nombre es Clara.
-Wanda: Bueno, lo más sabroso de aquí son los cachitos, son exquisitos.
-Clara: Genial. Muchísimas gracias.
-Wanda: A tu orden. Clara, toma mi número, si necesitas algún consejo sobre lugares o comidas o lo que sea, puedes escribirme y con gusto te aconsejare.
-Clara: Wao, significa mucho, gracias en serio.
-Wanda: No te preocupes. Espero saber de ti pronto.
-Clara: Seguro que sí.

Asking for Tourist Places - Preguntando lugares turísticos

English

-Clara: Good morning, my darlings. I'm here.
-Noah: Mom!
-Agatha: Mommy.
-Clara: Have you had breakfast?
-Agatha: No, room service came, but I didn't like anything.
-Clara: I have a surprise for you then... SANDWICHES!
-Noah: Yeeey.
-Agatha: Thanks, mom.
-Clara: I hope you like them. They were recommended to me by a local lady. Her name is Wanda, and she gave me her number so I could ask her anything.
-Agatha: Ask her where we can go for a walk.
-Clara: Good thinking. I'll call her.
...
-Clara: Hi Wanda, it's Clara.
-Wanda: Hi Clara, I'm glad you called.
-Clara: Thank you. I wanted to ask you, what are the tourist places in the area?
-Wanda: Well, you have the beach that is about 10 minutes from the bakery. The mountain is about 15 kilometers to the north, and there is also an amusement park that is 5 kilometers to the west.
-Clear: Perfect, there's a lot to visit then.
-Wanda: That's right, enjoy it.

Spanish

-Clara: Buenos días mis amores, ya llegue.
-Noah: ¡Mamá!
-Agatha: Mamii.
-Clara: ¿Ya desayunaron?
-Agatha: No, vino servicio a la habitación pero no había nada que me gustara.
-Clara: Les tengo una sorpresa entonces... ¡SANDUCHES!
-Noah: Yeeey.
-Agatha: Gracias mamá.
-Clara: Espero que les gusten, me los recomendó una señora de la zona, su nombre es Wanda, me dio su número para que le preguntara cualquier cosa.
-Agatha: Pregúntale a que lugares podemos ir a pasear.
-Clara: Bien pensado, ya la llamo.
...
-Clara: Hola Wanda es Clara.
-Wanda: Hola Clara, me alegra que llames.

-Clara: Gracias, quería preguntarte ¿Cuáles son los lugares turísticos que hay en la zona?
-Wanda: Bueno, tienes la playa que está a unos 10 minutos de la panadería; la montaña está a unos 15 kilómetros al norte y hay un parque de diversiones que está a 5 kilómetros al oeste.
-Clara: Perfecto, hay mucho que visitar entonces.
-Wanda: Así es, que lo disfruten.

Visit to the beach - Visita a la playa

English

-Clara: I just spoke to Wanda, and she told me that there is a beach 10 minutes from the bakery where I bought breakfast.
-Agatha: Great, I love the beach.
-Noah: Good, can I bring my snorkel?
-Clara: I know Agatha. Of course, you can, Noah.
-Agatha: Where are the bathing suits?
-Clara: In the big suitcase.
-Noah: What about my snorkel?
-Clara: It must be there too.
-Noah: Yes, here it is.
-Clara: Bring the towels, your sandals, sunscreen, water, caps, and sunglasses.
-Noah: I'll take my shovel to make sandcastles.
-Agatha: And I will bring my lifeguard.
-Clara: Perfect. Let's go. We have to be careful with the waves.
-Noah and Agatha: Ok.

Spanish

-Clara: Acabo de hablar con Wanda y me dijo que hay una playa a 10 minutos de la panadería donde compré el desayuno.
-Agatha: Genial, amo la playa.
-Noah: Que bien, ¿Puedo llevar mi snorkel?
-Clara: Lo sé Agatha. Claro que puedes Noah.
-Agatha: ¿Dónde están los trajes de baño?
-Clara: En la maleta grande.
-Noah: ¿Y mi snorkel?
-Clara: Debe estar ahí también.
-Noah: Si, aquí esta.
-Clara: Traigan las toallas, sus sandalias, el protector solar, agua, gorras y sus lentes de sol.
-Noah: Llevare mi pala para hacer castillos de arena.
-Agatha: Y yo mi salvavidas.
-Clara: Perfecto. Vamonos, hay que tener cuidado con el oleaje.
-Noah y Agatha: Ok.

Visit to the mountain - Visita a la montaña

English

-Clara: Yesterday on the beach was exhausting.
-Agatha: It was the best. I enjoyed it a lot.
-Noah: Are we going to the beach again today?
-Clara: No, I was thinking of going to the mountain that Wanda told me. What do you think?
-Agatha: I don't like the mountain.
-Noah: I've never been to one.
-Clara: That's why we're going to Agatha so that Noah knows it.
-Agatha: Good.
-Clara: To go to the mountain, we must wear sports clothes, a cap, glasses, mosquito repellent, and lots of water.
-Agatha: I hate mosquitoes.
-Clara: Then don't forget the repellent.
-Agatha: Okay.
-Noah: What do you do in the mountains, Mom?
-Clara: Walk, climb, exercise, and see the flora and fauna.
-Noah: I see.
-Clara: Walking in the mountains is also known as trekking.
-Agatha: I've heard about that before.
-Clara: Well, today, you'll see how it's done.
-Agatha: All right.
-Clara: Bring sneakers too, and jackets in case it rains.
-Noah: Ok.
-Agatha: Okay.
... On the mountain...
-Clara: Well children, here we are. Look at all those trees, flowers, and plants. Look at the birds and the insects that are there. Some say there are monkeys in certain parts of the mountain.
-Noah: Great, I want to see them.
-Clara: Let's open our eyes to see if we can see them.

Spanish

-Clara: El día de ayer en la playa fue agotador.
-Agatha: Fue lo máximo, lo disfrute mucho.
-Noah: ¿Vamos a ir hoy a la playa de nuevo?
-Clara: No, pensaba ir a la montaña que me dijo Wanda. ¿Qué opinan?
-Agatha: No me gusta la montaña.
-Noah: Yo nunca he ido a una.
-Clara: Por eso vamos a ir Agatha, para que Noah la conozca.
-Agatha: Bueno.

-Clara: Para ir a la montaña debemos llevar ropa deportiva, gorra, lentes, repelente de mosquitos y mucha agua.
-Agatha: Odio los mosquitos.
-Clara: Entonces no olvides el repelente.
-Agatha: Esta bien.
-Noah: ¿Qué se hace en la montaña, mamá?
-Clara: Caminar, escalar, ejercitarse y ver la flora y fauna.
-Noah: Ya veo.
-Clara: Caminar en las montañas también es conocido como treking.
-Agatha: Ya había oído sobre eso.
-Clara: Pues hoy veras como se hace.
-Agatha: Esta bien.
-Clara: Lleven zapatos deportivos también, y chaquetas por si llueve.
-Noah: Ok.
-Agatha: Esta bien.
... En la montaña...
-Clara: Bueno hijos, aquí estamos, miren todos esos árboles, flores, plantas, vean las aves y los insectos que hay. Algunos dicen que hay monos en ciertos lugares de la montaña
-Noah: Genial, yo quiero verlos.
-Clara: Abramos los ojos a ver si logramos verlos.

Visit to the Amusement Park - Visita al parque de diversiones

English

-Clara: Good morning, children. I'm sure today will be your favorite day.
-Noah: Why?
-Clara: We'll go to the amusement park.
-Agatha: YEEES!
-Noah: YUPIIII!
-Clara: Get dressed so we can leave early and be on time.
-Noah: Great mom.
... In the park...
-Clara: What do you think?
-Noah: This incredible, mom.
-Agatha: I love it. I want to get on everything.
-Clara: There are several rollercoasters. There's a mirror house, a haunted house, slides, swimming pools, horses, swimming with dolphins, karts, bumper cars, tennis courts, soccer courts, basketball courts, ping pong tables, video game rooms, trampolines, diving, simulators, climbing walls, paintball, a carousel, a wheel of fortune, and many other things.
-Noah: This is paradise, Mom.
-Agatha: The best. I want to stay and live here.
-Clara: There are certain rules and prohibitions for attractions.
-Agatha: How so?
-Clara: For some attractions, you have to be higher than a certain height. For others, you have to be older than a certain age.
-Noah: Damn.
-Clear: But come on, there are many attractions to try.

Spanish

-Clara: Buenos días hijos. Estoy segura que hoy será su día favorito.
-Noah: ¿Por qué?
-Clara: Iremos al parque de diversiones.
-Agatha: ¡SIIIII!
-Noah: ¡YUPIIII!
-Clara: Vístanse para salir temprano y poder aprovechar el tiempo.
-Noah: Genial mamá
... En el parque...
-Clara: ¿Qué les parece?
-Noah: Esta increíble mamá.
-Agatha: Me encanta, quiero subirme en todo.
-Clara: Hay varias montañas rusas, hay una casa de espejos, una casa embrujada, toboganes, piscinas, caballos, nado con delfines, kartings, carros chocones, canchas de tenis, de futbol, de baloncesto, mesas de ping pong,

salones de videojuegos, trampolines, buceo, simuladores, pared de escalada, paintball, un carrusel, una rueda de la fortuna y muchas otras cosas.

-Noah: Esto es el paraíso mamá.

-Agatha: Lo máximo, me quiero quedar a vivir aquí.

-Clara: Hay ciertas reglas y prohibiciones para las atracciones.

-Agatha: ¿Cómo así?

-Clara: Para algunas atracciones debes ser mayor de una altura, para otras, mayor de cierta edad.

-Noah: Rayos.

-Clara: Pero vamos, hay muchas atracciones que probar.

Visit to the Museum - Visita al Museo

English

-Clara: Kids, here we are. This is the city museum.
-Agatha: It's huge.
-Clara: Yes, usually, museums are big.
-Noah: What is a museum?
-Clara: It's a place where you keep artworks and objects related to history or artistic things.
-Noah: I get it.
-Clara: Generally, there are paintings and sculptures. In some museums, there are fossils. In others, there are objects that are important in histories such as swords, weapons, and other objects.
-Noah: And what do you do in museums?
-Clara: Generally, there is a guide that explains everything about objects, their history, importance, date, and other things. In museums, you learn about the things inside and appreciate the art and the evolution of things over time.
-Agatha: It sounds a little boring.
-Clara: It's not. Did you know there's a museum where they have the evolution and models of all airplanes? They have the model of the first plane that was invented.
-Agatha: That does sound more interesting.
-Noah: Can we go to that museum next?
-Clara: Sure, in the next holidays.
-Noah: Great.

Spanish

-Clara: Niños, aquí estamos, este es el museo de la ciudad.
-Agatha: Es enorme.
-Clara: Si, generalmente los museos son grandes.
-Noah: ¿Qué es un museo?
-Clara: Es un lugar donde se guardan obras y objetos relacionados con la historia o cosas artísticas.
-Noah: Ya entiendo.
-Clara: Generalmente hay pinturas, esculturas, en algunos museos hay fósiles, en otros hay objetos que son importantes en la historia, como espadas, armas y otros objetos.
-Noah: ¿Y qué se hace en los museos?
-Clara: Generalmente hay un guía que te explica todo sobre los objetos, su historia, importancia, fecha y otras cosas. En los museos se aprende sobre las cosas que hay dentro y aprecias el arte y la evolución de las cosas con el pasar del tiempo.
-Agatha: suena un poco aburrido.

-Clara: No lo es. ¿Sabías que existe un museo en donde tienen la evolución y modelos de todos los aviones? Tienen el modelo del primer avión que se invento.
-Agatha: Eso si suena más interesante.
-Noah: ¿Podemos ir luego a ese museo?
-Clara: Claro, en las próximas vacaciones.
-Noah: Genial.

Relax day - Dia de relajación

English

-Clear: Today, we will have a day of relaxation.
-Agatha: What do you mean?
-Clara: We'll go to a spa, get massages, bathe in hot springs, get masks, go into a sauna, and relax like never before.
-Agatha: Sounds very good.
-Noah: It is not interesting.
-Clara: We have already done many activities. The body must rest a little, and that's why we'll go.
-Noah: I'm not tired.
-Clara: You'll see that at the end of the day, you'll be more rested.
-Noah: I doubt it.

Spanish

-Clara: Hoy tendremos un día de relajación.
-Agatha: ¿A qué te refieres?
-Clara: Iremos a un spa, nos darán masajes, nos bañaremos en aguas termales, nos harán mascarillas, entraremos a un sauna y nos relajaremos como nunca antes.
-Agatha: Suena muy bien.
-Noah: No me llama la atención.
-Clara: Ya hemos hecho muchas actividades, el cuerpo debe descansar un poco y por eso iremos.
-Noah: Yo no estoy cansado.
-Clara: Veras que al finalizar el día, estarás más descansado.
-Noah: Lo dudo.

Pool day- Dia de piscina

English

-Clara: Today, we'll go to some pools. Bring your swimsuits, your floats, your inflatable ball, your water pistols, and Noah, you should bring your snorkel.
-Noah: Great mom, here it is.
-Clara: Perfect.
-Agatha: Which pools are we going to?
-Clara: Some that Wanda told me. They have a lot of pools where we go. They have a wave pool, a surf pool, and a natural pool. They have water games and a lot of other things you're going to like.
-Agatha: Do you have the giant balls that people get into?
-Clear: Yes.
-Agatha: Let's go.
-Clara: Remember not to go deep without the floats.
-Agatha and Noah: Okay.

Spanish

-Clara: Hoy iremos a unas piscina. Traigan sus trajes de baño, sus flotadores, su pelota inflable, sus pistolas de agua y Noah, deberías traer tu snorkel.
-Noah: Genial mamá, aquí lo tengo.
-Clara: Perfecto.
-Agatha: ¿A qué piscinas vamos?
-Clara: A unas que me dijo Wanda. Tienen muchas piscinas allí donde vamos, tienen una piscina con olas, una piscina para surfear, una piscina natural, tienen juegos acuáticos y muchas otras cosas que les van a gustar.
-Agatha: ¿Tienen las pelotas gigantes donde se mete la gente?
-Clara: Si.
-Agatha: Vamos ya.
-Clara: Recuerden no ir a lo profundo sin los flotadores.
-Agatha y Noah: Esta bien.

Day at the hotel - Día en el hotel

English

-Agatha: Good morning, mom. Do you think we can stay here at the hotel today?
-Clara: Why is that?
-Agatha: Yesterday, I read that they were going to do a rally for the children here at the hotel.
-Clara: I didn't know.
-Agatha: Yes, there will be races, table hockey, football tables, darts, team games, and they will reward the best.
-Clara: Sounds great. Can you take Noah with you?
-Agatha: Sure, but I hope he doesn't make me lose.
-Noah: I'm better than you at sports.
-Agatha: We'll see.
-Clara: Until what time is that?
-Agatha: It's until three o'clock in the afternoon, but after that, they're going to show a movie at the cinema, and I would like to see it.
-Clara: Excellent, so I can visit a friend.
-Agatha: Okay.
-Clara: Call me if you need anything.

Spanish

-Agatha: Buenos días mamá, ¿Crees que hoy podamos quedarnos aquí en el hotel?
-Clara: ¿Y eso?
-Agatha: Ayer leí que iban a hacer un rally para los niños de aquí del hotel.
-Clara: No sabía.
-Agatha: Si, habrá carreras, hockey de mesa, mesas de futbolito, dardos, juegos en equipos y premiaran al mejor.
-Clara: Suena genial. ¿Puedes llevar a Noah contigo?
-Agatha: Claro, pero espero que no me haga perder.
-Noah: Yo soy mejor que tú para los deportes.
-Agatha: Ya lo veremos.
-Clara: ¿Hasta qué hora es eso?
-Agatha: Es como hasta las tres de la tarde, pero después de eso darán una película en el cine y quería verla.
-Clara: Excelente, así yo puedo visitar a un amigo.
-Agatha: Vale.
-Clara: Llámame si necesitas algo.

Visit to friends - Visita a amigos

English

-Clara: Ray, it's Clara. I'm outside your house. I've already rung the doorbell, but I don't think it's working.
-Ray: I'm going to open it. It was damaged a few days ago, and I haven't had time to fix it.
-Clara: Okay. I'll wait for you.
...
-Ray: Clara, it's good to see you again after so many years.
-Clara: Ray, what an emotion. You are absolutely right.
-Ray: Please come in. Welcome to my house.
-Clara: Thank you very much. What a beautiful house.
-Ray: Thank you. This is my wife, Gaby, and these are my children, Magnolia and Aran.
-Clara: Nice to meet you. I'm Clara.
-Gaby: Nice to meet you.
-Clara: You have a very nice family, Ray. I didn't know you were married.
-Ray: The last time I saw you were 15 years ago, at the university.
-Clara: That's right.
-Ray: Would you like something to drink? Water, coffee, tea, or a glass of wine?
-Clara: A cup of coffee is fine. I brought cookies to share.
-Ray: It's good that you came to visit me.
-Clara: I was walking around here on vacation and I remembered that I knew you lived around here and I thought I'd stop by.
-Ray: You don't know how happy I am.

Spanish

-Clara: Ray, soy Clara, estoy afuera de tu casa, ya toque el timbre pero creo que no funciona.
-Ray: Ya te abro, se daño hace unos días y no he tenido tiempo para arreglarlo.
-Clara: Vale. Te espero.
...
-Ray: Clara, que gusto verte de nuevo después de tantos años.
-Clara: Ray, que emoción, tienes toda la razón.
-Ray: Pasa adelante por favor. Bienvenida a mi casa.
-Clara: Muchas gracias, que casa tan bonita.
-Ray: Gracias. Ella es mi esposa Gaby, y ellos mis hijos, Magnolia y Aran.
-Clara: Mucho gusto, soy Clara.
-Gaby: Encantada.
-Clara: Tienes una familia muy bonita Ray, no sabía que estuvieras casado.
-Ray: La última vez que te vi fue hace 15 años, en la universidad.

-Clara: Así es.
-Ray: ¿Quieres algo de beber? ¿Agua, café, té, una copa de vino?
-Clara: Un café está bien, yo traje galletas para compartir.
-Ray: Que bueno que hayas venido a visitarme.
-Clara: Paseaba por acá de vacaciones y recordé que supe que vivías por aquí y pensé en pasar.
-Ray: No sabes cuánto me alegra.

Camping - Acampando

English

-Clara: What do you guys want to do today?
-Noah: Yesterday, we did what Agatha wanted. Today, it's up to me to choose.
-Agatha: You choose boring things.
-Noah: Of course not.
-Clara: What do you want to do, Noah?
-Noah: I saw on TV that there's a park where you can camp. I want to go.
-Agatha: It doesn't sound boring.
-Clara: Excellent idea, Noah. I like it.
-Noah: Thanks, Mommy.
-Clara: To camp, we'll need a family tent and three sleeping bags or an inflatable mattress, canned food, repellent, flashlights, and charcoal or firewood to make the campfire.
-Noah: Don't forget the marshmallows and hot chocolate.
-Clara: Of course, my love, you're absolutely right.

Spanish

-Clara: ¿Qué quieren hacer hoy muchachos?
-Noah: Ayer hicimos lo que Agatha quería, hoy me toca a mí elegir.
-Agatha: Tú eliges cosas aburridas.
-Noah: Claro que no.
-Clara: ¿Qué quieres hacer Noah?
-Noah: Vi en la TV que hay un parque donde se puede acampar, quiero ir.
-Agatha: No suena aburrido.
-Clara: Excelente idea Noah. ME gusta.
-Noah: Gracias mami.
-Clara: Para acampar, necesitaremos una carpa familiar y tres bolsas para dormir o un colchón inflable, comida enlatada, repelente, unas linternas y carbón o leña para hacer la fogata.
-Noah: No olvides los malvaviscos ni el chocolate caliente.
-Clara: Claro mi amor, tienes toda la razón.

Chapter 3: Llegando a un nuevo país - Getting to a new country

Rent a House - Alquilar una casa

English

-Katy: Good morning. I want to rent a house.
-Agent: Good morning. Thank you for preferring our rental agency. What are you looking for?
-Katy: I want a townhouse or a one-floor house, with three bedrooms, two bathrooms, living room, garden, and two parking spaces.
-Agent: With these characteristics, we have three options.
-Katy: Let's see.
-Agent: You have this, a one-floor house, three bedrooms, two bathrooms, living room, garden, three parking spaces, and the right to use the swimming pool of the urbanization. It is located 15 minutes north of the Kendall bus station, at a cost of $650 per month, not including services and must give an advance of four months.
-Katy: What other options are there?
-Agent: You have this townhouse. It has the features you asked for. It is located further north than the previous one, but the rent is $500 per month, with the services included and you only have to give three months in advance.
-Katy: I like it, and the third option?
-Agent: A small house, three bedrooms, two bathrooms, living room, garden, and a single parking place. It costs $450 a month, includes the services, and must give three months in advance as in the previous one.
-Katy: I think I'll take the second option.
-Agent: Excellent choice. Let's do the paperwork.
-Katy: Thank you very much for your help.

Spanish

-Katy: Buenos días, quiero alquilar una casa.
-Agente: Buenos días, gracias por preferir nuestra agencia de alquiler. ¿Qué está buscando?
-Katy: Quiero un town house o casa de un piso, que tenga tres habitaciones, dos baños, sala de estar, jardín y dos puestos de estacionamiento.
-Agente: Con esas características tenemos tres opciones.
-Katy: A ver.
-Agente: Tiene esta, una casa de un solo piso, tres habitaciones, dos baños, sala de estar, jardín, tres puestos de estacionamiento y derecho al uso de la piscina de la urbanización. Está ubicada a 15 minutos al norte de la estación

de autobús de Kendall, con un costo de 650$ mensuales, sin incluir los servicios y debe dar un adelanto de cuatro meses.

-Katy: ¿Qué otras opciones hay?

-Agente: Tiene este town house, tiene las características que usted pidió, está más al norte de la anterior pero el alquiler son 500$ mensuales, con los servicios incluidos y solo debe dar tres meses de adelanto.

-Katy: Me gusta, ¿Y la tercera opción?

-Agente: Una casa pequeña, tres habitaciones, dos baños, sala de estar, jardín y un solo puesto de estacionamiento. Cuesta 450$ al mes, incluye los servicios y debe dar tres meses de adelanto igual que en la anterior.

-Katy: Creo que me quedare con la segunda opción.

-Agente: Excelente elección. Ya hacemos los trámites.

-Katy: Muchas gracias por su ayuda.

Asking About Traditions - Preguntando tradiciones

English

-Rod: Good evening. How are you?
-Alice: All right, Rod. What about you?
-Rod: Excellent, Alice. A little confused.
-Alice: Why?
-Rod: People are happy, like celebrating something but I don't know what.
-Alice: Today is the third Monday of February.
-Rod: What does that mean?
-Alice: Today is President's Day.
-Rod: I didn't know, I don't have much time living here. What other traditions do you have?
-Alice: Martin Luther King Day is celebrated on the third Monday in January. Memorial Day is celebrated on the last Monday in May. Labor Day is celebrated on the first Monday in September. Veteran's Day is celebrated on November 11th and Independence Day on July 4, and the other traditions like Christmas, Halloween, and Thanksgiving are the same as in other countries.
-Rod: I see, thank you very much for the explanation, Alice. Stay tuned for the next holiday.

Spanish

-Rod: Buenas noches. ¿Cómo estás?
-Alice: Muy bien Rod, ¿Y tú?
-Rod: Excelente Alice. Un poco confundido.
-Alice ¿Por qué?
-Rod: La gente está contenta, como celebrando algo pero no se qué.
-Alice: Hoy es el tercer lunes de Febrero.
-Rod: ¿Y eso que significa?
-Alice: Hoy se celebra el día del presidente.
-Rod: No sabía, tengo poco tiempo viviendo acá. ¿Qué otras tradiciones tienen?
-Alice: El día de Martin Luther King se celebra el tercer lunes de Enero, el Memorial Day se celebra el ultimo lunes de Mayo, el Labor Day se celebra el primer lunes de Septiembre, el Veteran's Day se celebra el 11 de Noviembre y el día de la independencia que celebramos el 4 de Julio, las otras como Navidad, Halloween y acción de gracias si son igual que en los otros países.
-Rod: Ya veo, muchas gracias por la explicación.
- Alice: Está pendiente de la próxima festividad.

Asking About Typical Foods - Preguntando comidas típicas

English

-Martin: Good morning, boys. How are you?
-Luis: All right, how are you?
-Carlos: I'm fine.
-Alex: Very good.
-Martin: I'm glad. Today, I wanted to do a sharing in my house and have dinner there.
-Carlos: Great. What do we have to bring?
-Martin: Since each one of us is from a different country, I thought that everyone should bring food typical of their country.
-Luis: Excellent idea.
-Alex: I think it's spectacular.
-Martin: Since I'm from Italy, I'll make different types of pasta with their sauces. What are the typical dishes in your countries?
-Carlos: I'm from Argentina, and the typical dishes I can take are a provoleta, a little chimichurri, and some alfajores for dessert.
-Alex: I'm from the United States and I can take some hamburgers and apple pie.
-Luis: I'm from Japan and I'll take sushi, sashimi, udon, and some soba.
-Martin: Great, I'll see you at my house at eight at night.
-Carlos and Luis: Ok.
-Alex: I'll be a little early, is there a problem?
-Martin: Not at all. That way, you will help me with the preparations.

Spanish

-Martin: Buenos días muchachos, ¿Cómo están?
-Luis: Todo bien, ¿Y tú?
-Carlos: Estoy bien.
-Alex: Muy bien.
-Martin: Me alegro. Hoy quería hacer un compartir en mi casa y cenar todos alla.
-Carlos: Genial, ¿Qué hay que llevar?
-Martin: Como cada uno de nosotros es de un país diferente, pensé que cada quien llevara comida típica de su país.
-Luis: Excelente idea.
-Alex: Me parece espectacular.
-Martin: Como yo soy de Italia, hare distintos tipos de pastas con sus salsas. ¿Cuáles son los platos típicos de sus países?
-Carlos: Yo soy de Argentina y los platos típicos que puedo llevar son una provoleta, un poco de chimichurri y unos alfajores para el postre.
-Alex: Yo soy de Estados Unidos y puedo llevar unas hamburguesas y un pie de manzana.

-Luis: Yo soy de Japón y llevaré sushi, sashimi, udon y un poco de soba.
-Martin: Genial, nos vemos en mi casa a las ocho de la noche.
-Carlos y Luis: Ok.
-Alex: Llegare un poco antes, ¿Hay algún problema?
-Martin: Para nada, así me ayudas con los preparativos.

Asking about Taxes - Preguntando Sobre impuestos

English

-German: Good morning.
-Peter: Good morning. What can I do for you?
-German: I checked my account yesterday, and I have a lot of deductions and I want to know what they are.
-Peter: Give me your account number.
-German: 8888777755555559999.
-Peter: Okay, this deduction is for income tax. This is for rent taxes, and these are for social security taxes.
-German: I understand. Do you know what the income tax is?
-Peter: Yes, it's 30% of monthly income.
-German: Thank you very much for the information.

Spanish

-German: Buenos días.
-Peter: Buenos días, ¿En qué puedo ayudarle?
-German: Revise mi cuenta ayer y tengo un montón de deducciones y quiero saber de que son.
-Peter: Dame tu número de cuenta.
-German: 88887777555559999.
-Peter: De acuerdo, esta deducción es por impuesto sobre ingresos, esta es por impuestos sobre la renta y estas por impuestos de seguro social.
-German: Entiendo. ¿Sabe cuánto es el impuesto sobre ingresos?
-Peter: Si, es del 30% de los ingresos mensuales.
-German: Muchas gracias por la información.

Buy a House- Comprar una casa

English

-Nora: Good afternoon.
-Calvin: Good afternoon, how are you?
-Nora: Very well, and you?
-Calvin: Excellent.
-Nora: I saw that you have your house for sale. Can I see it inside?
-Calvin: Sure, come on in.
-Nora: Thank you very much.
-Calvin: The house was built 20 years ago and remodeled 10 years ago. It has four bedrooms, a maid's room, an office type room, two bathrooms upstairs and one downstairs, a living room, garage, garden, and a Jacuzzi.
-Nora: I love it. How much do you want?
-Calvin: I am asking $70,000.
-Nora: Is there any possibility of financing?
-Calvin: Maybe.
-Nora: If I want to pay for 5 years, how much would I have to pay monthly?
-Calvin: With an interest of 15%, you would have to pay $1345 per month.
-Nora: No initial, right?
-Calvin: That's right.
-Nora: I will buy it.
-Calvin: Perfect, let's sign the papers and close the deal.

Spanish

-Nora: Buenas tardes.
-Calvin: Buenas tardes, ¿Cómo esta?
-Nora: Muy bien, ¿Y tú?
-Calvin: Excelente.
-Nora: Vi que tiene su casa en venta. ¿Puedo verla por dentro?
-Calvin: Seguro, pase adelante.
-Nora: Muchas gracias.
-Calvin: La casa fue construida hace 20 años y remodelada hace 10, tiene cuatro habitaciones, un cuarto de servicio, un cuarto tipo oficina, dos baños arriba y uno abajo, una sala, garaje, jardín y un jacuzzi.
-Nora: Me encanta. ¿Cuánto pide?
-Calvin: Pido 70.000$.
-Nora: ¿Hay posibilidad de financiación?
-Calvin: Quizas.
-Nora: Si quiero pagarle a 5 años, ¿Cuánto tendría que pagar mensual?
-Calvin: Con intereses del 15%, tendría que pagar 1345$ mensuales.
-Nora: Sin inicial, ¿correcto?
-Calvin: Asi es.
-Nora: La compro.
-Calvin: Perfecto, firmemos los papeles y cerremos el trato.

Buy a Car- Comprar un carro

English

-Alexander: Good morning. I want to buy a car.
-Seller: Excellent. Come on in.
-Alejandro: Thank you very much.
-Seller: Do you know what kind of car you want?
-Alejandro: I want a family car with good autonomy and a trunk.
-Seller: We have these large cars, a range of 10 kilometers per liter, with a trunk, air conditioning, assisted steering, abs brakes, and HID lights.
-Alexander: I like it, but isn't it better to have a van or an SUV?
-Seller: We have these, but the autonomy is not so good. The autonomy of this van is 7.7 kilometers per liter, and this SUV is 8.5 kilometers per liter.
-Alejandro: I see. How much does the large car you told me cost?
-Seller: It has an initial value of $10,000, and you can ask for extras such as improvements to the sound system, leather seats, luxury rims, sunroof, special colors, and cup holders.
-Alexander: How much does it cost with all the extras?
-Seller: Its final value would be 12.599$.
-Alexander: And to pay it in 36 months?
-Seller: You would have to pay 405$ per month.
-Alejandro: Does the cost include maintenance?
-Seller: Correct. When you buy the vehicle with us, you will get 2 years of free maintenance.
-Alexander: Excellent. We have a deal then.

Spanish

-Alejandro: Buenos días. Quiero comprar un carro.
-Vendedor: Excelente. Pase adelante.
-Alejandro: Muchas gracias.
-Vendedor: ¿Sabe qué tipo de carro quiere?
-Alejandro: Quiero un carro familiar, con buena autonomía y que tenga maletero.
-Vendedor: Tenemos estos carros grandes, una autonomía de 10 kilómetros por litro, con maletero, aire acondicionado, dirección asistida, frenos abs y luces HID.
-Alejandro: Me agrada pero, ¿No es mejor una van o un SUV?
-Vendedor: Tenemos estas, pero la autonomía no es tan buena, la autonomía de esta van es 7.7 kilómetros por litro y de esta SUV es de 8.5 kilómetros por litro.
-Alejandro: Ya veo. ¿Cuánto cuesta el carro grande que me dijiste?
-Vendedor: Tiene un valor inicial de 10.000$ y puede pedir extras como mejoras en el sistema de sonido, asientos de cuero, rines de lujo, quemacoco, colores especiales y portavasos.

-Alejandro: ¿Cuánto cuesta con todos los extras?
-Vendedor: Su valor final seria 12.599$.
-Alejandro: ¿Y para pagarlo en 36 meses?
-Vendedor: Tendría que pagar 405$ mensuales.
-Alejandro: ¿El costo incluye mantenimiento?
-Vendedor: Correcto. Al comprar el vehículo con nosotros usted obtendrá 2 años de mantenimiento gratis.
-Alejandro: Excelente. Tenemos un trato entonces.

Car maintenance - Mantenimiento del carro

English

-Adam: Hey, is everything all right, Vladimir?
-Vladimir: Hey, all excellent, you?
-Adam: No complaints.
-Vladimir: What are you doing here?
-Adam: I've come to ask you to maintain the car.
-Vladimir: Perfect. Full or normal maintenance?
-Adam: What are the differences?
-Vladimir: Full maintenance includes oil filter change, fuel filter, air filter, oil change, engine wash, disc, and brake pad changes, spark plug and cable changes, alignment, and balancing.
-Adam: I see why you call it full. And the normal?
-Vladimir: The normal includes only oil change, oil filter change, alignment, and balancing.
-Adam: Which one do you recommend?
-Vladimir: You have time without maintenance, right?
-Adam: That's right.
-Vladimir: I think full is better then.
-Adam: Great, if you say so.

Spanish

-Adam: Hey, ¿Todo bien Vladimir?
-Vladimir: Hey, todo excelente, ¿Tú?
-Adam: No me quejo.
-Vladimir: ¿Qué haces aquí?
-Adam: Vengo pedirte que le hagas mantenimiento al carro.
-Vladimir: Perfecto. ¿Mantenimiento full o normal?
-Adam: ¿Cuales son las diferencias?
-Vladimir: El mantenimiento full incluye cambio de filtro de aceite, filtro de gasolina, filtro de aire, cambio de aceite, lavado del motor, cambios de discos y pastillas de freno, cambio de bujías y sus cables, alineación y balanceo.
-Adam: Ya veo porque le dicen full. ¿Y el normal?
-Vladimir: El normal incluye solo cambio de aceite, cambio de filtro de aceite, alineación y balanceo.
-Adam: ¿Cuál me recomiendas?
-Vladimir: Tienes tiempo sin hacerle mantenimiento, ¿Cierto?
-Adam: Asi es.
-Vladimir: Creo que es mejor el full entonces.
-Adam: Genial, si tu lo dices.

Asking for a loan/credit - Pidiendo un crédito

English

-Daniela: Good afternoon.
-Bank agent: Good afternoon.
-Daniela: I would like to ask for a loan to buy a house.
-Bank agent: How much do you want to ask for?
-Daniela: $50,000.
-Bank Agent: I will check your credit history.
-Daniela: It's impeccable.
-Bank Agent: That's what I see.
-Daniela: Will you approve?
-Bank agent: How long do you want to pay the credit?
-Daniela: Five years.
-Bank agent: For that term, the interest rate is 25%.
-Daniela: And ten years?
-Bank agent: The interest would be 35%.
-Daniela: I think I will choose 10 years.
-Bank agent: Perfect.
-Daniela: Thank you very much.
-Agent: Banker: If any of the payments are late, you will be charged an extra fee of 10% in that period.
-Daniela: I understand.

Spanish

-Daniela: Buenas tardes.
-Agente bancario: Buenas tardes.
-Daniela: Me gustaria pedir un crédito para comprar una casa.
-Agente bancario: ¿Cuánto desea pedir?
-Daniela: 50.000$.
-Agente bancario: Chequeare su historial de créditos.
-Daniela: Esta impecable.
-Agente bancario: Eso veo.
-Daniela: ¿Si lo aprobara?
-Agente bancario: ¿A cuánto tiempo desea pagar el crédito?
-Daniela: A cinco años.
-Agente bancario: Para ese plazo el interés es de 25%.
-Daniela: ¿Y a diez años?
-Agente bancario: El interés seria de 35%.
-Daniela: Creo que elegiré a 10 años.
-Agente bancario: Perfecto.
-Daniela: Muchas gracias.
-Agente: bancario: Si alguno de los pagos tiene retraso se le cobrara una cuota extra de 10% en dicho plazo.
-Daniela: Entiendo.

Clean the pool - Limpiar la piscina

English

-Elias: Love, the children want to invite their friends to play in the pool.
-Elizabeth: When?
-Elias: Tomorrow afternoon.
-Elizabeth: I don't think they can.
-Elias: Why?
-Elizabeth: The pool is very dirty; it hasn't been cleaned for months.
-Elias: And what should be done to it?
-Elizabeth: It needs to be emptied, to clean the tiles that already have mold, to fill them, to clean the filters, to put chlorine and all the detergents that it needs, and to repair the heater so that the water is not so cold.
-Elias: It's a lot to do. But I think that if I start now, it will be ready for tomorrow.
-Elizabeth: Start once and for all then.
-Elias: Perfect. Where are the utensils to clean it?
-Elizabeth: In the storeroom.
-Elias: Ok.

Spanish

-Elias: Amor, los niños quieren invitar a sus amigos a jugar en la piscina.
-Elizabeth: ¿Cuándo?
-Elias: Mañana por la tarde.
-Elizabeth: No creo que puedan.
-Elias: ¿Por qué?
-Elizabeth: La piscina está muy sucia, no se ha limpiado desde hace meses.
-Elias: ¿Y qué hay que hacerle?
-Elizabeth: Hay que vaciarla, limpiar la losa que ya tiene moho, llenarla, limpiar los filtros, ponerle cloro y todos los detergentes que necesite y reparar el calentador para que el agua no esté tan fría.
-Elias: Es mucho que hacer. Pero creo que si empiezo ya, estará lista para mañana.
-Elizabeth: Empieza de una vez entonces.
-Elias: Perfecto. ¿Dónde están los utensilios para limpiarla?
-Elizabeth: En el depósito.
-Elias: Ok.

Moving - Mudanza

English

-Lucius: Wake up. Today is the day to move.
-Karl: Great, I can't wait to get to the new house.
-Lila: I don't want to leave here. I love my house.
-Lucio: Lila, your little sister is about to be born, and the dog is going to have her puppies. We need a bigger house. Wait till you see the new house, you'll love it.
-Lila: I doubt it.
-Lucio: Give it a chance.
-Karl: Think Lila. A bigger room, a bigger closet, a bigger garden, and we'll be closer to the mall.
-Lila: Well, that doesn't sound so bad.
-Pike: The moving truck should arrive in half an hour, bring all your luggage, your boxes, your bags, your pillows, mattresses, bring absolutely everything. Once we move, we won't be able to come back for anything.
-Lila: I know Dad, you've been saying it all week.
-Lucio: The boxes have names and numbers. Let's be organized with moving.
-Karl: All right.

Spanish

-Lucio: Despiértense, hoy es el día de mudarnos.
-Karl: Genial, no puedo esperar a llegar a la nueva casa.
-Lila: Yo no quiero irme de aquí, me encanta mi casa.
-Lucio: Lila, tu hermanita ya va a nacer, y la perra ya va a tener a sus cachorros, necesitamos una casa mas grande. Espera que veas la nueva casa, te encantara.
-Lila: Lo dudo.
-Lucio: Dale una oportunidad.
-Karl: Piensa Lila, un cuarto más grande, un closet más grande, un jardín más grande y estaremos más cerca del centro comercial.
-Lila: Bueno, así no suena tan mal.
-Lucio: El camión de la mudanza debe llegar en media hora, traigan todo su equipaje, sus cajas, sus bolsos, sus almohadas, colchones, traigan absolutamente todo. Una vez que nos mudemos no podremos regresar a buscar nada.
-Lila: Lo sé papa, lo has dicho toda la semana.
-Lucio: Las cajas tienen nombre y número, seamos organizados con la mudanza.
-Karl: De acuerdo.

Laws - Leyes

English
-Miley: Good evening, neighbor. How are you?
-Lucy: Very well, my child, and you?
-Miley: Well, a little worried.
-Lucy: Why?
-Miley: As you know, I just moved here, and I don't know anything about the laws and regulations here.
-Lucy: Don't worry. The laws are the most common. Don't make too much noise at night, don't drive drunk, be respectful, use your seat belt, don't make racist or sexist comments, don't mistreat children, don't steal, don't drive without a license, and other rules that are common sense.
-Miley: I see.
-Lucy: There are so many other laws and rules that you have to follow, but as long as you follow those rules, you won't have any problems here.
-Miley: Thank you very much, Mrs. Lucy.
-Lucy: At your service, young lady. If you want, you can come another day, and I'll teach you more about laws and rules here.
-Miley: Thanks, anyway I'll take a course about it to be aware of all the laws as soon as possible. I do not want to get into trouble.
-Lucy: You're a very smart girl.

Spanish

-Miley: Buenas noches vecina, ¿Cómo esta?
-Lucy: Muy bien mi niña, ¿Y tú?
-Miley: Bien, un poco preocupada.
-Lucy: ¿Por qué?
-Miley: Como usted sabe, me acabo de mudar para acá, y no sé nada de las leyes y normas que hay aquí.
-Lucy: Tranquila, las leyes son las más comunes, no hacer mucho ruido en las noches, no manejar ebrios, ser respetuosos, utilizar el cinturón de seguridad, no hacer comentarios racistas ni sexistas, no maltratar a los niños, no robar, no conducir sin licencia y otras normas que son de sentido común.
-Miley: Ya veo.
-Lucy: Hay muchísimas otras leyes y normas que debes seguir, pero mientras cumplas esas no tendrás problemas por estos lados.
-Miley: Muchísimas gracias Sra Lucy.
-Lucy: A tu orden joven. Si quieres vienes otro día y te enseño mas sobre leyes y normas de acá.
-Miley: Gracias, de todas maneras yo tomare un curso sobre eso para estar al tanto de todas las leyes lo más pronto posible, no quiero meterme en problemas.
-Lucy: Eres una chica muy inteligente.

Penalty fees/ fines - Multas

English

-Police: Good afternoon.
-Mark: Good afternoon.
-Police: Do you know why this citation is?
-Mark: No idea, sir.
-Police: We're going to take away your driver's license.
-Mark: What? Why?
-Police: You are reckless driving.
-Mark: Of course not.
-Police: Here, I have all the recordings of you committing reckless acts.
-Mark: Let's see them.
-Police: Here, you drove too fast. You were fined and never paid it. Here you ran a red light, you were fined and never paid it. When you are driving drunk, you were fined and never paid it. When you are changing lanes without using dipped headlights, you were fined and never paid it. When you are speeding again. I think there are enough reasons to take away your license.
-Mark: If I pay the fines, won't you take it away from me?
-Police: I have to remove it because you have many fines. Pay the fines, wait for your six-month penalty without a license, and you can apply for it again.
-Mark: Six months without a license? It's an abuse. How am I going to pick up the kids at school? How am I going to go to the supermarket?
-Police: You should have thought of all that before you committed those violations.

Spanish

-Policía: Buenas tardes.
-Mark: Buenas tardes.
-Policía: ¿Sabe usted porque es esta citación?
-Mark: Ni idea señor.
-Policía: Vamos a quitarle su licencia de conducir.
-Mark: ¿Qué? ¿Por qué?
-Policía: Es imprudente conduciendo.
-Mark: Claro que no.
-Policía: Aquí tengo todas las grabaciones de usted cometiendo imprudencias.
-Mark: A verlas.
-Policía: Aquí condujo a exceso de velocidad, se le colocó una multa y nunca la pagó; aquí pasó un semáforo en rojo, se le colocó una multa y nunca la pagó; aquí está conduciendo ebrio, se le colocó una multa y nunca la pagó; aquí esta cambiándose de carriles sin utilizar las luces de cruce, se le colocó una multa y nunca la pagó; aquí está de nuevo a exceso de velocidad. Creo que hay razones suficientes para quitarle su licencia.

-Mark: ¿Si pago las multas no me la quitas?

-Policía: Se la tengo que quitar porque tiene muchas multas. Pague las multas, espere su penalización de seis meses sin licencia y puede volver a solicitarla.

-Mark: ¿Seis meses sin licencia? Es un abuso. ¿Cómo voy a buscar a los niños al colegio? ¿Cómo iré al supermercado?

-Policía: Debió pensar en todo eso antes de cometer esas infracciones.

Asking about Schools - Preguntando sobre colegios

English

-Mia: Hi, Abby. How are you?
-Abby: Mia, good to see you. I'm a little busy. I'm looking for schools where I can enroll my kids; you know some?
-Mia: Sure, I have my kids at Orlando High School. They have classes every day from 8 a.m. to 3 p.m., and they see extra subjects like cooking, art, economics, design, and some others.
-Abby: Sounds great, but that one's a bit far away. Do you know any more to the south?
-Mia: There is the Plantation High School. My sister has her kids there. The hours are from 8:30 a.m. to 2:30 p.m. and they have their swimming, basketball, baseball, and soccer teams. They also give extra classes like music, theater, and gardening.
-Abby: I like that one better. My kids love sports.
-Mia: That's very good. It's very nice and big, too.
-Abby: Maybe I'll see it this week. Will you come with me?
-Mia: I don't think so. I'll be busy.
-Abby: It's okay.

Spanish

-Mia: Hola Abby, ¿Cómo estás?
-Abby: Mia, que bueno verte. Ando un poco ocupada, estoy buscando colegios donde pueda inscribir a mis hijos, ¿Sabes de algunos?
-Mia: Claro, yo tengo a mis hijos en el Orlando High School, tienen clases todos los días de 8 a.m. a 3 p.m. y ven materias extras como cocina, arte, economía, diseño y algunas otras.
-Abby: Suena genial, pero esa me queda un poco lejos, ¿Sabes de alguna más al sur?
-Mia: Esta la Plantation High School, mi hermana tiene a sus hijos ahí, el horario es de 8:30 a.m. hasta las 2:30 p.m. y tienen su equipo de natación, de básquet, de beisbol y de futbol; además dan materias extras como música, teatro y jardinería.
-Abby: Esa me agrada mas, a mis hijos les encantan los deportes.
-Mia: Esa es muy buena, es muy bonita y grande también.
-Abby: Puede que vaya a verla en la semana. ¿Me acompañas?
-Mia: No creo, estaré ocupada.
-Abby: Esta bien

Asking about a Gym - Preguntando sobre Gimnasio

English

-Will: Hello, little brother. How are you?
-Wade: Brother, all right, and you?
-Will: Well, I'm glad.
-Wade: I see you with more muscles. Are you still training in the gym?
-Will: Sure, I go every day to train. It's routine.
-Wade: That's good.
-Will: You should sign up, and we train together.
-Wade: You say?
-Will: Sure, that way, we spend more time together, you train and gain some muscle.
-Wade: Maybe.
-Will: That's how you get muscle too because you're already thin.
-Wade: Hahahaha, which gym are you going to?
-Will: To the Power GYM.
-Wade: And what's in there?
-Will: It's all the machinery necessary to train all the muscles like biceps, triceps, back, shoulders, legs, abdominals, and chest. There is also a classroom where they give classes of many things like fit combat, TRX, CrossFit, boxing, dance, and taekwondo.
-Wade: Ready, on Monday, I will sign up and start training.

Spanish

-Will: Hola hermanito, ¿Como estas?
-Wade: Hermano, todo bien, ¿Y tú?
-Will: Bien, me alegro.
-Wade: Te veo con más músculos, ¿Sigues entrenando en el gimnasio?
-Will: Claro, voy todos los días a entrenar, ya es rutina.
-Wade: Que bueno.
-Will: Deberías inscribirte y entrenamos juntos.
-Wade: ¿Tú dices?
-Will: Claro, así pasamos más tiempo juntos, tú entrenas y ganas algo de músculo.
-Wade: Puede ser.
-Will: Así sacas musculo tu también, que ya te veo delgado.
-Wade: Jajajaja, ¿A qué gimnasio vas tú?
-Will: Al Power GYM.
-Wade: ¿Y qué hay allí?
-Will: Esta toda la maquinaria necesaria para entrenar todos los músculos como bíceps, tríceps, espalda, hombros, piernas, abdominales y pecho. También hay un salón donde dan clases de muchas cosas como fit combat, TRX, crossfit, boxeo, baile y tae kwon do.
-Wade: Listo, el lunes me inscribo y empiezo a entrenar.

Supermarkets - Supermercados

English

-Rachel: Thank you for dinner. It was exquisite.
-Dom: On your order. I'm glad you liked it.
-Rachel: It was very tasty. All the ingredients were very fresh and nice.
-Dom: Thank you very much.
-Rachel: Which supermarket are you going to? Where did you buy all these things?
-Dom: Actually, I buy in several supermarkets. In the supermarket in the north, I usually buy only the cleaning products because there they have good offers on those products always. In the supermarket in the south, they have everything very expensive, so I don't buy anything there. In the supermarket in the east, I buy fruits and vegetables. They are at a good price, and they are always very fresh. I don't buy the meat because although it is at a good price, it is not as nice or as fresh as the meat of the supermarket in the west.
-Rachel: You travel a lot to buy, don't you?
-Dom: It's the best way to buy good products and save a little money.

Spanish

-Rachel: Gracias por la cena, estaba exquisita.
-Dom: A la orden. Me alegra que te haya gustado.
-Rachel: Quedo muy sabrosa, todos los ingredientes estaban muy frescos y bonitos.
-Dom: Muchas gracias.
-Rachel: ¿A qué supermercado vas tú? ¿Dónde compraste todas estas cosas?
-Dom: En realidad compro en varios supermercados, en el supermercado del norte usualmente compro solo los productos de limpieza porque ahí tienen buenas ofertas en esos productos siempre; en el supermercado del sur tienen todo muy caro así que no compro nada allí; en el supermercado del este compro las frutas y verduras, están a buen precio y siempre están muy frescas, ahí no compro la carne porque aunque esta a buen precio no es tan bonita ni tan fresca como la carne del supermercado del oeste.
-Rachel: Recorres mucho para comprar, ¿Cierto?
-Dom: Es la mejor manera de comprar buenos productos y ahorrar un poco de dinero.

Daycares - Guarderias

English

-Emma: How are you, Gianna? How's your baby?
-Gianna: Hi Emma. We are well, thank God.
-Emma: I'm glad.
-Gianna: In two months, I have to go back to work, and I'm worried because I don't know who to leave my baby with.
-Emma: What about your mother?
-Gianna: She has a trip. I was thinking of leaving him in daycare, do you know any?
-Emma: Where I used to leave my children. It's spectacular. They have a ball pool, a lot of nannies, and the service and attention are excellent. They have a website on the internet that you can visit and see all the nannies, all the areas, the nanny certificates, and the opinions of the other mothers.
-Gianna: Well, send me the link for a text message.
-Emma: That's what I'll do. They also have an application for phones with which you can access the cameras of the daycare and see your child in real-time.
-Gianna: What? That's unbelievable.
-Emma: Yes, the technology advances very fast, and they knew how to take advantage of it.
-Gianna: I love that. What worried me the most was not knowing about my son the whole day, but that solves it.

Spanish

-Emma: ¿Cómo estas Gianna? ¿Cómo está tu bebe?
-Gianna: Hola Emma; estamos bien gracias a Dios.
-Emma: Me alegro.
-Gianna: Ya en dos meses debo volver a trabajar y estoy preocupada porque no se con quien dejar a mi bebe.
-Emma: ¿Qué hay de tu mamá?
-Gianna: Tiene un viaje. Estaba pensando en dejarlo en una guardería, ¿Conoces alguna?
-Emma: Donde yo dejaba a mis niños. Es espectacular, tienen una piscina de pelotas, muchas niñeras, el servicio y atención son excelentes. Tienen una página en internet donde puedes meterte a ver a todas las niñeras, todas las áreas, los certificados de las niñeras y las opiniones de las otras madres.
-Gianna: Que bien, pásame el link por un mensaje de texto.
-Emma: Eso hare. También tienen una aplicación para teléfonos con la que puedes acceder a las cámaras de la guardería y ver a tu hijo en tiempo real.
-Gianna: ¿Qué? Eso es increíble.
-Emma: Si, la tecnología avanza muy rápido y ellos supieron aprovecharlo.

-Gianna: Me encanta eso. Lo que más me preocupaba era no saber de mi hijo en todo el dia, pero con eso está solucionado.

Medical Insurances - Seguros Medicos

English

-Stevie: How are you?
-Francis: Good, you?
-Stevie: Good, coming out of the hospital.
-Francis: Why's that?
-Stevie: I fell down the stairs and fractured my wrist.
-Francis: When?
-Stevie: Two weeks ago.
-Francis: Are you better now?
-Stevie: Yes, I went to the doctor, and they put a cast on me.
-Francis: Thank goodness.
-Stevie: Yes, the best thing is that it's covered by medical insurance.
-Francis: That's good. Which one do you use?
-Stevie: I have private insurance, but I think I'll switch to Trumpcare or Obamacare. This is very expensive.
-Francis: I use Trumpcare. It's quite good.
-Stevie: That's what I'm researching.
-Francis: I have a friend who can give you information.
-Stevie: Great, I'll let you know so you can go see him.

Spanish

-Stevie: ¿Cómo estás?
-Francis: Bien, ¿Tu?
-Stevie: Bien, saliendo del hospital.
-Francis: ¿Y eso?
-Stevie: Me caí por las escaleras y me fracture la muñeca.
-Francis: ¿Cuándo?
-Stevie: Hace dos semanas.
-Francis: ¿Ya estas mejor?
-Stevie: Si, fui al doctor y me pusieron un yeso.
-Francis: Menos mal.
-Stevie: Si, lo mejor es que lo cubre el seguro medico.
-Francis: Que bueno. ¿Cuál usas?
-Stevie: Yo tengo un seguro privado, pero creo que me cambiare al Trumpcare u Obamacare, este es muy costoso.
-Francis: Yo uso el Trumpcare, es bastante bueno.
-Stevie: Eso estoy averiguando.
-Francis: Tengo un amigo que puede darte información.
-Stevie: Genial, te aviso para ir a verlo.

Car Insurances - Seguros de carros

English

-Chris: How are you, neighbor?
-Luke: Fine, everything's fine.
-Chris: What happened to your car?
-Luke: I was hit the other day.
-Chris: Really?
-Luke: Yes, sadly.
-Chris: And the one who hit you won't pay you?
-Luke: No, he crashed and ran away.
-Chris: I'd be upset.
-Luke: I am.
-Chris: And the insurance won't fix it for you?
-Luke: I don't have insurance. I never knew how that worked.
-Chris: Big mistake.
-Luke: Yeah, that's what I've been thinking.
-Chris: I can help you with that.
-Luke: Thank you very much. Which one do you use?
-Chris: The private insurance I have has services like property damage liability, bodily injury liability, medical payment, uninsured drivers coverage, collision damage, and full coverage.
-Luke: Sounds perfect, protection for all cases.
-Chris: That's right. Too bad, you didn't know.
-Luke: I will keep it very much in mind for the next vehicle or for this one if I manage to fix it.

Spanish

-Chris: ¿Cómo estas vecino?
-Luke: Bien, todo bien.
-Chris: ¿Qué le paso a tu carro?
-Luke: Me chocaron el otro día.
-Chris: ¿En serio?
-Luke: Si, tristemente.
-Chris: ¿Y el que te choco no te va a pagar?
-Luke: No, me choco y huyo.
-Chris: Yo estaría molesto.
-Luke: Lo estoy.
-Chris: ¿Y el seguro no te lo arregla?
-Luke: No tengo seguro, nunca supe cómo funcionaba eso.
-Chris: Gran error.
-Luke: Si, eso he estado pensando.
-Chris: Yo te puedo ayudar con eso.
-Luke: Muchas gracias. ¿Tu cual usas?

-Chris: El seguro privado que yo tengo tiene servicios como responsabilidad por daño a la propiedad, responsabilidad por daño corporal, pago medico, cobertura de conductores sin seguro, daños por colisión y cobertura completa.

-Luke: Suena perfecto, protección para todos los casos.

-Chris: Así es, lástima que no sabias.

-Luke: Lo tendré muy en cuenta para el próximo vehículo, o para este si logro arreglarlo.

Postal Service - Servicio de correo

English

-Charles: Hi, Olivia, are you busy?
-Olivia: Hello, Charles, not much. Why?
-Charles: I wanted to ask you something.
-Olivia: Sure, tell me.
-Charles: I bought something online, and I'd like to have it delivered to my house, but I have no idea which postal service to use.
-Olivia: There are many. I use the USPS. It has a lot of services like express mail, first-class mail, priority mail, delivery confirmation, certified mail, insurance, and paid response. It's pretty good.
-Charles: Perfect. I think I'll use that one. It has quite a few interesting services.
-Olivia: That's the one I use.
-Charles: Thank you very much. I'll let you know how I'm doing with them.

Spanish

-Charles: Hola Olivia, ¿Estas ocupada?
-Olivia: Hola Charles, no mucho, ¿Por?
-Charles: Quería preguntarte algo.
-Olivia: Claro, dime.
-Charles: Compre algo por internet y me gustaría que me llegara a la casa, pero no tengo idea de cuál servicio postal utilizar.
-Olivia: Hay muchos, yo uso el USPS, tiene un montón de servicios como correo express, envio de primera clase, correo de prioridad, confirmación de entrega, correo certificado, seguro y respuesta pagada. Es bastante bueno.
-Charles: Perfecto, creo que usare ese, tiene bastantes servicios interesantes.
-Olivia: Ese es el que yo uso.
-Charles: Muchas gracias, te aviso como me va con ellos.

Subscriptions- Suscripciones

English

-Ana: Hi, Tatiana, good day. How are you doing with the moving?
-Tatiana: Hi, everything's fine. Here we are, it's good that you're interested. Do you think you can clarify some doubts with the matter of subscriptions? You know I'm new in the country, and I have doubts about it.
-Ana: Of course, let's take the chance that still not many people have arrived at the office to talk.
-Tatiana: Which do you have?

-Ana: I am subscribed to entertainment services such as Netflix, Hulu, and Youtube. I am subscribed to Amazon prime for internet shopping, and I am subscribed to Home magazine because they give good tips on things for the home.
-Tatiana: I understand, thank you very much.
-Ana: Is there anything that interests you?
-Tatiana: I've heard about Spotify. What's that for?
-Ana: That's very good. It's for listening to music. A lot of people use it. I don't because I use Apple Music.
-Tatiana: Ah, it's good. We'll talk later. People are arriving, and we have to work.
-Ana: All right, let me know anything.

Spanish

-Ana: Hola Tatiana buen día, ¿Cómo van con la mudanza?
-Tatiana: Hola todo bien, ahí vamos, que bueno que te interese. ¿Crees que me puedas aclarar unas dudas con el asunto de las suscripciones? Sabes que estoy nueva en el país y tengo dudas al respecto.
-Ana: Si claro, aprovechemos que aun no llega mucha gente a la oficina para hablar.
-Tatiana: ¿Cuáles tienes tú?
-Ana: Yo estoy suscrita a servicios de entretenimiento como Netflix, Hulu y Youtube red; estoy suscrita al Amazon prime para compras por internet y estoy suscrita a la revista Home, porque dan buenos tips de cosas para el hogar.
-Tatiana: Entiendo, muchas gracias.
-Ana: ¿Hay algo que te interese?
-Tatiana: He escuchado sobre Spotify. ¿Para qué es esa?
-Ana: Esa es muy buena, es para escuchar música. Mucha gente la usa, yo no porque yo uso Apple Music.
-Tatiana: Ah está bien. Seguimos hablando luego, ya está llegando gente y hay que trabajar.
-Ana: Esta bien, cualquier cosa me avisas.

Chapter 4: Conversaciones del día a día- Day-to-Day conversations

Ordering a pizza- Pidiendo una pizza

English

-Max: Good afternoon, Pizzeria Loca?
-Telephone operator: Correct. How can I help you?
-Max: I would like to know if you have a delivery service.
-Telephone operator: That's right.
-Max: Excellent. How long is the delivery time?
-Telephone operator: Depends on where it should be delivered.
-Max: Four blocks from your store.
-Telephone operator: Approximately ten minutes.
-Max: Perfect. What pizza sizes do you have?
-Telephone operator: Small, medium, large, extra-large, and super large.
-Max: How many people are they for?
-Telephone operator: The small one is for one person, the medium one for two, the big one for four, the extra big one for six, and the super big one for eight.
-Max: Excellent. What additional ingredients do you have?
-Telephone operator: Corn, onion, paprika, mushrooms, extra cheese, ham, pineapple, jalapeños, pepperoni, sausages, meat, chicken, french fries, cheddar cheese, olives, and anchovies.
-Max: I understand. I'm going to order a super large one with corn, onion, paprika, extra cheese, and ham; an extra-large one with fries and pepperoni and a small one with anchovies and pineapple.
-Telephone operator: Annotated. Would you like something to drink?
-Max: What do you have?
-Telephone operator: Soft drinks, iced tea, coffee, and natural juices.
Max: Three 2-liter soft drinks.
-Telephone operator: Ready. Your order will arrive in forty minutes.
-Max: All right, to pay?
-Telephone operator: You can pay the delivery boy in cash, by card, or through our app.
-Max: Thank you very much.

Spanish

-Max: Buenas tardes, ¿Pizzería Loca?
-Operador telefónico: Correcto. ¿En que lo puedo ayudar?
-Max: Me gustaría saber si tienen servicio de entrega.

-Operador telefónico: Así es
-Max: Excelente. ¿Cuánto es el tiempo de entrega?
-Operador telefónico: Depende del lugar donde deba ser entregada.
-Max: A cuatro cuadras de su tienda.
-Operador telefónico: Aproximadamente diez minutos.
-Max: Perfecto. ¿Qué tamaños de pizza tiene?
-Operador telefónico: Pequeña, mediana, grande, extra grande y súper grande.
-Max: ¿Para cuantas personas son?
-Operador telefónico: La pequeña es para una sola persona, la mediana para dos, la grande para cuatro, la extra grande para seis y la súper grande para ocho.
-Max: Excelente. ¿Qué ingredientes adicionales tienes?
-Operador telefónico: Maíz, cebolla, pimentón, champiñones, extra queso, jamón, piña, jalapeños, pepperoni, salchichas, carne, pollo, papas fritas, queso cheddar, aceitunas y anchoas.
-Max: Entiendo. Voy a querer una súper grande con maíz, cebolla, pimentón, extra queso y jamón; una extra grande con papas fritas y pepperoni y una pequeña con anchoas y piña.
-Operador telefónico: Anotado. ¿Desea algo para tomar?
-Max: ¿Qué tiene?
-Operador telefónico: Gaseosas, té helado, café y jugos naturales.
-Max: Tres gaseosas de 2 litros.
-Operador telefónico: Listo. Su orden llegara en cuarenta minutos.
-Max: Muy bien, ¿para pagar?
-Operador telefónico: Puede pagarle al chico de entregas en efectivo, con tarjeta o a través de nuestra app.
-Max: Muchas gracias.

Shopping Mall - Centro comercial

English

-Andrea: Look! They've already opened the new shopping center.
-Penelope: WOW! It looks incredible.
-Andrea: We should go in and see.
-Penelope: I find it excellent.
-Andrea: Let's go then.
... Inside the mall...
-Andrea: I'm just coming in, and I love it already.
-Penelope: The entrance is spectacular.
-Andrea: That's right. Look at all the stores it has.
-Penelope: Yes, that's what I was seeing. It has shoe stores, perfumeries, ice cream shops, hairdressers, barbershops, beauty salons, clothing stores, and even a dance academy.
-Andrea: So exciting. It also has a cinema, an arcade, an electronics store, a video game store, a supermarket, bakeries, children's parks, restaurants, and they are remodeling a fast food store.
-Penelope: I love this place. I think I'll spend a lot of time here.
-Andrea: I feel the same way.
-Penelope: Let's come every Friday to visit a new store.
-Andrea: Ready. I'll put it in my schedule.
-Penelope: Today, let's have ice cream in that store over there.
-Andrea: What's your favorite flavor?
-Penelope: I love strawberry, and what about you?
-Andrea: I love Swiss cake.
-Penelope: Have you tried the hazelnut chocolate one?
-Andrea: I'm going to try it today.

Spanish

-Andrea: ¡Mira! Ya abrieron el nuevo centro comercial.
-Penélope: ¡WAO! Se ve increíble.
-Andrea: Deberíamos entrar a ver.
-Penélope: Me parece excelente.
-Andrea: Vamos entonces.
... Dentro del centro comercial...
-Andrea: Apenas estoy entrando y ya me encanta.
-Penélope: La entrada esta espectacular.
-Andrea: Así es. Mira todas las tiendas que tiene.
-Penélope: Si, eso estaba viendo. Tiene zapaterías, perfumerías, heladerías, peluquerías, barberías, salones de belleza, tiendas de ropa y hasta una academia de baile.

-Andrea: Que emoción. Tiene también un cine, un arcade, tienda de electrónicos, tienda de videojuegos, un supermercado, panaderías, parques para niños, restaurantes y están remodelando una tienda de comida rápida.

-Penélope: Amo este lugar. Creo que pasare aquí mucho tiempo.

-Andrea: Opino igual.

-Penélope: Vengamos todos los viernes a visitar una tienda nueva.

-Andrea: Listo. Lo pondré en mi agenda.

-Penélope: Hoy comamos helado en esa tienda de allí.

-Andrea: ¿Cuál es tu sabor favorito?

-Penélope: Me encanta el de fresa, ¿Y a ti?

-Andrea: Amo el de torta suiza.

-Penélope: ¿Probaste el de chocolate de avellanas?

-Andrea: Lo voy a probar hoy.

Ordering a coffee- Pidiendo un café

English

-Andrew: Good morning. How are you today?
-Seller: Very well, thank you for asking. And you?
-Andrew: Good too.
-Seller: How will you want your coffee?
-Andrew: I want something new today. What are the options?
-Seller: I have coffee with milk, frappuccino, cappuccino, late vanilla, coffee with chocolate, coffee with cream, iced coffee, and extra strong coffee.
-Andrew: Which one do you recommend?
-Seller: I like them all. Extra strong coffee is bitter, coffee with cream is too sweet, iced coffee is delicious, and frappuccino, cappuccino, and late vanilla are the specialties.
-Andrew: Then give me an iced coffee.
-Seller: On the way.
-Andrew: Thank you very much. Take this tip.
-Salesman: Thank you, sir, have a good day.

Spanish

-Andrew: Buenos días. ¿Cómo está hoy?
-Vendedor: Muy bien, gracias por preguntar. ¿Y usted?
-Andrew: Bien también.
-Vendedor: ¿Cómo va a querer su café?
-Andrew: Hoy quiero algo nuevo. ¿Qué opciones hay?
-Vendedor: Tengo café con leche, frapucino, capucino, late vainilla, café con chocolate, café con crema, café helado y café extra fuerte.
-Andrew: ¿Cuál me recomiendas?
-Vendedor: A mí me gustan todos. El café extra fuerte es amargo, el café con crema muy dulce, el café helado es delicioso y el frapucino, capucino y late vainilla son la especialidad.
-Andrew: Dame entonces un café helado.
-Vendedor: En camino.
-Andrew: Muchas gracias. Toma esta propina.
-Vendedor: Gracias señor, que tenga un buen día.

Using a bus - Usando un autobus

English

-Brad: Good evening.
-Katy: Good evening.
-Brad: Is this the Brickell bus station?
-Katy: No, this is Miami Beach Station.
-Brad: How do I get to Brickell Station?
-Katy: Wait for the bus that says route 3.
-Brad: Okay, thank you very much.
-Katy: On your order.
-Brad: And, to get to Davie Station?
-Katy: You can go to Brickell station and take the bus from route 5 or wait here and take the bus from route 7.
-Brad: Do you know what time the buses leave?
-Katy: There is the schedule. You can check there.
-Brad: Excellent. See you later.
-Katy: See you later.

Spanish

-Brad: Buenas noches.
-Katy: Buenas noches.
-Brad: ¿Esta es la estación de autobús de Brickell?
-Katy: No, esta es la estación de Miami Beach.
-Brad: ¿Como llego a la estación de Brickell?
-Katy: Espera al autobús que diga ruta 3.
-Brad: Ok, muchas gracias.
-Katy: A tu orden.
-Brad: Y, ¿Para llegar hasta la estación de Davie?
-Katy: Puedes ir a la estación de Brickell tomar el autobús de la ruta 5 o esperar aquí y tomar el autobús de la ruta 7.
-Brad: ¿Sabes a qué hora salen los autobuses?
-Katy: Allá está el horario. Puedes chequear allí.
-Brad: Excelente. Hasta luego.
-Katy: Hasta luego.

Buying food food - Comprando alimentos

English

-Eric: Love, I invited my friends to eat tomorrow.
-Sheila: Good, what are you going to cook?
-Eric: I thought I'd make a grill, maybe a salad, and some dessert.
-Sheila: You have to go to the supermarket to buy.
-Eric: Will you come with me?
-Sheila: Let's go.
... At the supermarket ...
-Eric: We have to buy meat, sausages, potatoes, onions, tomatoes, cucumbers, zucchini, sugar, salt, beer, soft drinks, flour, milk, eggs, and olive oil.
-Sheila: Okay, you also need to buy more vegetables for the week's salads like broccoli, lettuce, eggplant, cauliflower, and spinach. We are already short on rice and pasta.
-Eric: Let's go to the discount section and see what's on today.
-Sheila: Ok.
-Eric: We should buy some sweets for my friends' kids like chocolates, marshmallows, and stuff.
-Sheila: Good thinking.
-Eric: We also have to buy charcoal.
-Sheila: I'll get it.

Spanish

-Eric: Amor, invite a mis amigos a comer mañana.
-Sheila: Que bueno, ¿qué vas a cocinar?
-Eric: Pensaba hacer una parrilla, quizás una ensalada y algo de postre.
-Sheila: Debes ir al supermercado a comprar.
-Eric: ¿Me acompañas?
-Sheila: Vamos.
... En el supermercado...
-Eric: Hay que comprar carne, salchichas, papas, cebollas, tomate, pepino, calabacín, azúcar, sal, cervezas, refrescos, harina, leche, huevos y aceite de oliva.
-Sheila: Esta bien, también hay que comprar más verduras para las ensaladas de la semana como brócoli, lechuga, berenjenas, coliflor y espinaca. Ya tenemos poco arroz y pasta.
-Eric: Vayamos a la sección de descuentos a ver que ofertas hay hoy.
-Sheila: Ok.
-Eric: Deberíamos comprar unas chucherías para los hijos de mis amigos como chocolates, malvaviscos y esas cosas.
-Sheila: Bien pensado.
-Eric: También hay que comprar carbón.
-Sheila: Ya lo busco.

Buying Clothes - Comprando ropa

English

-Daniela: Brittany! What are you doing tomorrow?
-Brittany: I guess nothing, why?
-Daniela: In the new mall, there is a clothing store that offers discounts of up to 50% every Wednesday and Thursday.
-Brittany: That's crazy.
-Daniela: Absolutely, I wanted to go tomorrow. Are you coming?
-Brittany: Sure, what time?
-Daniela: At three o'clock in the afternoon.
-Brittany: See you there.
... In the clothes shop the next day ...
-Daniela: Everything is beautiful, and it's super cheap.
-Brittany: I don't know what to buy from everything there is.
-Daniela: What do you need?
-Brittany: I need pants. I saw some blue jeans and some black ones that I liked. I also saw some colored Lycras that I liked and some beautiful dotted leggings.
-Daniela: I saw the leggings and they're beautiful. There are some camouflage sweatshirts that would look spectacular with them. There are some striped t-shirts that I don't like.
-Brittany: I think I know which ones. Are they near the scarves?
-Daniela: Those.
-Brittany: Shoes and purses are normal, I've seen prettier things.
-Daniela: Did you see the skirts and the dresses?
-Brittany: No, where are they?
-Daniela: Behind the dressing rooms, near the box.
-Brittany: I'll go and see them.
-Daniela: First, look at these unicolored shirts. There are red, green, purple, pink, black, turquoise, and white.
-Brittany: They're pretty. They look like the flannels over there.
-Daniela: You're right. Now, let's see the dresses and skirts.

Spanish

-Daniela: ¡Brittany! ¿Que haras mañana?
-Brittany: Creo que nada, ¿Por?
-Daniela: En el nuevo centro comercial hay una tienda de ropa que hace descuentos de hasta el 50% todos los miércoles y jueves.
-Brittany: Eso es una locura.
-Daniela: Absolutamente, quería ir mañana. ¿Vienes?
-Brittany: Seguro, ¿A qué hora?
-Daniela: A las tres de la tarde.
-Brittany: Nos vemos allá.
... En la tienda de ropa al día siguiente...

-Daniela: Todo es hermoso, y esta súper barato.
-Brittany: No se que comprarme de todo lo que hay.
-Daniela: ¿Qué necesitas?
-Brittany: Necesito pantalones, vi unos jeans azules y unos negros que me gustaron. También vi algunas licras de colores que me gustaron y leggins punteados bellísimos.
-Daniela: Si yo vi los leggins y están bellos. Hay unas sudaderas de camuflaje que quedarían espectaculares con ellos; hay unas camisetas de rayas que no me gustan.
-Brittany: Creo que se cuales son, ¿Están cerca de las bufandas?
-Daniela: Esas.
-Brittany: Los zapatos y las carteras están normales, he visto cosas más bonitas.
-Daniela: ¿Viste las faldas y los vestidos?
-Brittany: No, ¿Dónde están?
-Daniela: Detrás de los probadores, cerca de la caja
-Brittany: Ya iré a verlos.
-Daniela: Primero mira estas camisas unicolores, hay rojas, verdes, moradas, rosadas, negras, turquesas y blancas.
-Brittany: Estan bonitas, se parecen a las franelas de allá.
-Daniela: Tienes razón. Ahora, veamos los vestidos y faldas.

Go to a Restaurant - Ir a un restaurant

English

-Valeria: Thank you so much for inviting me to dinner today.
-Domin: You don't have to thank me. You deserve it.
-Valeria: Okay.
-Domin: Good evening. Table for two, please.
-Waiter: Good evening. This way, please.
-Domin: Thank you.
-Valeria: Thank you.
-Waiter: Have a seat.
-Domin: Thank you very much. Please bring me the menu when you can.
-Waiter: Sure. Just a moment.
-Valeria: What a beautiful place. Very quiet and luxurious.
-Domin: That's what I like.
-Waiter: Here's the menu.
-Doma: Great.
-Valeria: Can you get me a glass of water?
-Waiter: Right away.
-Domin: Did you check the menu?
-Valeria: Everything looks very nice, the soups, the appetizers, the dishes, the drinks, the desserts.
-Domin: I'll order a caesar salad, a lasagna, a mojito, and for dessert, I thought of a cake.
-Valeria: I think I'll order a capresa salad, a pizza. I'll have a glass of wine and I don't think I'll eat dessert.
-Domin: Good thinking.
-Waiter: Here's your water, miss.
-Valeria: Thank you.
-Domin: We're ready to order.
-Waiter: Tell me your order.
-Domin: I'm going to want this, this, this, and this for dessert.
-Waiter: And the lady?
-Valeria: I'll ask for this, this, and this.
-Waiter: Excellent. I'll be right back.
-Domin: Thank you very much. Bring me the bill once, please.
-Waiter: Of course.

Spanish

-Valeria: Muchas gracias por invitarme a cenar hoy.
-Domin: No tienes que agradecer, te lo mereces.
-Valeria: Esta bien.
-Domin: Buenas noches, mesa para dos por favor.
-Mesonero: Buenas noches, por aquí, por favor.

-Domin: Gracias.
-Valeria: Gracias.
-Mesonero: Tomen asiento.
-Domin: Muchas gracias, muy amable. Me trae el menú cuando pueda por favor.
-Mesonero: Seguro. Un momento.
-Valeria: Que lugar tan bonito. Muy tranquilo y lujoso.
-Domin: Eso es lo que me gusta.
-Mesonero: Aquí tiene el menú.
-Domin: Genial.
-Valeria: ¿Me puede traer un vaso de agua?
-Mesonero: En seguida.
-Domin: ¿Chequeaste el menú?
-Valeria: Se ve todo muy rico. Las sopas, las entradas, los platos, las bebidas, los postres.
-Domin: Yo pediré una ensalada cesar, una lasaña, un mojito y de postre pensaba en una torta.
-Valeria: Yo creo que pediré una ensalada capresa, una pizza, tomare una copa de vino y no creo que quede espacio para el postre.
-Domin: Bien pensado.
-Mesonero: Aquí tiene su agua señorita.
-Valeria: Gracias.
-Domin: Ya estamos listos para ordenar.
-Mesonero: Dígame su orden.
-Domin: Yo voy a querer esto, esto, esto y de postre esto.
-Mesonero: ¿Y la señora?
-Valeria: Yo pediré esto, esto y esto.
-Mesonero: Excelente. Vuelvo en un momento.
-Domin: Muchas gracias. Me trae la cuenta de una vez, por favor.
-Mesonero: Como no.

Walk the Dog - Pasear al perro

English

-Matt: Mom, I'm going out to walk the dog.
-Mother: Be careful.
-Matt: Don't worry, I'm going with Heather.
-Mother: Tell him I said hi.
-Matt: All right.
... In the dog park...
-Matt: Hi Heather, how are you?
-Heather: Very well, how are you?
-Matt: Excellent. How's Rosi?
Heather: She's very well. Look at her. Yesterday, I bathed her with anti-flea soap.
-Matt: Well, I want to bathe Roll. He's got a lot of fleas.
-Heather: He's got long hair.
-Matt: Because of his breed, it grows fast.
-Heather: What breed is it?
-Matt: It's a golden Labrador.
-Heather: Rightly so.
-Matt: They say that some breeds get more fleas than others.
-Heather: Which ones?
-Matt: See that dog? He's a German shepherd. They have many.
-Heather: What about that one?
-Matt: That's a Beagle. They don't have many.
-Heather: I see.
-Matt: Look, Heather. Rosi made poop.
-Heather: Here's the bag. I'll pick it up.

Spanish

-Matt: Mamá voy a salir a pasear al perro.
-Madre: Ve con cuidado.
-Matt: Tranquila, voy con Heather.
-Madre: Mandale saludos de mi parte.
-Matt: Esta bien.
... En el parque de perros...
-Matt: Hola Heather, ¿Cómo estás?
-Heather: Muy bien, ¿Y tú?
-Matt: Excelente. ¿Cómo está Rosi?
-Heather: Esta muy bien, mírala, ayer la bañe con jabón anti pulgas.
-Matt: Que bueno, yo quiero bañar a Roll, tiene muchas pulgas.
-Heather: Es que ya tiene el pelo muy largo.
-Matt: Es que por su raza le crece rápido.
-Heather: ¿Qué raza es?

-Matt: Es un labrador.
-Heather: Con razón.
-Matt: Dicen que a algunas razas les caen mas pulgas que a otras.
-Heather: ¿Cuáles?
-Matt: ¿Ves aquel perro? Es un pastor alemán. Ellos tienen muchas.
-Heather: ¿Y ese?
-Matt: Ese es un Beagle. Ellos no tienen muchas.
-Heather: Ya veo.
-Matt: Mira Heather, Rosi hizo pupú.
-Heather: Aquí tengo la bolsa, ya lo recojo

Carwashes - Autolavados

English

Tony: Good afternoon.
-Luis: Good afternoon, Mr. Tony, how are you doing?
-Tony: Very well, Luis. And you?
-Luis: All good, thank God.
-Tony: I'm glad. Are you busy?
-Luis: A little, what do you need?
-Tony: Can you take my car to the car wash?
-Luis: Sure, in a few minutes.
-Tony: Perfect, thank you very much.
-Luis: Are you going to want it washed, vacuumed, and polished?
-Tony: That's right. To be washed with a lot of foam. And let them wash the rims and the upholstery well.
-Luis: Understood. Let me have the keys, and I'll take it when I can.
-Tony: Here you go. Thank you.
-Luis: To serve you.

Spanish

-Tony: Buenas tardes.
-Luis: Buenas tardes Sr Tony, ¿Cómo le va?
-Tony: Muy bien Luis, ¿Y a ti?
-Luis: Todo bien gracias a Dios.
-Tony: Me alegro. ¿Estás ocupado?
-Luis: Un poco, ¿Qué necesita?
-Tony: ¿Puedes llevar mi carro al autolavado?
-Luis: Seguro, en unos minutos.
-Tony: Perfecto, muchas gracias.
-Luis: ¿Va a querer que lo laven, lo aspiren y lo pulan?
-Tony: Correcto. Que lo laven con mucha espuma. Y que laven bien los rines y la tapicería.
-Luis: Entendido. Déjeme las llaves y lo llevo cuando pueda.
-Tony: Aquí tienes. Gracias.
-Luis: Para servirle.

Make an Appointment - Pedir una cita

English

-Mac: Good morning. Is this Dr. Lewis' office?
-Secretary: Correct. How can I help you?
-Mac: I'm calling to make an appointment.
-Secretary: When do you want to make the appointment?
-Mac: I'm free this Thursday and Friday.
-Secretary: For those days, there are no more appointments.
-Mac: When then?
-Secretary: Monday afternoon or Tuesday morning.
-Mac: What time on Monday?
-Secretary: 4:30 PM.
-Mac: What about Tuesday?
-Secretary: Tuesday would be at 7:00 am.
-Mac: Put me on Tuesday at 7:00 am then.
-Secretary: Perfect. Don't forget it.
-Mac: I won't.

Spanish

-Mac: Buenos días. ¿Es este el consultorio del Dr. Lewis?
-Secretaria: Correcto. ¿En qué puedo ayudarle?
-Mac: Estoy llamando para pedir una cita médica.
-Secretaria: ¿Para cuándo desea pedir la cita?
-Mac: Estoy libre estos Jueves y Viernes.
-Secretaria: Para esos días ya no hay citas.
-Mac: ¿Cuándo entonces?
-Secretaria: El lunes en la tarde o el martes en la mañana.
-Mac: ¿A qué hora el lunes?
-Secretaria: A las 4:30 PM.
-Mac: ¿Y el martes?
-Secretaria: El martes seria a las 7:00 am.
-Mac: Pongame la cita el martes a las 7:00 am entonces.
-Secretaria: Perfecto. No lo olvide.
-Mac: No lo hare.

Visiting the bank - Visitando el banco

English

-Jake: Hi, excuse me. Is the bank manager in?
-Watchman: Yes, who's asking?
-Jake: Jake Smith, a friend of his.
-Watchman: One moment.....
-Watchman: Come in.
-Jake: Thank you.
-Phil: Welcome Jake.
-Jake: How are you? What do you tell me?
-Phil: All right. A lot of work here at the bank, but I guess you know what it's like.
-Jake: I can imagine. You're always in a hurry.
-Phil: More or less. What are you doing here?
-Jake: It was to ask for a balance of my accounts and to ask about the new interest and taxes.
-Phil: You could have called me for that. I'll pass all that on to you by email.
-Jake: Thanks Phil, you're the best.
-Phil: Take it easy, anytime.

Spanish

-Jake: Buenas, disculpe, ¿Se encuentra el gerente del banco?
-Vigilante: Si, ¿Quién pregunta?
-Jake: Jake Smith, un amigo suyo.
-Vigilante: Un momento....
-Vigilante: Pase adelante.
-Jake: Gracias.
-Phil: Bienvenido Jake.
-Jake: ¿Qué tal? ¿Qué me cuentas?
-Phil: Todo bien. Mucho trabajo aquí en el banco, pero supongo que sabes como es.
-Jake: Me imagino. Siempre te veo apurado.
-Phil: Mas o menos. ¿Qué haces por aquí?
-Jake: Era para pedir un balance de mis cuentas, y preguntar sobre los nuevos intereses e impuestos.
-Phil: Pudiste haberme llamado para eso. Ya te paso todo eso por correo electrónico.
-Jake: Gracias Phil, eres el mejor.
-Phil: Tranquilo, cuando quieras.

Visiting the School- Visitando la escuela

English

-Jason: Excuse me. Do you have time to talk?
-Teacher: Sure, tell me.
-Jason: I'm Jason Thompson, Mike's father.
-Teacher: Nice to meet you.
-Jason: Nice to meet you. I wanted to ask you, how's my son doing in class?
-Teacher: He's going great. He's an outstanding student.
-Jason: I'm glad to hear it. He works very hard studying at home.
-Teacher: His effort is paying off. Follow me, the principal has been wanting to meet you for a long time.
-Jason: What's that for?
-Teacher: To learn more about your child's study method and use it with other students.
-Jason: Okay. Let's go.
... In the principal's office...
-Teacher: Principal, this is Mr. Thompson, Mike's dad. The boy who does very well in class.
-Principal: Nice to meet you. I have been wondering who Mike's father was.
-Jason: My pleasure.
-Principal: Your son is brilliant. I'd like to talk to you about a few things.
-Jason: Thank you very much, I'm flattered. Of course, I'm on your orders.

Spanish

-Jason: Disculpe, ¿Tiene tiempo para hablar?
-Profesora: Claro, dígame.
-Jason: Soy Jason Thompson, el padre de Mike.
-Profesora: Mucho gusto.
-Jason: Mucho gusto. Quería preguntarle ¿Cómo va mi hijo en clases?
-Profesora: Va excelente. Es un alumno sobresaliente.
-Jason: Me alegra oírlo, el se esfuerza mucho estudiando en casa.
-Profesora: Su esfuerzo está dando resultados. Sígueme, la directora quiere conocerlo desde hace tiempo.
-Jason: ¿Y eso para qué?
-Profesora: Para saber más sobre el método de estudio de su hijo y usarlo con los otros alumnos.
-Jason: De acuerdo. Vamos.
... En la oficina de la directora...
-Profesora: Directora, este es el Sr Thompson, el papa de Mike, el niño que sale muy bien en clases.

-Directora: Encantada de conocerlo. Tenía tiempo preguntándome quién era el padre de Mike.
-Jason: Un placer.
-Directora: Su hijo es brillante. Me gustaría conversar con usted sobre varias cosas.
-Jason: Muchas gracias, me halaga. Por supuesto, estoy a la orden.

Going to the cinema - Ir al cine

English

-Samuel: Alo, Dari?
-Dari: Yes, who is it?
-Samuel: It's me, Samuel.
-Dari: Ahh, hello, Samuel, how are you?
-Samuel: All right, how are you?
-Dari: I'm fine, resting.
-Samuel: That's good. Today, the new horror movie you wanted to see is released.
-Dari: Really?
-Samuel: Yes, shall we go to the movies to see it?
-Dari: I'd love to.
-Samuel: Perfect. I'll pick you up at 4:30 p.m. to buy the tickets.
-Dari: Isn't it better if you come by at 5:00 and I buy them online?
-Samuel: Good thinking. At 5:00 then.
-Dari: Great.
-Samuel: Can you get some popcorn online?
-Dari: I think so. I'll try.
-Samuel: Thank you. See you later.

Spanish

-Samuel: Alo, ¿Dari?
-Dari: Si, ¿Quién es?
-Samuel: Soy yo, Samuel.
-Dari: Ahh hola Samuel, ¿Cómo estás?
-Samuel: Todo bien, ¿Y tú?
-Dari: Bien, descansando.
-Samuel: Que bueno. Hoy estrenan la nueva película de terror que querías ver.
-Dari: ¿En serio?
-Samuel: Si, ¿Vamos al cine a verla?
-Dari: Me encantaría.
-Samuel: Perfecto, paso por ti a las 4:30 de la tarde para ir a comprar los boletos.
-Dari: ¿No es mejor que pases a las 5:00 y yo los compro por internet?
-Samuel: Bien pensado. A las 5:00 entonces.
-Dari: Genial.
-Samuel: ¿Puedes apartar unas palomitas por internet?
-Dari: Creo que sí, ya intentare.
-Samuel: Gracias. Nos vemos más tarde.

Going to a Football Match - Yendo a un partido de futbol

English

-Alan: Hi! How's it going?
-Nicolas: Brother, everything's fine, you?
-Alan: Very happy. Yesterday, in training, I was elected captain for today's match.
-Nicolas: Excellent news. I'm happy for you. You worked very hard for that.
-Alan: It was many months of hard work, but I did it.
-Nicolas: That's right.
-Alan: I'm on my way to the game. Are you going to do something right now?
-Nicolas: I don't think so, why?
-Alan: Come with me to watch the game.
-Nicolas: Sounds good.
-Alan: The team is also happy. We've practiced a lot.
-Nicolas: We've all noticed.
-Alan: Today, we will play with a 4-3-3 formation, with Pedro as goalkeeper; Jack, Buck, and Joey as strikers, Victor, Hector, and Javier as midfielders, and Luis, José, Cesar, and myself as defenders.
-Nicolas: I'm sure you're going to win.
-Alan: Me too.
-Nicolas: Let's hope the field is in good condition, grass cut, no holes, and no swamps.
-Alan: Yesterday, it was fine.

Spanish

-Alan: ¡Hola! ¿Cómo te va?
-Nicolás: Hermano, todo bien, ¿Tu?
-Alan: Muy contento. Ayer en el entrenamiento me eligieron capitán para el partido de hoy.
-Nicolás: Excelente noticia. Me alegro por ti, te esforzaste mucho por eso.
-Alan: Fueron muchos meses de trabajo duro, pero lo logre.
-Nicolás: Así es.
-Alan: Voy camino al partido, ¿Vas a hacer algo ahorita?
-Nicolás: No creo, ¿Por?
-Alan: Ven conmigo para que veas el partido.
-Nicolás: Suena bien.
-Alan: El equipo también está contento, hemos practicado mucho.
-Nicolás: Todos lo hemos notado.
-Alan: Hoy jugaremos con una formación 4-3-3, con Pedro como portero; Jack, Buck y Joey como delanteros; Víctor, Héctor y Javier como mediocampistas y Luis, José, Cesar y yo como defensas.
-Nicolás: Estoy seguro que van a ganar.
-Alan: Yo también.

-Nicolás: Esperemos que el campo este en buenas condiciones, grama cortada, sin huecos y sin pantanos.
-Alan: Ayer estaba bien.

Asking for a Book at the Library - Pidiendo un libro en la biblioteca

English

-Emma: Good afternoon.
-Roxana: Good afternoon. Welcome to the municipal library.
-Emma: Thank you very much.
-Roxana: Are you going to read here or are you going to borrow a book?
-Emma: It's my first time here. What kind of books do you have?
-Roxana: We have all kinds of books, horror, suspense, comedy, biographies, sciences, politics, history, fiction, romance, and so on.
-Emma: And how is your lending policy?
-Roxana: It depends on the history of the person. As you are new, we can lend you a book for a week. Passed that week, if you do not return the book, we will begin to apply sanctions for your future loans.
-Emma: I see. My favorites are horror. Which one is the best?
-Roxana: The most requested horror book is "The Monster in the Attic."
-Emma: Perfect, I'll take it.
-Roxana: I'll get it for you.

Spanish

-Emma: Buenas tardes.
-Roxana: Buenas tardes. Bienvenida a la biblioteca municipal.
-Emma: Muchas gracias.
-Roxana: ¿Vas a leer aquí o vas a pedir un préstamo para un libro?
-Emma: Es primera vez que vengo, ¿Qué clase de libros tiene?
-Roxana: Tenemos todo tipos de libros, de terror, de suspenso, de comedia, biografías, de ciencias, de política, de historia, de ficción, de romance, etcétera.
-Emma: ¿Y cómo es su política de préstamos?
-Roxana: Depende del historial de la persona, como tú eres nueva, te podemos prestar un libro por una semana, pasada esa semana, si no regresas el libro comenzaremos a aplicar sanciones para tus futuros prestamos.
-Emma: Ya veo. Mis favoritos son los de terror. ¿Cuál es el mejor que tiene?
-Roxana: El libro de terror mas pedido es "El Monstruo del ático".
-Emma: Perfecto, me lo llevo.
-Roxana: Ya te lo busco.

Asking for Wifi's Password - Pidiendo la clave del wifi

English

-Gabriela: Good evening, are you all right?
-Lucy: Good evening, not really, I feel a little dizzy.
-Gabriela: Is there anything I can do to help you?
-Lucy: Would you be so kind as to search on the Internet what to do in these cases?
-Gabriela: I would, but I don't have an internet connection at the moment.
-Lucy: Ask that lady for the wifi password, she's my neighbor.
-Gabriela: Perfect, on my way.
-Lucy: Thank you...
-Gabriela: Good evening. Excuse me, but could you give me the password of your wifi? Your neighbor Lucy is feeling bad and I need to get on the Internet as soon as possible.
-Gladys: Sure, honey. The password is 1234567891. What's wrong with Lucy?
-Gabriela: She's feeling a little dizzy and I see her weak. I'll search the internet for what it could be and how to solve it.
-Gladys: Let me know if you need anything else. Tell her to let me know when she gets better.
-Gabriela: Sure.

Spanish

-Gabriela: Buenas noches, ¿Está usted bien?
-Lucy: Buenas noches, en realidad no, me siento un poco mareada.
-Gabriela: ¿Hay algo que pueda hacer para ayudarla?
-Lucy: ¿Serias tan amable de buscar en internet que hacer en estos casos?
-Gabriela: Lo haría, pero no tengo conexión a internet en este momento.
-Lucy: Pídele la clave del wifi a aquella señora, ella es mi vecina.
-Gabriela: Perfecto, ya voy.
-Lucy: Gracias....
-Gabriela: Buenas noches, disculpe pero, ¿Podría darme usted la clave de su wifi? Su vecina Lucy se está sintiendo mal y necesito entrar a internet tan pronto como sea posible.
-Gladys: Claro cariño, la clave es 1234567891. ¿Qué tiene Lucy?
-Gabriela: Se está sintiendo un poco mareada y la veo débil. Buscare en internet que puede ser y como solucionarlo.
-Gladys: Hazme saber si necesitan algo más. Dile que me avise cuando mejore.
-Gabriela: Seguro.

Asking for a Ride- Pidiendo un aventón

English

-Troy: Hey Alice, how are you?
-Alice: Troy, all right, how are you?
-Troy: All right, a little worried really.
-Alice: Why?
-Troy: I have to walk home but it's raining a lot.
-Alice: Why don't you ask for a ride?
-Troy: You think so?
-Alice: Of course, someone from here must go there.
-Troy: Good thinking.
-Alice: Where are you going?
-Troy: 4th Avenue and 13th Street.
-Alice: Okay. I think Ron uses that road.
-Troy: Can you ask him?
-Alice: Hey, Ron. Do you go down 4th Avenue and 13th Street to your house?
-Ron: Hello, Alice. Yes, but I'm not going home today.
-Alice: Do you know of anyone passing by? Troy needs a ride because of the rain.
-Ron: I'm pretty sure Amanda does.
-Alice: Great. Thanks a lot. Come on Troy.
-Troy: Thanks anyway, Ron.
-Ron: Some other time.
-Troy: Sure.
-Alice: Hi, Amanda. Are you leaving already?
-Amanda: Alice, yes, I'm going home.
-Alice: Ron told me that you're going through 4th Avenue and 13th Street, right?
-Amanda: That's right, why?
-Troy: Do you think you can give me a ride? The rain won't let me walk there.
-Amanda: Of course, with pleasure. But I'm leaving now, so hurry.
-Troy: Okay, thank you very much, and thank you, Alice. See you tomorrow.
-Alice: See you tomorrow.

Spanish

-Troy: Hey Alice, ¿Cómo estás?
-Alice: Troy, muy bien, ¿Y tú?
-Troy: Todo bien, un poco preocupado en realidad.
-Alice: ¿Por qué?
-Troy: Tengo que caminar a casa pero está lloviendo mucho.
-Alice: ¿Y porque no pides un aventón?
-Troy: ¿Tú crees?
-Alice: Claro, alguien de acá debe ir hacia allá.

-Troy: Bien pensado.
-Alice: ¿A dónde vas tú?
-Troy: A la Avenida 4 con calle 13.
-Alice: Ok. Creo que ron usa esa vía.
-Troy: ¿Puedes preguntarle?
-Alice: Hey Ron, ¿Tu pasas por la avenida 4 con calle 13 para ir a tu casa?
-Ron: Hola Alice, si, pero hoy no voy a mi casa.
-Alice: ¿Sabes de alguien que pase por ahí? Troy necesita un aventón por la lluvia.
-Ron: Estoy casi seguro que Amanda.
-Alice: Genial. Muchas gracias. Vamos Troy.
-Troy: Gracias de todas maneras Ron.
-Ron: En otra oportunidad será.
-Troy: Seguro.
-Alice: Hola Amanda. ¿Ya te vas?
-Amanda: Alice, si, ya voy saliendo a casa.
-Alice: Me dijo ron que pasas por la Avenida 4 con calle 13, ¿Correcto?.
-Amanda: Así es, ¿Por?
-Troy: ¿Crees que me puedas dar un aventón? La lluvia no me dejara caminar hasta allá.
-Amanda: Claro, con mucho gusto. Pero ya me voy, así que apúrate.
-Troy: Ok, muchas gracias, y gracias a ti también Alice. Nos vemos mañana.
-Alice: Hasta mañana.

Visiting the Doctor - Visitando al doctor

English

-Donald: Good morning, Doctor. How are you?
-Doctor: Very well, you?
-Donald: Good. I'm here for the monthly checkup.
-Doctor: All right, although the last one went quite well.
-Donald: Thank God. But I had a cold, that's why I came.
-Doctor: All right, let's start with the consultation and checkup then.
-Donald: Thank you.

Spanish

-Donald: Buenos días Doctor. ¿Cómo esta?
-Doctor: Muy bien, ¿Usted?
-Donald: Bien. Vengo por el chequeo mensual.
-Doctor: Esta bien, aunque la ultima salió bastante bien.
-Donald: Gracias a Dios. Pero me he sentido resfriado, por eso vine.
-Doctor: Muy bien, empecemos con la consulta y chequeo entonces.
-Donald: Gracias.

Wrong Number - Número equivocado

English

-Thalia: Hi, is this Noah's number?
-Stranger: Good afternoon. I'm afraid not, you're wrong.
-Thalia: I called the wrong number, excuse me.
-Stranger: Okay, bye.

Spanish

-Thalia: Hola, ¿Es este el numero de Noah?
-Extraño: Buenas tardes, me temo que no, está equivocado.
-Thalia: Llame al número equivocado, disculpe.
-Extraño: Vale, adios.

Apply for a job - Aplicar para un trabajo

English

-Vanessa: Good afternoon. I came for the newspaper ad that says you're looking for a salesman and I'd like to apply for the job.
-Secretary: Good afternoon, welcome. Take a seat and you will be attended in a moment.
-Vanessa: Thank you very much...
-Secretary: You can go to the interview.
-Vanessa: Tha-Thank you.
-Secretary: Don't be nervous. Smile. You'll be fine.
-Vanessa: Fine.
...
-Vanessa: Good afternoon.
-Interviewer: Good afternoon. Please sit down.
-Vanessa: Ok.
-Interviewer: The secretary told me that you are here to apply for the position of the saleswoman, is that right?
-Vanessa: Yes, sir.
-Interviewer: Why should we hire you?
-Vanessa: I have my resume here. You can see that I'm the right person for the job, and I'm very responsible and committed.
-Interviewer: I see. I'd like to interview you another day more slowly.
-Vanessa: Okay, there's my phone number. You call me.

Spanish

-Vanessa: Buenas tardes. Vengo por el anuncio del periódico de que buscan un vendedor y me gustaría aplicar para el puesto.
-Secretaria: Buenas tardes, bienvenida. Toma asiento y serás atendida en un momento.
-Vanessa: Muchas gracias....
-Secretaria: Puedes pasar a la entrevista.
-Vanessa: Gra-gracias.
-Secretaria: No estés nerviosa, sonríe, te irá bien.
-Vanessa: De acuerdo.
...
-Vanessa: Buenas tardes.
-Entrevistador: Buenas tardes, siéntate por favor.
-Vanessa: Ok.
-Entrevistador: Me dijo la secretaria que estas aquí para aplicar por el puesto de vendedora, ¿es cierto?
-Vanessa: Si señor.
-Entrevistador: ¿Por qué deberíamos contratarte?

-Vanessa: Aquí tengo mi curriculum, puede ver que soy la indicada para el puesto, además, soy muy responsable y comprometida.

-Entrevistador: Ya veo. Me gustaría entrevistarla otro día con más calma.

-Vanessa: De acuerdo, ahí está mi número de teléfono, me llama.

Chapter 5: Conversaciones Communes De Trabajos - Common Jobs Conversations

Secretary - Secretaria

English

-Secretary: Good morning, boss. How are you?
-Boss: No complaints, you?
-Secretary: Well, a little busy.
-Boss: Why is that?
Secretary: I'm making the itinerary of your trip, sending e-mails to the other members, asking for quotations from hotels and restaurants, making copies of certain documents, and organizing meetings for Friday.
-Boss: You're very busy, do you need help?
-Secretary: A helper for this week would be very helpful.
-Boss: Perfect, I'll get you one.
-Secretary: Thank you very much. Don't forget to send me the numbers of the people I have to call to get them to pay.
-Boss: All right, I'll give them to you.

Spanish

-Secretaria: Buenos días jefe, ¿Cómo esta?
-Jefe: No me quejo, ¿Usted?
-Secretaria: Bien, un poco ocupada.
-Jefe: ¿Y eso?
-Secretaria: Estoy haciendo el itinerario de su viaje, enviando correos electrónicos a los otros miembros, pidiendo cotizaciones de hoteles y restaurantes, sacando copias de ciertos documentos y organizando las reuniones para el viernes.
-Jefe: Esta muy ocupada, ¿Necesita ayuda?
-Secretaria: Sería muy útil un ayudante para esta semana.
-Jefe: Perfecto, ya le consigo uno.
-Secretaria: Muchísimas gracias. No se olvide de enviarme los números de las personas a quienes debo llamar para que paguen.
-Jefe: Esta bien, ya se los entrego.

Driver - Chofer

English

-Esther: I'm leaving my driver's here.
-Aura: I'll see you later. Take care
-Esther: You too my friend.
-Driver: Good evening, miss. Where do you want me to take you?
-Esther: Good evening. What time is it?
-Driver: It is 7:30 p.m., ma'am.
-Esther: It's still early. Can you please take me to the pharmacy to buy some medicines and then to the supermarket to buy ice cream for my son who feels sick?
-Driver: With pleasure, which pharmacy and supermarket do you want to go to?
-Esther: To the nearest pharmacy, but the supermarket I would like the one near the house because there they sell the ice cream that my son loves.
-Driver: Understood.
-Esther: Thank you very much.

Spanish

-Esther: Me voy, ya llego mi chofer.
-Aura: Hasta luego, que estés bien.
-Esther: Tu igual amiga.
-Chofer: Buenas noches señorita, ¿A dónde desea que la lleve?
-Esther: Buenas noches, ¿Qué hora es?
-Chofer: Son las 7:30 p.m. señora.
-Esther: Aun es temprano, ¿Puedes por favor llevarme a la farmacia para comprar unas medicinas y luego al supermercado para comprarle un helado a mi hijo que se siente mal?
-Chofer: Con gusto, ¿A qué farmacia y supermercado desea ir?
-Esther: A la farmacia más cercana, pero al supermercado si me gustaría el que está cerca de la casa porque ahí venden el helado que le encanta a mi hijo.
-Chofer: Entendido.
-Esther: Muchas gracias.

Teacher - Profesor

English

-Teacher: Very good morning, class.
-Students: Good morning, teacher.
-Teacher: Happy first day of classes. Welcome to my subject.
-Students: Thank you very much.
-Teacher: Before I begin to give my subject, do any of you know what a teacher's duty is?
-Student 1: Teach.
-Teacher: Anyone else?
...
-Teacher: Yes, teach, but also learn and create content and methods for students to learn. I must help them understand my classes, make them like it, entertain them, and make them feel attracted to learning.
-Student 2: It's a lot more than I thought.
-Teacher: That's right. Well, get ready to start.

Spanish

-Profesor: Muy buenos días clase.
-Estudiantes: Buenos días profesor.
-Profesor: Feliz primer día de clases. Bienvenidos a mi materia.
-Estudiantes: Muchas gracias.
-Profesor: Antes de comenzar a dar mi materia, ¿Alguno de ustedes sabe cuál es el deber de un profesor?
-Estudiante 1: Enseñar.
-Profesor: ¿Alguien más?
...
-Profesor: Si, enseñar, pero también, aprender, crear contenido y métodos para que los estudiantes aprendan. Debo ayudarlos a entender mis clases, hacer que les guste, que se entretengan, que se sientan atraídos por aprender.
-Estudiante 2: Es mucho más de lo que yo pensaba.
-Profesor: Así es. Bueno, prepárense para comenzar.

Doctor - Doctor

English

-Child: Mommy, why do I have to come to the doctor so much?
-Mother: Here comes the doctor. Ask him yourself.
-Boy: All right.
-Doctor: Hello, little one. How are you?
-Boy: Hello, doctor. Very well.
-Doctor: I'm glad.
-Mother: Do you want to ask the doctor something, son?
-Child: Yes, Mommy, thank you for remembering me. Doctor, why do I have to come to see you so much?
-Doctor: That's a good question. How do you feel?
-Child: Better.
-Doctor: How did you feel when you came here four days ago?
-Child: Sick.
-Doctor: Your mom gave you medicine, didn't she?
-Child: That's right.
-Doctor: And you felt better taking the meds, right?
-Boy: I hadn't thought of that, but yes.
-Doctor: I'm in charge of taking care of your health, of sending you medication when you get sick, of making you always feel good, and making sure you grow up healthy and strong.
-Child: I get it.
-Mother: You see, son? That's why it's important to come to the doctor often.
-Child: Yes, Mommy. We can come every week.
-Mother: Hahahaha
-Doctor: Hahaha, you don't need it so often, once a month is fine.
-Child: It's okay.

Spanish

-Niño: Mami, ¿Por qué tengo que venir al doctor tanto?
-Madre: Ahí viene el doctor. Pregúntaselo tu mismo.
-Niño: Esta bien.
-Doctor: Hola pequeño, ¿Cómo estás?
-Niño: Hola doctor. Muy bien.
-Doctor: Me alegro.
-Madre: ¿Quieres preguntarle algo al doctor, hijo?
-Niño: Si mami, gracias por recordarme. Doctor, ¿Por qué tengo que venir tanto a verlo?
-Doctor: Esa es una buena pregunta. ¿Cómo te sientes?
-Niño: Mejor.
-Doctor: ¿Cómo te sentías cuando viniste hace cuatro días?
-Niño: Enfermo.

-Doctor: Tu mamá te dio medicinas, ¿Verdad?
-Niño: Así es.
-Doctor: Y te sentiste mejor al tomar las medicinas, ¿Correcto?
-Niño: No había pensado en eso, pero si.
-Doctor: Yo estoy a cargo de cuidar tu salud, de mandarte medicamentos cuando te enfermes, de hacer que siempre te sientas bien y de asegurarme de que crezcas sano y fuerte.
-Niño: Ya entiendo.
-Madre: ¿Ya ves, hijo? Por eso es importante venir frecuentemente al doctor.
-Niño: Si mami. Podemos venir todas las semanas.
-Madre: Jajajaja.
-Doctor: Jajaja, no hace falta tan seguido, una vez al mes está bien.
-Niño: Esta bien.

Librarian - Bibliotecaria

English

-Laura: Hello, aunt, blessings, how do you do?
-Yanny: Hello, darling, very well, you?
-Laura: Everything's fine.
-Yanny: I'm glad.
-Laura: Aunt, I wanted to ask you. What do you do for a living?
-Yanny: I'm a librarian.
-Laura: And what do you do as a librarian?
-Yanny: Maybe you think I do little. But I organize books according to their year, author, subject, volume, take control of book loans, receive donated books, and see which ones are useful and which ones are not to be used in the library and other things.
-Laura: Okay, one day I'll come with you and help you.
-Yanny: I'd love to.

Spanish

-Laura: Hola tía, bendición, ¿Cómo amaneces?
-Yanny: Hola mi vida, muy bien, ¿Tu?
-Laura: Todo bien.
-Yanny: Me alegro.
-Laura: Tía, quería preguntarte, ¿Tu de que trabajas?
-Yanny: Soy bibliotecaria.
-Laura: ¿Y qué haces como bibliotecaria?
-Yanny: Quizás pienses que hago poco. Pero yo organizo los libros según su año, autor, tema, tomo, llevo control de los préstamos de libros, recibo libros donados y veo cuales sirven y cuáles no para ser usados en la biblioteca y otras cosas.
-Laura: Esta bien, un día iré contigo a ayudarte.
-Yanny: Me encantaría.

Businessman/ Entrepreneur - Empresario

English

-Abreu: Good morning. How are you?
-Ashley: Good morning, very good.
-Miguel: Excellent.
-Abreu: I'm glad. I asked you to attend this meeting because I want to talk to you.
-Ashley: About what?
-Abreu: I'm looking for partners to open a new business.
-Miguel: A new business from what?
-Abreu: Clothing.
-Ashley: What do you propose?
-Abreu: I propose that the company will have 100 shares. I will keep 51 and you will buy the other 49 as you wish.
-Miguel: And how do we benefit?
-Abreu: The number of shares you have will be the percentage you get of the profits.
-Ashley: I am in. You have experience in companies and businesses and I know that everything will be fine.
-Abreu: Thank you very much Ashley, and you, Miguel?
-Miguel: I will if Ashley is 25, you are 50 and I am 25.
-Abreu: All right, we're partners then.
-Ashley: A new association.

Spanish

-Abreu: Buenos días. ¿Cómo están?
-Ashley: Buenos días, muy bien.
-Miguel: Excelente.
-Abreu: Me alegro. Les pedí que asistieran a esta reunión porque quiero hablar con ustedes.
-Ashley: ¿Sobre qué?
-Abreu: Estoy buscando socios para abrir un nuevo negocio.
-Miguel: ¿Un nuevo negocio de qué?
-Abreu: De ropa.
-Ashley: ¿Qué propones?
-Abreu: Propongo que la empresa tenga 100 acciones, yo me quedo con 51 y ustedes compran las otras 49 según deseen.
-Miguel: ¿Y en que nos beneficiamos?
-Abreu: El número de acciones que tengan será el porcentaje que obtengan de las ganancias.
-Ashley: Yo entro, tienes experiencia en empresas y negocios y sé que todo saldrá bien.
-Abreu: Muchas gracias Ashley, ¿Y tú, Miguel?

-Miguel: Lo hare si Ashley tiene 25, tu 50 y yo 25.
-Abreu: De acuerdo, somos socios entonces.
-Ashley: Una nueva asociación.

Designer - Diseñador

English

-Eliezer: Good afternoon.
-Chel: Good afternoon.
-Eliezer: What can I do for you?
-Chel: I saw in your social networks that you are a designer, is it true?
-Eliezer: Yes.
-Chel: Excellent, what kind of work do you do?
-Eliezer: I do all kinds of designs such as logos, images, videos, presentations, advertisements, book covers, posters, image editions, and many other things.
-Chel: What programs or tools do you use?
-Eliezer: The one I like the most is Photoshop, but I can use any program, in case you want me to do a job in a specific program.
-Chel: No, don't worry.
-Eliezer: What are you going to need me to do?
Chel: I'm going to need a banner, with many colors, contours, and well-defined figures of a battle for a special event that will be next Sunday.
-Eliezer: All right, what sizes does the banner have to be?
-Chel: 3.5 meters wide and 2 meters high.
-Eliezer: Perfect, send me more details through my social networks and coordinate over there.
-Chel: Excellent. Thank you.

Spanish

-Eliezer: Buenas tardes.
-Chel: Buenas tardes.
-Eliezer: ¿En que lo puedo ayudar?
-Chel: Vi en tus redes sociales que eres diseñador, ¿Es verdad?
-Eliezer: Si.
-Chel: Excelente, ¿Qué tipo de trabajos haces?
-Eliezer: Hago todo tipo de diseños como logos, imágenes, videos, presentaciones, publicidades, portadas de libros, posters, ediciones de imágenes y muchas otras cosas.
-Chel: ¿Qué programas o herramientas utilizas?
-Eliezer: El que más me gusta usar es Photoshop, pero se utilizar cualquier programa, en caso de que desees que haga un trabajo en un programa específico.
-Chel: No, tranquilo.
-Eliezer: ¿Qué vas a necesitar que haga?
-Chel: Voy a necesitar un banner, con muchos colores, contornos y figuras bien definidas de una batalla, para un evento especial que habrá el próximo domingo.
-Eliezer: Esta bien, ¿De qué medidas tiene que ser el banner?

-Chel: 3.5 metros de ancho y 2 metros de alto.
-Eliezer: Perfecto, envíame más detalles a través de mis redes sociales y coordinamos por allí.
-Chel: Excelente. Muchas gracias.

Janitor - Conserje

English

-Alex: Good morning, Mr. Arturo, how are you?
-Arturo: Good morning, Alex, very tired.
-Alex: Why?
-Arthur: Yesterday, I started working as a janitor in a school.
-Alex: Good, I'm glad you got the job.
-Arturo: I was happy too, but these children are very disastrous.
-Alex: Really? What did they do?
-Arturo: They throw garbage on the floor, they drop food and don't pick it up, they throw the pencil sharpener garbage on the floor, they don't clean their desks...
-Alex: Sounds terrible.
-Arturo: The worst thing is the bathrooms. They pee outside the poceta and the papers, they don't put them in the trash.
-Alex: How unpleasant.
-Arthur: Disgusting.
-Alex: You should talk to the principal so he can talk to them.
-Arthur: Yes, I'll talk to him today.
-Alex: Propose a system of rewards for the cleanest students.
-Arturo: That or I quit. It's very disgusting to work like that.
-Alex: I can imagine it, Mr. Arturo. I couldn't work like that.
-Arthur: I doubt anyone can.

Spanish

-Alex: Buenos días Sr Arturo, ¿Como esta?
-Arturo: Buenos días Alex, cansadísimo.
-Alex: ¿Por qué?
-Arturo: Ayer comencé a trabajar de conserje en una escuela.
-Alex: Que bueno, me alegra que obtuvo el trabajo.
-Arturo: Yo también estaba feliz, pero esos niños son muy desastrosos.
-Alex: ¿En serio? ¿Qué hicieron?
-Arturo: Tiran la basura al piso, se les cae comida y no la recogen, botan la basura del sacapuntas en el piso, no limpian sus escritorios...
-Alex: Suena terrible.
-Arturo: Lo peor son los baños, hacen pipi afuera de la poceta, los papeles no los meten en la papelera.
-Alex: Que desagradable.
-Arturo: Asqueroso.
-Alex: Debería hablar con el director para que hable con ellos.
-Arturo: Si, hoy hablare con él.
-Alex: Propón un sistema de recompensas para los estudiantes mas limpios.
-Arturo: Eso o renuncio, es muy asqueroso trabajar así.

-Alex: Me lo imagino Sr Arturo. Yo no podría trabajar así.
-Arturo: Dudo que alguien pueda.

Gardener - Jardinero

English

-Betty: Good afternoon, Brad, how are you?
-Brad: Good afternoon, Betty, ready to work.
-Betty: I find it excellent.
-Brad: What do you want me to do with your garden today?
-Betty: Well, mow the lawn, water the trees, plant these avocado seeds, fertilize the plants that need it, and insecticide the fruit trees that I have.
-Brad: Got it. I won't cut the grass very much because we are in a hot season and it's better to leave it a little long for that. I'll plant the avocado seeds away from the other plants because that tree grows a lot, and I can't throw the insecticide into the orange grove because it's bad for it.
-Betty: Well, you're the gardener. You know what's best for my garden.
-Brad: That's right. Don't worry. Your garden is in excellent hands.
-Betty: I know. You are such a good gardener that I recommended you to the neighbors, so show them today how well you work so they will hire you in the future.
-Brad: I will, thank you very much for your help.
-Betty: Thank you.

Spanish

-Betty: Buenas tardes Brad, ¿Como estas?
-Brad: Buenas tardes Betty, listo para trabajar.
-Betty: Me parece excelente.
-Brad: ¿Que quiere que haga hoy con su jardín?
-Betty: Bueno, corta la grama, riega los arboles, planta estas semillas de aguacate, échale fertilizante a las plantas que lo necesiten e insecticida a los arboles de frutas que tengo.
-Brad: Entendido. La grama no la cortare mucho porque estamos en periodo de calor y es mejor dejarla un poco larga por eso; las semillas de aguacate las plantare lejos de las otras plantas porque ese árbol crece bastante y el insecticida no se lo puedo echar a la mata de naranjas porque es malo para ella.
-Betty: Bueno, tu eres el jardinero, tu sabes lo que es mejor para mi jardín.
-Brad: Así es, no se preocupe, su jardín esta en excelentes manos.
-Betty: Lo sé, eres tan buen jardinero que te recomendé con los vecinos, así que lúcete hoy para enseñarles lo bien que trabajas y que te contraten en el futuro.
-Brad: Lo hare, muchas gracias por su ayuda.
-Betty: Gracias a ti.

Salesman/ Seller - Vendedor

English

-Rafael: Good afternoon, chief. This is Sebastian, the cousin I told you about to be a salesman here.
-Stefan: Good afternoon. Nice to meet you, Sebastian. Thank you very much, Rafael, I'll talk to him.
-Rafael: Thank you, Stefan. Bye Sebastian, good luck.
-Sebastian: Thank you, cousin, take care.
-Stefan: Tell me, Sebastian, do you have experience working as a salesman?
-Sebastian: That's right. I worked for two years as a salesman in a household towel company.
-Stefan: How did it go?
-Sebastian: All right, I had the highest sales rate in the company.
-Stefan: Amazing.
-Sebastian: The company had a good system of rewards, for each sale you were given a 5% commission on the total amount of the sale.
-Stefan: Here you will be happy. We give 6% fixed commission and depending on your sales and amounts, sometimes, we give 8% of sales.
-Sebastian: Sounds incredible, sir.
-Stefan: I'll test you for a week. If you do as well as you say, the job is yours.
-Sebastian: Sounds fair.
-Stefan: Do we have a deal?
-Sebastian: You can count on me.

Spanish

-Rafael: Buenas tardes jefe, este es Sebastián, el primo del que le hable para que sea vendedor de acá del negocio.
-Stefan: Buenas tardes, mucho gusto Sebastián, muchas gracias Rafael, hablaré con él.
-Rafael: Gracias a usted Stefan. Chao Sebastián, suerte.
-Sebastián: Gracias primo, cuídate.
-Stefan: Dime Sebastián, ¿Tienes experiencia trabajando de vendedor?
-Sebastián: Así es, trabaje dos años como vendedor en una empresa de toallas para hogar.
-Stefan: ¿Y cómo te fue?
-Sebastián: Muy bien, tenía el índice de ventas más alto de la empresa.
-Stefan: Asombroso.
-Sebastián: La empresa tenía buen sistema de recompensas, por cada venta te daban un 5% de comisión del monto total de la venta.
-Stefan: Aquí serás feliz, nosotros damos 6% de comisión fija y dependiendo de tus ventas y los montos, en algunas ocasiones damos el 8% de las ventas.
-Sebastián: Suena increíble señor.

-Stefan: Te pondré a prueba una semana. Si te va tan bien como dices, el puesto es tuyo.
-Sebastián: Suena justo.
-Stefan: ¿Tenemos un trato?
-Sebastián: Cuente conmigo

Mechanical - Mecánico

English

-Jorge: Good morning. Go ahead.
-Thais: Good morning. Thank you very much. Where do I park?
-Jorge: There on the left, next to the green car.
-Thais: Ok.
-Jorge: Tell me, why are you coming?
-Thais: I went away for the weekend and the car started to fail.
-Jorge: Do you have any idea about what might be?
-Thais: Not a bit. That's why I brought it to you. You're the most honest mechanic I know.
-Jorge: I'm flattered. Did you check the oil level?
-Thais: Yes, it was low and I filled it up.
-Jorge: Did you check the spark plugs and their cables?
-Thais: No, no idea how it's done.
-Jorge: Okay, did you check the coolant?
-Thais: Yes, everything was fine. It didn't overheat.
-Jorge: Perfect. When did you change the gas filter?
-Thais: A few months ago, you changed it.
-Jorge: Right, I didn't remember.
-Thais: Can you also check the brakes?
-Jorge: Sure. As far as I can see, your tires are worn. You should buy others.
-Thais: I have it in mind, but I don't have any money. I bought the shock absorbers before I left for the trip and I ran out of money.
-Jorge: It happens. Well, I'll start by checking the spark plugs. I'll let you know when I'm ready.
-Thais: Thank you very much. We're in touch.

Spanish

-Jorge: Buenos días. Adelante.
-Thais: Buenos días. Muchas gracias, ¿Dónde me estaciono?
-Jorge: Allá adelante a la izquierda, al lado del carro verde.
-Thais: Ok.
-Jorge: Cuéntame ¿Y eso que vienes?
-Thais: Me fui de viaje el fin de semana y el carro comenzó a fallar.
-Jorge: ¿Tienes idea de lo que pueda ser?
-Thais: Ni un poco, por eso te lo traje a ti, eres el mecánico más honesto que conozco.
-Jorge: Me halagas. ¿Chequeaste el nivel de aceite?
-Thais: Si, estaba bajo y lo llene.
-Jorge: ¿Revisaste las bujías y sus cables?
-Thais: No, ni idea de cómo se hace.
-Jorge: Ok, ¿Revisaste el refrigerante?

-Thais: Si, estaba todo bien, no recalentó.

-Jorge: Perfecto. ¿Cuándo cambiaste el filtro de gasolina?

-Thais: Hace unos meses, lo cambiaste tú.

-Jorge: Cierto, no recordaba.

-Thais: ¿Puedes también revisar los frenos?

-Jorge: Seguro. Por lo que veo ya tus cauchos están gastados, deberías comprar otros.

-Thais: Lo tengo en mente, pero no tengo dinero, le compre los amortiguadores antes de irme de viaje y me quede sin dinero.

-Jorge: Suele pasar. Bueno, comenzare revisando las bujías, te aviso cuando esté listo.

-Thais: Muchísimas gracias. Estamos en contacto.

Pharmacist - Farmaceuta

English

-Anabella: Hello, are you a pharmacist?
-Martin: That's right. I'm one of the pharmacists in this pharmacy. How can I help you?
-Anabella: I came from the doctor's appointment and the doctor gave me this prescription.
-Martin: Let's see it.
-Anabella: Here you are.
-Martin: I don't have the brand of the antibiotic he prescribed. I have another brand but the same component.
-Anabella: If it's the same, give me that one.
Martin: Here's the antacid, the gastric protector, the anti-inflammatory, and the serum.
Anabella: Thank you very much. Do you also have band-aids, cotton, and alcohol? Now that I remember, my son fell a few days ago and I'm out of them.
-Martin: I'll look for them.
-Anabella: Great.
Martin: Here are the Band-Aids and the cotton. I'm out of alcohol.
-Anabella: Don't worry. I'll look at another pharmacy.
-Martin: Here's the bill. Will you pay in cash or by credit card?
-Anabella: In cash.
-Martin: Will you want a bag?
-Anabella: No thanks.

Spanish

-Anabella: Hola, ¿Es usted farmaceuta?
-Martin: Así es, soy uno de los farmaceutas de esta farmacia, ¿En qué puedo ayudarla?
-Anabella: Vengo de la cita médica y el doctor me dio este récipe.
-Martin: A verlo.
-Anabella: Aquí tiene.
-Martin: No tengo la marca de antibiótico que le receto, tengo otra marca pero del mismo componente.
-Anabella: Si es lo mismo, deme ese.
-Martin: Aquí está el antiácido, el protector gástrico, el desinflamatorio y el suero.
-Anabella: Muchísimas gracias, ¿Tienes también curitas, algodón y alcohol? Ahora que recuerdo mi hijo se cayó hace unos días y ya se me acabaron.
-Martin: Ya lo busco.
-Anabella: Genial.
-Martin: Aquí tienes las curitas y el algodón, alcohol no me queda.

-Anabella: No te preocupes, yo busco en otra farmacia.
-Martin: Aquí tiene la cuenta. ¿Va a pagar en efectivo o con tarjeta?
-Anabella: En efectivo.
-Martin: ¿Va a querer bolsa?
-Anabella: No gracias.

Lawyer - Abogado

English

-George: Good morning.
-Esteban: Good morning, can I help you?
-George: I took your number from the newspaper. It said you were a lawyer, is that correct?
-Esteban: That's right.
-George: Well, I'd like to know what kind of paperwork you do, because there are several kinds of lawyers.
-Esteban: I'm in charge of divorces, advice, defenses, business matters, inheritances, and other similar matters.
-George: Perfect, I'd like you to advise me with a divorce.
-Esteban: All right, come to my office and I'll be happy to help you.
-George: Where are you located?
-Esteban: I'm sending you the information by text message to this number you're calling me from.
-George: Excellent. I'll see you.

Spanish

-George: Buenos días.
-Esteban: Buenos días, ¿En qué puedo ayudarlo?
-George: Tomé su número del periódico, decía que usted era abogado, ¿Es correcto?
-Esteban: Así es.
-George: Bueno, me gustaría saber qué tipo de trámites realiza usted, porque hay varios tipos de abogados.
-Esteban: Yo me encargo de divorcios, asesorías, defensas, temas empresariales, herencias y otros temas parecidos.
-George: Perfecto, me gustaría que me asesore con un divorcio.
-Esteban: Muy bien, venga a mi oficina y con gusto le atenderé.
-George: ¿Dónde está ubicado?
-Esteban: Ya le envío la información por mensaje de texto a este número del que me llama.
-George: Excelente. Nos vemos.

Watchman - Vigilante

English

-Matt: Good morning, Jesus. How are you?
-Jesus: Good morning, very tired. The night was difficult.
-Matt: Why?
-Jesus: Because there were so many noises. I thought they were thieves.
-Matt: And you found out what they were?
-Jesus: Yes, a lot of cats fighting and running around.
-Matt: Thank goodness they weren't thieves.
-Jesus: Yes, but they made noise and knocked things down all night. I was worried.
-Matt: Calm down, Jesus. With you as the watchman, nobody will want to enter here to steal.
-Jesus: I hope so, sir.
-Matt: I'm sure.
-Jesus: Could you ask another guard to stay tonight?
-Matt: So you can rest?
-Jesus: That's right, sir.
-Matt: Sure, no problem.

Spanish

-Matt: Buenos días Jesus, ¿Como estas?
-Jesus: Buenos días, muy cansado, la noche fue difícil.
-Matt: ¿Por qué?
-Jesus: Porque hubo muchos ruidos, pensé que eran ladrones.
-Matt: ¿Y descubriste que eran?
-Jesus: Si, un montón de gatos peleando y corriendo por todos lados.
-Matt: Menos mal no eran ladrones.
-Jesus: Si, pero hicieron ruido y tumbaron cosas toda la noche. Estaba preocupado.
-Matt: Tranquilo Jesus, contigo como vigilante nadie querrá entrar aquí a robar.
-Jesus: Eso espero señor.
-Matt: Estoy seguro.
-Jesus: ¿Podría pedirle a otro vigilante que se quede esta noche?
-Matt: ¿Para que tú descanses?
-Jesus: Así es señor.
-Matt: Claro, no hay problema.

Policeman - Policía

English

-Police: Good afternoon, do you know why I pulled you over?
-Robert: No idea, sir.
-Police: Have you been drinking?
-Robert: No, Officer.
-Police: Are you sure?
-Robert: Well, maybe a little.
-Police: That's what I thought. Please get out of the vehicle.
-Robert: Wait a minute.
-Police: I'll ask you to take the alcohol test.
-Robert: Of course.
-Police: Blow here.
-Robert: Ready.
-Police: Look, your alcohol level is above the limit for driving.
-Robert: Strange, it was just a beer.
-Police: Sir, I've been following you for half an hour. You've stopped at three liquor stores and out of the three, you've gone out drinking.
-Robert: Are you sure?
-Police: Yes, I have the recordings here. Besides, in one of the liquor stores, you stole chocolate. While driving, you exceeded the speed limit and didn't put the cross-lights on at any time. I'm afraid I'll have to stop you and take you to the station.
-Robert: The chocolate was very expensive and I wasn't going to pay as much for chocolate and about the speed limit, I was late to watch the game.
-Police: They're not excuses, get on the patrol and be quiet.
-Robert: All right.

Spanish

-Policía: Buenas tardes, ¿Sabe usted porque lo detuve?
-Robert: Ni idea señor.
-Policía: ¿Ha usted estado bebiendo?
-Robert: No oficial.
-Policía: ¿Está usted seguro?
-Robert: Bueno, quizás un poco.
-Policía: Eso supuse. Por favor bájese del vehículo.
-Robert: Un momento.
-Policía: Le pediré que haga la prueba de alcohol.
-Robert: Por supuesto.
-Policía: Sople aquí.
-Robert: Listo.
-Policía: Mire, su nivel de alcohol está sobre el límite permitido para conducir.

-Robert: Que extraño, solo fue una cerveza.

-Policía: Señor, vengo siguiéndolo desde hace media hora, se ha parado en tres licorerías y de las tres ha salido bebiendo.

-Robert: ¿Esta seguro?

-Policía: Si, aquí tengo las grabaciones, además, en una de las licorerías se robó un chocolate; manejando excedió el límite de velocidad y no puso las luces de cruces en ningún momento. Me temo que tendré que detenerlo y llevarlo a la estación.

-Robert: Es que el chocolate estaba muy caro y no iba a pagar tanto por un chocolate y sobre el límite de velocidad, se me hacia tarde para ver el partido.

-Policía: No son excusas, súbase a la patrulla y guarde silencio.

-Robert: De acuerdo.

Fireman - Bombero

English

-Adam: Good morning, team. How are you?
-Team: Good, sir.
-Adam: Glad to hear it. Today, I will divide you into three teams. Team 1, put out a fire at the south of the forest. Team 2, there's a gas leak in a mall. Investigate and fix it, and team 3 stays here at the station with me to fix the fire truck. Understood?
-Team 1: Yes sir.
-Team 2: Loud and clear, sir.
-Team 3: Sir, yes sir.
-Adam: Let's get to work then. Pay attention to your radios, we're communicating over there.

Spanish

-Adam: Buenos días equipo, ¿Cómo están?
-Equipo: Bien Señor.
-Adam: Me alegra oírlo. Hoy los dividiré en tres equipos. Equipo 1, apaguen un incendio que hay al sur del bosque; equipo 2, hay una fuga de gas en un centro comercial, investiguen y arréglenla y el equipo 3 se queda aquí en la estación conmigo para arreglar el camión de bomberos. ¿Entendido?
-Equipo 1: Si señor.
-Equipo 2: Fuerte y claro, señor.
-Equipo 3: Señor, sí señor.
-Adam: A trabajar entonces. Presten atención a sus radios, nos comunicamos por allí.

Baker - Panadero

English

-Pablo: Good morning. Welcome to the opening of my bakery.
-Katherine: It is very beautiful, Pablo.
-Pablo: Thank you very much.
-Katherine: It smells delicious, what is it?
-Paul: It must be what they're baking.
-Katherine: And what's that?
-Paul: I don't know, let's ask the baker.
-Katherine: Come on.
-Paul: Hi, Ricky.
-Ricky: Hi, Mr. Pablo, how are you?
-Paul: All right, this is my friend Katherine. I invited her to the opening of the bakery.
-Katherine: Nice to meet you.
-Ricky: Nice to meet you.
-Pablo: I was showing her the bakery and she told me that it smelled very tasty and wanted to know what it was. What are you baking?
-Ricky: I'm baking chocolate cake, brownies, apple pie, strawberry pie, passion fruit cake, some cinnamon rolls, French bread, and sandwich bread.
-Katherine: It must be the cinnamon rolls or the brownie that smells so good.
-Pablo: Come on, here's some freshly baked. Try it.
-Katherine: God, this is delicious.
-Ricky: Thank you very much.
-Paul: I'm glad you like it.

Spanish

-Pablo: Buenos días, bienvenida a la inauguración de mi panadería.
-Katherine: Esta muy bonita Pablo.
-Pablo: Muchas gracias.
-Katherine: Huele riquísimo, ¿Qué es?
-Pablo: Debe ser lo que están horneando.
-Katherine: ¿Y qué es eso?
-Pablo: No se, preguntémosle al panadero.
-Katherine: Vamos.
-Pablo: Hola Ricky.
-Ricky: Hola Sr Pablo, ¿Cómo esta?
-Pablo: Muy bien, ella es mi amiga Katherine, la invite a la inauguración de la panadería.
-Katherine: Mucho gusto.
-Ricky: Encantado de conocerla.
-Pablo: Le estaba enseñando la panadería y me dijo que olía muy sabroso y quería saber que era. ¿Qué estas horneando?

-Ricky: Estoy horneando torta de chocolate, brownies, pie de manzana, pie de fresa, torta de parchita, unos roles de canela, pan francés y pan de sanduche.
-Katherine: Deben ser los roles de canela o el brownie lo que huele tan bien.
-Pablo: Vamos, aquí hay unos recién horneados, prueba.
-Katherine: Dios, esto esta delicioso.
-Ricky: Muchas gracias.
-Pablo: Me alegra que te guste.

Chef - Chef

English

-Bratt: Hi, how are you?
-Joyce: Hello, very well, how are you?
-Bratt: Very good. I'm here because I'd like to be a kitchen assistant.
-Joyce: Excellent. I will call the chef to talk to him. MARCO!
-Marco: Yes, love?
-Joyce: This guy wants to be a kitchen assistant.
-Marco: That's good. Come with me.
-Bratt: Right away.
-Marco: This is my kitchen. Here I have my utensils like knives, forks, teaspoons, spoons, ladles, pots, and pans. On this side, I have ingredients like salt, sugar, oregano, vinegar, basil, flour, milk, cumin, laurel, curry, and onoto. Here in this fridge, I have vegetables such as carrot, potato, cucumber, tomato, onion, paprika, zucchini, eggplant, beetroot, chili, and others. While here in this fridge, I keep meat, chicken, fish, and cheese.
-Bratt: You are very organized.
-Marco: That's right. If you want to be my assistant, you'll have to be too.
-Bratt: Okay.
-Marco: I prepare all kinds of food including Italian, French, Colombian, Mexican, Venezuelan, Argentinean, German, Dutch, and many others.
-Bratt: I would love to learn with you.
-Marco: If you do your job well, you'll do it over time.

Spanish

-Bratt: Hola, ¿Como esta?
-Joyce: Hola, muy bien, ¿Y tú?
-Bratt: Muy bien. Vengo porque quisiera ser asistente de cocina.
-Joyce: Excelente; ya llamo al chef para que hables con él. ¡MARCO!
-Marco: ¿Si amor?
-Joyce: Este chico quiere ser asistente de cocina.
-Marco: Que bueno. Acompáñame.
-Bratt: En seguida.
-Marco: Esta es mi cocina. Aquí tengo mis utensilios como cuchillos, tenedores, cucharillas, cucharas, cucharones, ollas y sartenes; en este lado tengo los ingredientes como sal, azúcar, orégano, vinagre, albahaca, harina, leche, comino, laurel, curry y onoto; acá en esta nevera tengo las verduras como zanahoria, papa, pepino, tomate, cebolla, pimentón, calabacín, berenjena, remolacha, ají y otras; mientras que aquí en esta nevera guardo la carne, pollo, pescados y quesos.
-Bratt: Es muy organizado.
-Marco: Así es. Si quieres ser mi asistente deberás serlo.
-Bratt: De acuerdo.

-Marco: Yo preparo comidas de todo tipo como italianas, francesas, colombianas, mexicanas, venezolanas, argentinas, alemanas, holandesas y muchas otras.

-Bratt: Me encantaría aprender con usted.

-Marco: Si haces bien tu trabajo, lo harás con el tiempo.

Dog Walker - Paseador de perros

English

-Leila: Good morning, Mrs. Nancy?
-Nancy: Yes, tell me.
-Leila: It's Leila, the girl who you hired to walk your dog. I'm out here waiting for you.
-Nancy: I'll be right out.
-Leila: I'll wait for you here.
...
-Nancy: Good morning, Leila. Sorry I'm late.
-Leila: Don't worry.
-Nancy: This is Capi, my little puppy.
-Leila: He's very cute.
-Nancy: Yes, I take good care of him. I hope you do, too.
-Leila: Don't doubt it.
-Nancy: Well, I need you to walk him for half an hour or three kilometers. Give him plenty of water and two fists of food after walking.
-Leila: I understand.
-Nancy: Here's the food, the water, and two bags for you to pick up his poop.
-Leila: Perfect. I'll write to you when I am back.
-Nancy: Thank you very much.

Spanish

-Leila: Buenos días, ¿Sra Nancy?
-Nancy: Si, dígame.
-Leila: Es Leila, la muchacha que contrato para pasear a su perro, estoy acá afuera esperándola.
-Nancy: Ya salgo.
-Leila: Aquí la espero.
...
-Nancy: Buenos días Leila, disculpa la tardanza.
-Leila: No se preocupe.
-Nancy: Este es Capi, mi pequeño cachorro.
-Leila: Es muy lindo.
-Nancy: Si, lo cuido muy bien, espero que tu también lo hagas.
-Leila: No lo dude.
-Nancy: Bueno, necesito que lo pasees durante una media hora o que camine tres kilómetros, le des bastante agua y dos puños de comida después de caminar.
-Leila: Entiendo.
-Nancy: Aquí tienes la comida, el agua y dos bolsas para que recojas su pupú.
-Leila: Perfecto, le escribo entonces cuando este de regreso.
-Nancy: Muchas gracias.

Babysitter/Nanny - Niñera

English

-Mother: Good day, Maria. It's good that you arrived early. The children are awake. Let's go to the kitchen and talk.
-Nanny: Yes. Today, I didn't have any problems with transportation.
-Mom: Did you have breakfast?
-Nanny: Yes, before leaving home.
-Mom: Well, let's have a cup of coffee and talk about today's chores.
-Nanny: Perfect, thank you.
-Mother: Here on the blackboard are all the activities and schedules for the children. It's important that you follow the schedules of Samuel's medicines. He spent the whole weekend with a lot of flu fever.
-Nanny: Ok, and where are the medicines?
-Mother: They are all here in this cabinet. He takes them without any problem. They don't taste bad. He has had little appetite. Don't force him to eat. Offer them juices and fruits during the day, and some yogurt or cookie.
-Nanny: It's okay, ma'am. I'll do it.
-Mom: Thanks, I'm going to work. I'll see you in the afternoon. You can call me if anything goes.

Spanish

-Mama: Buen día María, que bueno que llegaste temprano, ya los niños están despiertos, vamos a la cocina y conversamos.
-Niñera: Si, hoy no tuve problemas con el transporte.
-Mama: ¿Desayunaste?
-Niñera: Si, antes de salir de casa.
-Mama: Bueno, tomemos un café y hablemos de las tareas de hoy.
-Niñera: Perfecto, gracias.
-Mama: Aquí en la pizarra están todas las actividades y horarios para los niños, es importante que sigas los horarios de las medicinas de Samuel, pasó todo el fin de semana con mucha fiebre por la gripe.
-Niñera: Ok y, ¿En donde están las medicinas?
-Mama: Aquí en este gabinete están todas, él se las toma sin ningún problema, no saben mal, ha tenido poco apetito, no lo obligues a comer, ofréceles jugos y frutas durante el día y algún yogurt o galleta.
-Niñera: Está bien señora, así lo hare.
-Mama: Gracias, voy saliendo al trabajo, nos vemos en la tarde, cualquier cosa me llamas.

Conclusión

Gracias por llegar hasta el final de Aprender inglés para principiantes: más de 100 conversaciones en inglés fáciles y comunes para aprender inglés.

Esperemos que sea informativo y pueda brindarle todas las herramientas que necesita para lograr sus objetivos.

Con el contenido cubierto en este libro, podrá defenderse y hablar con hablantes de inglés sobre temas y conversaciones básicos.

El siguiente paso es seguir practicando todas las conversaciones que aquí se presentan, seguir leyéndolas y analizándolas, aplicándolas en situaciones cotidianas para tener más retención de lo escrito en este libro. Ahora que ha terminado el libro Aprenda inglés para principiantes: más de 100 conversaciones en inglés fáciles y comunes para aprender inglés, puede pasar a otro libro con conversaciones más avanzadas y técnicas sobre otros temas para mejorar su conocimiento del idioma inglés.

Por último, si este libro le resultó útil de alguna manera, ¡siempre se agradece una reseña en Amazon!

Aprende inglés con historias cortas

Mejore su idioma inglés con historias fáciles y haga crecer su vocabulario (Vol. 1)

Introducción

Felicitaciones por descargar Aprenda inglés con historias cortas: mejore su idioma inglés con historias fáciles y haga crecer su vocabulario (Vol. 1) y gracias por hacerlo.

El siguiente libro contiene varias historias breves y sencillas en inglés. Cada una de estas historias tiene un resumen en inglés al final con su respectiva traducción al español. Asimismo, al final de cada resumen, hay una sección de vocabulario con la que puedes aprender y repasar el vocabulario desconocido y poco común utilizado en la historia. Esos cuentos cortos están escritos con palabras, frases y oraciones simples, fáciles y comunes en el idioma inglés porque el libro está dirigido a personas que están aprendiendo el idioma inglés desde cero o que ya tienen un conocimiento principiante.

El propósito de este libro es enseñarte a aprender, de manera entretenida e interactiva, cómo usar y manejar los principios básicos del idioma inglés como verbos, adjetivos, adverbios, tiempo pasado y otros recursos literarios del idioma. Es necesario aclarar que este libro debe complementarse con otros recursos y actividades para lograr un buen dominio y comprensión del idioma inglés, como ver videos o escuchar audios para comprender e imitar la pronunciación, los diferentes usos de las palabras y los usos verbales. conjugaciones.

Hay muchos libros sobre este tema en el mercado, ¡gracias nuevamente por elegir este! Se hizo todo lo posible para garantizar que esté lleno de tanta información útil como sea posible, ¡disfrútelo!

A different day – Un dia diferente

It was two in the afternoon on a Tuesday when the phone rang. Matt and Max knew what that sound meant. His father was supposed to go to work, just like every Tuesday that summer, so they would be left alone in the house. However, that Tuesday was different, the weather was rainy, cloudy and very cold. Matt and Max's father picked up the phone, listened to what the other person was saying and immediately answered:

-Are out.

She grabbed her brown leather coat, her night-black umbrella, the keys to her electric blue Camaro that made it hard to miss her and went to do business. As the door closed, Matt and Max were excited, because, like every Tuesday, they would be home alone and could play and eat as much as they wanted.

-Matt: What are we going to play today?
-Max: What do you think if we play video games for a while and then go out on the bike?
-Matt: Great. I was going to eat the cereal Mom brought yesterday.
-Max: It seems to me an excellent idea, I'm going to look for them.
-Matt: I'll wait here to start playing.
-Max: Ok.

And so they did, Max searched for the cereal his mother had hidden in that old cupboard in his room, and they played video games for two hours. When they stopped playing, they went to get their bikes. Matt's was white, freshly painted and looked very bright, with flame stickers everywhere and yellow ribbons moving in the strong breeze that afternoon; Max's was green, the paint had deteriorated and a little rusted, he had a basket where Max kept the thermos of travel water and some cereal that was left over. They wore helmets, elbow pads and knee pads, but when they opened the garage door they were surprised to see the time. The day was completely gray, cold and wet.

-Max: And now?
-Matt: How strange, the weather forecast didn't mention anything about rain.
-Max: It rarely rains in the summer at this time.
-Matt: I guess we'll have to stay here today.
-Max: What a pity.

Matt and Max did not leave the house, they stayed playing video games, watching television and talking while waiting for the parents to arrive. It was starting to get dark when the weather got worse, a big rain with strong wind and a lot of thunder broke out, what the boys didn't know was that a strong storm was forming. As time went by, the night became darker and the storm grew stronger and stronger. It got so strong that it knocked down a pole, leaving the street where Matt and Max lived without electricity.

Just before the electricity went out, Matt and Max's father had called to let him know that he was with his mother, trapped by the storm, in a shopping mall.

Brothers Matt and Max were then alone at home, at night, with a horrible storm outside and without electricity, when suddenly there was a loud bang on the roof and attic of the house.

-Matt: Did you hear?
-Max: Yes, what is it?
-Matt: I don't know.
-Max: Maybe it's the witches Mike talks about.
-Matt: I don't think so.
-Max: Mike told me they hunt when there are storms like that.
-Matt: Witches don't exist!
-Max: Are you sure?
-Matt: Not entirely, but I don't think they exist.
-Max: Go find out then.
-Matt: Come with me!
-Max: No ... I'm afraid to go up to the attic, and without light I'm even more afraid.
-Matt: Come on, you take the flashlight and I carry the baseball bat.
-Max: Ok. But if anything happens to me, it's your fault.

Then they looked for the flashlight and baseball bat and went to the attic when suddenly there was a knock on the windows. Frightened, they walked away from the attic.

-Max: We are surrounded.
-Matt: I think so.
-Max: She knew we were going for her and asked for backup and now they cornered us Matt, I'm very scared. I want mom and dad to come right away.
-Matt: Calm down Max, I'm terrified too but if we panic it will be even worse. Let's think about what we can do.

As they talked, they saw two shadows crossing one of the windows, and they stood still and watched as those shadows headed for the door. When they got to the door they started knocking desperately, so Matt and Max, who were paralyzed with fear, reacted and ran to hide in their room. They ran through the house at full speed towards the parents' room; as they ran, they heard lightning, noises in the attic, bangs on the windows and then on the door.

They reached the parents' room, got under the bed and turned off the flashlight.

-Matt: Don't make any noise Max. Maybe they won't find us like that.
-Max: I'm trying Max! He said crying.

And there they remained, every minute seemed to them hours of suffering. They hoped the storm would subside. After a long period of waiting, the storm seemed to gradually calm down until the electricity returned. When he returned, they were a little happier, as they could already turn on the lights and see everything better. But to their surprise the front door of the house opened.

-Max: Matt, they are already in!
-Matt: Don't make noise Max!

They remained there, under their parents' bed, silent, still and frightened. They heard footsteps getting closer and closer, until someone tried to open the door to the room they were in, but it was locked. There was absolute silence for a few seconds, the storm had stopped, nothing could be heard from the attic, there was no banging on the windows and no footsteps approaching. After the silence, the boys heard a familiar voice say their names ...

-Matt: Mom? Pope?
-Max: Is it you?

And a voice replied:
- Of course, children, open the door.

-Max: How can we know they are not witches?
-Matt: We have to risk Max!

Matt got up and walked carefully to the door, opening it very slowly. They were their parents. Matt and Max ran up to them and hugged them.

-Max: Luckily you arrived, we didn't have the light, the witches were everywhere and I was very afraid.

Puzzled, the parents looked at each other and then burst out laughing. They told them that the witches did not exist and that those knocking on the door were the ones who were getting wet outside and couldn't find the keys because they couldn't see anything.

-Max: Of course they exist! There is one in the attic, let's go and see it.

They all went to the attic and what they found was a cat, which entered through a hole in the ceiling. Then they went to investigate the windows and saw that it was the branches of the trees that made noise because of the wind.

Summary

English

Matt and Max were two children who waited for Tuesdays with a lot of emotion because their father had to go out to the store leaving them alone at home to play and eat as much as they wanted. On Tuesday, everything was normal until they decided to go out and ride their bicycles and saw that there was bad weather. What they didn't know was that this bad weather was a storm that would leave them without their parents and without electricity for several hours. During the storm, the children heard many noises and hits, first in the attic and then on windows and doors. Thinking that they were witches coming for them, they finally decided to hide under their parents' bed. After waiting for the electricity to come back and the storm to end, it turned out that the knocks on the door were their parents because they couldn't find the keys to enter because everything was too dark. The noises on the attic came to be a cat and the hits on the windows were the branches of the trees.

Espanol

Matt y Max eran dos niños que esperaban los martes con mucha emoción porque su padre tenía que salir a la tienda dejándolos solos en casa para jugar y comer todo lo que quisieran. El martes todo fue normal hasta que decidieron salir a andar en bicicleta y vieron que hacía mal tiempo. Lo que no sabían era que este mal tiempo era una tormenta que los dejaría sin sus padres y sin electricidad durante varias horas. Durante la tormenta, los niños escucharon muchos ruidos y golpes, primero en el ático y luego en ventanas y puertas. Pensando que eran brujas que venían por ellos, finalmente decidieron esconderse debajo de la cama de sus padres. Después de esperar a que volviera la luz y cesara la tormenta, resultó que los golpes en la puerta eran sus padres porque no pudieron encontrar las llaves para entrar porque todo estaba demasiado oscuro. Los ruidos en el ático llegaron a ser de un gato y los golpes en las ventanas fueron las ramas de los árboles.

Vocabulary

English

Store, summer, rainy, cloudy, umbrella, keys, cereal, wardrobe, stickers, flames, ribbons, wind, rusty, helmets, elbow pads, knee pads, weather, wet, forecast, thunder, storm, roof, attic, witches, hunt, fear, flashlight, surrounded, shadows.

Espanol

Tienda, verano, lluvioso, nublado, paraguas, llaves, cereal, guardarropa, pegatinas, llamas, cintas, viento, oxidado, cascos, coderas, rodilleras, clima, mojado, pronóstico, trueno, tormenta, techo, ático, brujas, caza, miedo, linterna, rodeado, sombras.

Have you seen Luke? - ¿Has visto a luke?

Once upon a time there was a little girl named Cindy, she had long curly red hair, her skin was fair, she had big blue eyes and a lot of freckles on her face. Cindy has loved animals since birth. He always fed him when he found them on the street, gave them drinks and asked his parents to visit them again to make sure they were okay.

One day, Cindy was walking with her parents when in the distance she saw a box moving on the floor, with great curiosity she observed it for a long time, until she told her father to accompany her to see what it was. As they stood in front of the box, Cindy and her father saw what it was that made it move. A small, white, hairy, brown-spotted dog that appeared to be a Cocker breed.

-Cindy: Dad, what is that puppy doing in that box?
-Father: I don't know Cindy, maybe someone left it there.
-Cindy: Why did they abandon it?
-Father: Maybe they don't want it, they don't have the time to care for it or they don't have the food to feed it.
-Cindy: I already fell in love with him and I also have a lot of time to take care of him.
-Father: What do you mean?
-Cindy: You could buy him food and I will take care of him and love him. Can we adopt it?
-Father: Having a puppy is a big responsibility Cindy, are you sure you want to?
-Cindy: Sure dad, I won't let him live there in that box hungry and in the cold.
-Father: You're right, come on, take it out of the box and let's tell your mother.
-Cindy: Thank you so much dad.
-Father: No problem, but you will see that this is a great responsibility.
-Cindy: I can do it.
-Father: He's a boy, what will you call him?
-Cindy: I've always liked the name Luke.
-Father: It's a nice name. We hope he likes it.

And that's how Luke was saved from the street by Cindy, and that he became her best friend.

Then Cindy, along with her father, introduced the puppy Luke to his mother, who was fascinated by the idea of adopting and saving a dog in need. They went home, everyone was happy. Cindy was for saving a puppy; Luke was happy because he was no longer on the street, and Cindy's parents because that animal would help Cindy to become more responsible.

Gradually, as time passed, Luke was still very small, so he was very active and wreaked havoc; he broke furniture, shoes, magazines, bags and everything that was within his reach. He ate all the food that fell to the ground, peed and poo everywhere. Cindy was a little disappointed that raising a puppy was much more difficult than she thought. However, her parents always supported and guided her so that she wouldn't give up and therefore, with a lot of patience and dedication, Cindy managed to get Luke better.

Now Luke ate only what was served on his plate, he no longer broke furniture, magazines or bags. Sometimes he broke a shoe, but it was still a big improvement. Cindy taught him how to toilet on newsprint and taught him to go to the yard to get them out.

Two years later, Cindy decided to throw a birthday party for Luke, as it was the second anniversary of the day he was saved. Luke was still a puppy, but much more educated. He had a bell near his plate of food that rang when he was hungry, a device that gave him water by resting his paw on a button, and a dog door through which he went out into the garden when he needed to free himself.

-Cindy: Dad! Mom and I go to the pet shop to buy Luke a new toy.
-Father: Good luck. He likes toys that make sounds.
-Cindy: I know.
-Father: Buy him some of that special grilled food he likes so much.
-Cindy: I was thinking about buying him a packet of dog cake that I saw the other day, I think he'd like to try something new.
-Father: Okay.
-Cindy: See you later dad.
-Father: Wait Cindy, which pet shop do you go to?
-Cindy: The one that is three streets north.
-Father: There is a pharmacy on the street, do you know what it is?
-Cindy: Yes, why?
-Father: Can you buy me some pills there?
-Cindy: Sure, give me the prescription and I'll buy them.
-Father: Thank you very much.
So Cindy went out with her mother to buy Luke's gifts and her father's medicines, but what she didn't know was that she'd be in for an unpleasant surprise when she returned. When Cindy went out with her mother, Luke went to the window to see them, but as soon as he looked out he saw a cat that was always chasing when he went out into the garden, and Luke ran to get it. Cindy's father, seeing the situation, ran to try to catch Luke, but he was too slow and as he ran, he watched Luke go further and further until he lost sight of him. After an hour, Cindy and her mother returned home and saw Cindy's father crying. Worried, they ran to him to find out what had happened.

-Mother: What happened?
-Father: I couldn't avoid it, I ran and ran but I couldn't reach it.
-Mother: What are you talking about?
-Cindy: Luke .... He didn't come out to greet me. Where is it?
-Mother: Is it for Luke? He ran away?
-Father: Yes, he went out to chase the cat he always chases but he didn't stop, he ran and ran until I lost sight of him.
-Cindy: It's not possible, which path did you take?
-Father: He ran north for two blocks, then he turned left, went on for another block, then right, and there I lost him.

Cindy was very sad, she didn't understand how Luke was able to escape after two years of many games, so much love and food they shared. Quickly, Cindy remembered that Luke had been given a tracking necklace, so she ran to get the phone to try and locate Luke. So he did, he opened the app on his phone and saw the route that Luke had taken in the last few hours and Cindy's father was right, he went north for two blocks, then he turned left and then right, he continued like this about two blocks, then he turned right again, reached the square and stopped there. Then Cindy, along with her parents, hurried to look for him, and when they reached the square Luke started moving again, but this time much faster than before. As they crossed the square, they saw the cat that Luke had chased over a tree and several people were trying to get him down, so Cindy stopped and walked over to ask them if they had seen their dog.

-Cindy: Have you seen Luke?
-Straniero 1: Who?
-Cindy: Excuse me, did you happen to see a dog chasing this cat?
-Straniero 1: No girl, sorry.
-Straniero 2: Maybe I do, how is it made?
-Cindy: It is a white dog with brown spots, very hairy and looks like a cocker spaniel.
-Straniero 2: I think I saw him get in the car with someone.
-Cindy: HOW !?
- Stranger 2: I remember someone gave him food and water and put him in his vehicle.
-Cindy: Thank you very much.

Cindy ran back to her parents' car and told them what the stranger had told her and started crying because she thought someone had stolen her dog. Her parents tried to calm her down but couldn't. In tears, Cindy told them to catch the dog thief using the locator on Luke's collar, and they did. Cindy entered the app and they followed the path shown by the app until she finally stopped moving.

-Cindy: Hurry up dad, it stopped moving! Turn left here and continue right.

-Father: This leads us to ...
-Cindy: Hurry up, which brings us to Luke.

Unexpectedly, the GPS path brought them home. Puzzled, they quickly got out of the car to see if Luke was there incredibly ... Luke had come home! But how was that possible? How did Luke manage to get home after so far? The answer was related to Luke's collar. There was a letter that said:

"Hello Struss family,

I was walking around town when her dog ran after me chasing the neighbor's cat. Realizing that none of you were with him, I followed him to see where he would go. I tried to call you but I had left my phone at home. I followed Luke to the park, where the cat climbed a tree and the game ended. I saw that his collar had a locator, so I waited a bit to see if you would come to the square to look for it. Since you didn't arrive and Luke was friendly to me, I decided to put him in the car to take him back to his house. Here is Luke, safe and sound.

Regards, Francis "

Now it all made sense, the neighbor was the one who had found Luke and who had brought him home. Cindy was so happy to see Luke again, she thought she had lost him forever. In recognition, Cindy and her parents decided to invite the neighbor to Luke's "birthday party", where everyone ate and played with Luke.

Summary

English

There was a girl named Cindy who was an animal lover. One day, while walking with her father, she picked up a street puppy that had been abandoned in a box. She named the puppy, Luke. At first, Luke was very disastrous and did not pay attention to what Cindy or her parents told her. Cindy was disappointed in herself for not being able to train a puppy, but her parents motivated her to continue trying with patience and dedication and the effort paid off. Luke had learned and improved a lot. He no longer broke things and went to do his needs where he had to, and not just anywhere. On the second anniversary of Luke's rescue, Cindy decided to throw him a party. So she went out to buy him a gift along with her mother. Luke stayed at home with his father. However, Luke, seeing the neighborhood cat, ran out to catch him and Cindy's father couldn't stop him. When Cindy came back and heard that Luke had escaped, she decided to go out and look for him using the locator on his necklace. They followed the GPS path to a square, where a stranger told Cindy that someone had taken Luke in his vehicle. Cindy was very worried because she thought her dog had been stolen. She continued to follow the GPS path until she strangely returned home, where Luke was. Wondering how Luke had come home, they found a note on his dog's collar explaining that it was the neighbor who returned him, so they invited him to Luke's party and enjoyed it all together.

Espanol

Había una chica llamada Cindy que era una amante de los animales. Un día, mientras caminaba con su padre, recogió un cachorro callejero que había sido abandonado en una caja. Llamó al cachorro, Luke. Al principio, Luke fue muy desastroso y no prestó atención a lo que le dijeron Cindy o sus padres. Cindy estaba decepcionada de sí misma por no haber podido entrenar a un cachorro, pero sus padres la motivaron a seguir intentándolo con paciencia y dedicación y el esfuerzo valió la pena. Luke había aprendido y mejorado mucho. Ya no rompía cosas y se iba a hacer sus necesidades donde tenía que hacerlo, y no solo en cualquier lugar. En el segundo aniversario del rescate de Luke, Cindy decidió organizarle una fiesta. Así que salió a comprarle un regalo junto con su madre. Luke se quedó en casa con su padre. Sin embargo, Luke, al ver al gato del vecindario, corrió a atraparlo y el padre de Cindy no pudo detenerlo. Cuando Cindy regresó y se enteró de que Luke se había escapado, decidió salir y buscarlo usando el localizador de su collar. Siguieron el camino del GPS hasta una plaza, donde un extraño le dijo a Cindy que alguien se había llevado a Luke en su vehículo. Cindy estaba muy preocupada porque pensó que le habían robado a su perro. Continuó siguiendo la ruta del GPS hasta que extrañamente regresó a casa, donde estaba Luke. Preguntándose cómo había llegado Luke a casa, encontraron una nota en el collar de su perro que explicaba que fue el vecino quien lo devolvió, así que lo invitaron a la fiesta de Luke y lo disfrutaron todo juntos.

Vocabulary

English

Box, curiosity, puppy, hairy, abandoning, responsibility, disastrous, furniture, magazines, handbags, disappointed, giving up/quitting, newspaper, party, birthday, bell, paw, pet, toys, cake, pharmacy, recipe, window, love, quickly, locator, chase, spots, stolen, hurry.

Espanol

Caja, curiosidad, cachorro, peludo, abandono, responsabilidad, desastroso, muebles, revistas, bolsos, decepcionado, renunciar / renunciar, periódico, fiesta, cumpleaños, campana, pata, mascota, juguetes, pastel, farmacia, receta, ventana, amor , rápido, localizador, persecución, manchas, robado, prisa.

The Library Thief - El ladrón de la biblioteca

The main library of the city of Munich was the ideal library for lovers of reading, it was a veritable paradise of books. The library was gigantic, had more than four floors, one floor with science books, one floor with religion books, one floor with literature books, and one floor with entertainment books. There were many large tables with chairs for those who wanted to read in groups, small desks with chairs for those who wanted to read alone, hammocks for those who wanted to read more comfortably, a dining room on each floor where readers could go to eat and drink something (obviously without books) and air conditioning or heating depending on the time of year.

Carlos was an engineer, a lover of science and discovery, he went to the library three times a week to study and reread books on various subjects such as physics, mathematics, biology, chemistry, geography, thermodynamics and the like. He was looking for something to help him complete his project for a water-powered automobile engine. Carlos had all the features of a scientist; He was tall, thin, with glasses, short black hair, long arms and legs, big ears and a pointed nose.

Lila was a theologian, her passion was the different religions and beliefs that were around the world. Lila went to the library every day from 2 to 6 pm to read books on religion. He perfectly knew the history of each of the gods of Greek mythology such as Zeus, Poseidon, Hades, Apollo, Athena, Ares and others; He also knew the different gods of Norse mythology such as Odin, Thor, Balder, Tyr, Bragi and others; He knew very well the principles of religions such as atheism, Judaism, Buddhism, Islam, Christianity and Hinduism. Lila was brownish, with wavy black hair, brown eyes, tall and with a very athletic body, as she went to the gym every day when she left the library. She was a beautiful brunette who, upon entering the library, all eyes fell on her.

Sam and Brenda were a young couple who went to the library on Tuesdays and Thursdays after training for the college baseball team. Sam was part of the team and Brenda was part of the cheerleaders. Sam was young, tall, with straight blond hair, blue eyes that were hard to miss, and he was muscular because he trained hard to be in good baseball condition. Brenda was short, had very long brown hair, dropped to her waist, green eyes and probably the perfect body of a cheerleader. They went to the library to relax and unwind by reading entertainment books, such as comedies or crime and crime stories.

One day, Sam, Brenda, Lila and Carlos were all in the library, each in the usual ward, reading the books they liked, when suddenly an alarm started ringing very loud throughout the library, and so all the people headed towards the exit to evacuate the building. However, at the exit there were several security guards checking the people. While he was leaving, Carlos saw Lila and was amazed by her beauty. He was paralyzed to see the figure and the beautiful hair of that brunette girl.

-Carlos: Oh ... Hi ...
-Lila: Hi.
-Carlos: You know ... Do you know what happened?
-Lila: No, I arrived now just like you.
-Carlos: I understand. Wh ... what's your name?
-Lila: Another one ... Why do men have to be so perverted and harassing?
-Carlos: Hey ... sorry, I was just asking.
-Lila: Don't bother me.

Sam and Brenda were nearby and saw what was happening between Carlos and Lila.

-Sam: Look, the nerd is talking to the brunette everyone sees when he passes by.
-Brenda: Poor girl, she must be tired of being bothered by men.
-Sam: And that nerd might have no chance to be with her.
-Brenda: It depends, maybe he can do it.
-Sam: I don't think so.
-Brenda: What do you think happened? Did you see that the guards are checking people?
-Sam: There was probably a theft.
-Brenda: A book theft?
-Sam: Maybe. I do not know.

Eventually, everyone in the library went out and the guards made it clear that there was a thief. Someone had stolen several people's belongings in the library and the security cameras had no record of what had happened. There was a five-minute interval in which the cameras had stopped recording, and it coincided with the moment the thief committed the theft. The fact that a thief robbed several people inside the library in less than five minutes was unusual, no one could imagine how that was possible.

However, for a time, people were more careful about their belongings, and as there were no more thefts, people felt confident and safe in the library again.

But that peace and trust didn't last long ...

One day, Carlos, Lila, Brenda and Sam were back in the library when suddenly the alarm went off. All the people got out quickly and again there were guards at the exit checking the people, but this time Carlos was with them.

-Sam: Look, the nerd is with the guards today.
-Brenda: Do you think something has been stolen from him?
-Sam: Maybe, let's ask him ...
-Brenda: Okay.
-Sam: Hi, how are you?
-Carlos: Hi, I don't have time to talk, I need to find my hard drive.
-Sam: Was it stolen from you?
-Carlos: Yes, I was sitting reading and I fell asleep for a moment and when I woke up it was gone and there was no one around.
-Sam: Crazy.
-Carlos: That hard drive is my life, there are my years of research, my projects, my knowledge and my ideas, I need to recover it at all costs.
-Sam: My girlfriend and I have read a lot of books about crime and stuff, we have to trap the thief to catch him.
-Carlos: It's a good idea, we have to work together! Guardians don't and I don't think they will do anything about it.
-Brenda: Great, our names are Sam and Brenda.
-Carlos: My name is Carlos.

At that moment Lila was coming to the exit, walking fast and pushing all the people, until she got to where the guards were and shouted:

-Lila: LISTEN TO ME, WHOEVER YOU ARE! IT WILL BE BETTER FOR YOU THAT I FIND MY WATCH IN THE BAG BY TOMORROW. IF I DON'T FIND IT, I WILL COME TO LOOK FOR AND PRACTICE ALL THE FIGHTING LESSONS I DO IN THE GYM ON YOU!

Seeing her so upset, Sam, Brenda and Carlos realized that she too had been the victim of a theft, so they approached to talk to her.

-Carlos: Hey ... Hi again!
-Lila: Stop it, stop talking to me, I don't want any relationship or anything at all from you.
-Carlos: Wait ... I came here to tell you that me and the guys (Sam and Brenda) are going to set a trap to catch the thief, I will notify you when we catch him so you can get your watch back.
-Lila: Oh, I'm sorry, it wasn't my intention to treat you like that, I'm very upset, that watch is what I use for my workouts and many other things.
-Carlos: I know how you feel, my hard drive has been stolen.
-Lila: It shouldn't happen, a thief inside a library ... Absurd! How are they going to take it?
-Carlos: We will set a trap, a bait, and when he steals again we will catch him.
-Lila: I'm joining your group.
-Sam: Welcome to the library detectives.
-Brenda: Who said they called us that?

-Sam: Sounds good to me.
-Brenda: Not for me.
-Lila: No.
-Carlos No.

The four then began to reunite, creating a perfect plan to catch the thief. Sam and Brenda did some brainstorming about what they had read in the mystery books, Carlos was studying ways to create trap mechanisms and Lila was inventing the perfect bait based on the tricks that the gods of deception were making.

-Sam: I think Brenda and I should be the bait, since we're the ones who weren't stolen.
-Brenda: I think the same thing.
-Carlos: Sounds reasonable, but we have to give the thief the perfect time to commit the theft.
-Lila: I'll take care of this! I'll be the distraction, I'll pretend I'm falling in the middle of the library, then all the people will turn to see me, like they always do, and the thief will have the perfect time to steal and so we'll catch him.
-Carlos: Good idea.
-Lila: I need you to stand by me to help me get up.
-Carlos: Me?
-Lila: Yes, since I know you. Otherwise, if another man comes to help me, then he'll want to ask for my number or invite me for a coffee.
-Brenda: How annoying.
-Lila: Really.
-Carlos: Or ... Okay. But do we have any idea who the thief is?
-Sam: I think so, it must be someone working here in the library, because every time someone is robbed, the security cameras are disabled.
-Lila: It makes sense, that's why they didn't get it, when I was robbed, I watched every person acting suspiciously, but I didn't check the employees.
-Brenda: Right. So we're going to do this show every time there's a library employee around.
-Carlos: Perfect. Ok, this is the object is that we will let ourselves be stolen, a cell phone. As you know, when they steal a cell phone, the first thing they do is turn it off so it cannot be located, so I took this old cell phone I had at home, I took it apart and installed a small black ink pump in it. which is activated by pressing the key to switch off. This way, when the thief picks up the phone and tries to turn it off, the ink pump will explode, filling our thief with indelible ink. So at the exit, the person who will be covered in ink will be guilty of the thefts.
-

Lila: Wow, what a great invention, you are very smart.
-Carlos: Gra ... Thanks.

-Lila: When we recover your hard drive, you should show me all your projects. If they are as interesting as the cell phone comes out, I would really like to see them all.
-Carlos: Ok.

Carlos and Lila continued talking when Brenda whispered to Sam:

-Brenda: I told you.
-Sam: What?
-Brenda: Maybe they could get together.
-Sam: Do you think?
-Brenda: Yes, they are both very intelligent people, with opposite tastes and passions, he is a man of science and she is a fanatic of religions. Also, he's not like other stalkers who talk to her, he's respectful and kind, he's not an idiot.
-Sam: We'll see if you're right, that would be great.

Then they put their plan into action to catch the library thief. Everything was in place, the cell phone came out on the table, Sam and Brenda were nearby, Lila was preparing to fall and Carlos was ready to help her. They just had to wait for a library employee to arrive. The first employee who walked by was the doorman and the team didn't hesitate to test their plan. Everything went perfectly, Lila's fall attracted everyone's attention, Sam and Brenda turned away from the cell phone to see what had happened and Carlos helped Lila, but the plan failed, because the porter also approached to help Lila.

A few days later, they put the plan into action again, this time with one of the guards, however, the cell phone still remained there on the table.

The third time they put the plan into action, it was with the librarian. They weren't convinced it was her, but they did it anyway and to their surprise, when Sam and Brenda returned to the table, the cell phone was going off. Someone had taken it. They ran from surveillance to report that the thief had struck again, the guards immediately activated the alarms and everyone who was present began to evacuate the library. Sam, Brenda, Carlos and Lila were looking for the librarian, but there was no sign of her anywhere. They waited until the library was empty but they never saw it leave. Disappointed by the failure of their plan, they were on their way home when the completely ink-stained librarian suddenly emerged from the women's bathroom. The team was filled with excitement about unmasking the thief but were very disappointed that she was the librarian, whom they had known for a long time.

As she was about to leave, Carlos questioned her.

-Carlos: How are you doing? What happened to your clothes?

- Librarian: Eehmm nothing, this is nothing, it is .... it is the fault of a pen that exploded.
-Carlos: Are you sure?
- Librarian: Yes, sure.
-Carlos: Guards, check her bag please.
- Librarian: Don't you dare control me, I'm your boss.
-Carlos: She's the thief, check her out.

After a few quarrels, the guards were able to check her bag and realized that she was the thief. They took her cell phone and gave it to Sam and Brenda, then they went to her office and analyzed it completely and found all the other things she had stolen on a shelf. There were watches, wallets, Lila's watch, Carlos's hard drive and many other personal possessions.

At the end of the day, everyone was very happy to have caught the library thief, who turned out to be the librarian. To celebrate they decided to dine in a restaurant where all four had a great time.

-Lila: I have to go now, I'm late.
-Sam: Oh, you're right! We must go too.
-Brenda: Right.
-Carlos: Where are you going?
-Lila: I'm going home, three blocks from here.
-Carlos: You shouldn't walk alone on the street so late, I'll accompany you.
-Lila: I was hoping you would say that.
-Carlos: From ... Really?
-Lila: Yes, let's go my knight.
-Sam: Hi, good luck.
-Brenda: Hi.

When Lila and Carlos left, Sam and Brenda stayed talking.

-Brenda: Who was it that was right?
-Sam: You, as always.
-Brenda: This is what I wanted to hear.
-Sam: Hahaha

Summary

English

In the immense and perfect central library of Monaco, which consists of four floors; four people: Carlos, Lila, Brenda, and Sam will be the protagonists of this story. Carlos was an engineer who read many science books, Lila a theologian who read books about religions every day, and Sam and Brenda a couple of young university students who went to the library to read books for entertainment. The four of them didn't know each other, until one day; there was a first robbery in the library. The alarms started ringing and everyone was sent to evacuate. The guards were standing at the exit checking all the people to see if they could find the thief. When Carlos sees Lila, and because of how beautiful she was, he tries to talk to her, but she rejects him. When Sam sees the scene, he laughs at the nerd that is trying to talk to that beautiful brunette. However, Brenda said not to laugh, that it was possible that they liked each other.

Things settled down a bit, but the second robbery happened at some time later, when Carlos was robbed of a hard drive that was very important to him. Sam and Brenda, who read many crime books, offered to help him to set a trap for the thief. That same day, Lila's smartwatch was stolen, so Carlos decided to offer her to be on the team to catch the guilty.

They created a master plan, which was simple. Carlos created a cell phone that by pressing the power button would explode an ink bomb that would stain the thief. To give the thief a chance to steal it, Lila would be the distraction, falling in the middle of the library. Sam and Brenda would get up from the table where they would leave the cell phone trap to steal. The plan was put into practice several times. The first time they set the trap to a doorkeeper, who was innocent; then to a guard who was also innocent, and the last time, they set the trap to the librarian, who turned out to be the library thief.

After so much time together planning and perfecting the plan, the team ended up being friends. So the day they caught the thief, they decided to go celebrate at a restaurant. At the end of dinner, Lila got up to leave and Carlos offered to go with her and she gladly accepted. So Brenda reminded Sam that she had told him that there was a chance that they would be together.

Espanol

En la inmensa y perfecta biblioteca central de Mónaco, que consta de cuatro pisos; cuatro personas: Carlos, Lila, Brenda y Sam serán los protagonistas de esta historia. Carlos era un ingeniero que leía muchos libros de ciencia, Lila una teóloga que leía libros sobre religiones todos los días, y Sam y Brenda una pareja de jóvenes universitarios que iban a la biblioteca a leer libros para entretenerse. Los cuatro no se conocieron, hasta un día; hubo un primer robo en la biblioteca. Las alarmas empezaron a sonar y todos fueron enviados a evacuar. Los guardias estaban parados en la salida revisando a toda la gente para ver si podían encontrar al ladrón. Cuando Carlos ve a Lila, y por lo guapa que era, intenta hablar con ella, pero ella lo rechaza. Cuando Sam ve la escena, se ríe del nerd que está tratando de hablar con esa hermosa morena. Sin embargo, Brenda dijo que no se riera, que era posible que se agradaran.

Las cosas se calmaron un poco, pero el segundo atraco sucedió algún tiempo después, cuando a Carlos le robaron un disco duro que era muy importante para él. Sam y Brenda, que leyeron muchos libros sobre crímenes, se ofrecieron a ayudarlo a tenderle una trampa al ladrón. Ese mismo día, le robaron el reloj inteligente de Lila, por lo que Carlos decidió ofrecerle estar en el equipo para atrapar a los culpables.

Crearon un plan maestro, que era simple. Carlos creó un teléfono celular que al presionar el botón de encendido haría explotar una bomba de tinta que mancharía al ladrón. Para darle al ladrón la oportunidad de robarlo, Lila sería la distracción, cayendo en medio de la biblioteca. Sam y Brenda se levantaban de la mesa donde dejarían la trampa del celular para robar. El plan se puso en práctica varias veces. La primera vez que le tendieron la trampa a un portero, que era inocente; luego a un guardia que también era inocente, y la última vez le tendieron la trampa al bibliotecario, que resultó ser el ladrón de la biblioteca.

Después de tanto tiempo juntos planeando y perfeccionando el plan, el equipo terminó siendo amigo. Así que el día que atraparon al ladrón, decidieron ir a celebrarlo a un restaurante. Al final de la cena, Lila se levantó para irse y Carlos se ofreció a acompañarla y ella aceptó con mucho gusto. Así que Brenda le recordó a Sam que le había dicho que existía la posibilidad de que estuvieran juntos.

Vocabulary

English

Library, perfect/ideal, lovers, paradise, giant, floors, desks, hammocks, cafeteria, air conditioning, engineer, discovery, review, engine, automobile, appearance, scientist, theologian, passion, religion, belief, history, Greek mythology, Nordic mythology, brunette, couple, team, muscled, cheerleader, comedy, alarm, evacuate, stalker, thief, steal, belongings, cameras, record, rare, confident, quickly, hard drive, whoever, wherever, smartwatch, trap, catch, upset, decoy, detectives, distraction, pretend, suspicious, guilty, invention, bomb, explode, ink, librarian, struggle, celebrate, late.

Espanol

Biblioteca, perfecto / ideal, amantes, paraíso, gigante, pisos, escritorios, hamacas, cafetería, aire acondicionado, ingeniero, descubrimiento, revisión, motor, automóvil, apariencia, científico, teólogo, pasión, religión, creencia, historia, mitología griega, Mitología nórdica, morena, pareja, equipo, musculoso, animadora, comedia, alarma, evacuar, acosador, ladrón, robar, pertenencias, cámaras, grabar, raro, confiado, rápido, disco duro, quien sea, donde sea, reloj inteligente, trampa, captura, trastornar, señuelo, detectives, distracción, fingir, sospechoso, culpable, invención, bomba, explotar, tinta, bibliotecario, luchar, celebrar, tarde.

Lost in the Woods – Perdidos en el bosque

It was 2009 when a group of friends decided to organize a trip to the woods near the outskirts of the city, where they would walk, reach rivers and waterfalls, enter caves, climb mountains and camp. The idea came from a TV show that all of them watched, in which a man, together with his family, faced nature in different situations in places like jungles, forests, deserts, snow-capped mountains and other ecosystems.

The group consisted of eight friends, Fred, Michael, Hugh, Brad, Lindsey, Carolina, Daniela and Esther. Fred was the youngest of them all, but he was the bravest and the boldest, and it was he who had had the idea of making the trip; Michael was the greatest of all, he was a lover of nature and wanted to know it and live it fully; Hugh was a little older than Fred, but he was the opposite, that is, he was fearful and cowardly, and he was afraid of everything; Brad was older than Hugh and was the hippie of the group. As for women, Carolina was the youngest, she was Fred's partner and she loved her boyfriend's adventurous and risky ideas; Daniela was very similar to Hugh, she was terrified to get out of her comfort zone, she was always very negative for everything that was new to her; Esther was a lover of extreme sports, she was the one who planned all the activities they would do during the trip, among which she had proposed "abseiling" and other things, but the others did not approve. Finally Lindsey, she was the daughter of a very rich couple, so she had always lived between luxury, which is why she wanted to go on a trip with them, to have a new and stimulating experience.

In 2009 when they started planning the trip, Fred and Carolina were still 16 years old, so to travel without adults they would have to wait another two years and be of age. So they did. The whole group planned every moment of the journey during these two years of waiting. They bought non-perishable food and essentials such as tents, bags, lanterns, ropes, coats and various utensils.

Then came the year 2011, Carolina had turned 18 before Fred, so everyone got ready to go camping one day after Fred's birthday. When his birthday then came, they decided not to party to have more energy for the next day's trip. They all stayed home, went to bed early so that the big day would come sooner. Fred at home celebrated his birthday with his parents and he too went to bed early. The next day, Michael woke up at 5:00 in the morning because he was driving his father's car and taking everyone into the woods. He checked the tire pressure, checked the coolant, oil, gasoline, spare tire and loaded all his stuff. Then he went to get each of his friends.
Hugh and Brad were neighbors, so he picked them both up at the same time. It was 6:00 am when he came to pick them up, they were still half asleep, so

they got in the car and said nothing. Then he took Carolina, who lived nearby, she was very energetic as she had drunk several cups of coffee before leaving.

-Carolina: Hi guys, how are you? Aren't you excited? I am very much! But how are you sleepy? How can you be sleepy? The big day has finally arrived! Finally we leave for this journey, I couldn't wait any longer!
-Michael: Carolina, calm down! It's 6:15, relax a bit, first we have to take the others and then we start the journey.
-Carolina: Oh, how boring you are, there are people who get up early puts them in a bad mood, you must be one of them. I'm not, I'm perfect.
-Michael: As you say.

So Michael went to get Esther, Daniela and Lindsey. Carolina kept talking and talking while the others tried to get some more sleep. They finally got to Fred's house at 6:45 am

-Fred: Good morning, how are you? You're right on time, as expected.
-Michael: Right, all according to plan.
-Carolina: Hello my love, good morning. How did you spend your birthday yesterday? I missed you a lot, I couldn't wait for the big day to come! The others are boring, today our journey finally begins and those lazy ones just want to sleep.
-Fred: Love, did you have coffee right?
-Carolina: Yes, a little, why?
-Fred: How many cups?
-Carolina: Only one.
-Fred: Tell the truth.
-Carolina: Maybe three, hehehe
-Fred: Are you sure?
-Carolina: Okay, I had four cups of coffee, I was very sleepy and after taking the first I woke up a bit, but then without realizing it while I was waiting for Michael I poured another one and another ...
-Fred: You took too much, try to calm down a bit.
-Carolina: Okay, uffa! You appreciate neither my energy nor my good mood. And so began the journey they had planned for so long. They had three routes recorded in the GPS, option A, option B and option C. If used well, each of them would take them to their destination at 9:15 am.
As they approached the place of arrival, they were losing sleep and everyone began to get excited little by little, except Carolina who had been excited since she left her house.

They had planned to spend five days there in the woods. They had already bought everything: hamburger bread, hot dog bread, sausages, meat for the grill, a grill for cooking over the fire, charcoal, sodas, water, chocolates, marshmallows, insect repellent, sunscreen and many other resources that they would use it during their stay.

As expected, they arrived at their destination at 9:15 am. They parked the car in a safe place, collected all the things they had brought for the camp and started walking. Esther was in charge of reading the map, she had experience with it because she had already gone camping several times with her father, who had taught her to read maps, and this made her the right person to lead the group of friends. After walking for two and a half hours they arrived in the area where they were going to camp the first night. They each set up their own tent, unpacked and ate sandwiches, as it was already 1.30pm. Just as planned.

-Michael: It's already 1:30 pm it's time to eat sandwiches.
-Fred: Finally, I was starving.
-Lindsay: Mine are wholemeal sandwiches.
-Esther: I thought you came here to get out of your fantasy world and enjoy nature, something different and new.
-Lindsay: This is what I have in mind, but I can't get out of my diet.
-Daniela: I want plain sandwiches please, I don't want my stomach to hurt here in the middle of nowhere.
-Esther: It would have been better to come with my little brother, he doesn't complain and asks for less.
-Hugh: Your little brother is unaware of the risks of such a trip.
-Brad: Quiet brother, nature will do nothing to us if we do nothing to it. Feel our energies.
-Michael: You don't want to start with your mystical and weird hippie stuff, do you?

In addition to eating and talking, they rested a little, because walking in the forest for two and a half hours with the unevenness of the ground was not an easy task. After getting enough rest (always according to plan), they all went into tents and changed their clothes, put on their bathing suits and put on sunscreen and repellent, as they would go to some lakes about 15 minutes away from where they were. camp on the map. They all came out of the tents wearing their bathing suits, Esther grabbed the map and started walking. After about 10 minutes they could see the lake and it was something impressive. The lake was amazing, everyone was speechless to see so much beauty, the perfection of nature.
The water was calm, and it was so clear and clean that it appeared to be glass. They immediately rushed to that wonderful place so they could swim and play there in the water.

Upon reaching the lake, Brad was the first to jump into the water.

-Brad: Quick guys, dive in! The water is delicious.
-Hugh: Brad, we don't know if there are fish or parasites in that water, or if there are leeches, or if it's contaminated.

-Daniela: Hugh is right, we can't just get in the water and ...
Fosso: Go inside Daniela!

Fred had pushed Daniela into the lake.

-Fred: Hugh, do you have anything else to say?
-Hugh: No Fred, I dive too.
-Fred: Here.
-Lindsey: I hope I don't get an allergy or a rash for coming here, if anything happens to me it's your fault.
-Esther: It's the clean water of a lake, what can happen to you?
-Carolina: Come on, nothing will happen to us, we are not the first to take a bath here, look over there.

Carolina pointed to a place where there were the remains of a bonfire and a pile of garbage on the ground.

-Michael: I don't understand why people have to be so dirty, it costs nothing to pick up trash.
-Brad: Human beings are dirty by instinct, they don't feel part of nature and that's why they don't care about dirtying and contaminating.
-Michael: In this I support you.
-Esther: We have brought enough garbage bags, we can collect what they left there, so the place will not be contaminated and we can continue our journey.
-Fred: Good idea, we should also leave a sign that says: "Don't leave the garbage here, take care of the environment"
-Carolina: I love this idea, love, how smart you are.
-Fred: Thanks baby, never as much as you.
-Daniela: Please don't start. Yes, you are both smart, that's enough.
-Carolina: What I hate.
-Daniela: Hahahaha you are cloying.
-Carolina: Of course not, do you think we are cloying?
-Lindsey: Ehhmm, what time is it?
-Michael: It's 2:30 pm, we will stay here until 5:30 pm and then we will go back to the camp, as scheduled, do you agree?
-Carolina: Don't ignore me.
-Brad: Yes Michael, perfect.
-Hugh: Got it.
-Esther: Let's enjoy the moment then.
-Daniela: Get in the water, it's great, Brad was right.
-Carolina: Guys? You are ignoring me.
-Michael: Go for it!
-Lindsay: Here I am.

And so everyone, ignoring Carolina's question, entered the water of that beautiful lake, where they swam, played, tried to fish, jumped off some very high rocks that were there and enjoyed immensely. The time to leave was approaching, and although they didn't want to leave because of how much fun they were having, they had to because it would get dark soon and they hadn't brought their torches with them, because according to the plan they had made, they would return to the camp still the sunlight. When they arrived there was hardly any light left, so they hastened to take their flashlights to change. They put on dry clothes and searched for charcoal, firewood, and everything they needed to make a fire so they could cook sausages for the hot dogs they were going to eat for dinner.

Esther, once again, was the wisest, thanks to her camping experiences with her father, and so it was she who decided to light the bonfire. However Lindsey asked Esther if she could help her, as she always wanted to learn how to do it. Daniela and Hugh had obviously drifted a little away from the place, because they were afraid that the fire would spread uncontrollably and that they might burn.

-Esther: So Lindsay, first make sure neither the wood nor the coal is wet, okay?
-Lindsay: Got it.
-Esther: Then make a circle with the largest pieces of firewood, put the smaller pieces inside and finally put coal on top of that wood. So.
-Lindsay: Okay. I got it.
-Esther: Then, you can put the newspaper to start lighting the fire or use some gasoline. Sometimes the newspaper is better so it doesn't smell like gasoline, but with gasoline it's faster. Light the fire and keep it burning until the coals turn red, and the bonfire is ready.
-Lindsay: It's easier than I thought.
-Esther: I wouldn't be so sure, try it yourself.
-Lindsay: Great, thank you very much.
To everyone's surprise, Lindsay managed to start a nice fire, so she was very happy. Michael and Brad cooked the sausages for dinner, Carolina and Lindsey cut the bread for the hot dogs while Fred and Hugh poured the sauces over them. Daniela and Esther were talking to themselves in one of the tents.

-Esther: Still not telling him?
-Daniela: No, I'm sorry.
-Esther: Don't be silly, tell him, I'm sure he feels the same thing.
-Daniela: I don't think so, he is unlikely to like someone like me.
-Esther: What are you saying? You are made for each other. You and Hugh are very similar, I'm sure he likes you.
-Daniela: Do you believe?
-Esther: I'm sure, I saw how he looks at you, and he's always close to you.
-Daniela: I hope it's true.
-Esther: You have to tell him while we're here on the road.

-Daniela: I'll keep that in mind ...
-Brad: Daniela and Esther come and eat, dinner is ready.

Esther and Daniela left the tent and sat down to eat. The food was delicious, they talked about how much they enjoyed the trip, that it was worth waiting for, checked the next day's schedule, looked at the stars together for a while and then went to sleep. While everyone was sleeping, it started raining. It rained a lot for several hours and suddenly thunder fell and woke Esther. Esther, half asleep, listened to the rain and thought, "I think I left something out, something important that shouldn't get wet, will it be my shoes? The bag? I don't remember, it's probably nothing "and he went on sleeping. The next morning, everyone woke up, left the tents, greeted each other and saw that there was a lot of mud. They had breakfast and dismounted the whole camp, because according to the itinerary, that day they had to walk 17 km to the next point of the journey, where they would set up the camp, and then they would go to visit a cave near that place and they would see the waterfall they would go to on the third day. While they were gathering their things, Esther kept thinking about what she had forgotten outside, which was so important but she couldn't remember what it was. When everything was collected, and everyone was ready to go, Fred spoke.

-Fred: We're ready Esther, guide us.

At that moment Esther remembered him; She remembered having forgotten the map outside her tent, she had taken her out the night before to check the route and had moved near the fire to take advantage of the light but then Daniela told her to speak and they entered the tent without the map.

-Esther: Oh my God ...
-Fred: what?
-Esther: it can't be, it can't be.
-Daniela: What's going on Esther?
-Hugh: Speak, what is it?
-Esther: I'm so sorry, I ruined everything, the whole trip is ruined.
-Hugh: Explain yourself better.
-Esther: You remember that yesterday I was looking at the map before going to talk to Daniela, right?
-Michael: Right.
-Esther: And then we had dinner ...
-Carolina: Exactly.
-Esther: And then we saw the stars and went to sleep.
-Brad: Sure, then?
-Esther: I never took the map back, I didn't put it in place.
-Hugh: Oh no.
-Daniela: Are you kidding?
-Esther: I wish it were so.

-Lindsay: You mean that ...?
-Hugh: WE ARE LOST! We got lost in the middle of this forest! WE ARE ABOUT TO DIE! I knew it was not a good idea to come here, I should have stayed at my house!
-Daniela: WHAT HAPPENED TO YOU ESTHER !? YOU HAVE NOT COLLECTED THE MAP, THE MOST IMPORTANT THING OF OUR TRIP! YOU COULD FORGET THE WATER, YOU COULD FORGET THE CHOCOLATE, YOU COULD FORGET A TROUSERS, BUT YOU FORGOTTEN THE MAP!
-Brad: Hey calm down, there is no point in looking for the culprits, everything has a solution and we have to find it. Esther is not to blame, we all should have been careful of the map! The eight of us are in the forest, not just Esther.
-Carolina: Exactly, let's calm down and think a bit, let's look for solutions, we still have food and supplies for another two days, it took two hours to get here from the car, I doubt it will take us more than three days to get back.
-Fred: Exactly, however, if someone has some battery in their phone we can use the GPS to guide us, it's not very accurate, but it will give us an idea of where we should go.
-Michael: Exactly, who still has some battery?
-Lindsay: I have 34%, my phone has the best battery of current phones on the market.
-Michael: Perfect, how long does it last?
-Lindsay: About 6 hours.
-Michael: Well, let's not waste time and let's go.
-Brad: Well said brother. Seen? Everything has a solution.
-Lindsay: I'm already activating the GPS.

Lindsay activated the GPS of her cell phone and little by little they were returning to where they had left the car, sometimes they had to go back because they took the wrong path as the GPS was not very accurate. They walked and walked and three of the six hours had passed when they were about halfway there. There was already 19% battery left on Lindsay's phone, as active GPS drained the battery faster. They kept walking and it was already 12:30. The sun was very strong, Lindsay checked her cell phone and said that the perceived temperature was 43 ° C. So the boys decided to stop for a while to hydrate and rest, as they had been walking for more than three hours without stopping. They rested for half an hour, didn't talk much, were exhausted, upset and a little worried about getting lost forever in the woods. After the break, they continued on their way, walking for another half hour when Lindsay stopped.

-Hugh: What's wrong?
-Lindsay: Bad news.
-Hugh: Again?

-Lindsay: I have lost the connection to the GPS, I have no signal on my mobile.
-Hugh: It can't be, now we're going to die.
-Daniela: We were missing this.
-Michael: Does anyone with a little battery have the signal?
-Brad: No.
-Fred: Not a bit.
-Carolina: Not even.
-Daniela: Nothing.
-Esther: I don't even have battery anymore.
-Hugh: Me too nothing.
-Lindsay: What do we do now?
-Fred: In the TV program we watch they said that the sun always hides towards a certain cardinal point.
-Esther: Right, it was east.
-Michael: I think it's west.
-Brad: Me too.
-Carolina: I don't remember.
-Fred: We have to go northwest from here, so the east is towards the side opposite which the sun is hidden, so we have to follow the sun and walk a little towards the right side of what is hidden. Hopefully, then we should get to Michael's car and be able to leave.

They followed the sun and were moving north as well, but they had no idea how far north or how far they had to go, they just knew they had to follow the sun. They walked and walked until 4pm. They no longer had the strength to keep walking, so they decided to stay there and wait for the next day. They began to set up the camp. Daniela and Hugh were upset by Esther, still accusing her of losing the map and getting lost because of her. Esther, super sorry and repentant, kept apologizing for making that mistake.

Brad, Michael and Fred secretly met to discuss the situation, Michael was starting to worry, they had no idea how long it would take to get back to the car, they didn't know if they were on the right track, they didn't have resources for more than two days; they had to get back to the car before the third day or they would have no more food or water. Brad proposed that if they couldn't get to the car the next day, they would start rationing their food better so they could have a third day with the necessary resources. Michael and Fred thought it was a good idea, but they were sure that Hugh and Daniela would care a lot about it, and besides, they doubted Lindsay was willing to stop eating, which she used to do. On the other hand, Daniela and Hugh were talking about how negligent and irresponsible Esther was ...

-Daniela: I still can't believe Esther has forgotten something as important as the map.

-Hugh: It's a fatal mistake. We can die here by getting lost, we could die of hunger, of thirst, we could be prey to wild animals.
-Daniela: Don't say these things anymore please, I'm terrified just thinking about it.
-Hugh: Sorry, I'm very afraid something will happen to you.
-Daniela: How?
-Hugh: Ehh yes, I'm afraid that something will happen to all of us, that we will go home and one will be missing.
-Daniela: Ahh, so it's not just me?
-Hugh: Well, I care about everyone, but I care more about you.
-Daniela: I care a lot too.
-Hugh: Really?
-Daniela: Yes, you are the one I like the most in this group, I love the way you talk and how you treat me.
-Hugh: You know, I didn't know whether to tell you in case you didn't feel the same thing, but given the situation we're in, I want you to know.
-Daniela: What?
-Hugh: That I like you.
-Daniela: I like you too.

After saying this, Daniela grabbed Hugh by the hand and kissed him on the cheek. Esther, who was watching them, smiled at Daniela, but she was still angry and did not return the smile. Carolina sat next to Esther talking.

-Carolina: In the end they said it.
-Esther: Yes, I'm happy for them.
-Carolina: We just had to get them lost in a forest hahaha
-Esther: I don't think it's funny, it's my fault, Daniela is very angry with me.
-Carolina: You know she's like that. Don't worry, when we get out of here he'll forget.
-Esther: Do you think we can get out?
-Carolina: Absolutely, we still have two days, even three if we manage food and water well. And I no longer think we are very far from the finish.
-Esther: I hope so. I couldn't stand the guilt if something happened to any of you.
-Carolina: Don't worry, like Brad said, it's everyone's fault for not helping you.
-Brad: Hey, did you say my name?
-Carolina: No, you're crazy.
-Lindsay: I'm impressed, Brad always hears everything.
-Brad: Thanks.

Then they all had dinner together, talked and joked a little to improve the spirits and went to bed early, because the next day they had to keep walking to get out of that forest. No one had a battery in cell phones anymore, so whether or not there was a signal was no longer important.

It was already dawn when they heard music coming from somewhere. They all got up quickly to have breakfast and clear the field to go to the place where the music was coming from. They walked around for about half an hour until they found a park where people could camp, which had a swimming pool, soccer fields and all those things. They immediately ran to talk to the people.

-Fred: Good morning, how are you?
- Stranger: Good morning, do I know you?
-Fred: No sir, but we got lost in the forest. Where are we?
- Foreign: This is Adventure Camp Park.
-Fred: Do you know where the parking lot is on the hill?
- Foreign: About an hour and a half south. Do you have your car there?
-Fred: Yes, sir
- Stranger: Do you have a way to get there? Will you call a taxi?
-Fred: No sir, we don't have battery in any of our phones
- Stranger: Are you eight?
-Fred: Right.
- Stranger: Come on, I'll take you.
-Fred: Don't worry, we don't want to bother you.
-Hugh: Yes sir, take me please, I can't take it anymore.
- Stranger: Come on, I'll take you all, don't worry, you look exhausted and hungry. No problem.
-All: Thank you very much sir.

The stranger took the boys to their car, left them there, lent them his phone to call their parents and left. The boys put all their luggage in the car and drove home. They were shocked and disappointed that the trip did not go as planned.

-Brad: Guys, don't worry, we didn't miss the trip, we walked, we exercised, we camped two nights, we bathed in the lake, we survived the forest and nobody got hurt, Hugh and Daniela are finally together, Lindsay has learned how to make a bonfire and now we know that we have to bring more than one map for the next adventure.

With that motivating message, the kids were a little happier and decided to plan another trip for next year this time, taking better precautions.

Summary

English

It all started in 2009 when a group of friends watching a TV survival program together decided to take a trip to the forest to do various activities. They had to wait two years to make the trip because Fred, the youngest of them all, was still a minor in 2009. During those two years, they bought food and all the equipment, and they planned everything perfectly; everything had a start time and an end time. When Fred's 18th birthday arrived, everyone was excited to go on the trip they had planned so much. Fred didn't throw any birthday parties to get enough energy to go on the trip the next day.

When the day of the trip arrived, Michael got up early to check that everything related to the car they were going to travel in was in order, and then he went out to pick up his friends and travel for two and a half hours to the parking lot where they would leave the vehicle. They arrived at the parking lot, took everything related to the trip out, and started walking into the woods until they reached the place where they had decided to camp. They set up the camp and went for a walk to a beautiful lake nearby, enjoyed it there until the day began to get dark, and returned to the camp. In the camp, Esther was going to light the fire, but Lindsay asked her to teach her how to make one because she had always wanted to learn and Esther, without hesitation, did. When the bonfire was done, while some people were making dinner, Esther told Daniela that she should talk to Hugh and declare her feelings before it was too late. They had dinner and talked and went to bed. During the night, it rained a lot and thunder woke up Esther, who, half asleep, felt that she had forgotten something important that should not get wet. The next day, she realized that what she had forgotten was the map, so now they would be lost.

Michael was smart and thought about using the GPS on their cell phones and Lindsay offered to use hers until somewhere it lost the signal and the GPS stopped working. They walked following the sun for the rest of the day and when the sun went down, they set up camp and stayed there. That night, Hugh told Daniela how important she was to him, and so did she.

The next morning, they woke up listening to music coming from somewhere, had a quick breakfast and picked up the camp, and followed the sound of the music until they reached Camp Park Adventure, where an unknown man helped them to the car. They all returned home safe and secure.

Espanol

Todo empezó en 2009 cuando un grupo de amigos que veían juntos un programa de supervivencia en televisión decidieron hacer un viaje al bosque para realizar diversas actividades. Tuvieron que esperar dos años para hacer el viaje porque Fred, el más joven de todos, todavía era menor de edad en 2009. Durante esos dos años, compraron alimentos y todo el equipo, y planearon todo a la perfección; todo tenía una hora de inicio y una hora de finalización. Cuando llegó el cumpleaños número 18 de Fred, todos estaban emocionados de ir al viaje que tanto habían planeado. Fred no organizó ninguna fiesta de cumpleaños para tener suficiente energía para hacer el viaje al día siguiente.

Cuando llegó el día del viaje, Michael se levantó temprano para comprobar que todo lo relacionado con el coche en el que iban a viajar estuviera en orden, y luego salió a recoger a sus amigos y viajar durante dos horas y media a la estacionamiento donde dejarían el vehículo. Llegaron al estacionamiento, sacaron todo lo relacionado con el viaje y empezaron a caminar hacia el bosque hasta llegar al lugar donde habían decidido acampar. Montaron el campamento y fueron a caminar a un hermoso lago cercano, lo disfrutaron allí hasta que el día comenzó a oscurecer y regresaron al campamento. En el campamento, Esther iba a encender el fuego, pero Lindsay le pidió que le enseñara a hacer uno porque siempre había querido aprender y Esther, sin dudarlo, lo hizo. Cuando terminó la hoguera, mientras algunas personas preparaban la cena, Esther le dijo a Daniela que debería hablar con Hugh y declarar sus sentimientos antes de que fuera demasiado tarde. Cenaron, hablaron y se acostaron. Durante la noche llovió mucho y un trueno despertó a Esther, quien, medio dormida, sintió que se le había olvidado algo importante que no debía mojarse. Al día siguiente, se dio cuenta de que lo que había olvidado era el mapa, por lo que ahora estarían perdidos.

Michael era inteligente y pensó en usar el GPS en sus teléfonos celulares y Lindsay se ofreció a usar el de ella hasta que en algún lugar perdió la señal y el GPS dejó de funcionar. Caminaron siguiendo el sol durante el resto del día y cuando se puso el sol, acamparon y se quedaron allí. Esa noche, Hugh le dijo a Daniela lo importante que era para él, y ella también.

A la mañana siguiente, se despertaron escuchando música proveniente de algún lugar, tomaron un desayuno rápido y tomaron el campamento, y siguieron el sonido de la música hasta llegar a Camp Park Adventure, donde un hombre desconocido los ayudó a subir al auto. Todos regresaron a casa sanos y salvos.

Vocabulary

English

Walk, forest, city outskirts, rivers, waterfalls, caves, ecosystems, young, brave, opposite, fearful, coward, save, tents, non-perishable food, indispensable, ropes, lanterns, coats, drive, refrigerant, oil, spare tire, neighbours, excited, boring, miss, lazy, routes, approaching, hamburger bread, hot dog bread, sausages, coal, soft drinks, insect repellent, sunscreen, map, guide, unpack, luggage, hunger, very hungry, swimsuits, lakes, beauty, perfection, clear, clean, fish, parasites, leeches, pushing, garbage, filthy, sign, get in, dive, fishing, sunlight, firewood, dinner, learn, uncontrollably, burn, secure, wet, sauces, shame, silly, like, stars, rain, thunder, forgotten, sorry, ruined, lost, die, guilty, accurate, wrong way, thermal sensation, cardinal point, east, west, north, error/mistake, swimming pool, exhausted

Espanol

Caminata, bosque, afueras de la ciudad, ríos, cascadas, cuevas, ecosistemas, joven, valiente, opuesto, miedoso, cobarde, salva, carpas, comida no perecedera, indispensable, sogas, linternas, abrigos, drive, refrigerante, aceite, llanta de refacción , vecinos, emocionado, aburrido, señorita, perezoso, rutas, acercándose, pan de hamburguesa, pan de hot dog, salchichas, carbón, refrescos, repelente de insectos, protector solar, mapa, guiar, desempacar, equipaje, hambre, mucha hambre, trajes de baño, lagos belleza, perfección, claro, limpiar, pescado, parásitos, sanguijuelas, empujando, basura, sucio, firmar, entrar, bucear, pescar, luz del sol, leña, cena, aprender, incontrolablemente, quemar, seguro, mojado, salsas, vergüenza, tonto, me gusta, estrellas, lluvia, trueno, olvidado, lo siento, arruinado, perdido, morir, culpable, exacto, camino equivocado, sensación térmica, punto cardinal, este, oeste, norte, error / error, piscina, agotado

I am getting old – Me estoy poniendo viejo

Hi dear reader, this is my story, my name is Adam Williams, I am currently 55 years old, I am from Toronto, Canada. In these few pages I want to tell you about my life, what I have done and what I still have to do, I hope you like it and it will serve as a motivation to give a change to your present and therefore have a completely different future, full of fun and of good memories.

It all started when I was 7, my parents had jobs where they were paid enough to live on. When they were paid, they bought food, paid taxes and other things and the money ran out, there were no luxuries in our family like holidays or toys. One day, while I was going to the market with my father to buy food, I saw several of my friends playing in the square with their bicycles, I went to greet them and talk to them while my father went shopping. My friends were happy because David had bought the new bike and they were all playing with it to try it out. They told me that the next day they would go out again for cycling, that I could go with them if I wanted. I would have liked to go, but I didn't have a bike and I knew there was no chance my parents would buy me one, however, I told my dad. With tears in his eyes, he told me that he was very sorry, but that I knew they didn't have the money to buy me a bicycle. I understood that they worked all day, every day, to earn money and to be able to buy food and other things, but I did not understand why my friends' parents worked the same way or even less and they could buy new toys. I was very disappointed, because my friends would ride their bikes without me and they would have a lot of fun. A few months later, I was walking with my father and a lady nearby pulled a bicycle out of her house and was about to throw it in the garbage. My father and I were in awe, why was a woman about to throw away a bicycle? I immediately ran to her and asked her.

-Adam: Madam, why are you throwing that bike away?
-Lady: My son no longer liked him and I bought him another one.
-Adam: Just for that?
-Lady: Yes.
-Adam: Can I take it?

When I asked, my father, who was next to me, gave me a pinch.

-Adam: What?
-Father: Nothing
- Lady: Sure, no problem.
-Adam: Thank you very much, seriously.
-Lady: Don't worry.
-Adam: Really, thank you very much.

-Lady: Hey boy, do you want to earn some money? The grass is already a little tall. I have a lawnmower, if you mow my lawn I will pay you, if your father has nothing against it.
-Adam: Can I dad?
-Father: I think so, so you learn to work and see how hard it is to earn things.
-Adam: Great. When I come?
-Lady: Are you okay tomorrow, are you free?
-Adam: Yes.

I was decided, the next day I would go to that lady's house to mow the lawn, even if I didn't know very well how it was done, all the work would be done by the lawnmower, I just had to go through the whole garden. I went home rolling the new bike I had, as I'd never ridden one. My father tried to teach me, but one day was too little time to learn to ride a bicycle. The next day I went to that nice lady to mow the lawn, that day her husband was there, who explained to me how the lawnmower worked and what I should do with the lawn. I started mowing the lawn and in two hours I had almost the whole garden done, but suddenly a boy came out on a golden bicycle, the most beautiful bicycle I have ever seen, approached me looking at me and greeted me.
-Stan: Hi, I'm Stan, nice to meet you!
-Adam: Hi, I'm Adam, nice to meet you.
-Stan: My mom told me you took my old bicycle
-Adam: Right, thank you very much.
-Stan: Well, I'm glad you have it and not someone else.
-Adam: I see you changed it for a more beautiful one.
-Stan: Thanks, I love this. You should bring yours someday and let's ride here in the garden.
-Adam: Great, I'd love to, even if I don't know how to drive it yet.
-Stan: Put wheels on it and that's how you learn little by little.
-Adam: I hadn't thought about it.
-Stan: Well, I'll let you conclude that you are close to it.
-Adam: Thanks.

When I finished mowing the lawn, I picked up the garbage and went to tell the lady that I was finished, when, after ringing the bell, the lady's husband came out and told me that I had done a good job of being my first time. I wanted to go in and wait for my father, but just at that moment I heard my father's voice behind me, he had come to get me. The lady's husband gave me a $ 20 bill.

-Adam: Sir, that's a lot of money.
-George: Call me George. And it's not a lot of money, you used your time and tried to get everything right, even if you never did it before. You deserved them. Our time is our most important thing, it is what is worth more than any amount of money.

-Adam: I understand, thank you very much sir.
-George: Call me George. Will you come another day to play with Stan? He said he invited you to ride a bike.
-Adam: Yes, but first I have to learn how to drive it.
George: I understand. You can ring the doorbell of our house whenever you want, we are almost always here at home.
-Adam: I understand, thank you very much.

I left with my father, exhausted, but with my $ 20. My father asked me how I had gone and if I liked it, I told him it was something difficult, but I was very happy to see the pay. Walking home with my father, we passed a bicycle shop, where I saw that they were selling bicycle wheels, I asked my father if we could enter and he said yes with pleasure. Inside the shop, I went straight to see the price of the wheels, they were $ 5.99 and I also saw several cans of spray paint to paint the bikes. There were all the colors, what I liked best was the silver, because it reminded me how beautiful Stan's bike was all gold, and so I said I wanted mine in silver. I spent $ 14 in total purchasing the wheels and spray paint. My father congratulated me, he told me that I had seen a bit of how life works, which is to work hard to earn money and then spend it on things we want or need. We went home and put the wheels on the bike and started practicing. I drove for a while and then asked my dad to remove the wheels. It hadn't been fun at all, nor had I experienced any thrill riding a bike with wheels without the risk of falling. My father took off the wheels and I started practicing. I fell several times, some even quite hard. When I was able to ride my bike without falling, I asked my dad to paint my bike silver so I could go to Stan's house and ride a bike together.
As soon as I finished, my bike looked as beautiful as Stan's, so I rode my bike to his house and rang the bell. Stan's mom opened it to me.

-Adam: Good afternoon lady, how are you?
-Katy: You can call me Katy. I'm fine and you?
-Adam: Very good. Is Stan there?
-Katy: Sure, come on, I'll call him.
-Adam: Can I leave the bike here?
-Katy: Sure. Is that the bicycle I gave you?
-Adam: Yes.
-Katy: I see you repainted it, it's very nice.
-Adam: Thank you very much.
-Katy: Wait here, I'm going to find Stan.

As he went to find Stan, I took a look around the house. It was a simple house, but it was very clean and had very nice decorations and things. Everything sparkled and shone no matter how clean it was. Then Stan's mom came back.

-Katy: I wanted to tell you that the neighbors were impressed with the work you did with my garden.
-Adam: Well, I'm very happy.
-Katy: My husband asked me to tell you to prune the garden for the other neighbors, and if you get paid $ 30, $ 20 would be yours to prune the garden and $ 10 would be ours because we would loan you the lawn mower. What do you say?
-Adam: It sounds very good.
-Katy: Think about it and let me know if you're interested.
-Stan: Hi Adam, I'm ready, have you already learned to ride a bike?
-Adam: Come out so you can see.
-Stan: Okay. Is that my old bike?
-Adam: Right.
-Stan: You painted it silver, it's very beautiful, it looks like mine.
-Adam: I know.
That day I rode my bike for hours with Stan, I was happy, he was a good friend, sometimes I went out with my other friends, but I liked Stan more than them. Of course, I accepted the deal Mrs. Katy had proposed to me, worked a few hours and managed to save $ 100. I became so good friends with Stan that his parents invited my parents to lunch. My parents did not want to go there because they were sorry to go to them with worn out clothes. I still had the $ 100 aside, so I offered to buy them some sweaters and pants so they could go well dressed to eat with Stan's family and they did.
Being in their home, his parents started talking about work and how they made a living. Knowing that my parents worked with so much effort and were paid with so little money, they offered them a job in one of the businesses they had, my parents, with tears in their eyes but happy, took the job and it was then that everything. began to change for the better.

From that moment they worked less and earned more. Little by little our situation was improving, and at the end of each month there was always some money left that my parents saved. They could buy one or two pairs of shoes a month for each one, they could go to the cinema, to some park and so on. I also continued to be a gardener for Stan's family and his neighbors, so I also made my own money.

One day Mr. George called me, I was already 9 years old. He told me he wanted to talk to me about very important things.

-George: I want to ask you, what do you do with the money you earn as a gardener?
-Adam: I save them and buy things I need sometimes, why?
-George: Do you want to know why Katy and I are doing so well?
-Adam: What are you talking about?
- George: Of our activities.
-Adam: Ah ok. Because?

-George: We are not happy with working for money. We don't save money, we invest it.
-Adam: I don't understand.
-George: How much money have you saved?
-Adam: $ 100
-George: If you don't spend it, how many will be in 3 years?
-Adam: $ 100.
-George: That's right, the money saved is money that will always stay the same. On the other hand, if you invest it, it will generate more money.
-Adam: I think I understand.
-George: The lawn mower is an example, it cost me $ 150 and we lent it to you 18 times, and you give us $ 10 for every time we lend it to you. So we already have $ 180 which will keep increasing more and more if we keep lending it. This is an investment.
-Adam: I understand.

That day, I didn't really understand why Stan's dad explained that concept to me, I just wanted to ride a bike and go out and play sports with my friends. One day I went to Stan's house and they had bought him a new video game console, so expensive that none of my friends had it. Playing with Stan, I remembered George's speech to me and I remembered how much money he had saved. So, I came up with the idea of buying a console like that and renting it out so that others could play it for $ 5 an hour.

I did and in five days I had already got my money back.

When I turned 10, skateboards were all the rage, so Stan and I bought them and went there all day. We also signed up for swimming, and we were on a soccer team. In short, we practiced many sports. I kept investing my money and so I bought new things to play or to play sports.

At 14, I loved the beach, bought a surfboard and diving gear, and went to the beach every weekend with Stan. We played whatever sport there was, as our parents had taught us very well that video games damaged the brain and made people sedentary. Despite everything Stan and I did, our favorite sport was cycling, we had bikes of all kinds, road bikes, mountain bikes, cross and downhill bikes. We went out driving them every day, even if it was raining.

Growing up, I came up with good ideas for investing my money, when I was 18 I was earning $ 1,300 a month from my investments. Stan and I had joined the gym to gain muscle mass and meet some girls. Little by little we were changing our nights. We preferred spending evenings out with the girls and weekends at parties and clubs rather than riding a bike.
After graduating from high school, everyone went to different universities, Stan was studying medicine in the north and I was studying engineering there in Toronto. Stan left and so we communicated via video calls and texts,

but with how much I studied and how busy I was managing my investments, I sometimes didn't have time to answer him. I was in the third year of my school career when on a boring afternoon I was watching Xgames from motocross racing on TV. I loved that sport, so I checked my finances and bought a motorcycle to practice motocross. In the beginning it was great, the thrill of running, jumping and not falling was something completely new for me, on the bike there were a lot of things that couldn't be done because of the bike itself. Over time I got bored, because I was always alone, because Stan was gone and I didn't have time to make new friends.

Eventually I became sedentary, left the gym to take care of my studies and left sports to take care of business, and so the years passed. After my school career, I graduated as an electronic engineer. I married a very nice girl I met at the gym with whom I had a beautiful daughter and two sons.

I was about 35 when one day, while I was at home with the children, the doorbell rang, I got up from the recliner I had and opened the door. At first I didn't recognize the person in front of me, until he started talking and so I recognized his voice immediately.

-Stan: Aren't you going to say hello?
-Adam: STAN!
-Stan: Hehehe, how are you, old friend?
-Adam: All very well, I didn't recognize you, it's been a lot of time. Come, welcome to my home.
-Stan: I'm happy, that's right, I've been very busy traveling to medical conferences. You have a nice house, it reminds me a little of mine.
-Adam: Hahaha, you noticed, I borrowed some ideas.
-Stan: I understand.
-Adam: These are my children, Lucy, Aaron and Lucas.
-Stan: Lucas looks like you as a kid.
-Adam: That's what everyone says. My wife isn't here, she went out on errands.
-Stan: Quiet, I'll be staying here in the city for several months.
-Adam: Really?
-Stan: I'm on vacation and I came to visit my parents.
-Adam: Well, I visited them a few weeks ago and they didn't tell me you were coming.
-Stan: They didn't know, it was a surprise for them too.
-Adam: What a great surprise.
-Stan: Right, my mom cried with excitement when she saw me.
-Adam: I guess.
-Stan: You haven't trained anymore from what I see.
-Adam: Why are you saying that?
-Stan: You are no longer the muscular Adam I knew, I also see you a little fat, no offense.

-Adam: Hahaha, don't worry. You're right, I haven't trained anymore, I don't have time, between work, home and children's activities I don't have too much time for hobbies.
-Stan: I don't think so, there is always time. Also, in a few years you will turn 40, if you want to avoid heart attacks and other diseases it is good to resume exercises, I tell you as a friend and as a doctor.
-Adam: I'll consider it hahaha
We kept talking and talking, meanwhile my wife came home, I introduced her to my dearest friend Stan, whom I have always talked about and asked him to stay for dinner, who would prepare something tasty for that special occasion. He made some chicken wings that Stan loved, and jokingly said:

-Stan: If you cook everything like this, I understand why my friend is overweight hahahaha.

We all laughed, kept joking and talking until Stan realized how late it was and at midnight he returned to his house, a few blocks from mine. When Stan left, I helped my wife collect everything we had used during dinner and then we went to sleep as we were quite sleepy.

At 7:30 the next day my phone started ringing, it was an unknown number and I decided to decline the call. Within minutes the same number called again, so I refused the call again, but that time I turned off the phone. After fifteen minutes the doorbell rang, perplexed, I went to open it. It was Stan, wearing beach shorts, a T-shirt and sandals.

-Stan: Today is Saturday.
-Adam: I know, I was sleeping.
-Stan: Get ready quickly.
-Adam: For what?
-Stan: To go to the beach as you did when you were young and had fun, no offense.
-Adam: Are you serious?
-Stan: Of course, I never stopped going there, except when I didn't have any beaches nearby
-Adam: And my family?
-Stan: Bring them, when was the last time you went to the beach?
-Adam: Let me ask my wife ... Honey, do you want to go to the beach with the kids? STAN INVITED US WITH HIM.

My wife accepted immediately, she loved the beach, I remember that on a couple of occasions she told me to buy a house by the sea, but I told her it was not a good idea. He quickly prepared the children, settled down and we left. While we were at the beach, Stan pulled two surfboards out of his car, the old one he was sailing with years ago and a seemingly new one. He came up to me with the new one and gave it to me saying:

-Stan: Let's see if you still remember how to use it. I'll use my old one, you know it always draws good waves.

Enthusiastic, I remembered doing it every weekend about 16 years ago. We went in the water, there were good waves, but I didn't remember how to surf. Stan was surfing some nice waves, while I was out there in the water watching him and waiting for the perfect moment to catch a wave. When I finally did, I fell off the board, it was no longer the same, I had a lot less balance and a lot less skill. I tried several times, but ended up exhausted after several falls off the board. Stan scoffed at me and called me old, while my wife and children watched from the shore. After surfing, Stan pulled out two full sets of scuba gear, gave me one, put them on and dived. I could hardly hold my breath, and if I held it several times, I would end up feeling sick. My wife and kids loved the beach, the waves and the sand very much; On the other hand, I was a bit troubled by the fact that I couldn't surf or dive as I did before, I thought it was due to lack of practice. We went home and Stan greeted us, said the number I blocked was his, so I unblocked it. I turned off the phone at night so that she wouldn't call me early the next day hahaha.

The day after the beach, Stan didn't call me, nor did I see him all day, so at night I called him to see if he was doing something and told me he was busy, but he already had something planned for the next day and that he would have called me.

The next day, I waited for his call all morning, all afternoon, and nothing, I thought he was still busy visiting your old friends in the neighborhood. I resigned myself to knowing nothing about him when at one point the doorbell rang. Happy, I went to open to my old friend, although when I saw him I had regretted a little of the emotion and I think it appeared on my face because Stan said:

-Stan: What's wrong? Aren't you happy to see me anymore?
The first thing I saw when I opened the door was Stan wearing clothes to ride a bike.

-Adam: Ehhmm yes, I just don't have a bike anymore.

In fact, I wasn't that keen on going out with Stan anymore, I hadn't ridden a bike for years, I was afraid the same situation would happen to me as surfing or diving and I would end up being fooled by him.

-Stan: Don't worry, I know, that's why I rented it to you. Come, join me for a walk like we did before.
-Adam: Ok.

I went up to my room, grabbed a sports shorts that I usually used as pajamas, put on a shirt and went out. Stan also brought me a helmet. A little disappointed, I left the house with Stan, took the bike he had rented for me and got on. At that moment I felt that I had not forgotten anything about how to ride a bicycle. And so I was there, after 15 years, cycling as if it had been the day before. We walked around the streets for a while, then went up the dirt road we used to take when we were young. Stan was happy, he had no signs of being tired or anything like that, but I couldn't take it anymore, I was about to pass out. As much as I could, I stopped, got off the bike and sat down on the side of the road. Stan, seeing me there, turned around, put his bike aside and sat down beside me without saying a word. Not only was he not tired, he wasn't even sweating, while I felt like I was going to die there. It was at that moment that I thought, "I'm getting old ..." After a few minutes of silence, while I was recovering, Stan spoke.

-Stan: You already figured it out, right?
-Adam: What?
-Stan: That's not the same anymore.
-Adam: What?
-Stan: Nothing is like before, life is not the same. We get older, every day that passes is one less day left to live.
-Adam: I didn't think so.
-Stan: You should. Every day you lie in your chair and watch TV for hours is a day your body takes its toll.
-Adam: What are you talking about?
-Stan: We are no longer teenagers, and our bodies are not as good as they used to be. The lungs and heart begin to deteriorate, which is why so many adults have heart attacks and respiratory attacks. You sure felt like you were going to die right now, right?
-Adam: Yes.
-Stan: You have a nice family, don't get caught up in laziness and alleged lack of time. You don't know how many times I've seen men aged 45 to 50 suffer from heart attacks and leave their children and wives alone.
-Adam: I never would have imagined.
-Stan: Right.
-Adam: I really don't have time.
-Stan: Stop lying to yourself, yesterday I didn't call you and you have been worrying all day, right? So you had some free time! The day we went to the beach, you were also free! And now, while we're here on our bikes, you still are.
-Adam: Wow. You are right. I used all the other things as excuses to stay home and do nothing.
-Stan: Right. When I saw you fat, I knew I should have shown you the mistake you were making of not exercising and not taking care of your health.
-Adam: You don't know how much I appreciate it.

-Stan: Don't worry. Many people see exercise as something to entertain themselves, distract themselves from their daily activities and find any excuse not to do it. Exercise really means taking care of your health.

Since that moment, my life has changed, I realized that not everything was money and work. I joined the gym again, bought a bicycle that I used every night to go for a walk with some friends I had found. I resumed going to the beach every weekend with my wife and children. I became active again like many years ago.

My message to you, dear reader, is never to neglect your health, never neglect your family. It's okay to have business and other things, but never forget to seek your well-being and happiness. As I write this story, I am on a plane with my wife on the way to Venezuela. We will visit Angel Falls, the tallest waterfall in the world, and as I said at the beginning, I'm 55 years old.

Summary

English

This story is told by the protagonist, Adam Williams, who tells that when he was a child, his parents did not have a job to pay for expensive rides or new toys. They only earned what was necessary for food and basic needs. One day, while out on the street with his dad, Adam saw his friends riding bikes. They invited him to ride the next day, but he didn't have one. He asked his father for one even though he knew his father wouldn't have the money to buy it for him, which is what he told him. Sometime later, Adam was walking with his father when a lady threw a bicycle in the trash. Adam, seeing that, ran to her and asked if he could keep it. The lady gave it to him with pleasure and also offered him a job as a gardener. Adam was 7 years old, so he asked his father if he could do it. His father accepted so that Adam would learn to earn money and value his effort. The next day, Adam went and mowed the lawn. When he was about to finish, the lady's son came out, introduced himself as Stan, and invited Adam to ride bicycle another day.

Adam didn't know how to ride a bike, so he had to learn to drive first before he could accept Stan's invitation. When he had learned, he went to Stan's house. Stan's mom told him that the other neighbors were amazed at how well his garden had turned out and that, if he wanted, she would rent him the mower to mow the other gardens and both of them would win. Adam agreed and went out to ride the bike with Stan, with whom he made such a good friend. Later, Stan's parents would invite Adam's parents to dinner where they offered him better jobs and wages.

One day, Stan's father tells Adam that he wanted to talk to him. When they are reunited, Stan's father recommends Adam not to save money. He said it is better to make investments so that the money becomes more. He made their mower an example of a good investment. Adam didn't understand that conversation very well. One day, when Stan had a video game that no one else had because it was too expensive, he remembered that conversation. So with his savings, he went and bought a similar video game and rented it to the kids in the neighborhood for a small price every hour. In less than five days, Adam had recovered his money and already understood what Stan's dad was referring to.

Adam and Stan were always very close and did a lot of sports and activities together because they were taught not to use video games too much because they damage the brain. Sadly, they split up when they went to college because Stan would go north and Adam would stay in town. Adam said he stopped exercising and doing recreational activities because he didn't have time for his business and studies. The business and his family left him no time to do any of the things he did in his youth.

One day, when Adam was 34 years old, the doorbell rang in his house. He went to open the door, and when he opened it, it turned out to be Stan. He was on vacation in the city and went to surprise his old friend. Adam introduced him to his children. They talked and joked. Adam's wife arrived and invited Stan to dinner for a special dish. After dinner, since the food was too good, Stan jokingly said that he knew why his friend was a little fat, and everyone laughed. It was midnight when Stan left because it was already late.

That same day, early in the morning, an unknown number called Adam several times. He blocked that number, but then the doorbell rang. It was Stan who invited Adam and his family to the beach. They all went. On the beach, Adam realized that he no longer remembered how to surf and it was too difficult to dive as he did years ago. They enjoyed their day very much and then returned home.

The next day, Adam didn't hear from Stan, so he called him at night to see if they would do anything, but Stan said he was busy and he would call him the next day.

Adam waited all morning and all afternoon for Stan's call, but Stan never called him. It was already dark and Adam thought his friend wouldn't call him, however, the doorbell rang. Stan had arrived with a rented bicycle and his own, to go out and ride a bicycle. Adam, at first didn't want to because he was afraid that it would happen the same as with surfing and diving, but it didn't happen. After awhile riding, the road became difficult. Adam began to feel very bad, he was exhausted and had to stop to rest. At that moment he thought, "I'm getting old". Stan, who knew what was going on, spoke very seriously with him and told him that it wasn't all business and family. He had to exercise, more than to entertain himself, to have good health. From that moment on, Adam changed his lifestyle and became active again as he was when he was young, even when he was already 55 years old.

Espanol

Esta historia es contada por el protagonista, Adam Williams, quien cuenta que cuando él era un niño, sus padres no tenían trabajo para pagar paseos costosos o juguetes nuevos. Solo ganaban lo necesario para la alimentación y las necesidades básicas. Un día, mientras estaba en la calle con su padre, Adam vio a sus amigos en bicicleta. Lo invitaron a montar al día siguiente, pero no tenía. Le pidió uno a su padre aunque sabía que su padre no tendría dinero para comprarlo, que es lo que le dijo. Algún tiempo después, Adam caminaba con su padre cuando una señora tiró una bicicleta a la basura. Adam, al ver eso, corrió hacia ella y le preguntó si podía quedárselo. La señora se lo dio con gusto y también le ofreció un trabajo como jardinero. Adam tenía 7 años, así que le preguntó a su padre si podía hacerlo. Su padre aceptó para que Adam aprendiera a ganar dinero y valorara su esfuerzo. Al día siguiente, Adam fue y cortó el césped. Cuando estaba a punto de terminar, el hijo de la dama salió, se presentó como Stan e invitó a Adam a andar en bicicleta otro día.

Adam no sabía andar en bicicleta, por lo que primero tuvo que aprender a conducir antes de poder aceptar la invitación de Stan. Cuando se enteró, fue a la casa de Stan. La mamá de Stan le dijo que los otros vecinos estaban asombrados de lo bien que había salido su jardín y que, si él quería, ella le alquilaría la podadora para cortar los otros jardines y ambos ganarían. Adam estuvo de acuerdo y salió a montar en bicicleta con Stan, con quien hizo tan buen amigo. Más tarde, los padres de Stan invitarían a los padres de Adam a cenar, donde le ofrecieron mejores trabajos y salarios.

Un día, el padre de Stan le dice a Adam que quería hablar con él. Cuando se reencuentran, el padre de Stan le recomienda a Adam que no ahorre dinero. Dijo que es mejor hacer inversiones para que el dinero sea más. Hizo de su cortacésped un ejemplo de buena inversión. Adam no entendió muy bien esa conversación. Un día, cuando Stan tenía un videojuego que nadie más tenía porque era demasiado caro, recordó esa conversación. Entonces, con sus ahorros, fue y compró un videojuego similar y se lo alquiló a los niños del vecindario por un pequeño precio cada hora. En menos de cinco días, Adam había recuperado su dinero y ya entendía a qué se refería el padre de Stan.

Adam y Stan siempre estuvieron muy unidos e hicieron muchos deportes y actividades juntos porque les enseñaron a no usar demasiado los videojuegos porque dañan el cerebro. Lamentablemente, se separaron cuando fueron a la universidad porque Stan se iría al norte y Adam se quedaría en la ciudad. Adam dijo que dejó de hacer ejercicio y realizar actividades recreativas porque no tenía tiempo para sus negocios y estudios. El negocio y su familia no le dejaron tiempo para hacer ninguna de las cosas que hizo en su juventud.

Un día, cuando Adam tenía 34 años, sonó el timbre de su casa. Fue a abrir la puerta y, cuando la abrió, resultó ser Stan. Estaba de vacaciones en la ciudad y fue a sorprender a su viejo amigo. Adam le presentó a sus hijos. Hablaron y bromearon. La esposa de Adam llegó e invitó a Stan a cenar por un plato especial. Después de la cena, como la comida era demasiado buena, Stan bromeó y dijo que sabía por qué su amigo estaba un poco gordo y todos se rieron. Era medianoche cuando Stan se fue porque ya era tarde.

Ese mismo día, temprano en la mañana, un número desconocido llamó a Adam varias veces. Bloqueó ese número, pero luego sonó el timbre. Fue Stan quien invitó a Adam y su familia a la playa. Todos se fueron. En la playa, Adam se dio cuenta de que ya no recordaba cómo surfear y que era demasiado difícil bucear como hacía años. Disfrutaron mucho su día y luego regresaron a casa.

Al día siguiente, Adam no tuvo noticias de Stan, así que lo llamó por la noche para ver si podían hacer algo, pero Stan dijo que estaba ocupado y que lo llamaría al día siguiente.

Adam esperó toda la mañana y toda la tarde la llamada de Stan, pero Stan nunca lo llamó. Ya estaba oscuro y Adam pensó que su amigo no lo llamaría, sin embargo, sonó el timbre. Stan había llegado con una bicicleta alquilada y la suya propia, para salir a andar en bicicleta. Adam, al principio no quería porque temía que le pasara lo mismo que con el surf y el buceo, pero no sucedió. Después de un rato, el camino se volvió difícil. Adam comenzó a sentirse muy mal, estaba agotado y tuvo que detenerse a descansar. En ese momento pensó, "estoy envejeciendo". Stan, que sabía lo que estaba pasando, habló muy seriamente con él y le dijo que no todo era negocios y familia. Tenía que hacer ejercicio, más que entretenerse, para gozar de buena salud. A partir de ese momento, Adam cambió su estilo de vida y volvió a ser activo como lo era cuando era joven, incluso cuando ya tenía 55 años.

Vocabulary

English

Reader, motivation, taxes, market, tears, toys, disappointment, throw away, keep it, pinch, lawn, mower, mow, garden, suddenly, golden, training wheels, doorbell, husband, money, possession, learn, exhausted, shop, paint (Object), aerosol/spray, silver, a while, fun, risk, fall, to paint (Verb), clean, shone, save, business, invest, investments, skateboard, swimming, soccer team, beach, surfboard, scuba diving, weekend, sedentary, sport, street bikes, mountain bikes, gym, muscles, parties, discos, high school, graduate, races, jumping, got bored, reclining sofa, voice, fat, cooking, Saturday, undoubtedly, accept.

Espanol

Lector, motivación, impuestos, mercado, lágrimas, juguetes, decepción, tirar, mantenerlo, pellizcar, césped, podadora, podar, jardín, de repente, dorado, ruedas de entrenamiento, timbre, marido, dinero, posesión, aprender, agotado, tienda , pintar (Objeto), aerosol / spray, plateado, un rato, diversión, arriesgar, caer, pintar (Verbo), limpiar, brillar, ahorrar, negocio, invertir, inversiones, patineta, natación, equipo de fútbol, playa, tabla de surf, buceo, fin de semana, sedentario, deporte, street bicis, mountain bike, gym, musculatura, fiestas, discotecas, bachillerato, posgrado, carreras, saltar, aburrir, sofá reclinable, voz, gordo, cocinar, sábado, sin duda, aceptar.

The Perfect Date – La cita perfecta

Samantha was a 23-year-old girl studying mechanical engineering, an industry where there were very few girls. Samantha was a tall girl, with brown hair, brown eyes, freckles on her cheeks and a perfect smile. She was thin and had a spectacular body. Since she entered college, all the guys were crazy about dating her, as she was a girl of unusual beauty. In the university he attended there was only the engineering faculty, which is why most of the students were boys. The year she entered college, 45 boys and only 5 girls undertook mechanical engineering including her, 2 of whom dropped out of college. Samantha was in her senior year, the other two girls who came in with her hated her, because she always caught the attention of the boys and they were never noticed.

Samantha almost always studied alone, because she had no mates to study with, since those in her class were louts who wanted to study with her just to invite her out and things like that. Samantha's college friends had taken up different faculties such as chemical engineering, where most were women or electrical engineering. Becky was her best friend, she studied chemical engineering. Becky was also very beautiful. She had black hair, blue eyes, was thin and a little shorter than Samantha.

Becky had a boyfriend, and he was one of the few who had no ulterior motives with Samantha, so they were good friends. On Becky's boyfriend's birthday, a party was organized at her house and of course Becky invited her best friend, Samantha. Becky and Samantha arrived at the party together, everyone began to admire them because they were beautiful, they had made up and dressed very well for the evening. Becky's boyfriend came and greeted her with a kiss, there some guys stopped staring at her, because she had a boyfriend. But they kept staring at Samantha. Becky's boyfriend was named Chad. Chad had some friends who looked good, but Samantha knew they were jerks, so she didn't talk to them. Since Samantha arrived at the party, many of the guys present would approach her to ask for her number or to ask her to dance, but Samantha turned them all away.

Suddenly, Samantha saw a guy she had never seen before, he looked quite attractive, and for a moment they exchanged a glance, but he stopped looking at her and continued joking and talking to his friends. Samantha was still being pestered by the guys at the party but suddenly ...

-Bruce: Hi, very pleased, I'm Bruce.
-Samantha: Hi.
-Bruce: I wanted to tell you that I can't stop staring at you because....
-Samantha: You too? Stop being so annoying, I know I'm beautiful, everyone has told me.

-Bruce: What are you talking about? I was going to tell you you have a runny nose.
-Samantha: What? Where is it? Really?
-Bruce: No, haha, I was kidding, it was to make you let your guard down, I saw you turning down the other guys all night.
-Samantha: Hahaha, you scared me for a moment. It's just that I'm fed up, everyone comes up with the same thing: "You are very beautiful" "You would make me very happy if you danced with me" "My cellphone doesn't have your number" They don't know what to invent anymore.
-Bruce: Maybe they should just tell you that you have snot on your nose to talk to you.
-Samantha: Hahaha, it sounds good.
-Bruce: Ahahah. You say everyone is looking at you but I know you've been looking at me for a while.
-Samantha: Of course not, that's not true.
-Bruce: I have a picture that says otherwise.
-Samantha: Oh yeah? Let me see.

Bruce pulled out his phone, walked into the gallery and opened an image with a white background and text that said "The opposite" and showed it to Samantha.

-Samantha: Hahahaha! I see you are very witty, right?
-Bruce: Exactly, I see that you can laugh and therefore you are not a robot that rejects men.
-Samantha: Haha apparently not. My name is Samantha.
-Bruce: Nice to meet you.

Samantha was talking and laughing at Bruce's jokes during the party. The other guys, seeing her having fun and laughing so much with Bruce, never came closer to ask her for her number or anything like that. Samantha was super happy, she had finally met a different, kind and nice guy. When the party ended, they said goodbye and although Samantha wanted to give him her number to keep talking, she didn't make it so he didn't think she was an easy girl.
Samantha told Becky everything about that cute and funny guy she met at the party, and who was different and very funny. She was angry that she hadn't asked for his number and therefore hadn't heard from him for days. Becky asked her why she hadn't given him her number or why she hadn't asked for hers, and Samantha explained that she didn't want to seem like an easy girl. Becky told her she had been silly, and that now she might not know anything about him now because of him.

A few days later, Samantha was studying when a message from an unknown number lit up her cell phone. "Hi, how are you? I was wondering if you have already managed to get rid of your mucus." Samantha, reading the message, immediately understood that it was Bruce and was very happy, so she called him.

-Samantha: Hi stalker, where did you get my number?
-Bruce: I asked Chad, it's just that I saw some mucus and I remembered your hahaha.
-Samantha: Hahaha, I've never had mucus.
-Bruce: But I made you believe it.
-Samantha: Fool.
-Bruce: Are you busy?
-Samantha: A little bit, I'm studying, why?
-Bruce: I was bored here at my house and I remembered how much I loved making you laugh at the party so you can invite me to go somewhere and I'll make you laugh in return.
-Samantha: Hahaha, I think you should invite me.
-Bruce: Then I guess you'll be the one making me laugh.
-Samantha: See you at 7:30 pm at the mall.
-Bruce: Perfect, don't have dinner.
-Samantha: Okay.

Enthusiastic, Samantha called Becky to tell her everything. Becky was very happy for her friend, she had never been like this for any guy before, she told her to go to her house and he would help her with her makeup, dress and look pretty.

When it was 7:30 pm, Samantha arrived at the mall and waited for Bruce. While waiting, she received a message saying: "You are beautiful tonight". Samantha read the message and looked up to look for Bruce all over the place, when another message reached her: "Stop looking for me." Samantha read the message and laughed and kept looking for Bruce when another message came. "I see you like the game, I'll give you a clue, I'm higher than you." Samantha then looked to the second floor and there was Bruce. He was also very well dressed, which Samantha liked very much. When they went up the stairs they met, Samantha punched Bruce.

-Samantha: This is for making me wait and coming looking for you.
-Bruce: It's not my fault you haven't seen me, I've been here for over twenty minutes haha.
-Samantha: Good.
-Bruce: Here, I brought you these chocolates, I remember you said they were your favorite on the day of the party.
-Samantha: Thank you very much, how kind you are.
-Bruce: You're welcome.
-Samantha: I'm very hungry. Where are we going to eat?
-Bruce: I was thinking about having caviar and lobster for dinner at that restaurant.

-Samantha: Really?
-Bruce: No, we can go eat pizza.
-Samantha: Thank goodness, I don't like any of that. The pizza is perfect
-Bruce: Let's go then.

They went to a restaurant and ordered pizza. Coincidentally, Samantha's favorite pizza was Bruce's second favorite pizza and Bruce's favorite pizza was Samantha's second favorite, so they ordered and shared their favorite pizza. After dinner, Bruce invited Samantha to the cinema to watch a movie, they saw a horror movie, as it was their favorite genre, and after the movie they went for a walk in the park. It was a little late and it was all dark so you could see the stars. They talked and told each other things and really enjoyed each other's company. When it came time to say goodbye, Bruce seemed a little nervous.
-Samantha: What have you got? You are silent and you never shut up hahaha.
-Bruce: Hahaha, there is something important I want to tell you.
-Samantha: What is it? You're not a lost cousin or brother, right?
-Bruce: Hahaha no no, nothing like that as far as I know. It's just that I love being with you because I can be myself and I know you are like that with me too.
-Samantha: I know, that's why I enjoyed being together so much. But there is nothing wrong with that.
-Bruce: There's something important that I haven't told you.
-Samantha: What?
-Bruce: Well, you know the mall we went to?
-Samantha: Sure, we come right from there silly.
-Bruce: Well ... My father is the owner.
-Samantha: How nice. And why was it so important to tell me?
-Bruce: Because he makes a lot of money and because I am his son, I have a lot of advantages in many of the stores in there.
-Samantha: I'm very happy for you.
-Bruce: You still don't get it right?
-Samantha: No.
-Bruce: All the friends I have, or at least most of them, are my friends just for interest. So they get things without paying and other things like that.
-Samantha: I understand. Are you afraid that I am like this?
-Bruce: Not at all, I saw that you are not. In fact, you even insisted a little on paying for movie tickets.
-Samantha: Of course, I don't like being offered things, men believe they should always pay them and that only then will we fall at their feet and do whatever they ask.
-Bruce: That's why I like you ...
-Samantha:?
-Bruce: What is it?
-Samantha: What would you have said?
-Bruce: That I like you!

Samantha didn't say a word, she just saw Bruce's face as he said it. She waited a few seconds, threw herself at him and kissed him.

-Samantha: I like you a lot too, you are the first guy I feel so calm and safe with, you are the first one who makes me laugh so much and stays between you and me ... This was my first kiss.
-Bruce: Who would have thought, the so famous and desired Samantha, who has thousands of suitors, had never given her first kiss.
-Samantha: If you tell someone I'll kill you.
-Bruce: I was just going to post it on my twitter hahaha.
-Samantha: You're a good guy Bruce, thank you for everything you did today. This was the perfect date.
-Bruce: Thanks to you Sam. You're not that hateful after all hahaha.
-Samantha: You too are different from others. You are not an idiot.

This is how Samantha, without imagining or looking for him, got the ideal guy for her, and that made her feel special and unique.

Summary

English

Samantha was a young girl of 23 years who studied mechanical engineering. She was very beautiful. Among the three girls who studied mechanical engineering, she was the most beautiful, so the boys only noticed her. She was sick and tired of the louts and all the boys always trying to have something with her. One day, at the birthday party of Becky's boyfriend, her best friend, Samantha was approached by all the boys at the party. A very handsome boy arrived and told her he couldn't avoid seeing her. Samantha, thinking he was one of the bunch, immediately rejected him, but he told her it was because she had snot on her face. Samantha, super embarrassed, asked him if he was serious and that where she had it. However, it was just his joke so that he could let her guard down. His name was Bruce. He was very funny and nice, so Samantha liked him and they talked for the rest of the party. Bruce left and Samantha didn't give her number or ask for his because she was afraid he thought she was an easy girl.

Excited by the boy she met; Samantha told Becky everything, who said she was a fool for not giving or asking for his number.

Days later, she received a message from an unknown number, joking about the snot. Samantha knew it was Bruce and called him. They agreed to go out to eat and see each other at the mall.

The date was wonderful. Bruce told Samantha his secret and also told her that he liked her very much. Samantha threw herself on him and kissed him, to thank him for being the best date she had ever had.

Espanol

Samantha era una joven de 23 años que estudiaba ingeniería mecánica. Ella era muy bella. Entre las tres niñas que estudiaron ingeniería mecánica, ella era la más hermosa, por lo que los niños solo la notaron. Estaba harta y cansada de los patanes y de todos los chicos que siempre intentaban tener algo con ella. Un día, en la fiesta de cumpleaños del novio de Becky, su mejor amiga, todos los chicos de la fiesta se acercaron a Samantha. Llegó un chico muy guapo y le dijo que no podía evitar verla. Samantha, pensando que él era uno más del grupo, lo rechazó de inmediato, pero él le dijo que era porque tenía mocos en la cara. Samantha, súper avergonzada, le preguntó si hablaba en serio y que donde lo tenía. Sin embargo, era solo su broma para poder bajar la guardia. Su nombre era Bruce. Era muy divertido y agradable, así que le agradaba a Samantha y hablaron durante el resto de la fiesta. Bruce se fue y Samantha no le dio su número ni pidió el suyo porque temía que él pensara que era una chica fácil.

Emocionada por el chico que conoció; Samantha le contó todo a Becky, quien dijo que era una tonta por no dar o pedir su número.

Días después, recibió un mensaje de un número desconocido, bromeando sobre los mocos. Samantha sabía que era Bruce y lo llamó. Acordaron salir a comer y verse en el centro comercial.

La cita fue maravillosa. Bruce le contó a Samantha su secreto y también le dijo que le gustaba mucho. Samantha se arrojó sobre él y lo besó, para agradecerle por ser la mejor cita que había tenido.

Vocabulary

English

Mechanical engineering, career, freckles, cheeks, smile, thin, crazy, going out/date, beauty, male, female, classmates, electronic engineering, chemical engineering, boyfriend, party, handsome, dancing, rejecting, glances, snot, nose, joking, lowering guard, tired, arrogant, photo, funny, happy, nice, funny, said goodbye, unknown, busy, make-up, cinema, movies, park, stars, enjoy, mutual, nervous, say goodbye, quiet, cousin, brother, owner, pay, invite, kiss.

Espanol

Ingeniería mecánica, carrera, pecas, mejillas, sonrisa, delgada, loca, salir /
salir, belleza, hombre, mujer, compañeros de clase, ingeniería electrónica,
ingeniería química, novio, fiesta, guapo, bailar, rechazar, miradas, mocos,
nariz, bromeando, bajando la guardia, cansado, arrogante, foto, gracioso,
feliz, agradable, gracioso, dijo adiós, desconocido, ocupado, maquillaje, cine,
películas, parque, estrellas, disfrutar, mutuo, nervioso, decir adiós, tranquilo,
primo , hermano, dueño, pagar, invitar, besar.

Lost Luggage – El equipaje perdido

December was approaching, so the Curtis family were starting to plan their annual year-end trip, the previous year they had traveled to Argentina and shared an apartment they had rented with a local family. They had learned a lot about Argentine culture and the big difference between celebrating Christmas and the New Year. The Curtis family lived in the United States and consisted of Stefan Curtis, his wife Leila Cooper and their children, Antonela and Noah. Antonela was the youngest, she was 14 and Noah was 16.

The Curtis family was looking for places to celebrate Christmas that year.

-Antonela: What do you think of Australia?
-Noah: Vhe boredom.
-Antonela: There are many kangaroos and many other species of exotic animals there.
-Noah: Yes, and mortals! Australia is the country with the strangest, most poisonous and deadly animals.
-Antonela: What a coward you are.
-Noah: The best is Germany, I read on the internet that there are motorways where there is no speed limit. Did you hear dad? We could rent a Ferrari and we would have no speed limits.
-Stefan: It sounds interesting, but we're not going to Germany just to rent a Ferrari.
-Leila: Your father is right, Noah.
-Noah: And what do you propose?
-Stefan: I had thought about Italy, they have many tourist places and I have friends there with whom we can stay.
-Leila: We could go by train from Italy to France, so we see the Eiffel Tower.
-Antonela: There is also Disneyland Paris.
-Noah: And we can also visit the stadiums of Paris Saint Germain, Olympique Marseille and Monaco.
-Stefan: Are we all in agreement then? We go to Italy and from there we go by train to France.
-Leila: I think so.
-Noah: I like it.
-Antonela: Couldn't we also include Spain in the list? I have a friend there that I would like to visit. So we would go through Madrid, Noah sees the Real Madrid stadium and you visit the tourist spots.
-Leila: Good idea. I would like to visit the Canary Islands, I heard that there is a beautiful water park in Tenerife.
-Noah: Real Madrid and water park. Let's go to Spain.
-Stefan: Remember that we will go there for 40 days, we have to organize ourselves well if we want to do everything we are saying.
-Leila: Exactly.

-Noah: Ok.
-Antonela: Perfect.

So it was then that the Curtis family decided to go on vacation to various cities in Europe. They bought airline tickets, booked hotels, bought water park ticket promotions, and organized all the activities.

When they arrived in December, they went to the airport, took the five suitcases from the car, one for each and one empty for the souvenirs and gifts for their friends. They went in, checked in, loaded their suitcases and waited. As soon as they got on the plane, they were warned that they would have to use a different plane, as apparently they would have to carry out checks on the plane they were about to travel on. Then they got on the other plane and left. It was a very long flight, it seemed endless, but eventually they arrived. Once in Italy, they got off the plane very excited but with back pain due to the long journey. All the passengers on the flight went to collect the bags but to the great surprise of all the bags they were not yet ready. People began to despair.

-Stefan: It takes a long time to get your luggage off the plane, don't you think?
-Antonela: Too much, we have already been waiting for a thousand hours here.
-Leila: Don't be an exaggerated daughter, it's only 30 minutes.
-Antonela: 30 minutes of lost fun.
-Noah: I'm actually getting a little worried, this shouldn't take that long.

They were all complaining when the following message sounded throughout the airport: "Passengers on Flight 1234 from Colorado, United States to Milan, Italy, please approach the security control area, I repeat, approach the security control area. safety"

-Stefan: Something is wrong.
-Leila: Oh no.

When they arrived in the designated area, they were told that there had been an error and that the plane's luggage had never left the departure airport. Their bags remained on the old plane and so they would arrive on the next flight the next day. He was also told that the airline, being responsible, would pay him room and board while waiting for his luggage to arrive. Many people were angry but the Curtis family took it very well. They collected the money for room and board and with them Stefan paid for a taxi that took them to his friend's house. His friend was very happy to see him and his family and immediately noticed that they didn't have any luggage so they told him everything that had happened and that they were surprised at the big mistake the airline had made, but still they would pay him. board and lodging for the entire waiting period. The next day, the Curtis family went to the airport to get the suitcases, collected them and everything was fine. These had labels with the names and surnames of each of them, including the identification number. They then began to enjoy their holidays in Italy as planned. They went to Rome and visited the Colosseum, they also visited the Tower of Pisa, a Ferrari factory, the city of Venice, and ate all kinds of pasta and pizza possible. They even went to a street food fair which was only there for one day.

As soon as their days in Italy were completed, they went to the train station to leave for France to discover Paris. They handed over their tickets, loaded their five suitcases onto the train and there they were, headed for France.

-Leila: This is the first time we travel by train.
-Stefan: That's right, it's something unique.
-Antonela: I like more than traveling by plane, I see the landscape more closely.
-Noah: I don't like it, it makes a lot more noise than the plane and we go much slower too.
-Stefan: It is a matter of taste.

The train journey was quite long. Despite the fact that France and Italy are neighboring countries, the distance to travel and the speed of the train, with all its stops, made the journey a bit heavy.

They had finally arrived in France. Stefan had woken Noah, who had fallen asleep a few hours earlier. Noah woke up, got up and took his suitcase, just like all the other members of the Curtis family. With our bags in hand, Stefan called a taxi to take them to the hotel where they had booked, just minutes from the train station. Arriving at the hotel, the receptionist greeted them, asked them for the reservation number and gave them the room key. When they saw them take the five suitcases, the receptionist told them not to worry as he would send someone to pick them up. The Curtis family then went up to their room and waited for the bags to be brought up to bathe, change, and go out to dinner at a restaurant.

The next morning, the Curtis family woke up very early, as they wanted to do a lot of things on their first day there in Paris. They got dressed and went for a walk, saw the houses, structures, streets, museums, shops and finally came to the famous Eiffel Tower. There they took photos, talked, toured the tower with a tour guide and then returned to the hotel because they had walked a lot and were tired.
The following days they walked and traveled by train to different parts of France. Noah visited the stadiums of the football teams he wanted to meet, went to Disneyland Paris, where Antonela climbed all the attractions and went to the Louvre museum, Notre Dame Cathedral, the Arc de Triomphe of Paris and the Palace of Versailles.

It was time to leave for Spain, they collected all their belongings from the hotel, went down to the reception, returned the room keys to the receptionist, thanked her for the excellent service and went to the train station to go to Spain. The train that took them to Spain was taken right there in Paris towards Madrid, but the Curtis family stopped first in Barcelona so that Noah could see the Camp Nou, the stadium of Barcelona F.C. After that, they returned to the train and headed for Madrid, where as soon as they got off the train they went directly to another hotel, where they rested because the journey and the journey to Barcelona had been exhausting.

The next day, Antonela got up very early, because her friend would come with her mother to take her for a walk. She got ready and asked her mother to accompany her to the place where they would take her. Stefan and Leila, after accompanying Antonela to her friend, talked to Noah.

-Stefan: Hey Noah, how are you feeling?
-Noah: Well, why?
-Leila: It is that your father and I are tired and we would like to stay here today in the hotel to rest a bit.
-Noah: Really?
-Stefan: Yes, son, and then we don't want to visit anything without your sister.
-Noah: And what could I do?
-Leila: Get off to see the hotel's activities.
-Stefan: You can go to the pool and see if you can find someone to have fun with.
-Noah: Okay, I'll do it.
After room service brought breakfast for everyone, Noah got dressed and went down to see the hotel. It had a soccer field, a swimming pool, tennis courts and a jacuzzi. He went up to the room, told his parents about the hot tub and everyone went down to relax and rest there. Noah, then went upstairs and put on sports clothes to go back down and play soccer and tennis. Antonela, on the other hand, was with her friend, went to her house, went to eat ice cream, her friend introduced her to other girls and went to a shopping center. It was already sunset and Stefan and Leila were in the room when their two children entered together.
-Stefan: What are you doing together?
-Noah: I was about to go up when Antonela arrived with her friend.
-Antonela: And I arrived and found Noah waiting for the elevator.
-Stefan: Ahh ok.
-Leila: I advise you to rest, tomorrow we will do many things.
The next morning Noah and Antonela were super tired and resting, but their parents woke them up and got ready to go out. They left and visited many tourist places such as the Plaza Mayor, the Retiro Park, the Prado National Museum, the Puerta del Sol, the Palacio de Cristal and the Real Madrid F.C

football stadium, the Santiago Bernabéu. In the following days they visited other tourist spots, as Madrid is full of them, and finally the day came to go to Tenerife.

The flight to Tenerife lasted almost three hours, so they decided to buy tickets for a flight that left at dawn to take advantage of each day, as they would only stay in Tenerife for three days. Once in Tenerife, they were waiting for the suitcases to come off the plane, everything was normal, until the suitcases ran out and the extra suitcase of the Curtis family where all the souvenirs and gifts were, was gone. Perplexed, they went to make a report of the loss.

-Stefan: Good afternoon, I want to make a complaint.
-Agent: What happened?
-Stefan: I went to collect my suitcases and I am missing one.
-Agent: Are you sure? I see you are four and you have four suitcases.
-Stefan: Yes, I'm sure I'm missing a suitcase.
Agent: What flight were you flying on?
-Stefan: The one who just arrived from Madrid.
-Agent: Flight 9876, correct?
-Stefan: Right.
Agent: Let me call the baggage handler for that flight and the airline to see what happened. Do you have the reference number of the suitcase?
-Stefan: Yes, 45646.
Agent: That suitcase is not registered on that flight.
-Stefan: What do you mean?
-Agent: No suitcase with that reference number entered that plane. Or at least it's not registered, let me speak to the manager. Wait here a moment.

The Curtis family waited for the agent to return with his suitcase or at least some clue as to where he might be. After a long period of waiting, the agent returned with the baggage handler and gave them the bad news of not knowing where his suitcase was. They were also told that if they wanted to they could leave a phone number and go enjoy the ride and when they found the suitcase they would call them. So they did, they were all upset because they had lost all the souvenirs and gifts they had bought. They knew that if they presented the invoices, the airline would refund the money for losing the suitcase, but they would also lose everything they bought during the holidays. They arrived at the hotel very discouraged and disappointed, they had not paid attention to the beautiful landscape of the island of Tenerife because they were thinking about their suitcase and what could have happened to them.

-Antonela: Hey, I know we're angry, but I think we should take advantage of what's left of the trip instead of being angry. Come on, let's take a walk, so we get distracted.
-Leila: Antonela is right, let's get ready and go out.
-Stefan: Right. Here we go.

They got ready and went for a walk on that beautiful island. They saw the beautiful beaches, the wonderful tourist spots and returned to the hotel just before sunset to swim in the pool.

The next day, Stefan got up and checked his phone to see if he had any messages or calls from the airline, but there was nothing, he got a little angry, but decided not to tell his family, so he didn't. they would be more worried. That day they went to the famous water park in Tenerife, Siam Park. They all woke up, had breakfast and got ready to leave. Noah grabbed his waterproof camera to photograph all the rides he would go on. Antonella took a hat, her sunglasses, a tanning lotion and a float to relax in one of the park's pools. They went to Siam Park, where they stayed all day, and had a lot of fun with all the slides, pools, rides and games that were there. In the afternoon they went back to the hotel, washed, dressed and went for a walk around the city again.

Arriving on the last day of their vacation, they went to the Tenerife airport, as they would take the flight Tenerife-Madrid and then Madrid-Colorado, but at some point they met the agent they had talked to days before about their lost luggage.

-Agent: I'm sorry to inform you that we haven't found your suitcase yet, the airline will give you a form to fill out so you can pay for the value of your lost luggage.
-Stefan: Well, we'd rather have our bags, but if there's no other way ...
-Agent: Sorry for the inconvenience.

They filled out the form, handed it over to the airline, and within a few hours they were given a check that covered the cost of the suitcase. They flew from Tenerife to Madrid and then from Madrid to Colorado, they were already home. They had had a lot of fun on the trip, but they were a little sad about the loss of the suitcase.

A couple of months later, when Leila was home, a young man from the postal service arrived with a suitcase, when Leila saw her he realized that it was the suitcase they had lost, and along with the suitcase came an envelope with a letter.

"Dear Curtis family.
From the airline, we are very sorry for everything that happened with your suitcase 45646. After several investigations, we noticed that by mistake your suitcase was sent on the wrong flight, a Madrid-Caracas flight that had the same schedule. of your Madrid-Tenerife flight. The suitcase was not claimed by anyone in Venezuela, so an investigation was launched to see who it was from and we have seen according to our records that it was yours. Thanks to the information provided for the purchase of tickets, we were able to obtain your home address. So we decided to send it. By way of compensation, if you have not yet cashed the check you received, you can keep it and if you have already cashed it, you do not have to return the money.

Our sincere apologies.

-The Air company ".

Summary

English

The Curtis family was a family who traveled during the December holidays. The last December, they had traveled to Argentina. This December, they decided to visit some European countries because it was easy to go from one country to another by train. The family went to the airport and had already boarded the plane that would depart from the United States to Italy. However, there was a problem with the plane they had boarded and all the passengers were asked to get off that plane and get on another one. When arriving in Italy, there was a problem with everyone's luggage. The suitcases had stayed on the other plane, so the airline would give the passengers money for lodging and food for one night since the suitcases would arrive the next day with the next flight. The Curtis family spent the night at the house of a friend of Stefan, the father of the Curtis family. They went the next day to pick up their suitcases and everything was perfect.

They walked and enjoyed all over Italy for several days, then traveled to France and finally to Spain. In each of those countries, they stayed for several days and visited several touristic places. Finally, in Spain, they would take a plane to Tenerife to stay there for the last days of their vacations. When they arrived in Tenerife and picked up their suitcases, one was missing. Stefan went and complained to the security agent, who said that he would look for it. The days passed in Tenerife and the suitcase did not appear, so the airline gave money to the Curtis family, taking responsibility for the loss of the suitcase.

It was already a couple of months back in the United States, at home, when the suitcase arrived by mail along with a letter from the airline explaining what had happened.

Espanol

La familia Curtis era una familia que viajaba durante las vacaciones de diciembre. El pasado diciembre habían viajado a Argentina. Este diciembre decidieron visitar algunos países europeos porque era fácil ir de un país a otro en tren. La familia se dirigió al aeropuerto y ya había abordado el avión que partiría de Estados Unidos hacia Italia. Sin embargo, hubo un problema con el avión que habían abordado y se pidió a todos los pasajeros que se bajaran de ese avión y subieran a otro. Al llegar a Italia, hubo un problema con el equipaje de todos. Las maletas se habían quedado en el otro avión, por lo que la aerolínea les daría dinero a los pasajeros para el alojamiento y la comida de una noche ya que las maletas llegarían al día siguiente con el siguiente vuelo. La familia Curtis pasó la noche en casa de un amigo de Stefan, el padre de la familia Curtis. Fueron al día siguiente a recoger sus maletas y todo fue perfecto.

Caminaron y disfrutaron por toda Italia durante varios días, luego viajaron a Francia y finalmente a España. En cada uno de esos países permanecieron varios días y visitaron varios lugares turísticos. Finalmente, en España, tomarían un avión a Tenerife para permanecer allí los últimos días de sus vacaciones. Cuando llegaron a Tenerife y recogieron sus maletas, faltaba una. Stefan fue y se quejó con el agente de seguridad, quien dijo que lo buscaría. Pasaron los días en Tenerife y la maleta no apareció, por lo que la aerolínea entregó dinero a la familia Curtis, responsabilizándose por la pérdida de la maleta.

Ya hacía un par de meses allá en Estados Unidos, en casa, cuando llegó la maleta por correo junto con una carta de la aerolínea explicando lo sucedido.

Vocabulary

English

Annual trip, end of year, rented, apartment, culture, celebration, Christmas, wife, kangaroos, species, exotic, deadly, poisonous, highways, speed limit, tourist places, stay, Eiffel Tower, stadiums, train, Spain, Italy, France, Canary Islands, aquatic park, plane tickets, to book, hotels, promotions, entrances, airport, suitcases, check-in, plane, boarding, flight, finally, back pain, passengers, desperate, exaggerated, tourism, speakers, box office, error, at first, picked up, lodging, labels, train station, noise, slower, woke up, reservation number, room, next morning, houses, structures, streets, museums, shops, tour guide, swimming pool, tennis court, football field, sportswear, elevator, manager, reference number, bills, refund, discouraged.

Espanol

Viaje anual, fin de año, alquilado, apartamento, cultura, celebración, Navidad, esposa, canguros, especies, exóticas, mortales, venenosas, carreteras, límite de velocidad, lugares turísticos, estancia, Torre Eiffel, estadios, tren, España, Italia, Francia, Islas Canarias, parque acuático, billetes de avión, reservar, hoteles, promociones, entradas, aeropuerto, maletas, check-in, avión, embarque, vuelo, finalmente, dolor de espalda, pasajeros, desesperados, exagerados, turismo, altavoces, caja oficina, error, al principio, recogido, alojamiento, etiquetas, estación de tren, ruido, más lento, despertó, número de reserva, habitación, mañana siguiente, casas, estructuras, calles, museos, tiendas, guía turístico, piscina, cancha de tenis , campo de fútbol, ropa deportiva, ascensor, gerente, número de referencia, facturas, devolución, desalentado.

The Zoo - El zoológico

A long time ago, there was a girl who was a veterinarian by profession and her name was Jacqueline. He lived on a farm with his father and younger brother. The farm had a gigantic piece of land, where nothing was usually planted because the type of soil was not suitable for planting any type of plant. Jacqueline has on many occasions found snakes, rats, foxes and even monkeys near the farm where she lived. Since she was a veterinarian, she took those she saw injured home and healed them, some even kept them. He had many pets, three rabbits, two goats, five dogs, a monkey and a snake. All those animals were rescued from the road and healed by her.

One day a friend called her:

-Tracey: Jacqueline?
-Jacqueline: Yes Tracey, what's up?
-Tracey: Can you come to my house right away? My cat is having kittens
-Jacqueline: Sure, I'm on my way. Do you have gloves and alcohol?
-Tracey: Yes.
-Jacqueline: Okay. Wait for me.

Jacqueline hurried and left for her friend's house. When he arrived, the cat had already had two kittens, but there were still more. Jacqueline put on her gloves and helped the cat finish the birth. After all the stress of work, she and Tracey talked for a while.

-Tracey: How are you?
-Jacqueline: Good. You?
-Tracey: I'm fine too.
-Jacqueline: I'm happy.
-Tracey: How are things on the farm?
-Jacqueline: A little complicated, it was difficult for me to find a job, there are many animals in the area but no one is willing to pay a vet to save them.
-Tracey: I get it. About that...
-Jacqueline: What?
-Tracey: I've heard of a mobile zoo going through town, maybe we could go see it when it comes and you can ask to be a vet for their animals.
-Jacqueline: It would be great, it will be a great challenge to take care of their different animals.
-Tracey: That was what I wanted to hear. The zoo will be here in two weeks, I'll call you to go together.
-Jacqueline: Great. Thank you so much for thinking of me Tracey.
-Tracey: Don't worry, you know we're friends.

This, for Jacqueline, was an incredible job opportunity.

When the zoo arrived, her friend Tracey called her and they went together to see the animals. When they got there, they noticed that the zoo was huge. They had a brown bear, a teddy bear, a tiger, two lions, several zebras, a leopard, a jaguar, a couple of pumas, a coyote, various types of monkeys, a gorilla, birds of different species and many other animals. Jacqueline was very excited because she had never seen any of those animals live, she had only seen them online and in books.

-Jacqueline: Are you looking at all the animals out there?
-Tracey: Yes, there are many.
-Jacqueline: Taking care of all of them has to be a lot of work.
-Tracey: Right, maybe too much.
-Jacqueline: Not at all, it's perfect, I could learn a lot by taking care of them and giving them the affection that each of these animals deserves. I would like this job with all my heart.

Then Jacqueline and Tracey looked for the owner of the circus.

-Jacqueline: Good afternoon. Are you the owner of the circus?
-Antonio: Exactly, my name is Antonio.
-Jacqueline: Nice to meet you, my name is Jacqueline.
-Antonio: Nice to meet you. Tell me how I can help you?
-Jacqueline: I am a vet, I take care of most of the animals here in the village, you can ask anyone about my experience and knowledge. I have visited all of their animals and I think it would be very helpful for both of you if you let me be your zoo vet. Your pets will be cared for and I will learn many new things by working steadily.
-Antonio: I think it can be done. But I have to verify that what you say is true, come with me.
-Jacqueline: Ok

Jacqueline followed Mr. Antonio in one of his trailers where they transported the animals. There, in a cage, was a small snake.

-Antonio: He stayed there in that corner for several days, he hardly moves at all, and he doesn't even want to eat.
-Jacqueline: Why?
-Antonio: And what I want to know. Examine it and tell me what it has.
-Jacqueline: I understand.

Jacqueline began to examine the snake calmly and carefully.

-Jacqueline: What I can see is her bowels are inflamed and she has a fever, it could be an infection from something she ate. I'll give him anti-inflammatories and antibiotics and he should be better by tomorrow.
-Antonio: Okay. Depending on how it is tomorrow, you will or will not have the job.

Jacqueline went home and told her father and her little brother what had happened and how it had gone. They were very happy and made lasagna to celebrate.

The next day Jacqueline went to the zoo to see the snake she had looked after.

-Jacqueline: Hello, how is the snake today?
-Antonio: Much better, he already moves more and wanted to eat.
-Jacqueline: I am very happy.
-Antonio: Welcome to the team.
-Jacqueline: Thank you very much, Mr. Antonio.

The zoo stayed in Jacqueline's village for a week. During that time Jacqueline stood out for her good care of the zoo animals. He bought and gave vitamins to all of them, I gave them wormers, washed them, treated them as if they were his pets. Since it was a mobile zoo, they had to collect all the animals to take them to another city. However, when they began to collect them, they were placed in small cages, mistreated and beaten. Jacqueline seeing this, was completely unhappy with the management of the zoo and went to complain to Mr. Antonio.

-Jacqueline: Do you know that you are mistreating animals?
-Antonio: What are you talking about?
-Jacqueline: You lock them in small cages, mistreat them and beat them to take them to another place.
-Antonio: And what did you expect? We are a walking zoo.
-Jacqueline: I didn't know you treated animals so badly, now I understand why some of them are afraid of humans.
-Antonio: They are just animals, they will forget it.
-Jacqueline: Maybe they do, but I don't.

Jacqueline, very upset by the way they treated the animals, went to report Mr. Antonio to the Animal Protection, who told her that they had already received several complaints about the case, but there was nothing they could do until they found a home for all animals. They told him that it was difficult for a zoo to accept so many animals all at once and that it was also difficult to send each animal to a different zoo. At that moment, Jacqueline had an idea; he ran to his home, where he talked to his father.

-Jacqueline: Dad, I was at the zoo today and saw how they mistreated the animals. I went to report the fact to Animal Protection but they told me that they cannot do anything because in order to intervene the animals should already have a place to stay. It is difficult for a single zoo to accept them all and it was even more difficult to send animals to separate zoos.
-Father: This is a problem! What are you going to do about it?
-Jacqueline: I was thinking of opening our own zoo here on the farm. We will accept all those animals, Animal Protection will fine the zoo owner, and with that public money we will open ours.
-Father: Are you sure?
-Jacqueline: Yes dad.
-Father: Let's try then. But we need the money.
-Jacqueline: Okay.
Jacqueline quickly went to speak with the Animal Protection officers and explained her plan to them; Animal Protection thought it was a great idea and they went out to arrest Mr. Antonio and his zoo. They arrested him and fined $ 500,000, which they gave to Jacqueline.

Jacqueline was then able to open her own zoo. Gradually it improved the facilities and received animals that were in a similar situation to that of Antonio's zoo and in a short time it became a very famous zoo for the diversity of animals it had and for the care with which they kept them. The zoo made enough money to keep expanding, and the animals had an excellent keeper.

Summary

English

Jacqueline was a veterinarian who lived on a farm in a small town. Jacqueline lived with her father and little brother and was unemployed, making it increasingly difficult to support the farm and her family. In the village, no one was willing to pay her to have their animals treated. One day, her friend asked her for help with the labor of her cat. That friend told her that a traveling zoo was coming in two weeks and that she should talk to the owner to be her vet. And so it happened. She applied to be her veterinarian and they gave her the position, however, the day they had to pick up the zoo, she realized that the animals were beaten and mistreated, so she denounced with animal protection. When she spoke with animal protection, they told her that they needed a home for all the animals. That was why they had not been able to do anything against that subject. Jacqueline quickly spoke to his father and convinced him to use part of the large farmland where they lived to keep the animals there and own the zoo. Jacqueline's father accepted and Jacqueline, with the help of animal protection, stopped the subject and set up her own zoo, which quickly grew and became famous for the large space it had and the good care the animals received there.

Espanol

Jacqueline era una veterinaria que vivía en una granja en un pequeño pueblo. Jacqueline vivía con su padre y su hermano pequeño y estaba desempleada, lo que hacía cada vez más difícil mantener la granja y su familia. En el pueblo, nadie estaba dispuesto a pagarle para que tratara a sus animales. Un día, su amiga le pidió ayuda con el parto de su gato. Esa amiga le dijo que en dos semanas llegaría un zoológico ambulante y que debería hablar con el dueño para que fuera su veterinario. Y así sucedió. Solicitó ser su veterinaria y le dieron el puesto, sin embargo, el día que tuvieron que ir a recogerlo al zoológico, se dio cuenta de que los animales eran golpeados y maltratados, por lo que denunció con protección animal. Cuando habló con protección animal, le dijeron que necesitaban un hogar para todos los animales. Por eso no habían podido hacer nada contra ese tema. Jacqueline habló rápidamente con su padre y lo convenció de que usara parte de la gran tierra de cultivo donde vivían para mantener a los animales allí y ser dueños del zoológico. El padre de Jacqueline aceptó y Jacqueline, con la ayuda de protección animal, detuvo el tema y montó su propio zoológico, que rápidamente creció y se hizo famoso por el gran espacio que tenía y el buen cuidado que los animales recibían allí.

Vocabulary

English

Girl, vet, farm, land, sow, soil, adequate, plant, snake, rat, fox, monkey, wounded, heal, keep, pets, rabbits, goats, rescued, gloves, alcohol, wait for me, give birth, childbirth/labor, get a job, traveling zoo, great challenge, care, attend, anxious, grizzly bear, tiger, lion, zebra, leopard, jaguar, puma, coyote, gorilla, birds, owner, examine, inflamed, intestine, fever, infection, anti-inflammatory, antibiotic, apply for a job, vitamins, cages, mistreat, hit/beat, upset, denounce, animal protection.

Espanol

Niña, veterinario, granja, tierra, sembrar, suelo, adecuado, planta, serpiente, rata, zorro, mono, herido, curar, guardar, mascotas, conejos, cabras, rescatado, guantes, alcohol, espérame, dar a luz, parto / trabajo, conseguir un trabajo, zoológico ambulante, gran desafío, cuidado, asistir, ansioso, oso grizzly, tigre, león, cebra, leopardo, jaguar, puma, coyote, gorila, pájaros, dueño, examinar, inflamado, intestino, fiebre, contagio, antiinflamatorio, antibiotico, postularse a un trabajo, vitaminas, jaulas, maltrato, golpe / paliza, enojo, denuncia, proteccion animal.

The Worst Boss – El peor jefe

Sebastian worked at one of the largest video game companies in the world. Sebastian was a computer engineer and had started working as a video game developer for that company. He excelled at everything he did and that is why he was respected by his colleagues.

One day, Alex's assistant, the administrator of the company, fed up with the abuse and humiliation of his boss, decided to resign. Unfortunately for Sebastian, his name was well known to everyone as he was an excellent employee, so Alex quickly asked him to come to his office to speak.

-Alex: Good morning Sebastian, how are you?
-Sebastian: Very well, you?
-Alex: I'm a little angry today.
-Sebastian: With me?
-Alex: No, not at all. With the company.
-Sebastian: Why?
-Alex: It's not possible that he doesn't have a replacement assistant.
-Sebastian: Mark resigned?
-Alex: Right, he just resigned and there is no one available for that position.
-Sebastian: I understand. I have an unemployed friend and maybe ...
-Alex: No. I've heard you're very good at what you do. I guess you will also be good as my assistant.
-Sebastian: But, Mr. Alex, I'm in the middle of an important project for the company and I have no idea what an assistant does.
-Alex: We will find who will take care of the project, I urgently need an assistant.
-Sebastian: But ...
-Alex: No "but". There is a lot to do instead of wasting time talking.
-Sebastian: Okay.

Sebastian went from second to second from lead developer of the company's most important project to owner's assistant and administrator. On the same day, Sebastian did all the things that Mr. Alex asked him to do; bring him coffee, find someone who could fix his desk chair, fix his cell phone, arrange an emergency meeting with company partners and many other things.

That night Sebastian came home exhausted, he had walked like never in his life, he had to go up and down stairs a thousand times, look for things all over the place, take photocopies, notifications, accompany Mr. Alex and entertain his 5 year old son who had come to see him while he was in a meeting.

His wife, realizing how strangely tired and upset Sebastian was, approached to talk to him.

-Wife: What's wrong honey?
-Sebastian: They changed my position at work.
-Wife: Well, did you get promoted to Chief Developer like you wanted?
-Sebastian: No, Mark resigned and now I have to be Mr. Alex's assistant.
-Wife: Really? What about the project you were working on?
-Sebastian: He said someone else would finish it.
-Wife: Wow, no wonder you're so upset.
-Sebastian: And that's not the worst, he appointed me his assistant but I
think I am his slave.
-Wife: Why?
-Sebastian: Because Mr. Alex doesn't do anything by himself. He stays all day
asking me for favors; find me this, bring me that, make copies, call Luis, find
Luisa, set me up here, entertain my son while I'm in a meeting, etc. It's a
nightmare.
-Wife: Now calm down, love, this is something temporary.
-Sebastian: I hope so because I don't think it will last long.

Days and weeks passed and Sebastian was still there, assisting Mr. Alex. He
always asked him when someone would come to replace him so he could
return to his old position, but Mr. Alex always replied the same way: "We are
already looking for someone, this will be your last week" and then, at the end
of the week, he would tell him : "We haven't found someone as good as you,
stay at the job for another week." Sebastian was getting more and more
frustrated by the situation, as Mr. Alex was becoming more confident,
demanding more and more and treating him worse and worse.
One day, in the middle of a meeting, Sebastian arrived to deliver some
documents requested by Mr. Alex.

-Sebastian: Here are the documents you requested.
-Alex: What are these?
-Sebastian: These are the required documents
-Alex: These aren't good. The letters are too small, do you think I can read
this stuff here? This is garbage, go get them again and this time get it right.
-Sebastian: Ok.

Sebastian was already fed up with that situation. The fact that Mr. Alex asked
for a lot of favors was something he could handle, but the fact that he yelled
at him and talked to him like that in front of other people he didn't tolerate.
He then decided to meet with him to discuss the situation and to tell him that
he should have treated him better if he wanted him to remain as his assistant.
But Mr. Alex didn't take it well.

-Alex: What do you think you're doing? Do you think you can come to me and
tell me how I should treat others?

-Sebastian: The only thing I asked is to respect me and not yell at me anymore because I don't deserve it.
-Alex: I can scream at you as much as I want, that's why I'm paying you.
-Sebastian: You believe that since you are the boss of this company, you are more important and valuable than us who work here, but you are not, we are all human beings and we are equally important.
-Alex: If you don't like how I treat you you can leave, just like your friend Mark.
-Sebastian: Ok. Hello. I'm leaving.
-Alex: You know where the door is.
-Sebastian: Better hurry up and find someone to pick up your kids from school or you will leave them on foot.

Those were Sebastian's last words as he left Mr. Alex's office. He started looking for another job because he was unemployed but a week later they called him on his cell phone, and the voice sounded familiar.

-Alex: Hi Sebastian, how are you? It's me, Alex, I wanted to apologize for how bad I have treated you and for how much I humiliated you, I would like you to come to my office to talk.
-Sebastian: Okay.

Sebastian went to the office and spoke to Mr. Alex, who was very sorry for what he had said and how he had behaved. He realized that Sebastian was right and that he should start treating people better, because he had lost an excellent employee because of his character. While they were talking, Mark walked into the office, as Mr. Alex had also called to apologize and offer him the assistant position again. Seeing this, Sebastian was quite happy, but also worried because he didn't know what position he would be assigned. But to his surprise they gave him the position he had long wanted, Lead Developer.

Summary

English

Sebastian was a computer engineer who worked for a major video game company as a developer. One day, the assistant of the owner and chief executive of the company couldn't stand the abuse and humiliation and resigned. As Sebastian was so good there at work, his name was well known. So, Mr. Alex, who owned the company, put him to work as his assistant "while looking for someone else". Little by little, Mr. Alex's requests increased and became more and more foolish. "Find me coffee, bring me water, distract my son while I enter a meeting" and other similar tasks. One day, Sebastian went in to give something to Mr. Alex and he mocked him and told him that what he had brought was useless and that next time he should do it well. That's why Sebastian decided to talk to him and tell him that he couldn't go through life treating badly and shouting at the people around him, that even if he owned the company, it didn't mean he had the right to treat everyone the way he wanted. Mr. Alex got upset and started treating Sebastian worse, so he resigned. A week later, while Sebastian was looking for another job, Mr. Alex called him and asked him to come to the office to talk and apologize for how badly he had treated him. In Mr. Alex's office, he acknowledged his mistakes and gave Sebastian the position he had always wanted, Chief Developer.

Espanol

Sebastian era un ingeniero informático que trabajaba como desarrollador para una importante empresa de videojuegos. Un día, el asistente del propietario y director ejecutivo de la empresa no pudo soportar el abuso y la humillación y renunció. Como Sebastian era tan bueno en el trabajo, su nombre era bien conocido. Entonces, el Sr. Alex, dueño de la empresa, lo puso a trabajar como su asistente "mientras buscaba a alguien más". Poco a poco, las solicitudes del Sr. Alex aumentaron y se volvieron cada vez más tontas. "Búscame café, tráeme agua, distrae a mi hijo mientras entro a una reunión" y otras tareas similares. Un día, Sebastián entró a darle algo al señor Alex y este se burló de él y le dijo que lo que había traído era inútil y que la próxima vez debería hacerlo bien. Por eso Sebastian decidió hablar con él y decirle que no podía pasar por la vida tratándose mal y gritándole a la gente que lo rodeaba, que aunque fuera el dueño de la empresa, eso no significaba que tuviera derecho a tratar a todos de la misma manera. de la manera que quería. El Sr. Alex se molestó y comenzó a tratar peor a Sebastian, por lo que renunció. Una semana después, mientras Sebastián buscaba otro trabajo, el Sr. Alex lo llamó y le pidió que fuera a la oficina para hablar y disculparse por lo mal que lo había tratado. En la oficina del Sr. Alex, reconoció sus errores y le dio a Sebastian el puesto que siempre había querido, Desarrollador Jefe.

Vocabulary

English

One of the biggest, companies, video games, computer engineer, developer, stand out/ highlight, very liked, assistant, abuse, humiliation, boss, resign, luck, known, employee, office, annoyed, position, project, urgently, chair, desk, organize a meeting, associates, promotion, slave, favors, copies, temporary, weeks, frustrated, documents, small print, treat better, shout, warned, apologize.

Espanol

Uno de los más grandes, empresas, videojuegos, ingeniero informático, desarrollador, destacar / destacar, muy querido, asistente, abuso, humillación, jefe, dimitir, suerte, conocido, empleado, oficina, molesto, cargo, proyecto, urgentemente, presidente , escritorio, organizar una reunión, asociados, promoción, esclavo, favores, copias, temporal, semanas, frustrados, documentos, letra pequeña, tratar mejor, gritar, advertir, disculparme.

Union Makes Strength - Unión hace fuerza

As we know, in most schools there is always at least one child who makes fun of others, who hits them and mistreats them. Montessori elementary school was no exception. Will was that child's name. He was taller and stouter than all the other kids, so he had no problem teasing them. He was always beating and nagging other children and taking away their snacks and pennies. The mothers had complained to the school but the school had already done everything it could to change Will. They had threatened to expel him and send him to a corrective facility, but that didn't work either. Mothers were furious that a single child caused so much trouble for everyone else, so much so that they no longer want to go to school to learn and have fun like all normal children do.

On Alex's birthday, all the mothers of the school children gathered to talk about it and find a solution.

-Mom 1: I'm tired of my son coming in every afternoon crying because of Will.

-Mom 2: It is torture, the poor children no longer know what to do.

-Mom 3: My son tried to deal with it and what he received was a strong bite in the arm.

-Mom 2: Your child is much smaller than him.

-Mom 3: Yes, but no one helped him.

-Mom 1: I have an idea.

-Mom 2: Which one?

-Mom 1: We tell all our kids that whenever Will bothers them, they all have to deal with him.

-Mom 3: I like it, it might work.

-Mom 1: It is the opposite of the saying that says: "Divide and you will win".

-Mom 2: My grandmother said "Unity is strength"

-Mom 1: Exactly, all our children have to come together to stop Will. Let's make him understand that if he messes with one, he messes with everyone. We agree?

All the mothers accepted the plan and when they got home they talked about it with their children and told them the idea. At first he didn't like having to face Will, they panicked, but after several days the children could no longer bear the abuse and decided to face it.

Like every day, Will was pestering the others, until the kids started dealing with him.

-Alex: Hey Will, leave Marco alone.

-Samuel: Right, stop bothering him.

-Jesus: Are you deaf? Leave him alone!

-Daniel: You have three seconds to leave it.
-Marco: Let me go or you will have big problems.
-Will: Hahaha, how afraid you make me. Losers.
-Federico: Last warning.
-Will: Come on, I'll wait for you here.

Will was confident, thinking the children wouldn't have the courage to face him, but he was wrong. The fight began, they were all against Will, pushing him, hitting him, trying to make him fall to the ground. The teachers came and stopped the fight. All the children felt a little guilty, but when they saw Will cry, they laughed a lot and celebrated because their mothers were right ...
"Unity is strength"
Will never bothered any of the school kids again and they all ended up being friends.

Summary

English

In one primary school, there was a bully child who bothered all the children. The mothers did everything they could to get the school to sanction him but nothing happened, so they decided to do justice by their own hands. They told their children that every time Will harassed someone, they would unite and harass him. At first, the children were afraid to do so, but as Will continued with his abuses, the children armed themselves with courage and confronted him, making him stop bothering others and ended up being friends.

Espanol

En una escuela primaria, había un niño acosador que molestaba a todos los niños. Las madres hicieron todo lo posible para que la escuela lo sancionara pero no pasó nada, por lo que decidieron hacer justicia con sus propias manos. Les dijeron a sus hijos que cada vez que Will acosara a alguien, se unirían y lo acosarían. Al principio, los niños tenían miedo de hacerlo, pero a medida que Will continuaba con sus abusos, los niños se armaron de valor y lo confrontaron, lo que hizo que dejara de molestar a los demás y terminaron siendo amigos.

Vocabulary

English

As we know, majority, primary school, robust, threatened, expelled, furious, birthday, face it/confront it, bite, proverb, accepted, please/like, panic, resist, seconds, confident, courageous, fight, teachers, crying, celebrate.

Espanol

Como sabemos, mayoría, escuela primaria, robusto, amenazado, expulsado, furioso, cumpleaños, afrontarlo / afrontarlo, morder, proverbio, aceptado, agradar / gustar, pánico, resistir, segundos, confiado, valiente, lucha, maestros, llanto , celebrar.

Conclusión

Gracias por llegar hasta el final de Aprenda inglés con historias cortas: mejore su idioma inglés con historias fáciles y desarrolle su vocabulario (Vol. 1). Esperemos que haya sido útil y pueda brindarle todas las herramientas que necesita para lograr una mejor comprensión, mejorar su vocabulario y aprender más sobre el idioma inglés.

Esperamos que este libro le sirva de motivación para seguir aprendiendo y mejorar su conocimiento del idioma inglés. Cada libro que leemos y cada habilidad que aprendemos y practicamos nos hace crecer como seres humanos y expande nuestros horizontes.

Por último, si este libro le resultó útil de alguna manera, ¡siempre se agradece una reseña en Amazon!

Aprende inglés con historias cortas
Mejore su idioma inglés con historias fáciles y haga crecer su vocabulario (Vol. 2)

Introducción

Bienvenidos al maravilloso mundo del inglés. Si realmente quiere mejorar sus habilidades en inglés, entonces ha venido al lugar correcto. En este volumen, encontrará una colección de historias basadas en varios temas que van desde actividades de tiempo libre hasta consejos profesionales. La mejor parte de todo es que cada historia contiene consejos, estrategias y sugerencias que te ayudarán a dominar el inglés.

Por supuesto, aprender cualquier idioma puede ser un desafío. Puede volverse aún más desafiante cuando no está realmente seguro de qué dirección tomar. Es por eso que este libro está destinado a brindarle una hoja de ruta que puede ayudarlo a descifrar el funcionamiento interno del idioma inglés. En otras palabras, el punto principal es brindarle los mejores medios para comprender la forma en que está estructurado el idioma.

En este sentido, podrá descubrir estrategias que pueden ayudarlo a comprender mejor este increíble lenguaje. Lo mejor de todo es que este volumen no trata en el lenguaje de los "libros de texto", es decir, el tipo de lenguaje que es gramaticalmente correcto pero que no coincide con la forma en que la gente real habla en un contexto de la vida real. Como resultado, se ha tenido mucho cuidado para asegurar que el lenguaje de este volumen refleje la forma en que las personas reales hablan tanto en situaciones formales como informales.

Como tal, este enfoque le ayudará a sentirse cómodo independientemente de las circunstancias.

Piense en eso por un momento...

Ciertamente es interesante considerar cómo se puede aplanar la curva de aprendizaje cuando se trata de un nuevo idioma. Tenga en cuenta que no se trata de tomar atajos. Se trata de aprender genuinamente un nuevo idioma de tal manera que pueda comprender los fundamentos sin tener que pasar semanas seguidas haciendo ejercicios de memorización de memoria o discutiendo temas gramaticales largos y complejos.

Pero lo mejor de todo es que tendrás la oportunidad de practicar el nuevo idioma que has aprendido, en contexto y con historias interesantes que sin duda te proporcionarán información útil además del tema en sí.

Entonces, comencemos con este nuevo viaje al mundo del inglés. Seguramente encontrará que cada vez que salte a un nuevo idioma, descubrirá un mundo que no sabía que existía. Descubrirás que hay innumerables formas en las que puedes aprender cosas nuevas, conocer diferentes culturas y descubrir gente increíble. También encontrará que estas personas increíbles están muy dispuestas a compartir su idioma y cultura con usted.

De hecho, aprender un nuevo idioma es el tipo de tarea que encontrará desafiante y gratificante. El resultado final serán sus habilidades llevadas a un nivel completamente nuevo. La perspectiva que logres definitivamente puede marcar la diferencia entre quién eres y quién te gustaría ser.

Comencemos con la primera lección. Sin embargo, una advertencia: una vez que empiece, no querrá dejar este libro.

Te veo dentro.

Getting to know a new city – Conocer a una nueva ciudad

I am really happy and excited, this is the first time I travel to Europe. I have always dreamed of visiting it and getting to know its famous and historical cities, especially Rome. It is a beautiful city full of culture, fashion and history.

Since I was a child I have seen television shows and films shot in Rome. I've always loved the places seen in these programs. They are so wonderful. They are places with many stories to tell. I feel so lucky to make one of my dreams come true.

But traveling from America to Italy is not easy. The flight takes about ten hours. This means that I need a good book, sleep (if possible) and some other activity. For this trip, I brought two good books with me. One book for the outbound flight and one for the return flight. I also got some sleep as the time change is also very complicated.

When I arrived in Rome, the first thing that struck me was the size of the airport. Sure, there are big airports in America, but Rome airport is really very nice. It is clean and very tidy. It's the kind of place where you can feel comfortable.

In general, the people who work at the airport are friendly and very helpful. They are always ready to support tourists and other foreigners. In the migration and customs department, I have had a great experience with the people who work there.

Perhaps the first, very good impression I got was with the taxi that took me from the airport to the hotel. The taxi driver, Giacomo, was very kind. This was my first conversation in English.

Giacomo: Where will I take you?
Kathy: At the Estrella Hotel in the center of Rome.
Giacomo: With pleasure. I leave immediately.
Kathy: How long does it take to get to the hotel?
Giacomo: About thirty minutes. There is some traffic at the moment.
Kathy: Oh, I understand. All right.
Giacomo: I'll do my best to get there as soon as possible.
Kathy: Thank you very much. I appreciate your effort.

After this little conversation, I was very happy. I managed to pass the first test!

When I arrived at the hotel, I greeted Giacomo.

Kathy: Thanks for everything. How much money do I owe you?
Giacomo: That's fifteen euros.
Kathy: Here you are.
Giacomo: Thank you very much. Very nice.
Kathy: Thanks to you. Goodbye.
Giacomo: See you soon.

After greeting Giacomo, I entered the hotel. The Estrella Hotel is very nice. It is large and has a very elegant decoration. It really is a great hotel.

I have a reservation for five nights and six days in this hotel for a single room. All my friends have booked their room as we like privacy and rest in peace. I like to sleep in the dark and in silence. So I prefer to sleep in my own room.

At the reception, the hotel employee welcomed me very kindly.

Clerk: Good afternoon, ma'am. What can I do for you?
Kathy: Good afternoon, sir. I have a reservation for tonight.
Clerk: Sure. I'll check right away. What is your surname?
Kathy: Jones.
Clerk: One moment, please. Yes, he has a reservation here for five nights starting today.
Kathy: Yes, that's correct.
Clerk: Perfect. In a single room.
Kathy: Yes, exactly.
Clerk: Very good. So, I need your ID, please.
Kathy: Here you are.
Clerk: Thanks. Done, his room is at number 325, on the third floor.
Kathy: Thanks. Where I go?
Clerk: He has to take the elevator to the third floor. His room is at the end of the corridor.
Kathy: Very nice.
Clerk: You're welcome. I'm here to serve you.

I have already passed the second test. Checking in at the hotel was easy. All my friends already have their rooms. So, let's rest for a couple of hours and then go to dinner. I am excited because I want to try local food. Whenever I go to a new country, I like to try authentic food from that place. That's why I prefer to eat in small restaurants.

I don't have a favorite food. I like them of all kinds. This is the best part of the trip, eating different types of dishes. It is something very special when you visit a new country. I am very eager to discover Italian food. My friends say it's the best ever. I hope.

There are also many places to visit. There are buildings, palaces and castles to see. All of these places are great. They are part of the history and culture of Italy. For many people, they are just nice places to take a photo. For me, they are places full of many stories to tell. It would be nice to hear them all.

Now we will see the Colosseum. This monument is one of the places I want to visit the most. It is one of the emblematic places of Rome, one of the places not to be missed when visiting Italy. There are many places just as beautiful, but the Colosseum is unsurpassed.

But we have a problem ... we can't find the monument. I think we should ask around where we can find the right path. Now I ask a couple walking down the street.

Kathy: Sir, good morning. I am looking for the Colosseum. Can you tell me where it is?

Lord: Sure, miss. Go to the corner, turn right and walk two blocks, then, turn right again. Walk another two blocks and you find the Colosseum, right in front of you.

Kathy: Okay. So, I go to the corner, turn right, walk two blocks, then turn right and walk two more blocks?

Sir: Yes, miss. It's right.

Kathy: Thank you so much for your help.

Lord: You're welcome. Good day.

Kathy: You too.

Well, now we have the right directions to find the palace. We are going as indicated, but we do not see the building anywhere. I think we got lost. I don't understand ... the directions were clear. Now that I see my map, I can't find the palace. I do not understand...

Oh, there's a police officer. I'll ask him.

Kathy: Good morning.

Agent: Good morning. How can I help you?

Kathy: I'm looking for the Colosseum. Can you help me?

Agent: Sure. The Colosseum is far from here.

Kathy: Really? It can not be.

Agent: Yes, you should go to the main road.

Kathy: Is it far from here?

Agent: A little.

Kathy: Can you walk?

Agent: Yes, but it would be a little tiring.

Kathy: I get it.

Agent: It would be better to take a taxi.

Kathy: How long does a taxi take?

Agent: Less than ten minutes.

Kathy: Oh, good. Thanks so much for your help.
Agent: You're welcome. Good luck.

Apparently we are not lost, we are just a little bit far but that's not a problem. We took a taxi and arrived early. With the directions of the police officer it was much easier to find the way to the monument.

It was a little hard to find but worth it. It is an impressive building. It is a wonder that you cannot miss if you go to Rome. But if you need directions, it's best to ask a police officer. I think it is the simplest solution to go anywhere.

I was very happy to have visited Rome. It is a dream that has come true. I know there are many places in the world to visit, but if you haven't done so yet, I recommend you visit Rome. You will not regret. The food is very good, the people are very friendly and the tourist spots are amazing.

Summary

English

Kathy is really happy because she is about to go to Rome. Visiting this city is a dream come true for her. For many years he dreamed of visiting Italy. The journey is long, about ten hours by plane from America to Italy, but it is worth coming to this wonderful city. He passed the first test in English. Had a great conversation with the taxi driver. Then afterward, she had no problem checking into the hotel. Kathy is eager to get to know all the places in Rome. There are many wonderful places to visit such as palaces, castles and monuments. The best is the food. Her friends tell her that Italian food is really very good, the best ever. She loves good food and is sure she will try all the dishes there are. She doesn't have a favorite food, but she likes all kinds of them. The place he wants to visit the most is the Colosseum. This is the most emblematic place in the city of Rome. There are so many beautiful places, but think that the best place to visit is the Colosseum. This is the one place not to be missed if you are visiting Rome. Today you will see this monument. She and her group are having trouble finding him. The directions a man gave her were incorrect. They follow his directions, but cannot find the Colosseum. They asked a police officer. The agent gave her the correct directions. They took a taxi which took them to the right place. They arrived at the Colosseum. It is an amazing place. It is worth coming to find out. He is very enthusiastic about visiting Rome. It's a dream come true for her.
I recommend you to visit Rome. You will not regret.

Espanol

Kathy está muy feliz porque va a ir a Roma. Visitar esta ciudad es un sueño hecho realidad para ella. Durante muchos años soñó con visitar Italia. El viaje es largo, son unas diez horas en avión desde América a Italia, pero vale la pena venir a esta maravillosa ciudad. Pasó la primera prueba en Inglés. Tuvo una excelente conversación con el taxista. Luego, después, no tuvo problemas para registrarse en el hotel. Kathy está impaciente por descubrir todos los lugares de Roma. Hay muchos lugares maravillosos para visitar, como palacios, castillos y monumentos. Lo mejor es la comida. Sus amigos le dicen que la comida italiana es realmente buena, la mejor de todas. Le encanta la buena comida y está segura de que probará todos sus platos. No tiene una comida favorita, pero le gustan todas las clases. El lugar que más quiere visitar es el Coliseo. Este es el lugar más emblemático de la ciudad de Roma. Hay muchos lugares hermosos, pero ella piensa que el mejor lugar para visitar es el Coliseo. Este es el único lugar que no debe perderse si visita Roma. Hoy verá este monumento. Ella y su grupo tienen problemas para encontrarlo. Las instrucciones que le dio un hombre eran incorrectas. Siguen sus instrucciones, pero no pueden encontrar el Coliseo. Le preguntaron a un oficial de policía. El agente le dio las instrucciones correctas. Tomaron un taxi que los llevó al lugar indicado. Llegaron al Coliseo. Es un lugar increíble. Vale la pena venir a descubrirlo. Está muy emocionada de visitar Roma. Es un sueño hecho realidad para ella.
Te recomiendo que visites Roma. No te arrepentirás.

Vocabulary

English
Palace, monument, building, hotel, airport, taxi, food, directions, sir, police, place, city, plane, dream, wonderful, discover, problem, best, visit, come, kind, alone, lady.

Espanol

Palacio, monumento, edificio, hotel, aeropuerto, taxi, comida, direcciones, señor, policía, lugar, ciudad, avión, sueño, maravilloso, descubrir, problema, mejor, visita, por venir, amable, solo, señorita.

My favorite hobbies – Mis pasatiempos favoritos

I am a young man of twenty five. Like any young person, I enjoy hanging out with my friends, watching movies in the cinema and meeting new people. I also like sports. I am passionate about tennis and football. Tennis in particular is a great passion for me. I've been playing tennis since I was little. My love for tennis is very big. I really enjoy playing it with my friends on weekends.

As for football, I really enjoy watching it on television. I also like playing with it, it's a good sport. Playing football for an hour is a great way to burn calories. Also, I have fun with my college friends. I follow all the teams, the tournaments and anything else related to football. I'm really passionate about it.

Although I like tennis and football, I have two other interesting hobbies. These hobbies are activities that I do when I am not working or have no university activities. These hobbies help me relax and focus on other activities I have to do each week. I can do them with my friends or I can do them myself. To be honest, I like doing them myself more because that way I can recharge my batteries after a full week of activities with all my friends.

My first hobby I have is collecting coins. I love to collect coins from different countries of the world. It is very interesting to know the forms of money of the different countries of the world. Each country has its own currencies. Some are fantastic, they have beautiful designs that tell a small part of the history of that country. Some other coins are simpler, but are representative of that nation's culture.

Whenever one of my friends goes on a trip, I always ask them to bring me a coin from the country they visit. My friends already know that I really enjoy collecting coins. So they help me enrich my collection. When I travel, I too take the coins of the countries I visit home. They are a great memory.

I currently have the currencies of fifty different countries. Some coins are in excellent condition. I keep these in an album and they are the coins I always show to my family and friends. I have other coins but they are in bad condition. These are stored in a plastic bag, which protects them from damage.

The other hobby I have is painting ... yes, painting. I love to paint pictures. My favorites are landscapes. I like trees and mountains. I think these are beautiful and relaxing. All my friends love them. My paintings are highly appreciated by both my friends and my parents. They always ask me if I have a new painting. Last month, I sold one for twenty-five dollars. It's not a lot of money, but it motivates me to continue my hobby.

These are my two hobbies and they are the activities I like to do when I'm not at work or university. They are also relaxing activities that I can do when I need to recharge my mind.

There are other types of hobbies. For example, some of my friends study languages. This is a nice pastime. But studying a language is not a goal for me at the moment. I speak Spanish and have been teaching English classes for many years. I would like to study another language, but I will one day.

Another popular hobby among my friends is traveling. At the moment, it's not one of my priorities. I am very busy and finishing university is very important to me. So I travel quite little. Maybe in the future it will be possible for me to travel more frequently. Sure, it's one of the coolest activities to do, but for now, I prefer short trips.

A very popular hobby these days is taking pictures. All my friends have good cameras or cell phones with a powerful camera. With these, they take pictures of all their activities, travels or people they know. Also, they take pictures of themselves. These photos are known as "selfies". I like selfies, but I don't take them very often. I prefer photographs where I am with all my friends or with my family.

And you, what is your favorite hobby?

You certainly have an activity that you enjoy doing often. These activities are very important in maintaining a healthy life. For example, you can play a sport. It does not matter which. What matters is playing a sport. Sports are essential for maintaining an active and interesting life. There are many sports to practice. Swimming, running or going to the gym are some examples of sports you can practice.

If you like to travel, you can collect souvenirs from each trip. Many people are used to collecting memories of all the trips they take. Some people collect pictures and paintings. Some others collect glasses, plates or handicrafts that are representative of the places they visit. These memories are actually a very special hobby.

For some other people, watches are more than just a hobby. They become a passion. Watches are items that serve much more than just knowing the time. Sure, that's the function of a watch, but when it becomes a hobby, you become passionate about the way they work, the mechanisms, the gears. I personally appreciate a nice watch, but I'm not a fan of it, so I don't care about the stories behind its making.

I also know some people who like to collect stamps. This hobby is similar to coins as you can learn more about the history and traditions of each country. Usually, countries produce stamps featuring important people of that country or in commemoration of special events such as their independence.

This hobby is no longer as popular as it used to be. Modern technology has revolutionized this sector, in fact thanks to e-mails, you hardly feel the need to send handwritten letters anymore. This is why stamps are getting scarcer. However, thanks also to this, if you have a collection of stamps, you can have a lot of money. Some are worth thousands of dollars.

But the most expensive hobby I know is collecting cars. These types of collections are for people with good taste and a lot of money. Cars, especially classic cars, cost a lot of money. Some collectors pay incredible amounts. For example, they pay hundreds of thousands of dollars for a classic car in good condition. There are other collectors who buy sports cars. These cars usually compete and develop high speeds. These are not the kind of cars you can use in the city. You need a special track to use their full speed.

Collecting cars is a hobby I would like to try. Of course, I can't do it right now as I don't have much money. For now, I only have a normal car. I need this for going to work, going out on weekends and traveling to nearby places. It is a good car but it is neither classic nor sporty. In the future I will have a lot of money and I will be able to collect all kinds of cars I want.

Maybe my coins can be worth a lot of money in the future. With my coin collection, I will be able to buy as many cars as I want! It would be a great hobby ... driving race cars on a track or driving a classic car in the places you travel. It is a very exciting idea.

Summary

English

There are all sorts of hobbies. Hobbies are activities that take place in free time, that is, in the time when you are not working or studying. This free time usually takes place on weekends. I have two hobbies. The first is to collect coins. I love knowing more about the history and culture of each country. Coins are a reflection of their history. I have currencies from fifty different countries. Every time my friends travel they bring me a coin from that country. The second hobby I have is painting pictures. I like to paint landscapes. It is a very relaxing activity. It helps me recharge my mind after a week of hard work and study. It's an activity I can do on my own. These are my two hobbies. These are the activities that I like to do the most. But it's not just these, there are many other hobbies. For example, many people collect postage stamps from different countries, take photos or have souvenirs from all the countries they visit. These hobbies are very interesting. Another very interesting hobby is traveling. At the moment, I cannot travel as I am very busy and I study a lot at the university so I don't have much time to do it. But the most interesting hobby I know is collecting cars. There are people with money who collect classic or sports cars. Classic cars can be driven like a normal car. Sports cars are generally race cars and are driven on the track. This type of car cannot be driven on the road as they develop high speeds. In the future I will have the money to collect classic and sports cars.

Espanol

Hay muchos tipos de pasatiempos. Las aficiones son actividades que se realizan en el tiempo libre, es decir, en el tiempo en el que no trabajas ni estudias. Normalmente, este tiempo libre se realiza los fines de semana. Durante los fines de semana, muchas personas tienen tiempo libre para realizar estas actividades. Tengo dos aficiones. La primera es recolectar monedas. Me encanta saber más sobre la historia y la cultura de cada país. Las monedas son un reflejo de la historia de ese país. Tengo monedas de cincuenta países diferentes. Cada vez que viajan mis amigos, me traen una moneda de ese país. El segundo pasatiempo que tengo es pintar cuadros. Me gusta pintar paisajes. Es una actividad muy relajante. Me ayuda a recargar mi mente después de una semana de arduo trabajo y estudio. Es una actividad que puedo hacer solo. Estos son mis dos pasatiempos. Estas son las actividades que más me gusta hacer. Pero estos no son los únicos. Hay muchas más aficiones. Por ejemplo, muchas personas coleccionan sellos postales de diferentes países, toman fotografías o tienen recuerdos de todos los países que visitan. Estos pasatiempos son muy interesantes. Otro pasatiempo muy interesante es viajar. Por ahora, no puedo viajar, estoy muy ocupado y tengo mucho estudio en la universidad. Entonces, no tengo mucho tiempo. Pero el pasatiempo más interesante que conozco es coleccionar coches. Hay gente con dinero que colecciona coches clásicos o exóticos. Los coches clásicos se pueden conducir como un coche normal. Los coches exóticos suelen ser coches de carreras y se conducen en una pista de carreras. Este tipo de automóviles no se pueden conducir en la calle ya que desarrollan altas velocidades. En el futuro tendré el dinero para coleccionar autos clásicos y exóticos.

Vocabulary

English

Collect, coins, paint, travel, photographs, cars, classic, exotic / sports, money, people, collector, hobby, sport, study, work, college, weekend, leisure, refill, mind, activity, interesting, important, di usually, often, souvenirs, places, to visit

Espanol

Coleccionar, monedas, pintar, viajar, fotografías, autos, clásico, exótico, dinero, gente, coleccionista, pasatiempo, deportes, estudio, trabajo, universidad, fin de semana, tiempo libre, recarga, mente, actividad, interesante, importante, usualmente, frecuentemente , recuerdos, lugares, visita

How to make new friends – Como hacer nuevos amigos

I love meeting new people. Everyone tells me that I am very sociable. I think they are right because I like to talk to everyone and learn more about them. I don't care if they're weird people, I always find something to talk to people about. It is the key to making new friends. Everyone has something interesting to say.

I recently met a very nice girl. He is from Germany and is visiting my country on vacation. She is a nice girl but a little shy. He is a very good person, but he has some problems starting a conversation. I talked to her because I saw her a bit lost in the city center. I approached her and offered my help.

Fernando: Hi, good morning. My name is Fernando. Do you need help?
Anna: Hi, good morning. My name is Anna. I am looking for Piazza Indipendenza.
Fernando: Sure, Independence Square is on that side. It's two blocks. You can't go wrong.
Anna: Thanks. I think the road is easy now.
Fernando: Yes, it's very simple. Where are you from?
Anna: I am from Germany.
Fernando: Interesting! Which part of Germany are you from?
Anna: I am from Berlin. Do you know Germany?
Fernando: I visited Berlin a few years ago with my family. It's a beautiful city.
Anna: Yes, it is.
Fernando: Are you here on vacation?
Anna: Yes, I'm with my brothers.
Fernando: How nice. Are you a student?
Anna: No. Actually, I work as a teacher in a school.
Fernando: Interesting. I work as a waiter in a restaurant while studying at university. Hey, your brothers would like to visit my restaurant? It is traditional cuisine.
Anna: Of course, that's not a bad idea.
Fernando: Great, you are all invited!

Anna came to my restaurant with her brothers. They are three brothers in total. We talked well, even though I was working. But still, they ate it very well and we had an interesting talk about their country, my city and many other things. It was a pleasure meeting Anna and her brothers.

I think that to make new friends easily, you have to be a positive and optimistic person. When you are pessimistic or negative, it is difficult to make new friends. People feel this if you are not a happy person and therefore look for other, more friendly people. This is not a problem for me. I am very friendly, I like to socialize with everyone. In short, I'm very outgoing.

Here are some helpful tips for making new friends.

First, it's important to smile. All people feel nervous or insecure when they meet a new person. If the first thing you do is smile, the other person will smile at you too. Smiling is the universal way to communicate with people. In all countries of the world, a smile is a very simple way to show that you are a good person. When you smile, others feel more relaxed, and this facilitates communication.

Then, keep your arms and hands open. If you cross your arms, you are demonstrating a defensive posture. This means that you have something to hide or you don't feel comfortable with other people. When you lower your arms or use your hands to speak, others see that you are sincere. This helps improve the first impression you make on other people. Your hands say much more than your words. If you use them effectively, you will always have a positive first impression.

Plus, eye contact allows you to be friendly, but without scaring your new friends. If you see a person in a direct, but friendly way, your new friend will feel comfortable. It is easy to do. You just have to look at the person normally. If, on the other hand, you don't look in the eyes, they will believe you have something to hide. This is why eye contact is important.

Likewise, your tone of voice is helpful in making new friends. You need to keep a firm but friendly tone of voice. This, combined with the right words, will help you improve your relationships with new people. This dialog is an example of how you can easily make new friends.

Fernando: Hi, what's your name?
Diego: My name is Diego. And you?
Fernando: My name is Fernando. My friends tell me Ferny.
Diego: Where are you from?
Fernando: I come from Spain. And you?
Diego: I come from Italy.
Fernando: How old are you?
Diego: I'm twenty three years old. How old are you?
Fernando: I'm nineteen years old.
Diego: Do you like football?
Fernando: Yes, and I also like basketball.
Diego: Really? I love basketball.
Fernando: How nice. We have a lot in common.

It is very important to ask your new friends interesting questions. With good questions, you can get to know your friends better. But you have to be careful not to ask too personal questions. If you ask questions that are too personal, you can make your new friends uncomfortable. That's why we need to talk about sports, hobbies, travel, work, family and other fun activities. With these conversations, he is sure that you will soon become good friends.

I personally like to listen to people. I ask questions and then listen to the answers. It is always a good idea to listen to people and then answer them with other questions. Virtually everyone likes to talk about their interests and experiences.

Conversely, if you talk too much and listen too little, other people don't feel comfortable. Nobody likes to talk to a person who doesn't stop talking. The ideal is to find a balance where everyone has the opportunity to speak. With this, you stand a good chance of having a good conversation.
So, here are some tips on what to do when meeting a new person.

First, it's a good idea to call your new friend by name. When he or she tells you his or her name, it's a good idea to repeat it. If you pronounce it incorrectly, your new friend will tell you the correct pronunciation. It's okay if you repeat it a few times, this way you make sure you pronounce it correctly.

So, when talking about your country or city, try to avoid inappropriate comments. For example, if you don't know a lot about your country, tell your new friend to explain where he is and to tell you a little about his country's history. These conversations are very interesting as you can learn something new.

Also, try to be positive at all times. That's why you should avoid negative comments or talk about bad things. Always talking about positive things is a good way to have a fun and interesting conversation. Above all, you help your friend feel comfortable.

Finally, try not to make awkward gestures with your face. Remember that smiling is the best thing you can do to maintain a positive atmosphere with your new friends. Smiles are contagious. So don't be surprised if your new friends smile at you too. Being a positive person is very important especially if the person you are talking to is from a different country.

As you can see, making new friends isn't difficult. The only thing it requires is a little attention and a lot of positivity. Being a good friend is easy when you have an interest in making people feel comfortable. You have the ability to make others feel good. With this, you can have good conversations.

Always remember that smiling is the most important thing you can do. Your smile is contagious. All people will react positively if you smile and speak in a friendly tone. Soon you will have many friends, even from all over the world.

Summary

English

Making new friends is easy when you know the best way to talk to people. The first thing you should do is smile. When you smile, other people also smile with you. Smiles are the universal form of communication. All people automatically recognize a smile when they see it. Also, it's always a good idea to ask interesting questions. Questions about countries, culture, weather, family, sports, and fun activities are the kind of questions that make conversations good. Try to avoid asking personal questions because personal questions can make your new friends uncomfortable. Likewise, if you listen more than you talk, you have a good chance of having a good conversation. Nobody likes to have a conversation with someone who doesn't stop talking. It is better to find a balance. This way, everyone has an equal opportunity to participate in the conversation. Another good tip is: always remember to ask the names of new people you know. If you have a hard time saying their name, they can surely help you say it correctly. It's also a good idea to ask interesting questions about your country, family, or job. But the most important thing is to keep a positive attitude. Just like smiling, it's important to keep a friendly tone of voice. Your voice is a very useful way to get a positive conversation going. Likewise, if you use your arms effectively, you can communicate correctly. If you hide your hands it is because you are hiding something. This creates distrust of others. That's why talking with your hands is an effective way to build trust in the people you meet. With these tips, you are ready to have a good conversation with new people and make lots of new friends quickly.

Espanol

Hacer nuevos amigos es fácil cuando conoce la mejor manera de hablar con la gente. Lo primero que debes hacer es sonreír. Cuando sonríes, otras personas también te sonríen. Sonreír es la forma de comunicación universal. Todas las personas reconocen automáticamente una sonrisa cuando la ven. Además, siempre es una buena idea hacer preguntas interesantes. Las preguntas sobre el país, la cultura, el clima, la familia, los deportes y las actividades divertidas son el tipo de preguntas que generan buenas conversaciones. Trate de evitar hacer preguntas personales porque las preguntas personales pueden hacer que sus nuevos amigos se sientan incómodos. Además, si escucha más de lo que habla, tiene muchas posibilidades de entablar una buena conversación. A nadie le gusta tener una conversación con alguien que sigue hablando. Lo mejor es encontrar un equilibrio. Por lo tanto, todos tienen la misma oportunidad de participar en la conversación. Algunos otros buenos consejos son: recuerde siempre pedir el nombre de una nueva persona. Si te cuesta pronunciar su nombre, seguro que te pueden ayudar a decirlo correctamente. También es una buena idea hacer preguntas interesantes sobre su país, familia o trabajo. Pero lo más importante es mantener una actitud positiva. Al igual que sonreír, es importante mantener un tono de voz amigable. Tu voz es una forma muy útil de lograr una conversación positiva. Del mismo modo, si usa sus brazos de manera efectiva, puede comunicarse de manera correcta. Si escondes tus manos es porque estás escondiendo algo. Esto genera desconfianza en los demás. Por eso, hablar con las manos es una forma eficaz de generar confianza en las personas que conoce. Con estos consejos, estará listo para tener una buena conversación con gente nueva y hacer muchos amigos rápidamente.

Vocabulary

English
Conversation, friends, smile, positive, attitude, tone, voice, hands, effectively, communication, hide, sincere, practically, balance, listen, speak, maintain, contact, eye, country, city, name, job, family, questions.

Espanol

Conversación, amigos, sonrisa, positivo, actitud, tono, voz, manos, efectivamente, comunicación, ocultar, sincero, prácticamente, balance, escuchar, hablar, mantener, contacto, visual, país, ciudad, nombre, trabajo, familia, preguntas.

Thanks for the compliment - Gracias por el cumplido

A compliment is a nice phrase that is said to a person when they do something good, look good, or on a special occasion. A compliment can be a word or a phrase that makes another person feel good. These words are meant to make them happy.

Generally, compliments are given on occasions such as birthdays, anniversaries, job promotions, or graduations. But there are also personal reasons for paying a compliment. For example, when a person looks good, a compliment can be well accepted. Even when a person does a good job, you can pay him a compliment. The important thing is to know what are the right occasions to get them.

When a person celebrates their birthday, you can say something like:

Best wishes! Have a good time.

This phrase is very common when someone turns a birthday. In fact, usually the answer is obtained:

Thank you so much!

Now, there is a very common confusion between the words "best wishes", "congratulations" and "congratulations".
The word "wishes" is used when it comes to a birthday or anniversary.

The word "compliments" is used when a person does something very well. For example, when a person does a good job, wins in a sport or achieves a goal, then this word is correct.

But if there is a very special event, like winning the lottery, or reaching a huge life goal, then the appropriate word is "congratulations".

If your best friend is getting married, you can also tell the newlyweds:

-Long life to the newlyweds!

This is a very common phrase when two people get married.

Another situation where you can compliment a person is when they do something right. This is rather however in the workplace, in sports, at school or at home. When a person does a good job, it is important to recognize it. For this, you can use phrases like:

-Good job
- You did it very well
-Congratulations
-Well done

All of these expressions serve as a compliment when you do a good job. For example, this dialogue is between a boss and an employee.

Boss: Great job. I am impressed with this report.
Employee: Thank you very much. You are very kind.

It's a short but effective exchange. The important thing is to recognize good work.

Another time you can compliment is when a person looks good. For example, it is customary to pay a compliment when someone improves their physical condition, perhaps losing weight. These sentences are some examples:

-You look great
-You are in great shape
-You look thinner
-How good are you
-Your efforts are paying off
- What a change!

With these expressions, you can comment on a person's physical appearance without making them feel uncomfortable. But if you want to compliment her on her clothes or shoes, you can use the following phrases:

-Those shoes fit you divinely.
-That blouse looks good on you.
- Those pants look great on you.
-That color goes well with your skin tone.
-That color makes you show off.

These are phrases that you can use for both men and women. The important thing is that they are friendly and do not cause any discomfort.

However, one thing to remember is not to ask questions about the prices of items your friends have bought. For example, if the watch he has is very nice but looks expensive, it's a bad idea to ask how much money it costs. But a good idea is to ask where he bought it instead. This can be a good way to start an interesting conversation. Many times, people feel uncomfortable talking about money, especially how much they paid for things.

Another time you can compliment is when it comes to a town or city. For example you can use some phrases like:

-Paris is a beautiful city.
-The United States is an interesting country.
-South America has many impressive places.
- England is full of history and tradition.

These are some examples of how you can compliment a country or city. With these phrases you mention the beautiful, positive and interesting things about a country. The most important thing is that you emphasize the most important aspects that you find interesting.

But you can also compliment places like a person's home. When visiting the home of a friend, colleague or client, you can use expressions such as:

-His house is very nice.
-What an elegant house.
-The paintings of your house look spectacular.
-What great family photos.
-The colors match very well.

In this case, you can use these expressions to show your liking for the house you visit. In this way you can manifest your education and good manners by finding yourself in the house of others.

Another time you can compliment is by making references to food. When you visit someone, you are in a restaurant or someone prepares food, you can compliment them to make them feel good. Here are some examples of phrases you can use in this case:

-The food is delicious.
- I love the soup. What is the secret ingredient?
-The pizza is wonderful. What's the recipe?
-This burger is the best.
-The food is very well seasoned.
-The meat is tender.
-The dessert is magnificent.

With these phrases, you can express your taste for the food you are trying. More importantly, you can do it in a polite and friendly way without sounding over the top.

It is also very important to know how to respond to compliments appropriately. A response like "thank you very much" is enough to show your appreciation for the positive comments. "Thank you very much" isn't the only way to respond to a compliment. You can use following phrases:

-I appreciate it
-So cute
-Thank you
-I really appreciate your words
-I really appreciate your gesture
-You are very kind

You can use any of these expressions when you really want to show your liking and appreciation for the compliments they've given you. Sometimes, for example, on a birthday, compliments can be accompanied by a gift. So these expressions are useful to indicate your appreciation, not only for the compliment, but also for the gift.

Now you can compliment and respond to them. Most importantly, you can do it naturally. With these phrases and expressions, you can show your appreciation in a sincere way. Your friends will surely appreciate your words. The important thing, in fact, is to be honest. Giving a sincere compliment is something very special. But false compliments can cause pain rather than pleasure for the other person. So a sincere compliment is a very valuable thing you can do to someone else.

Summary

English

Giving sincere compliments is a very nice thing you can do to a person. When your compliments are honest, you can please a friend, colleague, or family member. The important thing is to tell the truth. Such a compliment always pleases the person who receives it. Compliments are given on special occasions, such as a wedding, birthday, or anniversary. On these occasions, it is customary to say pleasant phrases to recognize the event that is happening. It is also a way to wish others the best. Compliments can also be given when a person does a good job. In these cases, a boss can compliment his employees. Similarly, you can compliment friends or colleagues who have done good things. You can also compliment a person on their physical appearance. You can compliment someone when they lose weight or wear clothes that make them more attractive. Another time you can compliment is when you visit the home of a friend, colleague, or even a client. It is in good taste to make pleasant comments about the house or the things you have in the house. Likewise, you can compliment the food you like.

It is also very important to know how to respond to compliments appropriately. In these cases, answering correctly pleases the person giving the compliments. That's why you need to know the appropriate phrases to answer correctly.

Espanol

Hacer cumplidos sinceros es algo muy bueno que puedes hacerle a una persona. Cuando sus cumplidos son honestos, puede complacer a un amigo, compañero de trabajo o familiar. Lo importante es decir la verdad. Un cumplido así siempre agrada a quien lo recibe. Los cumplidos se hacen en ocasiones especiales, por ejemplo, en una boda, cumpleaños o aniversario. En estas ocasiones se acostumbra decir frases agradables para reconocer el hecho que está sucediendo. También es una forma de dar buenos deseos a los demás. También se pueden hacer cumplidos cuando una persona hace un buen trabajo. En estos casos, un jefe puede hacer cumplidos a sus empleados. Del mismo modo, puede felicitar a amigos o colegas que hayan hecho cosas buenas. También puedes felicitar a una persona por su apariencia física. Puede felicitar a alguien cuando pierde peso o usar ropa que lo haga lucir bien. Además, otra ocasión en la que puedes hacer un cumplido es cuando visitas la casa de un amigo, pareja e incluso un cliente. Es bueno hacer comentarios agradables sobre la casa o sobre las cosas que tienen en su casa. De la misma manera, puedes hacer cumplidos sobre la comida que te gusta. Al igual que hacer cumplidos de manera adecuada, también es importante saber cómo responder a los cumplidos correctamente. En estos casos, responder de la manera correcta agrada a quienes están haciendo cumplidos. Es por eso que debes conocer las frases correctas para poder responder de la manera correcta.

Vocabulary

English
Compliment, fantastic, amazing, wonderful, magnificent, good, interesting, food, wedding, birthday, anniversary, occasion, event, sincere, honest, appropriate, correctly, appreciate, pleasure, sympathy, manners, congratulations, wishes, gift.

Espanol

Piropo, genial, increíble, maravilloso, magnífico, bueno, interesante, comida, boda, cumpleaños, aniversario, ocasión, evento, sincero, honesto, correcto, correcto, agradecer, placer, simpatía, modales, felicitaciones, deseos, obsequio.

Please come to my party - Por favor ven a mi fiesta

A party is a fun and special occasion. There are many reasons for throwing a party. For example, one of the reasons is a celebration, which is when special events such as a birthday or anniversary are celebrated. But there are also other types of celebrations, such as baptism, a bachelor party or a welcome for a new baby. On all these occasions, a party is organized in a person's home or in a large place with lots of decorations.

To throw a party you need food, music, drinks and a cake (usually). But the most important thing at a party is the guests. A guest is a person who attends the party, but does not organize it. A guest comes to the party, participates in the activities, eats and drinks, but does not prepare the festivities.

The people who organize the party invite the people who want to join the party. This is called making an invitation. There are many ways to make an invitation. Usually, it is done in person. You can invite your friends and family to join your party. It is also common to invite colleagues, fellow students or neighbors.

When inviting an invitation, you can use phrases like:

-Would you like to come to my party?
- I'm going to have a party on the weekend, do you want to come?
-We'll have a birthday party, I'd like you to join us.

Here are some phrases you can use to invite a friend or family member. But there are times when you need to make a more formal invitation, such as if you're going to invite your boss, client, or partner to a formal party or serious event. So, to make a formal invitation, you can say one of the following sentences:
-I would like to invite you to the launch party of our new brand.
-You are cordially invited to the welcome event for our general manager.
-I have the honor to invite you to our wedding.

These are all ways to make a formal invitation to an event or party. Likewise, formal invitations are generally made using the form of "you" rather than "you" as formal invitations should show a high level of respect towards the guest.

Some examples of formal events are a wedding, the launch of a new brand or company, a reception at a government or embassy office, or an awards or recognition ceremony for some cause. Charity events are also considered formal events.

However, not all invitations have to be formal. Sometimes the invitations are simple. The important thing is to know the correct way to do them. Below is an example of an invitation recently made to a friend.

Fernando: Hey Carla, do you have any plans for the weekend?

Carla: No, why?

Fernando: There is a new superhero movie. Do you want to come with me to see it?

Carla: Sure, sure. When?

Fernando: What do you think of Saturday night?

Carla: I think it's great. At what time?

Fernando: What do you say at eight in the evening?

Carla: Excellent. I'll see you.

This conversation is simple and informal, but uses the correct language. The most important thing is to communicate the reason for the invitation, when and at what time it will be. This lets your friend know exactly when the event or occasion will be.

We will now look at a more formal invitation. I made this invitation to a customer on the occasion of the launch of a new product from my company. The event was held in a hotel where only a select group of customers who we believe would be interested in learning about our new line were invited.

Fernando: Good morning, Mr. Rossi?

Mr. Rossi: Yes, tell me.

Fernando: Mr. Rossi, I am pleased to invite you to the launch of our new product next Wednesday at two in the afternoon.

Mr. Rossi: Oh, that's great. Thank you very much for the invitation. Where will it be?

Fernando: At the Excelsior Hotel. It is located three blocks from our offices.

Mr. Rossi: Great. I will be happy to participate.

Fernando: Thank you very much. We are waiting for you.

Mr. Rossi: With pleasure.

Fernando: Have a good day.

Mr. Rossi: You too.

As you can see, this invitation is more formal. You can see how there is respect for the customer. This is very important in business relationships as close friendships aren't always made at work.

Likewise, events at work can also be very informal. For example, when celebrating a colleague's birthday, a formal invitation is often not required. This is an example of an informal invitation for a birthday party in our office.

Fernando: Hey Daniele, we will organize a small party for Elisa's birthday. Tell your department that everyone is invited.

Daniele: Fantastic. When?

Fernando: Friday for lunch.

Daniele: Perfect. I'll tell everyone.

Fernando: Great. We are waiting for you.

In this conversation, we have kept a friendly but very informal tone. This is appropriate for co-workers or very close friends. Likewise, in this conversation I made an invitation to several people. But it is not necessary to invite everyone. Many times it is enough to tell one person so that everyone is officially invited.

As you can see, it is not difficult to make an invitation for any occasion. But there are times when you have to make a written invitation. In these cases, you can send an invitation by email or by post. Or, you can print the invitations and deliver them yourself.

A written invitation is a way to formalize your invitation. Even if your word is more than enough to invite someone, a written invitation is always a touch of good taste. Invitations are sent in writing for events such as weddings, birthday parties, corporate events or even some formal ceremony. Written invitations are often required to attend the event.

When you receive a written invitation, there are times when the invitation contains the letters "RSVP". These letters come from the French term that says "respondre s'il vous plait", that is, "answer please". The reason for including this is because the party organizers need confirmation on the number of people attending the event. The confirmation is used to prepare the event.

Now that you know how to make invitations, both formal and informal, you can make them to organize your next event, whether it's a birthday party, a friends reunion, or just hanging out with someone for a walk, watch a movie or eat something. The event or occasion doesn't matter. What matters is that you use the right words to make the invitation the right way.

Here are some tips for making invitations correctly.

First, it's a good idea to invite a week or two in advance when it comes to a formal event. This allows you to make the necessary arrangements for guests. For an outing with friends, it's always a good idea to do it a day or two earlier.

Then, keep in mind that in Italy people are not very punctual for formal events. People then start arriving at your event between thirty minutes to one hour after the time indicated on the invitation. But this does not happen in formal events.

Finally, don't worry about the details. People in Italy always find a way to have fun in any event!

Summary

English

An invitation is a request for people to attend an event or party. A party can be held for various reasons. For example, a birthday, wedding or baptism is celebrated. It is also customary to throw a party to welcome a new baby. Also, there are formal events where an invitation is made. These events include the launch of brands and products, the opening of a new office or a government or embassy ceremony. In all these cases, formal invitations are made for people related to the event to attend. Many times, you can make an invitation in person or with a phone call. In these cases, it is sufficient to provide information on the event to be held. The information refers to the day of the event, the time and place. This is basic information, but very important. In other cases, a written invitation must be sent. When you do this, it is to give more formality to the event you are organizing. In written invitations it is customary to include the letters "RSVP". These letters indicate that people need to confirm their presence. This confirmation is used by the event organizers to make the necessary preparations. On some occasions, the written invitation allows access to the place where the party takes place. Keep in mind that people are usually not on time for social events in Italy. So it shouldn't come as a surprise that they arrive at your party thirty minutes to an hour after the official time. But don't worry about the details. People in Italy always find a way to have fun.

Espanol

Una invitación es una solicitud para que las personas asistan a un evento o una fiesta. Una fiesta puede celebrarse por varias razones. Por ejemplo, se puede celebrar un cumpleaños, una boda o un bautismo. También se puede organizar una fiesta para dar la bienvenida a un nuevo bebé. Además, hay eventos formales en los que se realiza una invitación. Estos eventos incluyen lanzamientos de marcas y productos, la apertura de una nueva oficina o una ceremonia de gobierno o embajada. En todos estos casos, se realizan invitaciones formales a las personas relacionadas con el evento. Muchas veces, se puede hacer una invitación en persona o con una llamada telefónica. En estos casos, solo das la información sobre el evento que se realizará. La información se refiere al día del evento, la hora y el lugar. Esta es información básica, pero muy importante. En otros casos, debe enviar una invitación por escrito. Cuando haces esto, es para darle más formalidad al evento que estás organizando. En las invitaciones escritas se acostumbra incluir las letras "RSVP". Estas letras significan que las personas deben confirmar su asistencia. Esta confirmación es para que los organizadores del evento realicen los preparativos necesarios. En algunas ocasiones, la invitación escrita permite el acceso al lugar donde se realiza la fiesta. Tenga en cuenta que las personas no suelen ser puntuales para los eventos sociales en Italia. Por lo tanto, no debe sorprender que lleguen a su fiesta entre treinta minutos y una hora después de la hora oficial. Pero no se preocupe por los detalles. La gente en Italia siempre encuentra la manera de divertirse.

Vocabulary

English

Invitation, event, party, birthday, formal, informal, written, baby, government, embassy, client, confirmation, punctual, assistance, organize, preparations, information, celebration, ceremony, request, appropriate, officially, access, place, enter.

Espanol

Invitación, evento, fiesta, cumpleaños, formal, informal, escrito, bebé, gobierno, embajada, cliente, confirmación, puntual, asistencia, organizar, preparativos, información, celebración, ceremonia, solicitud, apropiado, oficialmente, acceso, lugar, ingresar.

How to get help in an emergency - Cómo obtener ayuda en caso de emergencia

Nobody likes an emergency. Emergencies are times when a person is in danger or there is an urgent situation such as a fire or a criminal act. In these cases, quick action is required. People in emergency situations need to think fast and solve the problem. Otherwise, they could suffer very serious consequences.

Often, the solution to an emergency is to ask for help. Of course, not all emergencies are a matter of life or death, but you often need help right away. When that happens, you should know who to call and what to say. If you know this information, you can ask for help correctly.

When you need help, you can call the police, fire department, paramedics or your embassy. In these places, get the help you need to solve the problem you are in. That's why we'll look at some examples and cases where you can ask for help. Likewise, we will look at the words and phrases that can be used in these cases.

One of the most common cases is when you should call the police. People call the police for various reasons. For example, the police are called in the event of a robbery, assault, fight or a very serious crime. When it comes to a serious crime, it is important to call the police immediately as some people's lives could be in danger.

When you call the police, you can do it over the phone. Each country has a special phone number that you can call in an emergency. You must always know this number when visiting a new country.

In some countries, the response operator is directly linked to the police or fire brigade. In other countries, a central operator is called and decides whether to report the emergency to the police, firefighters or paramedics. In an emergency call, the operator typically asks:

-What is your emergency?

In this case you can answer:

- They're robbing a shop.
- We are injured.
- There was a car accident.
-There is a fire

In all of these cases, you have to describe what is happening. Otherwise, the operator will not be able to help you. You can even add a direct request. For example:

- Please send an ambulance.
- Send the police over there.

- We need firefighters.
-An ambulance, it's urgent.
-Send the paramedics.

All of these ways to ask for help are fine. In fact, it's always good to say "please", but many times in an emergency, we forget to say it. It is enough to be direct without using offensive words. The operator understands that you are in a difficult situation.
Other important phrases that you can use in an emergency are:

-Help me!
-I need help
-This person needs an ambulance
-Call the police

With these phrases, you can communicate that you need help or you know someone else needs help. If you can't do this, someone else will see the situation and ask for help. Similarly, if you can't ask for help, these phrases are used to tell others to do it. The important thing is to communicate when a person is in danger.

When traveling, it's also important to contact your embassy in an emergency. In these cases, you may need help if your money or belongings are stolen, if you lose your passport or have a medical emergency. For these cases you can say:

- I need to contact my embassy.

If you are at an airport, you can easily find the contact information for your embassy. But if you are on the street, you can spot the police or military to tell them you need to contact your embassy for an emergency.

Some sentences in this case are:

-I need help. I've lost my passport.
-My money and my belongings have been stolen.
-I'm lost.
-I can't find my child / I can't find my parents.
-I have to block my credit card.

In other cases, you may have a medical emergency. In these cases, it is very important to communicate the information necessary to receive the information correctly. These are some very important phrases.

-I am allergic to _____.
-I take the medicine _____.
-I suffer from _____.
-I have problems with _____.
- I have an operation in _____.

With these phrases, you can indicate a medical condition. Some of the more common conditions are: diabetes, high blood pressure, or heart problems. You can also specify the problem you have, for example, you can say "I have back problems" or "I have heart problems".

When traveling through airports, it is always a good idea to know the name of your medication in English. Airport authorities may sometimes ask you what medicine you are taking. So, to avoid misunderstandings, it is a good idea to know the names in English. Often, airport security doesn't know much about drugs.

One of the most important aspects is to specify if you have allergies. Here are some phrases that will help you indicate your allergies.

-I am allergic to gluten.
-I'm allergic to penicillin.
-I am allergic to shellfish.
-I am allergic to peanuts.

It is also a good idea to carry a sheet with this information especially during a health crisis. That way, people who help you in the ambulance or hospital know they shouldn't give you penicillin, etc. The same is true in restaurants. If you know you are allergic to certain foods, you can ask before ordering:

- Does this food contain gluten?

This question is an example of how you can ask questions about the content of meals. This way, you can be sure that you are not eating something that will harm you. This is very important as no one wants to get sick on a trip.

When a crime occurs, it is always good to give a description of what happened. You can describe the events that happened. If the crime is a robbery, the following phrases can be used:

-A car was stolen.
-Someone is robbing a house.
-There are thieves in a shop.
-There are people who steal on the street.

This information is useful for the police to catch criminals. Providing information on criminals is also helpful. Here are some phrases you can use when talking to the police:

- There are three criminals.
-The thief is tall and fat.
-The thief is short and thin.
-He has a beard.
-He has long hair.
-He has tattoos.
-Wear black clothes.

When you talk to the police or the emergency operator, you need to tell them your location. Your location is based on the street or avenues you are on. For example, you can say:

- I'm in Piazza Grande.
- I'm in Viale Indipendenza number 9

But if you don't know exactly where you are, you can ask other people about your location. This sentence can help you:

- Where we are?
- Where I am?
- What's the name of this place?

With these phrases, you can find out your location and help the police know exactly where the emergency is. It's best to never have to ask for help, but if you have an emergency, you can now do it in English. The most important thing is to stay calm and provide the requested information. This way, the police, firefighters and paramedics can help you quickly.

Summary

English
An emergency is an event where a situation needs to be resolved quickly. If you can't resolve the situation, you need to ask for help. In these cases, you need to know who you can call for support. In an emergency, you can call the police, fire department, paramedics, or your embassy if you are traveling. In these cases, you need to know the emergency telephone number. All countries have a special number where help can be called. If you are traveling to another country, it is a good idea to know this number before you leave. You should also know your embassy's contact information when traveling. When a medical emergency occurs, it's a good idea to have written information about any food or drug allergies you have. It is also a good idea to have written information about the medications you take. Therefore, when you travel and go through airport security, they will understand what

medications you take and what kind of medications they are. With this you can avoid problems during your trip. When the emergency concerns a crime, it is important to describe it so that the police have information on the criminals. You can describe the number of criminals or the physical appearance of the criminal. Likewise, it's a good idea to know your location. With this information, the police can find you. If you don't know your location, you can ask people around you for street names. The best thing you can do is prepare for any emergency. Now that you know how to communicate in English, it's easier to express yourself when you need help. Nobody likes emergencies, but it's best to always be prepared. With the phrases in this lesson, you can get help in an emergency of any kind.

Espanol

Una emergencia es un evento en el que necesita resolver una situación rápidamente. Si no puede resolver la situación, debe pedir ayuda. En estos casos, es necesario saber a quién puede llamar para obtener apoyo. En caso de emergencia, puede llamar a la policía, los bomberos, los paramédicos o su embajada si está de viaje. En estos casos, debe conocer el número de teléfono de emergencia. Todos los países tienen un número especial al que puede llamar para pedir ayuda. Si viaja a otro país, es una buena idea conocer este número antes de salir de viaje. También debe conocer la información de contacto de su embajada cuando viaje. Cuando ocurre una emergencia médica, es una buena idea tener información escrita sobre las alergias que tiene a los alimentos o medicamentos. También es una buena idea tener información escrita sobre los medicamentos que toma. Entonces, cuando viaje y pase por la seguridad del aeropuerto, ellos comprenderán qué medicamentos toma y qué tipo de medicamentos son. Con esto podrás evitar problemas durante tu viaje. Cuando la emergencia se trata de un delito, es importante describir el delito para que la policía tenga información sobre los delincuentes. Puede describir el número de delincuentes o el aspecto físico del delincuente. Además, es una buena idea conocer su ubicación. Con esta información, la policía puede encontrarlo. Si no conoce su ubicación, puede preguntar a las personas que lo rodean sobre los nombres de las calles. Lo mejor que puede hacer es estar preparado para cualquier emergencia. Ahora que sabe cómo comunicarse en Inglés, es más fácil expresarse cuando necesita ayuda. A nadie le gustan las emergencias, pero es mejor estar preparado en caso de una emergencia. Con las frases de esta lección, puede obtener ayuda cuando tenga una emergencia de cualquier tipo.

Vocabulary

English

Emergency, help, support, medicine, medication, contact, criminals, theft, allergic, security, police, thieves, fire, ambulance, paramedics, embassy, passport, description, amount, operation, condition, penicillin, gluten, operator.

Espanol
Emergencia, ayuda, apoyo, medicina, medicación, contacto, delincuentes, robo, alérgico, seguridad, policía, ladrones, bomberos, ambulancia, paramédicos, embajada, pasaporte, descripción, monto, operación, condición, penicilina, gluten, operador.

Today is a nice day - Hoy es un buen día

The climate is very varied depending on which part of the world you live in. Depending on the country, the climate can be hot or cold. This is especially important if you are planning to travel to a new country. When traveling, it is always a good idea to check the climate of the place you are going to visit, this way, you can avoid an unpleasant surprise.

For example, if you are planning to travel to a hot country, it is important to know this first so that you can prepare yourself with the clothes you need to have fun. Likewise, if the country you are visiting is very cold, you need to bring warm clothes.

A very simple way to know the climate of a country you will visit is to consult it online. There are services where you can consult information on the current climate. Also, you can check the weather forecast for the following days. This will allow you to learn more about the weather conditions during the days you will spend in that town or city.

Another very useful way to know the weather conditions is through the use of an application on your mobile. A weather app can send you alerts, forecast updates, or notifications about a weather emergency. With the latter, you can be informed and prepared at any time.

In general, the weather can be described as sunny, cloudy, windy, foggy or rainy. In cold countries, snow also falls, which does not happen in tropical countries. In case of heavy rain or heavy snow, it is called a storm. A storm is a weather event in which conditions are severe.

When a rain storm falls, a lot of water falls from the sky. In this case, the storm usually includes a lot of wind, poor visibility and lightning. During a storm, it is best to avoid going out. The ideal is to stay at home. So you can avoid a car accident and put your life in danger.

In the event of a snowstorm, the situation can be very serious. During the snow storm it is very dangerous for people to leave the house because the roads become impassable.

But not all climatic conditions are dangerous. When the day is sunny and warm, it is a beautiful day. On nice days, people go out to the park, play sports, swim or have fun with family and friends. Warm and sunny days are usual during the summer. Summer is the favorite season for most people.

But summer isn't the only season. There are usually four seasons a year, summer, fall, winter and spring. In some countries, all four seasons are clearly marked, in others, they are slightly less marked. Likewise, the weather changes according to the season.

During the winter, the weather is colder than usual. In cold countries, snow falls and produces ice. In more tropical countries, the temperature drops and it rains. They also have a cloudy climate, so people should wear warmer clothing.

In spring, the weather is warmer, rain falls and plants and flowers begin to grow. This season, people start to feel better as the weather starts to improve. During the summer the climate becomes warm and very pleasant. This is many people's favorite season as they can do all their favorite activities. In tropical countries, the temperature becomes very high. That's why they need to drink a lot of water to avoid becoming dehydrated.

Autumn is the season that follows summer. Autumn is characterized by a lot of wind and cloudy weather. The leaves start falling from the trees. The plants slowly begin to prepare for winter. Likewise, the animals take refuge as winter is very cold.

The following dialogue is very useful for talking to someone about the weather.

Diego: How is the weather today?
Elisa: It's very hot. Wear a hat because it is very sunny.
Diego: Thanks. I'll be careful.

In this conversation, it is very hot and there is a lot of sun and consequently certain precautions must be taken. When it's very sunny, it's easy to get skin burns or feel fatigued from lack of water. This is another conversation with useful phrases.

Diego: Is it hot or cold?
Elisa: It is very cold. Cover up well.
Diego: Thanks. I'll wear the jacket with a sweater.

This dialogue is a good example of how you can talk in cold weather. Always remember that it is important to wear appropriate clothing for the cold season. When it's very cold, you can quickly take damage to your health.

When talking about the weather forecast, you can use the following phrases:
Diego: Hey, do you know what the weather will be this weekend?
Elisa: Yes, it will be cloudy with a high probability of rain.
Diego: Oh, then the weather will be bad. It would be a bad idea to go to the beach.
Elisa: Yes, it would be better to stay at home.

This is another conversation you can study.

- Diego: Hey, do you know what the weather forecast is for this week?
- Elisa: Yes, it will be very nice. Sunny and warm weather is expected.
- Diego: Great. Then I can go for a run.
- Elisa: Yes, you can also go out on a bicycle.
Diego: I think it's great.

These conversations are great examples to use with your friends or colleagues. Remember that asking questions about time is helpful. But it's also important to express your climate preferences.

For example, to express your tastes you can use the following phrases:

-I like it hot.
-I like the cold
-I don't like rain.
-I hate snow.
- I love snow.
-I like rainy days.

But you can also give your opinion on the weather. Here are some examples.

- The day is beautiful.
- It's bad weather.
- It's getting cold.
- It will rain soon.

These are useful phrases for giving your opinion. But when you describe the time in the moment you speak, you can use the following sentences.

-It's warm.
- It rains very hard.
-It's raining lightly.
-It's very cold.
-It's cloudy.
-It's foggy.

These expressions are used to describe the climate of that precise moment. They are also useful for describing the time when someone else asks you.

With the phrases we quoted in this story, you can perfectly talk about the weather with your friends and colleagues. You can ask questions and answer these questions. But remember that technology makes it easier for us to know the state of the climate. That is why I recommend that you have an application on your mobile so that you know the weather well, and so you can be prepared.

Furthermore, knowing the weather forecast is also important in the event of a storm or possible weather emergency. By preparing yourself, you can save your family from weather problems. That's why it's always good to have food and clothes ready in an emergency. For example, when a strong storm occurs, you can be prepared in case the current goes out. Another valuable tip is to keep a small radio that uses batteries. This way, you can always stay connected and aware of the latest information even when there is no electricity. Check local government recommendations in case of an emergency.

Summary

English
The weather can be varied depending on your country. In some countries, the weather is warm and sunny. In other countries, the weather is cold and also snowy. When the day is warm and sunny, it is said that the day is very beautiful. But when the day is cloudy and rainy, then it is said to be a bad day. In these cases, not much can be done. You can't do your favorite activities because the weather is bad. To know the state of the weather, you can check online. There are websites where you can learn more about weather conditions. There are also applications for mobile phones where you can learn more about the weather. The weather information in the future is known as the weather forecast. The forecast is very useful when traveling to a new country. It is very important to know the weather conditions in the country you will visit since it allows you to prepare with the appropriate clothes. For example, if it is hot, then you need light clothes. If it is very cold, then you can prepare yourself with warm clothes. There are also four seasons in the year, summer, autumn, winter and spring. Summer is the warmest season of the year. Most people prefer this season. Autumn is very windy, and the days are cloudy. It is cold in winter. In some countries snow falls. In the spring it rains, but the plants and flowers come back to life. The best season of the year is summer since during this season you can do all the favorite activities. The weather is the best to do any activity.

Espanol
El clima puede variar según su país. En algunos países, el clima es cálido y soleado. En otros países, el clima es frío y también con nieve. Cuando el día es cálido y soleado, se dice que el día es muy hermoso. Pero cuando el día está nublado y lluvioso, se dice que es un mal día. En estos casos, no se puede hacer mucho. No puedes hacer tus actividades favoritas porque hace mal tiempo. Para conocer el estado del clima, puede consultar en línea. Hay sitios web donde puede obtener más información sobre las condiciones climáticas. También hay aplicaciones para teléfonos móviles donde puedes aprender más sobre el clima. La información meteorológica en el futuro se conoce como pronóstico del tiempo. El pronóstico es muy útil cuando se viaja a un nuevo país. Es muy importante conocer las condiciones climáticas del país que visitarás ya que te permite prepararte con la ropa adecuada. Por ejemplo, si hace calor, entonces necesitas ropa ligera. Si hace mucho frío, puede

prepararse con ropa de abrigo. También hay cuatro estaciones en el año, verano, otoño, invierno y primavera. El verano es la estación más cálida del año. La mayoría de la gente prefiere esta temporada. El otoño es muy ventoso y los días están nublados. Hace frio en invierno. En algunos países cae nieve. En primavera llueve, pero las plantas y las flores vuelven a la vida. La mejor temporada del año es el verano ya que durante esta temporada se pueden realizar todas las actividades favoritas. El clima es el mejor para realizar cualquier actividad.

Vocabulary

English

Seasons, weather, summer, autumn, winter, spring, forecast, status, applications, online, snow, wind, heat, warm, cold, rainy, windy, foggy, plants, flowers, activities, beautiful, hot, light.

Espanol
Estaciones, clima, verano, otoño, invierno, primavera, pronóstico, estado, aplicaciones, en línea, nieve, viento, calor, cálido, frío, lluvioso, ventoso, brumoso, plantas, flores, actividades, hermoso, caluroso, ligero.

Remembering my childhood – Recordando mi infancia

A person goes through various stages of life. From birth, each stage is important and precious. In every part of life, essential lessons are learned for the development and growth of the person. The most important stage for a person's growth and development is childhood.

Childhood is the stage of life where a person grows from birth to a teenager. Typically, a person is considered a teenager when they are twelve or thirteen. From this point on, he stops being a child and becomes a boy.

Childhood is usually filled with good memories. These memories are about school, friends, games and family. It is during this stage that many of life's lessons are learned. But it is also necessary for children to use this stage to learn habits that will be useful throughout their lives.

Adults generally remember their childhood in a pleasant way. Sure, there are some people who haven't had a happy childhood. Indeed, there are people who faced a difficult childhood for various reasons. For this reason, their memories are not so pleasant.

When a person remembers his childhood, he remembers the past. So when you talk about the past, you can express these experiences in two ways. Each form is linked to the past, but expresses different ideas.

The first way to express the past is through the use of the simple past. This grammatical form refers to actions that have already finished and have remained in the past. For example, a person can talk about their place of origin in the following way:

- I grew up in Los Angeles, California.

The expression "I grew up" is an example of a simple past. This verb refers to the city where the person lived his childhood. Here are other examples of sentences that can be used in this context.

-I lived in a very large house.
-I lived in a small house.
-I studied in a public school.
-I studied in a private school.
-I played football when I was a child.
-I took dance lessons when I was a child.

These phrases reflect past actions on a person's childhood. The important thing is that they are actions that have already ended and are stored in the memories of the past. Therefore, they are expressed in this way.

Here is a small dialogue in which these phrases are used.

-Bianca: Where are you from?
-Lorenzo: I come from Argentina.

-Bianca: Interesting. Where have you grown up?
-Lorenzo: I grew up in Buenos Aires.
-Bianca: Oh, that's great. Where did you study?
-Lorenzo: I studied in a private school in my city.

This conversation is a good example of how you can use this verb to talk about your childhood. But also part of talking about childhood is mentioning the activities they used to do. This includes activities such as playing, walking, studying, vacations or any other usual activity.

For this type of activity, the imperfect past is used. This tense indicates actions that were usually performed in the past, but without specifying when they were performed. That is why it is called imperfect.

Here are some examples of using the imperfect past tense to talk about common actions in childhood.

-I used to play football during my free time at school.
-I was studying in a very nice school.
-I lived in a very quiet neighborhood.
-I ate a lot of sweets.
-I used to visit my grandparents often on weekends.

The difference between the imperfect past and the simple past is the frequency of the action. So when you talk about finite actions, which are just memories, the simple past is used. When you talk about regular actions in the past, you can use the imperfect past. With this, you can differentiate if you are just talking about a memory, or you are talking about an action that you often did in the past.

Other words you can use to talk about the frequency of actions are: always, never, sometimes. With these words you can be more specific about how often the actions were performed. Here are some examples that can help you in your conversations.

-I always got good grades in my exams.
-I never behaved badly in school.
- Sometimes I visited the lake during the holidays.

Below, here is a dialogue you can use to talk about your childhood.

-Bianca: How were you as a child?
-Lorenzo: I was very shy. I had to make a lot of effort to have friends. And you?
-Bianca: I was a very quiet girl. I had friends, but it took me a long time to learn to be sociable.

In this conversation you can see the adjectives, "shy" and "quiet" refer to the qualities of people. Of course, there are more qualities like: outgoing, funny, interesting, playful, calm, studious, mischievous, obedient and rebellious.

When a child is said to be "rebellious", it is because he has difficulty accepting the authority of adults. Conversely, when a child is said to be "calm", it is because it does not cause problems at home or at school.

This dialogue is a good example of how to talk about your childhood.

-Bianca: Hi Lorenzo. Tell me, how were you as a child?
-Lorenzo: Hi Bianca. I was a very studious boy. I have always enjoyed playing football. And you?
-White: I was a very calm girl. I went to the dance class and did all my homework after school.

In this conversation, you can see the use of the simple past tense for descriptions (I was a very studious child) and the use of the imperfect past tense to talk about habitual actions (I went to the dance class). Thus, you may notice the use of both tenses to refer to these actions.

The good news is that you can't necessarily use the simple past or the imperfect past to talk about your childhood. These tenses can also be used to talk about any event in the past. The important thing is to know the difference. With these times you can talk about any kind of past activity. For example:

-I worked in a small company.
-I worked in a small company.

What is the difference between both sentences?

Both sentences speak of the past. But the first one (I worked in a small company) refers to an action that has already finished. In the case of the second (I worked in a small company) you indicate that the action was habitual, that is, it was your routine to work in this company.

With this story, you are ready to talk about the past. Now you can express your ideas about your childhood or any past event. You can take time to remember the past with friends and family. You can relive pleasant moments or recall past experiences. You can also express your past experiences in a job interview. It is definitely a useful tool for making a good impression.

There is a saying that goes like this: "remembering is reliving". In short, remembering the past is a way to relive pleasant moments. But we want to forget the moments that were not pleasant. We just want to remember those wonderful moments we have with the special people in our lives.

Summary

English

Childhood is a stage of growth and development of all people. Usually, childhood is a stage where many things are learned for life. Being a child is a stage that lasts until the age of twelve or thirteen. From this age forward, the child becomes a teenager. After being a teenager, a young person becomes an adult. Usually, adults remember their childhood, the things they did and where they lived. Childhood memories include where they lived, the school where they studied and the activities they did. To express these ideas, the simple past is used. This tense is used to talk about activities that have already ended. So, these activities are only memories of the past. Likewise, they do not have a specific time in which they were done. It simply indicates that they happened. The other tense used in this case is the imperfect past. This other tense is used to talk about actions that usually happened. These actions can be of any type. The idea is to express the actions that always, sometimes, or were never done. The basic difference between both verb tenses is the frequency with which the actions were made. But these verb tenses are not only used to talk about childhood. They can also be used to talk about any action in the past. This is very useful in a job interview. So, you can use the simple past and imperfect past to talk about your experience.

Espanol
La infancia es una etapa de crecimiento y desarrollo de todas las personas. Por lo general, la infancia es una etapa en la que se aprenden muchas cosas de por vida. Ser niño es una etapa que dura hasta los doce o trece años. A partir de esta edad, el niño se convierte en un adolescente. Después de ser adolescente, un joven se convierte en adulto. Por lo general, los adultos recuerdan su infancia, las cosas que hicieron y dónde vivieron. Los recuerdos de la infancia incluyen el lugar donde vivieron, la escuela donde estudiaron y las actividades que realizaron. Para expresar estas ideas, se utiliza el pasado simple. Este tiempo se usa para hablar de actividades que ya terminaron. Entonces, estas actividades son solo recuerdos del pasado. Asimismo, no tienen un horario específico en el que se realizaron. Simplemente indica que sucedieron. El otro tiempo usado en este caso es el pasado imperfecto. Este otro tiempo se usa para hablar sobre acciones que generalmente sucedieron. Estas acciones pueden ser de cualquier tipo. La idea es expresar las acciones que siempre, a veces, o nunca se realizaron. La diferencia básica entre ambos tiempos verbales es la frecuencia con la que se realizaron las acciones. Pero estos tiempos verbales no solo se usan para hablar sobre la infancia. También se pueden usar para hablar sobre cualquier acción en el pasado. Esto es muy útil en una entrevista de trabajo. Por lo tanto, puede utilizar el pasado simple y el pasado imperfecto para hablar sobre su experiencia.

Vocabulary

English

Past, childhood, work, experience, frequency, habitual, school, always, sometimes, never, teenager, adult, both, usually, actions, verbs, interview, moments, ideas, simple, used, finished, shy, quiet, outgoing.

Espanol
Pasado, infancia, trabajo, experiencia, frecuencia, habitual, escolar, siempre, a veces, nunca, adolescente, adulto, ambos, habitualmente, acciones, verbos, entrevista, momentos, ideas, sencillo, usado, terminado, tímido, tranquilo, extrovertido.

Suggestions and recommendations - Sugerencias y recomendaciones

There are many occasions when we need to express our opinion on different things. It is common to give opinions on food, clothing, travel, music, books, and many other things. It is always a good idea to be honest when expressing opinions. Sincerity helps other people to know the reality of an object or service. For example, if you give your honest opinion about a restaurant, people will know if it's a good restaurant or if you don't want to go there. There are also cases where you should make a suggestion or recommendation regarding something. When doing this, it's important to be honest and realistic. Many times, our opinions are influenced by bad experiences. This is a classic example:

You go to a restaurant and order your food. Unfortunately, the service is slow, the food doesn't meet your expectations and the price is high. In short, it was a bad experience. So, your opinion of this place will be negative. If someone else asks you about this restaurant, it is very difficult for you to recommend it.

In this example, a bad experience makes a bad impression at the restaurant. When someone asks you for your opinion, you can use the following sentence:
-I don't recommend this restaurant. The service is slow, the food is bad and the prices are high.

This is a negative opinion about the restaurant you visited. However, opinion changes if, for example, you have a good experience with the restaurant. In that case you can use the following sentence:
-I recommend going to that restaurant. The food is good, the service is fast and the prices are fair.

Similarly you can counter your opinion.

-The food is expensive, but it is very good.

In this case, make it clear that the prices are high in your opinion, but still worth it. With this opinion, other people will consider whether they will go less to this restaurant.
But restaurants aren't the only places that get opinions and recommendations from others. Hotels, gyms and companies also receive opinions and criticisms. A criticism is when a person indicates an opinion about the good and bad things about that business. Simply put, try to show an objective side of that business. When a person is objective, he gives his opinion without including his personal thoughts.

Many people seek advice on restaurants, hotels, airlines, taxis, or any other type of service. Similarly, people try to get some insight into other people's experience in companies like beauty salons, spas, gyms, or schools. In such cases, it is common to see the following questions posted on social networks.

- Does anyone recommend a good gym?
-What do you think of the new beauty salon?
-I'm looking for a weekend restaurant. Some advices?
-I plan to travel next week, who knows a good hotel?
-What do you think of the restaurant?

All these questions are asked to get information from other people who know about these activities. Opinions can be negative or positive. In some cases, they can even be neutral. In such circumstances, a comment such as "it is neither good nor bad" is used to emphasize the neutral opinion.

There are also cases where you can make a suggestion to someone else. A tip is when you tell someone else what you think they should or should do. Every day, we make suggestions on many things.

For example, a friend wants to go on vacation but doesn't know where. In this example, your friend asks for a tip. In the following dialogue, we can observe this question.

-Fernando: Hey Karen, I want to go on vacation to a warm and beautiful place, but I don't know where. Some idea?
-Karen: What do you think of the beach?
-Fernando: I like it.
-Karen: Then you should go to Nova Beach. She's very pretty. I think your whole family will like it.
-Fernando: Hey, that's not a bad idea. I think I will bring my family. Thank you for your suggestion
-Karen: Imagine

In this conversation, the suggestion to go to the beach was expressed like this, "You should go to Nova Beach". This type of suggestion is very common among friends or family. It is a relatively informal way of making suggestions. But in cases where a formal opinion must be expressed, for example in the workplace, it is preferable to use a different type.

-Fernando: The company's situation is serious. I think some changes are needed.
-Karen: What changes do you suggest?
-Fernando: I suggest a cost reduction for this quarter.
-Karen: I understand, any other advice?
-Fernando: I recommend a 5% increase in our prices. This will help us balance our costs.

As you can see, in the previous dialogue the situation is much more formal. This is a formal business meeting where suggestions and recommendations should be made. The most important thing to remember is that it is not appropriate to use a phrase as "should" as it can be taken as an order rather than a formal recommendation.

Similarly, you can use these types of expressions when you want to give a hint to a person you don't know very well. This happens in business when a customer wants to pick up an item. In this case, the seller can suggest an item in a more subtle way. The following dialogue provides an example of this situation.

-Fernando: Good morning, I'm looking for a sweater.
-Karen: Good morning. We have these colors and styles.
-Fernando: Blue looks nice to me.
-Karen: Excellent choice. I recommend you get it today because we have a special discount.
-Fernando: Great. I'll take it.

In this case, the salesperson is very formal as they don't know their customer well. The conversation shows respect and kindness. But there are also cases where the seller can be more informal, especially if the type of shop or business is younger.

-Fernando: Good morning, I'm looking for a sweater.
-Karen: Good morning. Sure, we have these colors and styles.
-Fernando: Blue looks good to me,
Karen: How cool! You should get it today as we have it with a special discount.
Fernando: Really? I'll take it then.

This is a more informal conversation that shows how the salesperson behaves more relaxed with the customer. The conversation is appropriate, but make a direct recommendation by saying "You should get it." This tip is straightforward and refers to the store having the sweater on sale.

With the phrases that we have discussed in this story, you can now make suggestions and recommendations.

The only recommendation is to always be friendly. If you have a bad opinion about a restaurant, hotel or any other place, it's always nice to be polite and say something like "I don't recommend that place because I had a bad experience". If you trust people, you can provide more details. Otherwise, it's best to avoid bad mouthing a place. It is not appropriate to speak ill of other places. Just giving your negative opinion to let others know that a place is not good.

Summary

English

Many times, people seek opinions, suggestions and recommendations on places such as restaurants, hotels, airlines or any other type of business such as a beauty salon, gym or a school. Many times, it is common to see social media posts that ask about this type of business. With this, a person asks for the opinion of others. Then, the person decides if he goes to one of these places or not. The most common expression for giving a recommendation is "should." This expression indicates what a person believes is the best action for another person. It is commonly used among friends and colleagues. It is a direct and often informal expression. Therefore, it is not appropriate in a formal context. For example, in a business meeting, it is better to use expressions such as, "I think," "I suggest," or "I recommend." These types of expressions are appropriate to provide an opinion without giving orders to other people. This is important to remember when you talk to your boss or customers. When a seller talks to customers, they can be very formal, or they can be more informal. Usually, sellers are formal with their customers as it is a way of showing respect and manners. But in other cases, the business style can be more informal. In that case, the seller can take a more informal tone. Always remember to be polite when you give your opinions. If you had a bad experience with a company or a place, it is better to say something like, "I do not recommend it because I had a very bad experience." Of course, you can give more details if you talk to your friends or trustworthy people. But it is better to be polite and a little reserved when you give a negative opinion of a place. This makes you look like a polite and proper person.

Espanol

Muchas veces la gente busca opiniones, sugerencias y recomendaciones sobre lugares como restaurantes, hoteles, aerolíneas o cualquier otro tipo de negocio como un salón de belleza, un gimnasio o una escuela. Muchas veces, es común ver publicaciones en redes sociales que preguntan sobre este tipo de negocios. Con esto, una persona pide la opinión de los demás. Luego, la persona decide si va a uno de estos lugares o no. La expresión más común para dar una recomendación es "debería". Esta expresión indica lo que una persona cree que es la mejor acción para otra persona. Se usa comúnmente entre amigos y colegas. Es una expresión directa y a menudo informal. Por tanto, no es apropiado en un contexto formal. Por ejemplo, en una reunión de negocios, es mejor utilizar expresiones como "Creo", "Sugiero" o "Recomiendo". Este tipo de expresiones son adecuadas para dar una opinión sin dar órdenes a otras personas. Es importante recordar esto cuando hable con su jefe o sus clientes. Cuando un vendedor habla con los clientes, pueden ser muy formales o pueden ser más informales. Por lo general, los vendedores son formales con sus clientes, ya que es una forma de mostrar respeto y modales. Pero en otros casos, el estilo empresarial puede ser más informal. En ese caso, el vendedor puede adoptar un tono más informal. Recuerde siempre ser educado cuando dé sus opiniones. Si tuviste una mala experiencia con una empresa o un lugar, es mejor decir algo como, "No lo recomiendo porque tuve una muy mala experiencia". Por supuesto, puede dar más detalles si habla con sus amigos o personas de confianza. Pero es mejor ser educado y un poco reservado cuando se da una opinión negativa de un lugar. Esto te hace parecer una persona educada y adecuada.

Vocabulary

English
Customer, recommendation, suggestion, should, must, I think, I suggest, seller, tone, polite, respect, manners, boss, business, gym, restaurant, hotel, beauty salon, opinion, social networks, publication, reserved.

Espanol
Cliente, recomendación, sugerencia, debe, debe, creo, sugiero, vendedor, tono, cortés, respeto, modales, jefe, negocios, gimnasio, restaurante, hotel, salón de belleza, opinión, redes sociales, publicación, reservado.

A healthy diet and life - Una dieta y una vida saludables

Health is one of the most important aspects in a person's life. If a person is not in good health, it will be difficult to live a good life. In order to enjoy good health, a number of recommendations that are commonly made must be considered.

Personally, I like to eat a balanced diet. To achieve this, a balance is needed between meals rich in fat and carbohydrates and healthy meals. If you keep this balance between healthy and unhealthy meals, you have a high chance of achieving good health.

The first recommendation I always make to all my friends is that they should avoid a lot of junk food. Junk food is high in fat, salt and carbohydrates. It is usually food fried in a lot of oil or fat. Some examples of this type of food are burgers, pizza, french fries, fried chicken, and hot dogs. True, these foods are delicious, but they contain a lot of calories.

When we talk about calories, we are talking about the energy a person needs to function properly throughout the day. All people have a specific amount of calories they need to consume on a daily basis. Doctors usually recommend consuming two to three thousand calories per day. This is enough to do all your daily activities. With this, you can do all the activities you want.

But, if you consume a lot of calories, you will gain weight. I gained twenty kilos because I ate a lot of pizza and drank a lot of soft drinks. Also, I haven't trained much. This is a problem because if you eat a lot and don't exercise, you will gain weight.

So if you want to be in good shape, you need to eat healthy and exercise. One of the most common exercises is walking. When you walk, you train, but you don't make too much effort. This is a good exercise to get your body moving and burn off any excess calories you consume.

Doctors recommend regular exercise three to four times a week. For example, taking a walk is good exercise. I love taking a walk with my dog. We practice a lot besides getting to know our neighborhood and the people who live there better. My dog also needs exercise, so it's a good idea for both of us.

However, taking a walk isn't the only exercise you can do. There are many exercises that can help you lose weight and stay healthy. One of the most popular is swimming. This is a very interesting sport that serves to work the whole body. The only problem with swimming is having a pool near your home.

Many people go to the gym. A gym is a place where there are exercise machines and equipment. Also, many gyms have instructors who teach people how to do the exercises the right way. With these, you can train, lose weight and stay healthy.

The problem with gyms is that some are expensive while others are far from home. But if you find a gym near your home and at a good price, it might be a good option to improve your physical condition and be healthier.

I like to talk to my doctor often about how I can improve my health. When I talk to my doctor, this is the kind of conversation we have.

-Diego: Hi doctor, what do you think is the best way to lose weight?
-Doctor: A good way to lose weight is to eat a balanced diet and exercise regularly.
-Diego: What kind of exercise do you recommend, doctor?
-Doctor: Any kind of exercise is good. In particular, walking and yoga are good exercises to improve your physical condition.
-Diego: Sounds good to me. What Types of Foods Should I Avoid?
- Doctor: You should avoid foods high in fat and sugar. These ingredients are very bad for your health.
-Diego: So what foods do you recommend?
-Doctor: I recommend that you eat fresh fruit and vegetables. Lean meat is also a good way to consume protein without a lot of calories.
-Diego: Thanks doctor for your advice.
- Doctor: It's a pleasure.

This conversation with my doctor helped me a lot in learning about the best way to lose weight and be healthy. But I also like to talk to my friends about the best way to be in good physical condition.

My friend Pietro is an excellent athlete. He practices various sports, goes to the gym and is in excellent physical condition. With him we talk about sport and how to be fit. Here is an example of our conversations.

-Pietro: I go to the gym three times a week and play football on weekends.
-Diego: Wow! How beautiful it is. Do you play any other sports?

-Pietro: Not really. I really enjoy swimming.
-Diego: Me too. It's great exercise.
-Pietro: Yes, it also helps you work on your arms and legs.
-Diego: Really?
-Pietro: Yes, it is a low impact exercise. This means you don't get kicked in the legs like when running on the street.
-Diego: Oh, I understand. Thanks for the advice.
-Pietro: Imagine, when you want.

This was a very productive conversation. Pietro taught me a lot about different types of exercises and how to choose the best one for me. For now, I go to the gym three times a week and enjoy swimming on the weekends. Since I work Monday to Friday, it does me good to go swimming on Saturday mornings.
And you? What kind of exercise do you do?
The truth is, it doesn't matter what kind of exercise you enjoy. The important thing is that you are always on the move. I feel much better physically since I started my workout routine. Also, the diet has done me a lot of good. Not only have I lost twenty pounds, but I also feel much better. I feel like I have more energy and dress up my clothes better. Likewise, all my friends tell me I'm much better.
At work, I feel like I'm improving my performance. I think my boss has already noticed the difference. I hope to continue improving my results. This way, I will be able to apply for a promotion in my job. It would be great for me to get promoted and earn some extra cash.
But the best of all is to be healthy. Health is priceless. I don't like being sick. I feel like I am wasting time, money and effort. I love feeling energized and ready to do all my tasks for the day.
When you hear people say phrases like:

-I always feel tired.
-I can't sleep well.
- I have no energy.
- I don't have much appetite.

Can you suggest the ideas we have discussed in this story. You can offer them useful tips such as:

-Why don't you go for a fifteen minute walk a day?
If you reduce your consumption of coffee, sugar and fat, you can improve your health.
Exercise is a good way to improve your energy level.
-You can lose weight with a balanced diet and regular exercise.

These phrases are good advice you can give to people you know such as your friends and family.

Therefore, I advise you to change your diet, exercise and visit the doctor. If you don't know where to start, your doctor can give you many positive ideas on how to improve your health. The important thing is to maintain good communication with the doctor. This way, you can improve your physical condition, and look better and be healthier.

Summary

English
To look better, feel good and be healthy, it is a good idea to have a balanced diet and exercise regularly. This combination is ideal to maintain a good figure and be in good physical condition. The first thing you should do is eliminate junk food from your diet. Junk food is one that has many calories and is not very nutritious. Some examples of junk food are pizza, hamburgers and hot dogs. A balanced diet is based on fresh fruits and vegetables. In addition, you can consume meat that does not have much fat. With this, you can get protein without consuming a lot of calories. Also, regular exercise is very important to be healthy. A good exercise which you can do is go for a walk every day. With this, you can keep your body moving without doing a very complex exercise. Other good exercises are swimming and playing sports like football. There are many people who also go to the gym. But the gym can be very expensive or far away from home. But, if you find a gym close to home and at a good price, it would be a good idea to go three or four times a week. Finally, it is a good idea to talk with your doctor. Your doctor can give you good ideas on how to start exercising if you don't know where to start. In addition, your doctor can give you all the information you need about a balanced diet. That is why I recommend talking to your doctor to learn more about how you can change your habits and be in better physical condition. Best of all, you will have more energy, you will be in better health and you will feel much better overall. Do not wait anymore. Start today with your new exercise routine and a healthy diet.

Espanol
Para verse mejor, sentirse bien y estar saludable, es una buena idea llevar una dieta equilibrada y hacer ejercicio con regularidad. Esta combinación es ideal para mantener una buena figura y estar en buenas condiciones físicas. Lo primero que debes hacer es eliminar la comida chatarra de tu dieta. La comida chatarra es aquella que tiene muchas calorías y no es muy nutritiva. Algunos ejemplos de comida chatarra son la pizza, las hamburguesas y los perros calientes. Una dieta equilibrada se basa en frutas y verduras frescas. Además, puedes consumir carnes que no tengan mucha grasa. Con esto,

puedes obtener proteínas sin consumir muchas calorías. Además, el ejercicio regular es muy importante para estar sano. Un buen ejercicio que puedes hacer es salir a caminar todos los días. Con esto, puedes mantener tu cuerpo en movimiento sin hacer un ejercicio muy complejo. Otros buenos ejercicios son la natación y la práctica de deportes como el fútbol. Hay mucha gente que también va al gimnasio. Pero el gimnasio puede ser muy caro o estar lejos de casa. Pero, si encuentras un gimnasio cerca de casa y a buen precio, sería buena idea ir tres o cuatro veces por semana. Finalmente, es una buena idea hablar con su médico. Su médico puede darle buenas ideas sobre cómo empezar a hacer ejercicio si no sabe por dónde empezar. Además, su médico puede brindarle toda la información que necesita sobre una dieta equilibrada. Por eso te recomiendo hablar con tu médico para conocer más sobre cómo puedes cambiar tus hábitos y estar en mejor condición física. Lo mejor de todo es que tendrá más energía, gozará de mejor salud y se sentirá mucho mejor en general. No espere mas. Empiece hoy con su nueva rutina de ejercicios y una dieta saludable.

Vocabulary

English

Diet, exercise, weight, lose, calories, balanced, fruits, vegetables, doctor, swimming, walking, gym, times, advice, expensive, close, condition, combination, physical, healthy, sick, pizza, hamburgers, carbohydrates, fat, sugar.

Espanol

Dieta, ejercicio, peso, perder, calorías, equilibrado, frutas, verduras, doctor, natación, caminar, gimnasio, horarios, consejos, caro, cerrar, condición, combinación, físico, saludable, enfermo, pizza, hamburguesas, carbohidratos, grasa, azúcar.

Pets are wonderful - Las mascotas son maravillosas

Having a pet is a wonderful experience. Anyone who owns a pet knows how cute and special they are. A pet is more than just an animal. A pet is a companion, friend and support. A pet is always there with you, no matter what happens or however you feel.

Depending on the type of pet you have, it can help you in many situations. For example, dogs are supportive pets especially in difficult times. Although they cannot speak, dogs always serve as emotional support or can help you work. Furthermore, dogs are excellent observers. They always take care of the house they live in. Dogs are definitely great pets.

Another very common animal as a pet is the cat. Cats are great friends to have at home. They are intelligent and very playful. When a kitten becomes your friend, you know you have a friend for life. Cats are very loyal despite being very independent. In fact, people confuse cats' independence with a lack of loyalty or friendship. Generally, cats take care of their home but they do it in a very different way than dogs.

I recently had a nice conversation with a neighbor. This is what we talked about:

-Manuel: Hi Bianca, what a beautiful dog you have. What breed is he?
-Bianca: Hi Manuel. Thanks, it's a black labrador. And yours?
-Manuel: He is a German Shepherd. How old is your puppy?
-Bianca: She is four years old. And yours?
-Manuel: Mine is three years old. His name is Bruno. What is your puppy's name?
-Bianca: His name is Rocky.
-Manuel: We go to the park to play for a while. Come with us?
-Bianca: Sure! We come right away.

Manuel's puppy is very cute. He is very kind and playful. He got along very well with mine. Now Bruno and Rocky are good friends. I am happy that my dear puppy has a new friend to play with in the park.

I have a friend who is fascinated by cats. In fact, it has three! Her three puppies get along very well. They live in a very large house and therefore have space to play, run, hide and catch mice. Kittens are very happy when they play indoors and have all the space in the world to run around.

Also, my friend has a lot of games. There are some small trees for the kittens, which are used for climbing, jumping and scratching their claws. This helps prevent them from climbing on sofas or damaging furniture.

We had this conversation the other day.

-Bianca: Hey Roberto, how many cats do you have?
-Roberto: I have three.

-Bianca: Interesting. Why do you have three?
-Roberto: Because I saved each of them.
-Bianca: Saved?
-Roberto: Yes, there are bad people who don't like animals. So they abandon them. I saved them from mistreatment and give them a good home.
-White: Oh! This is very noble of you.
-Roberto: Thanks. Also, I love kittens.

As you can see, Roberto is a wonderful person with a big heart. He does his best to help poor kittens who don't have people to care for them. It is indeed a very noble action on his part.
On the other hand, there are people who have exotic pets. These types of pets are not as common as cats, dogs, fish, or birds. They are very strange animals like spiders, snakes and mice. This type of pets attracts a lot of attention as it causes fear among people. I mean, would you like to have a pet snake? Personally, I am not impressed with having such an animal in the house. However, there are people who love them.
I know a person who has pet spiders. Of course, he doesn't let them walk freely around his house. He has spiders in a glass fish cage. The most unusual is the way spiders feed. Spiders usually feed on insects such as ants, flies, and small beetles. It seems very strange to me. Not the kind of pet I want for me. When you see someone else's pet, you can compliment them. For example, you can use phrases like:

-What a nice dog (or cat).
-I like your pet.
-He's so cute.
-I love your kitten (or puppy)

You can also ask your friends questions about their pet. With these, you can have a more interesting conversation. Some examples are:

-What's your name?
-How old is he?
-How long have you had it?
-What does he like to play?
In the particular case of dogs, it is normal to ask, what breed is it?
The breed is the type of dog that it is. For example, common dog breeds are German Shepherd, Labrador, and Husky. These are some of the many dog breeds that exist in the world. There are also several breeds of cats. Many people have a particular preference for one breed of dog or cat over another. Some people prefer a smaller breed while others prefer a larger breed. Personally, I prefer a relatively small breed for a dog as I don't have a lot of space in the house. My house is quite small. So it is difficult to have a very large pet. Also, I work a lot and don't have a lot of time to devote to various

pets. That's why a dog is enough for me. I have a friend and companion who I can take care of and give everything I need.

If you have a large house, you can have multiple pets. I know some people who have dogs, cats, birds, and even other pets like rabbits, chickens and ducks. Sure, you need a very big house to have all those animals. Sure it's a lot of fun, but you have to give them a lot of food.

Pets are a wonderful thing in life. If you like animals in general, then you definitely like pets too. Of course, you need to find the ideal pet for you. Not all people love dogs. Other people prefer cats. Indeed, there are people who do not like dogs and therefore prefer to have birds. There are also people who like to have pets that don't make a lot of noise. So they prefer fish. The fish are beautiful and very quiet.

Well now, if you like exotic animals, I recommend that you study these types of animals. The important thing is to know how they are and the care they need. Many times, having an exotic pet can be dangerous. That is why it is necessary to take security measures. If you have a pet snake, it can injure a person. Therefore, it is best to be careful.

If you don't have a pet, I invite you to find one. If you haven't decided yet, there's a huge variety you can choose from. I am sure you will find a pet for you. Take some time to get to know each of them. The more you know about pets, the more you will learn which one is best for you. I'm sure you will find the perfect one for you. You can start your search online. You can read other people's experiences. When you find it you will surely be as happy as I am.

Summary

English

Pets are animals that serve as companions for humans. But, a pet is much more than just company. A pet is a friend who is loyal. This friend will accompany you everywhere. You can count on a pet for emotional support especially if you feel bad. Therefore, it is a good idea to have a pet in your life. The most popular pets are dogs and cats. Many people prefer dogs because they are playful. In addition, they serve as a company and for work. Some other people prefer cats as pets. Cats are more independent, but they are equally loyal and playful. Cats are an excellent company especially if you don't have much space. There are other people who have birds or fish. Birds are a good alternative for those who do not prefer cats or dogs. But for those who prefer quiet pets, fish are a good option. In fact, fish are beautiful animals and make no noise at all. Then, there are people who have exotic pets. Exotic pets are rare animals. For example, there are people who have spiders, snakes and mice as pets. These pets are unusual and can even be dangerous. If you like exotic pets, then you should be very careful because they can hurt people or hurt other animals. If you don't have a pet, I recommend doing an online search on the best pet for you. I'm sure there are many animals that would be a good option for you. The most important thing is to be sure that this is the ideal pet for you.

Espanol

Las mascotas son animales que sirven de compañía a los humanos. Pero una mascota es mucho más que compañía. Una mascota es un amigo leal. Este amigo te acompañará a todas partes. Puede contar con una mascota como apoyo emocional, especialmente si se siente mal. Por lo tanto, es una buena idea tener una mascota en su vida. Las mascotas más populares son perros y gatos. Mucha gente prefiere a los perros porque son juguetones. Además, sirven como empresa y para el trabajo. Algunas otras personas prefieren a los gatos como mascotas. Los gatos son más independientes, pero son igualmente leales y juguetones. Los gatos son una excelente compañía, especialmente si no tienes mucho espacio. Hay otras personas que tienen pájaros o peces. Las aves son una buena alternativa para quienes no prefieren perros ni gatos. Pero para aquellos que prefieren mascotas tranquilas, los peces son una buena opción. De hecho, los peces son animales hermosos y no hacen ningún ruido. Luego, hay personas que tienen mascotas exóticas. Las mascotas exóticas son animales raros. Por ejemplo, hay personas que tienen arañas, serpientes y ratones como mascotas. Estas mascotas son inusuales e incluso pueden ser peligrosas. Si te gustan las mascotas exóticas, debes tener mucho cuidado porque pueden lastimar a las personas o a otros animales. Si no tiene una mascota, le recomiendo hacer una búsqueda en línea sobre la mejor mascota para usted. Seguro que hay muchos animales que serían una buena opción para ti. Lo más importante es estar seguro de que esta es la mascota ideal para ti.

Vocabulary

English

Pet, dog, cat, mouse, snake, spider, fish, birds, careful, animal, loyal, independent, unusual, exotic, dangerous, common, prefer, quiet, playful, option, patient, search, ideal.

Espanol

Mascota, perro, gato, ratón, serpiente, araña, pez, pájaros, cuidadoso, animal, leal, independiente, inusual, exótico, peligroso, común, prefiero, tranquilo, juguetón, opción, paciente, búsqueda, ideal.

A difference of opinion among friends and colleagues - Diferencias de opinión entre amigos y colegas

It is completely normal to have a difference of opinion between friends and colleagues. In fact, it would be strange not to have it. Wherever you go, whether at home, to work or to school, you will always have some sort of difference of opinion. Often the differences are related to activities, preferences or decisions to be made.

In any situation where you have a difference of opinion, the important thing is to always be clear about the reality of things. It is natural that you always want to be right. But there are times when you are not right. In these cases, it is necessary to behave in a mature and purposeful way to achieve a correct way of doing things.

Plus, it's perfectly normal to have an emotional reaction when it comes to defending your opinion. However, you need to be careful not to offend other people. It is logical to think that you should defend your position, but it is also not necessary to offend or attack other people simply because they have a different opinion from yours.

In this sense, you must use expressions and ideas that demonstrate your education and culture even when others are not behaving on the same level as you. So, here are some phrases you can use to express your opinion in a polite way.

-In my opinion...
-I think that...
- I consider it a ...
-It is my opinion
-From my point of view

These expressions are very kind and polite ways to express your point of view. For example, you and your friends are deciding what you will have for dinner. In this discussion if you want to indicate your point of view you could use these types of expressions:

-In my opinion, Chinese food is the best.
-I think the pizza is delicious.
-I consider Italian food better than fast food.
-I believe that junk food is unhealthy.
From my point of view, fried chicken is too high in calories.

With these expressions you have indicated your opinion in a formal and friendly way. What if I wanted to express these ideas but in a less formal way? Well, in that case you can express your ideas in the following way.
-I think Chinese food is the best.
-For me the pizza is delicious.

-Italian food in my opinion is definitely better than fast food.
-In my humble opinion, junk food is unhealthy.
-It is logical to think that fried chicken is high in calories.

As you can see, the expressions above refer to your opinion in a minor way. But you have to remember that these types of expressions are used when you are with your friends or in trust. Don't use these types of expressions when talking to your boss or at a formal meeting. If you do it this way, you can cause a strong discussion among meeting attendees.
Speaking of a meeting, what happens when there is a difference of opinion in the middle of a meeting? How can you express your opinion without causing problems?
Here are some examples of how you can express your opinion correctly and appropriately.
-I appreciate your point of view, but I'm afraid I disagree.
-I understand your position, but I think we should act differently.
-You are right in what you say, but I do not completely agree.
-I understand why you think so, but I see things differently.

These sentences are formal and appropriate for a formal meeting. You can also use these expressions if you disagree with your boss or a client. These phrases are very important when you are in the middle of a negotiation. There are also expressions you can use in an informal situation. In these cases, you are in a more relaxed environment where it is not necessary to be so formal.

Here are some examples of less formal expressions.

-I do not think so!
-You are crazy?
-No it does not.
-What are you saying?

As you can see, these are extremely informal expressions, which can be used at a party, a gathering of friends or with family. Of course, be careful because if you use them in the middle of a strong argument, you can have a problem with other people.
Recently, I have had some discussions with various differences of opinion. I want to take this opportunity to show you what these conversations were like. One conversation is formal and the other is less formal.
-Boss: So the solution to our problem is to cut costs. We can reduce costs by laying off staff.
-Fernando: I believe that the dismissal of staff would be bad for the morale of our employees.
-Boss: But it's the only way to cut costs.

-Fernando: Yes, he's right, but I think we can find other ways to reduce costs. For example, we can renegotiate some contracts with our suppliers.
-Boss: It won't work.
-Fernando: I understand his point of view, but I think we could try it. If it doesn't work, then we can start with the layoffs.

In this conversation, a firm but friendly tone can be observed, even though my boss is confident in his point of view. Considering that this meeting was with my boss, it was necessary to maintain the appropriate level of conversation to avoid problems.

I had this conversation with a friend instead. We were discussing the movie we wanted to see in the cinema that weekend. Our tone is very informal, but we haven't had a strong argument.

-Fernando: Hey, what movie do you want to see?
-Manuel: I want to see "The Last Superhero". They say it's great.
-Fernando: I don't think so. I'm thinking about the new horror. It's "Scream 2" ... come on!
-Manuel: Absolutely not. Superheroes are much better.
-Fernando: What? You are crazy my friend. Superheroes are boring. This horror movie is definitely better.
-Manuel: Listen, why don't we watch another movie? There is a war one.
-Fernando: Hey, that's not a bad idea. Better see that.

In this conversation, my friend and I seriously discussed the film. But at no time did we fight. We are friends and we can have such a discussion without any problems between us. The important thing is to always reach an agreement between friends. This is the best way to solve the problems.
So the next time you have an argument at home, at work or with friends, you can now have it calmly and appropriately. Most importantly, you have the necessary expressions to do it without errors.
Likewise, I want to leave you some useful tips for solving problems in a polite and appropriate way. First, I think education is the most important thing. It is always best to avoid using strong and inappropriate expressions.
I believe that calm is the easiest way to reach a good agreement. When you stay calm, it is easier to talk and achieve a favorable outcome for everyone. This is very important especially in negotiations with customers.
Finally, I believe that the most effective way to talk to your boss is always the direct one, but with a lot of formality. Your boss will appreciate your confidence, but at the same time understand that you are a fair and formal person. This way, you will gain the respect of your boss and colleagues when they see that you are serious, honest and firm in your opinions.

Summary

English

It is completely normal to have a difference of opinion between your friends and colleagues. In fact, it would be a strange thing not to have them. Wherever you go, whether at home, at work or at school, you will always have some kind of difference of opinion. In any situation where you have a difference of opinion, the important thing is to always be clear about the reality of things. It is natural that you always want to be right. But there are times where you are not right. In these cases, it is necessary to behave in a mature and focused way in order to achieve the correct way of doing things. In addition, it is perfectly normal to have an emotional reaction when it comes to defending your opinion. However, you must be careful not to offend other people. In this sense, you need to use expressions and ideas that demonstrate your manners and culture even when others do not behave at the same level as you. Here are some useful tips to express your opinion in a correct and appropriate way. I think education is the most important thing. It is always better to avoid using strong and inappropriate expressions. It is my opinion that being calm is the easiest way to reach a good agreement. When you remain calm, it is easier to have a dialogue and reach a favorable outcome for everyone. I believe that the most effective way to talk to your boss is always to be direct, but very formally. If you express yourself this way often, you will have good results in your interpersonal relationships, achieving your goals consistently. Best of all, you will always have friends. This is especially important in a negotiation. When you reach agreements that benefit everyone, you will succeed in many aspects of your professional and personal life.

Espanol

Es completamente normal tener una diferencia de opinión entre sus amigos y colegas. De hecho, sería extraño no tenerlos. Vayas donde vayas, ya sea en casa, en el trabajo o en la escuela, siempre tendrás algún tipo de diferencia de opinión. En cualquier situación en la que tengas una diferencia de opinión, lo importante es tener siempre claro la realidad de las cosas. Es natural que siempre quieras tener la razón. Pero hay momentos en los que no tienes razón. En estos casos, es necesario comportarse de forma madura y centrada para lograr la forma correcta de hacer las cosas. Además, es perfectamente normal tener una reacción emocional a la hora de defender tu opinión. Sin embargo, debe tener cuidado de no ofender a otras personas. En este sentido, debe utilizar expresiones e ideas que demuestren sus modales y cultura, incluso cuando los demás no se comporten al mismo nivel que usted. A continuación se ofrecen algunos consejos útiles para expresar su opinión de forma correcta y adecuada. Creo que la educación es lo más importante. Siempre es mejor evitar el uso de expresiones fuertes e inapropiadas. En mi opinión, estar tranquilo es la forma más fácil de llegar a un buen acuerdo. Cuando se mantiene la calma, es más fácil dialogar y llegar a un resultado favorable para todos. Creo que la forma más eficaz de hablar con tu jefe es siempre ser directo, pero muy formal. Si te expresas de esta manera con frecuencia, tendrás buenos resultados en tus relaciones interpersonales, logrando tus metas de manera consistente. Lo mejor de todo es que siempre tendrás amigos. Esto es especialmente importante en una negociación. Cuando llegue a acuerdos que beneficien a todos, tendrá éxito en muchos aspectos de su vida profesional y personal.

Vocabulary

English
Agreement, opinion, difference, honest, direct, right, boss, calm, emotional, appropriate, proper, relations, interpersonal, clients, outcomes, offend, defend, reach, show, believe, perception, avoid, goals.

Espanol
Acuerdo, opinión, diferencia, honesto, directo, correcto, jefe, tranquilo, emocional, apropiado, adecuado, relaciones, interpersonales, clientes, resultados, ofender, defender, alcanzar, mostrar, creer, percepción, evitar, metas.

What's in the news? - ¿Qué hay en las noticias?

We listen to the news every day. It is common to know the most important events happening in our community. Indeed, the media constantly report incidents that occur in real time. In this way, we stay informed of the most relevant events, not only in our community, but also around the world. The media are television, radio and print, such as newspapers and magazines. Initially, newspapers were the most common way of reporting news. Many years ago, it was common to read the newspaper daily, in the morning and then in the afternoon. Typically, the morning paper reported the previous day's news while the afternoon paper reported the day's news. The newspapers therefore provided specific information on specific topics. These themes are varied, some examples being fashion, sport, home, food and travel. Newspapers have allowed readers to learn about a wide variety of topics. One of the most important features of newspapers is that they contain many images. Of course, the images were initially drawings. With the invention of photography, it was possible to include photographs.

Newspapers have been the most accessible way to get news for many years. But one invention that revolutionized the way of following the news was the radio. The radio is made up of people who speak on a station that is received by a device also called radio. With this device, people can hear what others have to say. This way you can get concrete information about the most important events, or listen to music or learn something new about a particular topic.

The radio made it possible to reach millions of homes in real time. When information is received in real time, it means that it is received immediately, instantly. This revolution has facilitated mass communication, that is, the communication of information to a large number of people, not just in one country, but around the world. In fact, this was a real revolution.

In short, radio was a significant invention in the history of communication. But the invention that marked an entire generation was television. Television was the first invention that allowed people to get vivid images in real time. When television was invented, cinema had been around for a few years. But the cinema had a very big limit: you could not get images and communications in real time. The news that was shown in theaters, many times, was weeks old. Although this was important to the people of his time, there was always this time difference between the news and the broadcast of the news in theaters.

With television, families around the world have been able to receive news in real time. In addition, entertainment and other types of educational, informational and advertising programs could be created. Quickly, television became part of the culture of many countries and a constant presence in homes. Therefore, television allowed a new cultural revolution where an entire generation of people had this technology in their lives.

But perhaps the biggest revolution has been the Internet. The internet emerged in the late 1980s. This invention offered an incredible opportunity to facilitate communication, send data and information, and connect the whole world.

A real revolution in communication was e-mail. E-mail was a way of communicating through written messages sent from one computer to another. The email communication was impressive. Messages arrive in seconds. When a letter took months to get from one point to another, an email message can travel the same distance in seconds. There is no doubt that this has made an impressive difference.

With the Internet, it has been possible to shift traditional media to an online model. Newspapers and magazines can now be easily read online. All you need is Internet access to access this information.

On the other hand, traditional radio, although it retains an important place in the world of communication, is now accessible online. This makes it easier for people all over the world to hear the information, content and music broadcast on these stations. Better yet, you can access many of these stations and their content twenty-four hours a day, seven days a week.

With the Internet came one of the most interesting inventions: social networks.

Social networks are virtual groups where people can communicate instantly. In addition, they can share messages, photos, content and documents. With these networks, information arrives even faster than on radio or television.

Also, traditional media has a presence on social networks as this is the easiest way to reach users. Not all people listen to the radio, not all watch television, not all people read the newspaper, but almost all people have some presence on social networks. This is why social media is so important in today's society.

How do you follow the news? What do you consult to receive information on the most relevant events?

If you read the newspaper, then you have recent information at a relatively low price. If you read magazines, you will certainly receive specific content on a certain topic. If you watch TV, you get useful information in real time.

But if you are on social networks, you can receive the information practically the moment it was generated. With this, you can reach a large number of people through these networks. You have the opportunity to become a journalist. If you are in the place of events and manage to capture information, you can share it on social networks. So you have the opportunity to help many people, especially if the events involve a large number of people. An example of this is traffic. When there is a traffic problem, people who are on the spot can share information on social networks.

So I invite you to read the newspapers and listen to the radio. You can do this in your free time, i.e. when you are not working or in a moment of concentration, for example when you drive your car in traffic. In these media, you can get a lot of useful information for your daily life. On the other hand, I invite you to subscribe to electronic versions of your favorite newspapers.

This way, if you have an Internet connection, you can access large amounts of information quickly and at very low cost.

Finally, if you have information that you think may be useful to others, don't be afraid to post it on social networks. Many people will thank you for your posts as this will allow them to learn more about the current situation. Maybe you can help people be safe or warn others of a danger that exists at that moment. In short, you now have the opportunity to make a difference in the lives of many people. Your contributions will surely be well received by interested people and served by information.

Summary

English
Every day we listen to the news. It is common to hear about the most important events that happen in our community. In fact, the media constantly reports the incidents that occur at the right time. In this way, we keep informed about the most relevant events, not only in our community, but also around the world. The media are television, radio and print media such as newspapers and magazines. Then, the magazines provided specific information on particular topics. These themes are varied. Print media was the most accessible way to get the news for many years. But an invention that revolutionized the way to get the news was the radio. The radio consists of people talking in a station which is received in an apartment that is also called radio. This revolution facilitated mass communication, that is, communicating information to a large number of people, not only in one country, but throughout the world. Actually, this was a revolution at the time. With television, families around the world were able to get news in real time. In addition, it was possible to create entertainment programs as well as other types of educational, informational and advertising programs. But perhaps the biggest revolution was the internet. The internet emerged in the late eighties of the twentieth century. This invention offered an incredible opportunity to facilitate communication, send data and information, and connect the entire world. With the internet, it has been possible to move traditional media to an online model. Now, newspapers and magazines can be easily read online. It is only enough to have access to the internet to get access to this information. Social networks are virtual groups where people can communicate instantaneously. In addition, they can share messages, photos, content and documents. With these networks, information arrives even faster than with radio or television.

Espanol
Todos los días escuchamos las noticias. Es común escuchar sobre los eventos más importantes que suceden en nuestra comunidad. De hecho, los medios informan constantemente de los incidentes que ocurren en el momento

adecuado. De esta manera, nos mantenemos informados sobre los eventos más relevantes, no solo en nuestra comunidad, sino también alrededor del mundo. Los medios son la televisión, la radio y los medios impresos como periódicos y revistas. Luego, las revistas proporcionaron información específica sobre temas particulares. Estos temas son variados. Los medios impresos fueron la forma más accesible de recibir noticias durante muchos años. Pero un invento que revolucionó la forma de recibir las noticias fue la radio. La radio consta de personas que hablan en una emisora que se recibe en un apartamento que también se llama radio. Esta revolución facilitó la comunicación masiva, es decir, la comunicación de información a un gran número de personas, no solo en un país, sino en todo el mundo. En realidad, esto fue una revolución en ese momento. Con la televisión, las familias de todo el mundo pudieron recibir noticias en tiempo real. Además, fue posible crear programas de entretenimiento, así como otro tipo de programas educativos, informativos y publicitarios. Pero quizás la mayor revolución fue Internet. Internet surgió a finales de los ochenta del siglo XX. Este invento ofreció una oportunidad increíble para facilitar la comunicación, enviar datos e información y conectar al mundo entero. Con Internet, ha sido posible trasladar los medios tradicionales a un modelo en línea. Ahora, los periódicos y revistas se pueden leer fácilmente en línea. Solo es suficiente tener acceso a Internet para acceder a esta información. Las redes sociales son grupos virtuales donde las personas pueden comunicarse instantáneamente. Además, pueden compartir mensajes, fotos, contenido y documentos. Con estas redes, la información llega incluso más rápido que con la radio o la televisión.

Vocabulary

English

Communication, mass, newspaper, news, print, magazine, radio, television, show, station, content, information, revolution, network, email, authentic, access, instantly, virtual, century, emerged, perhaps.

Espanol

Comunicación, misa, periódico, noticias, impresos, revista, radio, televisión, programa, estación, contenido, información, revolución, red, correo electrónico, auténtico, acceso, instantáneo, virtual, siglo, surgió, quizás.

Forgive me! – Perdóname!

One of the most common experiences in life is to apologize when you do something wrong or make a mistake. In these cases, the situation can be delicate or embarrassing. However, the ideal is to always acknowledge the mistake and apologize. When you apologize for the mistake made, you will have the opportunity to correct the problem situation.

Some examples of situations where you should apologize include accidentally hitting someone, interrupting someone while talking, spilling a liquid, forgetting something or information, and even making a mistake at work. In these circumstances, it's a good idea to apologize to people.

Consider this example: Go on public transport, for example a bus. You are walking among people and accidentally hit someone. You should apologize for the accidental action. These are phrases you can use in this situation.

- I'm sorry, it was an accident.
-Sorry. It was not my intention.
-Excuse me.

The first two expressions are very kind. With these expressions, you want to make it clear that it was not your intention to hurt the other person and that it was just an accident. With the expression "I'm sorry" you are pointing out your mistake in a direct and simple way. This is a very common expression that you can use without prolonging the conversation.

In such cases, you can answer as follows:

-No problem.
-Do not worry.
-Everything is alright. Thank you.

These are simple but polite ways of responding. They are a quick and easy way especially when going by public transport or to places where there are many people.

There are also occasions when you need to ask for permission to do something. For example, you are eating and you need salt. This is a very common case where you can ask for permission to get salt. Here is an example:

- Sorry, can you pass me the salt?

In this example you are asking the other person to pass you the salt. But if you want to get it yourself, you can say:

- Sorry, I just want the salt.

And then take the salt yourself. This is a simple sentence where the other people at the table can see what your intention is. In this case, your intention is to take the salt. Now, if someone asks you to give them salt, you can answer the following:

- Sure, here you go.

With this phrase, offer the salt and voila. You showed good table manners. As you can see, they are simple and easy to remember expressions. This way, you can show your education and manners especially in formal events.

There are also social situations where you can use expressions to say sorry. A common situation is when a person who is talking is interrupted. For example, they are talking about a topic, but suddenly you remember something important that you should tell your friend. If so, you can tell him:

- I'm sorry to interrupt, but I remembered one thing.

With this expression, you kindly apologized to your friend for the interruption. But the information you need to tell him is very important. So this sentence is an appropriate way to interrupt him while he speaks. Other phrases that can be used in this case are:

- Sorry for the interruption.
-Sorry, I have to tell you something.
-Oh, forgive me, I remembered something very important that I have to tell you.
When you use one of these phrases, you are making it clear that you have remembered something you need to say and that you cannot wait. Moreover, these expressions can be used in any situation or context, that is, it is possible to use them both in formal situations and in social situations. For example, if you are in a business meeting and there is some important information you should communicate, you can say something like:

- Sorry for the interruption, but there is something important I have to tell you.

Please note that "sorry" and "I have to tell you" refers to different people. Therefore, it is a phrase that you can use when speaking to a group of people. If you only use this phrase with one person, you can say it like this, "I'm sorry for the interruption, but there is something important I need to tell you." Now let's take a look at the use of the phrase "I'm sorry".

This phrase is used when you regret a situation. Some examples of such situations are: accidentally saying something inappropriate, forgetting a person's name, making a mistake at work, or forgetting something important.

It is also common to use "sorry" when coughing or sneezing, especially in the middle of a conversation.

Here are some examples of how to use this expression appropriately.

- Sorry it wasn't my intention.
-I'm sorry, it won't happen again.
- Sorry, I'm so sorry.
- Sorry, it was my mistake.

With these sentences, make it clear that it was not your intention to do what you did and that it was just a mistake. Also, the important thing about these examples is that you accepted that it was your fault and that is why you are apologizing for your mistake.
Now if something happens, but it wasn't your fault, you can use some phrases like:

- Sorry, but it wasn't my fault.
-I'm sorry for the situation, but I'm not the culprit.
-I am very sorry for what is happening, but it is not my responsibility.

In these examples you are making it clear that what happened is not your responsibility. Of course, you are not saying that you will do nothing, you are simply saying that the responsibility for what happened is not yours. Therefore, it is stressed that it is someone else who has to answer for the situation.

When something very bad or very embarrassing happens, you can use the following expressions to show a profound apology.

-I'm really sorry. I do not know what happened.
- I'll make you a thousand excuses.
-I am deeply sorry for the inconvenience.

As you can see, these sentences are a response to a very complicated situation. For example, your company made a mistake with a customer order. In this case, it doesn't matter who is responsible for the error. It is simply necessary to offer an apology to the customer and try to resolve the situation. These phrases demonstrate your regret for the negative situation that has arisen.
In addition to an apology, it is also important to respond appropriately. The ideal is to offer an adequate response that shows your education and kindness. Here are some expressions you can use when someone offers you an apology.

-Do not apologise

-It's nothing.
- Okay, nothing happened.
-Forget about it.

These are common phrases that you can use when you are in an informal situation or just in a public place. But there are also situations where it is necessary to formally respond to an apology. Consider these examples.

-It 'does not matter. I appreciate the apologies.
- Thanks for your concern.
-I appreciate your kindness.
-Thank you. I'm fine.

You can use these responses in formal situations where you need to show your kindness. Likewise, you show your generosity by preventing the situation from rising to another level. So the problem is solved.
If you find yourself in a situation, for example, in a company where employees are unable to solve your problem, you can use these phrases.

-Can I speak to the supervisor?
- I need to speak to customer service.
-Please, can you contact the director?

These phrases are very useful when you are in a company and need to get an answer. They can serve you both in an informal and formal context. So use them when needed. Often, you can get the answers you are looking for by talking to a supervisor or manager. Above all, the important thing is to be kind and courteous to others.

Summary

English
One of the most common experiences in life is to apologize when you do something wrong or make a mistake. In these cases, the situation can be delicate, or embarrassing. However, the ideal is always to acknowledge the error and apologize. When you apologize for the mistake made, you will have the opportunity to correct the problem situation. Some examples of situations where you should apologize include hitting a person accidentally, interrupting someone while talking, spilling a liquid, forgetting any object or information, and even making a mistake at work. There are also social situations where you can use expressions to ask for forgiveness. A common situation is when you interrupt a person who is speaking. The expression "I'm sorry" is used when you regret a situation that has happened. This may be the result of an error at work, or an accident. This expression is a polite and often

formal way to indicate that you have made a mistake or that the situation is negative. For example, an error is made with an order from a customer. In this case, it doesn't matter who is responsible for the error. It is simply necessary to offer an apology to the client and try to fix the situation. Actually, what is needed is to fix the problem and that's it. As well as apologizing, it is also important to respond appropriately. Ideally, offer an appropriate response that shows your education and kindness. Therefore, you can also show your manners and kindness by responding appropriately when someone apologizes. In general terms, I apologize is a very important part of the social interaction between people. When you use appropriate expressions, you can be sure that the problems will no longer happen. Of course, your kindness is something very important to avoid future problems with people.

Espanol

Una de las experiencias más comunes en la vida es pedir disculpas cuando haces algo mal o cometes un error. En estos casos, la situación puede ser delicada o embarazosa. Sin embargo, lo ideal es siempre reconocer el error y pedir disculpas. Cuando se disculpe por el error cometido, tendrá la oportunidad de corregir la situación problemática. Algunos ejemplos de situaciones en las que debe disculparse incluyen golpear a una persona accidentalmente, interrumpir a alguien mientras habla, derramar un líquido, olvidar cualquier objeto o información e incluso cometer un error en el trabajo. También hay situaciones sociales en las que puedes usar expresiones para pedir perdón. Una situación común es cuando interrumpe a una persona que está hablando. La expresión "lo siento" se usa cuando te arrepientes de una situación que ha sucedido. Esto puede ser el resultado de un error en el trabajo o un accidente. Esta expresión es una forma educada y a menudo formal de indicar que ha cometido un error o que la situación es negativa. Por ejemplo, se comete un error con un pedido de un cliente. En este caso, no importa quién sea el responsable del error. Simplemente es necesario ofrecer una disculpa al cliente e intentar arreglar la situación. En realidad, lo que se necesita es solucionar el problema y eso es todo. Además de disculparse, también es importante responder de manera adecuada. Lo ideal es ofrecer una respuesta adecuada que muestre su educación y amabilidad. Por lo tanto, también puede mostrar sus modales y amabilidad respondiendo de manera apropiada cuando alguien se disculpe. En términos generales, pido disculpas es una parte muy importante de la interacción social entre las personas. Cuando usa expresiones apropiadas, puede estar seguro de que los problemas ya no sucederán. Por supuesto, tu amabilidad es algo muy importante para evitar problemas futuros con las personas.

Vocabulary

English

Regret, I'm sorry, apology, error / mistake, inconvenience, problem, interruption, situation, circumstances, appropriately, manners, kindness, fix, case, therefore, happened, in fact, ideally, correct, hurt, avoid.

Espanol

Lamento, lo siento, disculpa, error / error, inconveniencia, problema, interrupción, situación, circunstancias, apropiadamente, modales, amabilidad, arreglar, caso, por lo tanto, sucedió, de hecho, idealmente, corregir, herir, evitar.

Social networks – Redes sociales

In our society, social networks are a phenomenon of great importance. Virtually everyone uses social networks.

In general, social networks are a means of communication. These networks serve to communicate between people who often live in different parts of the world. This made it easier for people to stay connected despite the distances. Simply put, social media is a way to unite the world.

When a person decides to join a social network, he must open an account. An account is your official participation in the social network. To achieve this, you need to enter an email address along with some personal information. In particular, users are asked to enter their name and their geographical location.

Usually, it is not checked whether the data is real or not. But in most cases, the system automatically detects the person's geographic location through their internet connection. Therefore, it's a bit difficult to hide a person's true geographic location ... at least from the platform they connect to.

The interaction on social networks is virtual, i.e. you don't interact in person. Hence, the conversations are carried out in a written way or can be carried out via a video call.

But when you meet someone in person and decide to interact on a social network, you can ask them the following question:
- What's your username?

With this question, you are asking your friend to tell you how you can find him on the social network. For example, the person may give you their name or some kind of nickname or pseudonym. A pseudonym is an alternate name that a person uses. That is, it is not a fake name, but simply a different name by which it is known. Many people use a nickname to protect their privacy and personal data.

There are some people who are against social networks. These people believe that they are unproductive and cause harm especially to young people. There are groups of parents who do not allow their children to use these networks. A few days ago I had an interesting conversation on this topic.

-Bianca: What do you think of social media?
-Elisa: I don't approve of these platforms. They are a danger to children as there is a lot of bad content and people who want to harm them.
-Bianca: What do you do to take care of your children?
-Elisa: I don't allow them to connect to these networks.
-Bianca: What do you recommend to other parents?
-Elisa: I advise parents to talk to their children to find out who they interact with on social networks. Furthermore, it is important to maintain good communication in case of problems.

This conversation was very interesting. I think my friend gave me very interesting and important tips to help our children be safe on social media. Personally, I agree that it is necessary to be careful, even if it is not always necessary to have close supervision. There are times when children can use the computer more freely.

In general, social networks are information platforms that have had a positive impact on the world. You can get urgent information and communicate with others in an emergency. In addition, the government can issue alarms in case of weather problems or natural disasters. These alerts save lives as citizens receive information directly from the authorities.

Another important function of social media is doing business. Buying and selling in groups is common on social media. These groups are a space where people who have something to sell and people looking for something to buy can join. So this becomes a virtual marketplace where buyers and sellers can do business safely.

Many companies operate this way today. You no longer need physical space to create a business. Now, with the tools of the Internet and social networks, you can start a business from home using a computer and a smartphone. A lot of people have made money working this way.

If you are thinking of starting your own business, social networks are an alternative for a good business. All you need is creativity is a computer. Otherwise, your imagination and knowledge will help you form a good company. Most importantly, you don't need a lot of money to start a business this way. In fact, you can start your own business with very little money.

Many people have started a business this way. They achieved success by combining their passion with their creativity and a little hard work. This allowed them to earn money and improve their lives. I advise you to inquire about these people. Their stories are full of good ideas that you can implement for your business. These stories can teach you a lot about the best way to start your business and achieve your personal goals.

Also, if you think you need to study hard or have many years of experience, it's not really necessary. What you need is to learn the correct way to start your business. The ideas other entrepreneurs can give you will help you start your business in the most effective way. So, you have nothing to lose and a lot to learn.

If you decide to start a business on social networks, I advise you to always be aware of communication with your customers. When your future customers are interested in your products or services, they will leave messages with questions about your business. Hence, you should be very careful and respond promptly. Thus, you will be able to get customers, earn a lot of money and improve the condition of your business. I am sure you will do a good job with your company.

Summary

English

In our society, social networks are a phenomenon of great relevance. Virtually everyone participates in some social network. In many cases, most people are active in multiple social networks. In general, social networks are a means of communication. These networks serve to communicate between people who often live in different parts of the world. This has made it easier for people to stay in touch despite the distances. Meanwhile, social networks are a way to unite the world. The interaction in social networks is virtual, that is, it does not interact in person. Then, the conversations are carried out in a written way, or it can be done through a video call. There are some people who are against social networks. These people believe that they are unproductive and that they cause harm especially to young people. There are groups of parents who do not allow their children to use these networks. In general, social networks are information platforms that have had a positive impact on the world. Urgent information can be obtained as well as communicating with other people in case of emergency. In addition, the government can issue alerts when there are problems with the weather, or a natural disaster. These alerts save lives as citizens receive information directly from the authorities. Another important function of social networks is to do business. Buying and selling groups are common in social networks. These groups are a space where people who have something to sell and people looking for something to buy can join. Then, this becomes a virtual market where buyers and sellers can do business quietly.

Espanol

En nuestra sociedad, las redes sociales son un fenómeno de gran relevancia. Prácticamente todo el mundo participa en alguna red social. En muchos casos, la mayoría de las personas están activas en múltiples redes sociales. En general, las redes sociales son un medio de comunicación. Estas redes sirven para comunicarse entre personas que a menudo viven en diferentes partes del mundo. Esto ha facilitado que las personas se mantengan en contacto a pesar de las distancias. Mientras tanto, las redes sociales son una forma de unir al mundo. La interacción en las redes sociales es virtual, es decir, no interactúa en persona. Luego, las conversaciones se llevan a cabo de forma escrita, o se puede hacer a través de una videollamada. Hay algunas personas que están en contra de las redes sociales. Estas personas creen que son improductivas y que causan daño especialmente a los jóvenes. Hay grupos de padres que no permiten que sus hijos utilicen estas redes. En general, las redes sociales son plataformas de información que han tenido un impacto positivo en el mundo. Se puede obtener información urgente así como comunicarse con otras personas en caso de emergencia. Además, el gobierno puede emitir alertas cuando hay problemas con el clima o un desastre natural. Estas alertas salvan vidas ya que los ciudadanos reciben información directamente de las autoridades. Otra función importante de las redes sociales es hacer negocios. Los grupos de compra y venta son habituales en las redes sociales. Estos grupos son un espacio donde las personas que tienen algo para vender y las personas que buscan algo para comprar pueden unirse. Entonces, esto se convierte en un mercado virtual donde compradores y vendedores pueden hacer negocios en silencio.

Vocabulary

English

Phenomenon, relevance, different, world, participate, account, users, geographic, verify, majority, interaction, virtual, nickname, pseudonym, alternate, against, young, damage, platforms, function, purchases, sales, creativity, entrepreneurs.

Espanol

Fenómeno, relevancia, diferente, mundo, participar, cuenta, usuarios, geográfico, verificar, mayoría, interacción, virtual, apodo, seudónimo, alterno, contra, joven, daño, plataformas, función, compras, ventas, creatividad, emprendedores.

Conclusión

Así que ahí lo tienes. Hemos llegado al final del viaje. El viaje hasta este punto nos ha llevado a través de una miríada de temas que tocaron una gran cantidad de temas y presentaron diálogos muy interesantes.

Entonces, en este punto, ¿cuál es el siguiente paso?

Si está interesado en profundizar en el idioma inglés, tómese el tiempo para repasar las partes que le parecieron particularmente atractivas o interesantes. Al mirar más de cerca, definitivamente descubrirás nuevas palabras, ideas y conceptos que te ayudarán a reducir tu enfoque en los diversos aspectos del idioma inglés.

Además, profundizar en cada historia le facilitará la comprensión del lenguaje que se presenta en este libro. Además, siempre es una buena idea rodearse del idioma. Al participar en una práctica constante, podrá perfeccionar aún más sus habilidades.

Una vez que se sienta cómodo con cada una de las historias, encontrará que su confianza habrá mejorado enormemente. Como tal, puede sentirse seguro en sus habilidades lingüísticas la próxima vez que viaje o simplemente conozca gente de habla inglesa. De hecho, se sentirá lo suficientemente cómodo como para interactuar con hablantes de inglés sin sentir la necesidad de un traductor o ser consciente de sus habilidades en inglés.

Ahora, una última cosa sobre el inglés: cuando te comprometes a aprender cualquier idioma, descubrirás que se convierte en un viaje para toda la vida. Los idiomas tienen una forma en la que están en constante cambio y evolución. Entonces, justo cuando pensaba que sabía todo lo que necesita saber, algo cambia de tal manera que lo hace pensar en todo lo que hay por descubrir.

De hecho, el lenguaje es una entidad viva y que respira. En consecuencia, siempre hay algo nuevo que aprender, algo nuevo que descubrir y, sin duda, gente nueva que le enseñará cosas en las que no había pensado antes.

Muchas gracias por tomarse el tiempo de leer este libro. Si lo ha encontrado útil e informativo, dígaselo a sus amigos y familiares. Aquellos que buscan aprender un nuevo idioma, o simplemente repasar sus habilidades en inglés, seguramente encontrarán una excelente manera de practicar sus habilidades.

Hasta la proxima